Newspaper Wars

Civil Rights and White Resistance in South Carolina, 1935–1965

SID BEDINGFIELD

**UNIVERSITY OF
ILLINOIS PRESS**
Urbana, Chicago, and Springfield

© 2017 by the Board of Trustees
of the University of Illinois
All rights reserved
1 2 3 4 5 C P 5 4 3 2 1
∞ This book is printed on acid-free paper.

Library of Congress Cataloging-in-Publication Data
Names: Bedingfield, Sid author.
Title: Newspaper wars : civil rights and white resistance in South
    Carolina, 1935–1965 / Sid Bedingfield.
Description: Urbana : University of Illinois Press, 2017. | Series: The
    history of communication | Includes bibliographical references and
    index. | Identifiers: LCCN 2017007860 (print) | LCCN 2017027116
    (ebook) | ISBN 9780252099830 (e-book) | ISBN 9780252041228
    (hardcover : alk. paper) | ISBN 9780252082788 (pbk. : alk. paper)
Subjects: LCSH: Civil rights movements—Press coverage—South
    Carolina—History—20th century. | African American
    newspapers—South Carolina—History—20th century. | South
    Carolina—Race relations—Press coverage—History—20th century.
    | Press and politics—South Carolina—History—20th century.
    | Racism in the press—South Carolina. | McCray, John Henry,
    1910–1987.
Classification: LCC PN4897.S64 (ebook) | LCC PN4897.S64 B44 2017
    (print) | DDC 070.4/493231196073—dc23
LC record available at https://lccn.loc.gov/2017007860

Contents

Newspaper Wars

THE HISTORY OF COMMUNICATION

Robert W. McChesney and John C. Nerone, editors

A list of books in the series appears at the end of this book.

Acknowledgments

I first met the journalist John Henry McCray in the pages of a poignant and influential book, *Days of Hope: Race and Democracy in the New Deal Era,* written by historian Patricia Sullivan. Since then, Sullivan has become a mentor and friend whose wise counsel has been invaluable in nudging this project forward. I owe a special debt to other historians as well, a number of whom I have never met. The works of Jack Bass, Katherine Mellen Charron, Peter F. Lau, Theodore Hemmingway, Edwin D. Hoffman, I. A. Newby, Wim Roefs, Miles Richards, and Barbara Woods are essential reading for anyone interested in South Carolina and its racial politics. I also must thank my former colleagues at the University of South Carolina School of Journalism and Mass Communications. That begins with Dean Charles Bierbauer, now a twice-former colleague and a class act in every way. Carol Pardun has been an especially helpful boss and mentor, and I consider her a model of what it means to be a scholar, educator, administrator, and friend. Ken Campbell introduced me to the study of media history, and his early guidance helped launch this book. Most of all, I want to thank Kathy Roberts Forde, who spent an enormous amount of her time and energy making my work better. Kathy is a brilliant scholar and an even better friend. Acquiring editor Danny Nasset and the staff at the University of Illinois Press improved this project significantly as they guided it to publication. I am especially thankful for the work of the manuscript reviewers, particularly historians Michael Stamm and Thomas F. Jackson. Both provided rich and detailed critiques that helped shape the final version. Jackson's frequent admonition to "show not tell" is perhaps the best advice a writer can hope to get. My new colleagues at the University of Minnesota supported my work as well, particularly Al Tims, outgoing director of the School of Journalism and Mass Communication. Finally, I owe a special debt to my wife, Dana, who endured more conversations about South Carolina and its history than she ever cared to during this process. Fortunately, she's a tough editor with a keen ear for nonsense. As always, her support has been essential.

Newspaper Wars

Introduction

In the spring of 1935, John Henry McCray graduated from college in Alabama and returned to Lincolnville, South Carolina, the tiny African American enclave near Charleston where he grew up. Brimming with ambition, McCray told friends that he wanted to launch a newspaper and use it to fight for equal rights in his home state.[1]

At the time, McCray's youthful optimism seemed dangerously misplaced. Mired in the Depression and demoralized by forty years of violent Jim Crow rule, black Carolinians struggled each day merely to survive. As one observer noted, they seemed trapped in a morass of economic exploitation and political hopelessness. The organizations that dominated black civic life in the state—churches, schools, and NAACP chapters—had grown either defeatist or moribund. The issue of white supremacy appeared to be settled. A prominent white newspaper editor assured readers at the time that the state's black leadership was now "educated" and "conservative" and had accepted the South's system of racial hierarchy. Most white politicians no longer bothered to talk about race when campaigning for office.[2]

Over the following decade, however, African Americans embraced social activism and emerged as a political force in South Carolina. NAACP membership increased from fewer than eight hundred in the mid-1930s to more than fourteen thousand in 1948, with a central state conference of branches coordinating activity across the organization's eighty-six chapters. McCray and his allies launched a political organization, the Progressive Democratic Party, and challenged the legality of the state's all-white Democratic Party. The PDP boosted black voter registration from fewer than four thousand in the early 1940s to more than seventy thousand by the end of the decade.

Serving as both cheerleader and commissar, McCray's newspaper stood at the center of this new black activism. The paper rallied support for a direct assault on white supremacy and demonized those in the black community who refused to join the fight.[3]

The new movement won a string of victories across the 1940s, both in the courts and at the ballot box. Black South Carolinians overturned the state's system of unequal pay for black teachers, won the right to participate in Democratic Party primaries, influenced the outcome of a U.S. Senate election, and filed a school desegregation suit that would lead to *Brown v. Board of Education,* the landmark Supreme Court case outlawing segregation in public schools. These successes served as a turning point in the political history of the state and the nation. As one historian put it, the NAACP activists who led the fight in South Carolina in the 1940s served as the "vanguard" of the massive civil rights struggle that would emerge across the South the following decade.[4]

The surge in activism that began in the late 1930s and accelerated through the 1940s raises an obvious question: How did a movement planted in such desolate terrain manage to take root and grow so quickly? Scholars who have studied the broader civil rights movement in the South trace its immediate origins to the demographic, economic, and social changes of the Depression and New Deal era. They note that the Great Migration accelerated during the 1930s, with more than 400,000 southern blacks moving north during the decade. The population shift increased the number of African American voters in the region, particularly in the large industrial states where national elections were often decided. The rise in black political clout in the North forced white liberal politicians to engage with the African American community and take black aspirations more seriously. At the same time, Franklin Roosevelt's presidency energized black activists and their white liberal allies in the South. As Patricia Sullivan has argued, Roosevelt's New Deal activism "stirred the stagnant economic and political relationships" that had ruled the South since the turn of the century.[5]

Additionally, industrialization and urbanization began to take hold in the South. With the arrival of the boll weevil and the collapse of the cotton crop in the late 1920s, African Americans began moving to cities in search of jobs. Literacy rates increased, and the proximity of urban life facilitated political mobilization by the church, the NAACP, and other civic institutions. Later, the spread of fascism in Europe and the Japanese attack on Pearl Harbor drew the United States into World War II, initiating a massive mobilization effort that further destabilized the social, political, and economic structures in the South. Finally, the arrival of the cold war helped rally black activism and recruit white allies by highlighting the hypocrisy of a society that demanded democratic self-determination abroad but accepted white supremacist rule at home.[6]

The changes that swept the nation during the 1930s and '40s created two of the three conditions social movement theorists believe are necessary for successful collective action. The black migration expanded political opportunities for African Americans in the North, and urbanization helped create new mobilizing structures in the South. Yet these developments alone did not ensure the rise of a robust civil rights movement. To achieve that, black communities in the South needed leaders who could infuse these social changes with political meaning. They required powerful new voices who could carry out what sociologist Douglas McAdam calls "the collective processes of interpretation, attribution and social construction that mediate between opportunity and action." More than a litany of court cases, protest marches, and voter registration drives, the battle over civil rights in the South was a cultural contest as well. Black activists and white segregationists crafted narratives that competed to interpret the meaning of the African American fight for political and social equality. They used the tools of mass communication and political symbolism to try to define citizenship and establish the proper boundaries of civic life. Both were pursuing a distinctly political goal: to mobilize supporters, persuade potential allies, and shape public opinion on the critical question of race and citizenship.[7]

In South Carolina, the black and white press operated at the heart of this meaning-making process. In the African American community, where a strategy of cautious accommodation of white supremacist rule remained prevalent, a radical newspaper emerged in the late 1930s to promote a new conception of what citizenship required. McCray's *Lighthouse and Informer* served as the public voice of a political reform movement that included an aggressive NAACP and a rising Democratic Party insurgency. Using the newspaper as a means of command and control, the movement mobilized black community support and launched a coordinated assault on the barriers white society had erected to block black participation in the state's civic life. Faced with this new challenge, white newspaper editors, often in collusion with political office holders, struggled to redefine the meaning of white democracy. They would continue to pursue what an earlier historian had called the "central theme of southern history"—the region's effort to remain a "white man's country." Yet the nation had changed since their forebears had fought to reimpose white supremacy during the rise of Jim Crow at the turn of the twentieth century. With northern public opinion turning in the years after World War II, white editors in the state worked to create a new defense of white rule in the South that would restore its legal and intellectual credibility within the nation's larger democratic narrative.[8]

Over the past three decades, the historiography of the civil rights movement has shifted from the study of national leaders and organizations to focus more narrowly on grassroots activism at the state and local level. Similarly, scholars have extended the movement's timeline beyond the so-called classical period—from the 1954 *Brown v. Board of Education* ruling through the 1965 Voting Rights Act—and have emphasized the continuity between earlier African American activism and the mass movements that emerged in the late 1950s. In the study of South Carolina, two works exemplify these changes. Peter F. Lau's *Democracy Rising* traces an enduring African American freedom struggle that had its roots in the Reconstruction era, and *Freedom's Teacher,* Katherine Mellen Charron's biography of educator Septima Clark, shines new light on grassroots organizing in the state. This book seeks to extend and build on this new historiography by emphasizing the role of mass communication and interpretation in facilitating social and political change. By focusing narrowly on the battle to shape public discourse, this study highlights a cultural struggle that dominated South Carolina politics during three critical decades: from the late 1930s, when McCray's newspaper joined the fight for back civil rights, through the 1950s and early 1960s, when white journalists mounted a sustained counterattack.[9]

By moving the state's newspapers from the periphery to the center of the political action, this book encourages readers to reconsider the role journalism played in the fight over civil rights. John McCray and his primary allies at the *Lighthouse and Informer*—Modjeska Monteith Simkins and Osceola E. McKaine—are significant historical figures who deserve more attention in the study of the nation's black press. At a time when most black newspapers in the Deep South were assumed to be cautious and conservative—much like the Scott family's *Atlanta Daily World* during the classical civil rights era—the *Lighthouse and Informer* called for direct confrontation with white supremacy. In the 1940s, McCray and his allies challenged their readers to "rebel and fight" for their rights as American citizens, to reject the "slavery of thought and action" that created "uncle Toms and aunt Jemimas" and become "progressive fighters for the emancipation of the race."[10]

This study also contributes new details about white journalists and their role in shaping the response to the movement McCray's newspaper helped launch. In South Carolina, journalists at white daily newspapers did more than document and interpret public events; they often served as independent and distinct political actors engaged directly in the state's political process. In the wake of the *Brown* decision, they editorialized in favor of massive resistance, but they also helped implement that policy through creation of White Citizens' Councils and other political organizations. When massive resistance began to fail, the same journalists turned to partisan politics and played central roles in creating a new political home for white segregationists in a conservative Republican Party in the South. In *The Race Beat,* Roberts and Klibanoff document the role northern white journalists played in shaping public opinion by forcing white northerners to confront the horrors of Jim Crow rule in the South. This book extends that familiar storyline to consider the period during the 1960s, when segregationist journalists worked to reverse that shift in national sentiment through deployment of new narratives designed to undermine the growing black political activism. It shows how South Carolina journalists joined forces with William F. Buckley Jr. and his political journal, *National Review,* to help develop a new rhetoric of so-called "color-blind conservatism" that could attract southern segregationists to the conservative cause without alienating northern supporters.[11]

This case study examines the press and its impact during a time of political change in one Deep South state. Yet it also raises larger questions about the role of journalism in the cultural contest that animates all democratic life. In doing so, it relies on sociologist Jeffrey C. Alexander's theory of the civil sphere, which emphasizes the power of interpretive communication to influence political and social change. In modern democracies, Alexander maintains, individuals construct narratives to help make sense of the world, and through these narratives they create the "social solidarity" that comprises the democratic public. It is within this civil sphere that democratic communities determine membership; they decide who has the right to full citizenship and who does not. In Alexander's view, this civil sphere is a space where cultural expression and interpretive communication can overcome narrow self-interest in shaping how members of the society make sense of their world. Within this solidary civil sphere, citizens share a deep emotional connection to the values embedded in the culture of the society. Powerful symbolic codes that grew out of the nation's founding documents convey these democratic ideals across society and help enhance a shared culture and sense of community. Much like Gunnar Myrdal's notion of an "American creed" or Gary Gerstle's conception of "civic nationalism," Alexander's civil sphere theory suggests the existence of a subtle but widely held belief that the American way is linked to such notions as liberty, justice, and equality.[12]

Yet Alexander emphasizes that the civil sphere has never been achieved in its ideal form. Members of the democratic public who comprise the civil sphere also participate in other spheres of everyday life—the market economy, most obviously, but also the bureaucratic state; racial, ethnic, and gender ties; family and religious sects; and other interest groups. Alexander argues that the power of these forces can invade and corrupt the democratic ideals of the civil sphere. The cultural codes that appeal to the nation's foundational ideals can be redeployed as weapons designed to maintain power and ostracize the weak, not to expand the circle of democratic life. Throughout U.S. history, powerful forces have emerged to deliver political arguments that seek to legitimize racism and other forms of repression as shared values embedded in the nation's democratic heritage. Civil sphere theory provides a rich framework for understanding how cultural narratives—both liberal and illiberal—have been mobilized to shape public discourse and influence public opinion [13]

With its emphasis on interpretive communication, civil sphere theory takes seriously the role journalists play in deploying and reifying the shared cultural narratives that shape much of our political discourse. In South Carolina, Mc-Cray's *Lighthouse and Informer,* working closely with NAACP allies, made strategic use of society's symbolic codes concerning freedom, justice, and equality to rally the black community and to elicit empathy from potential allies within the larger democratic public. The civil rights leaders won support by linking their struggle for equality to the most sacred traditions of the nation's democratic heritage—what one black activist called "things of the heart, things eternal." Yet across the 1950s and early 1960s, white journalists worked closely with the state's political leaders to develop a competing discourse, one that was used to taint the black political movement as anti-American and thus limit its gains.[14]

The political activism of the black press has been well documented. When the first African American newspaper was published in 1827, editors John B. Russworm and Rev. Samuel F. Cornish said black citizens must speak for themselves and "plead our own cause." Since then, historians have depicted black newspapers and magazines as a "fighting press" that worked closely with other community leaders to build social movements and bring about political change. The political activism of the modern white press has received far less scrutiny. In South Carolina, for example, white journalists played a more influential role in the state's politics during the mid-twentieth century than has been previously acknowledged. The state's leading white journalists carried their political engagement to an extreme level, but their activism should not be dismissed as an anomaly in an otherwise nonpartisan era of American journalism.[15]

The white journalists in South Carolina struggled to shape public opinion and dictate political outcomes, but they also proclaimed their commitment to the journalistic norms of independence and impartiality. Their efforts highlight a contradiction at the heart of the apolitical ideal that has shaped mainstream journalism in the second half of the twentieth century in the United States. As the South Carolina editors clearly understood, journalists contribute to the meaning-making process that is central to democratic life. They make dozens of subjective decisions about each story they cover. They decide which facts to include and which angles should be emphasized, downplayed, or ignored altogether. Through this selection process, journalists create interpretive cues that identify potential problems and propose possible solutions. Therefore, their work is inherently political in nature, even when they try to avoid that role. For the white, mainstream press, the professionalization of journalism across the twentieth century has obscured this reality. Much of the received scholarship has suggested that white daily newspapers—and later broadcast news—embraced their role as impartial, objective observers of public affairs. This study adds to the small but growing body of work showing how mainstream journalists often struggled with the tension between the new professional standards and their desire to shape cultural values and influence events, particularly during times of heightened political and cultural conflict in their communities.[16]

Partisan Journalism and the Mainstream Press in the Twentieth Century

Mainstream American journalism shed its openly partisan roots and slowly embraced the concepts of independence and impartiality in the years between 1870 and the 1920s. Before the Civil War, most American newspapers depended on political parties for financial support; they delivered a partisan message in return for a party subsidy. In the 1830s, New York's penny press began to break this mold. Penny press editors such as James Gordon Bennett published newspapers that were independent of political parties and produced some of the first hard news reporting. After the Civil War, more newspapers began to embrace this new model. As the industrial revolution accelerated, cities grew, the reading public expanded, and metropolitan newspapers prospered. New technology cut the cost of printing, and newspapers took advantage of an increased demand for advertising that accompanied the rising consumer culture. At the same time, readers began demanding more facts and less partisan opinion. In response, newspapers hired more reporters to gather hard news. Gradually, these newspapers evolved from political organs with party ties to independent and profitable businesses that supplied the public with a broad range of information.[17]

As the twentieth century approached, the rise of the nonpartisan newspaper quickened. Historian Michael McGerr contends that independent journalism grew naturally out of the progressive reform movement that emerged at the time. The reformers were educated elites who placed their faith in social science and empirical evidence. They were appalled by the corruption and the emotionalism of big-city machine politics. Reformers believed voters should be educated with facts, not inundated with opinion. The independent newspapers followed suit: They printed more straight news, exiled opinion journalism to the editorial page, and began to articulate the new norms of modern, independent journalism. An independent newspaper, one editor declared, should always put "fact before opinion, proof before inference, principle before partisanship."[18]

By the 1920s, the principles of independence and detachment were firmly established as the dominant paradigm in modern American journalism. Universities launched journalism schools to teach students the techniques of modern reporting, and journalists created professional associations such as the American Society of Newspaper Editors. Mainstream American journalism began to adopt what media theorists have described as the "monitorial" role in the democratic process. Journalists would provide neutral and objective reporting and allow some interpretation, but their role prohibited partisan advocacy or direct involvement in political activism. As Borden and Pritchard contend, the public began to expect journalists to carry out their "essential function" as purveyors of unbiased political information without violating the public trust or concealing any conflicts of interest.[19]

Nudged along by Walter Lippmann and other intellectuals of the 1920s, newspaper editors also began to articulate the concept of "objective" news reporting. Michael Schudson says that the notion of objectivity—the separation of facts from values—rested in part on the post–World War I belief that scientific inquiry was the only path to truth given the complexity of the modern world. But the rise of objectivity had a political component as well. Richard L. Kaplan maintains the claim of objectivity became a sort of cover that granted journalists a significant voice in political discourse without forcing them to embrace a partisan point of view. To justify their editorial decisions, journalists "elaborated an occupational ethic" that granted them sweeping authority to serve as arbiters in the public sphere.[20]

Across the twentieth century, newspapers that aspired to join the mainstream of American journalism embraced the new standards of independence, detachment, and objectivity. The ethical rules were often murky, especially for editorial writers and columnists. Opinion and interpretation did have an acknowledged role in the press, but some opinion journalists continued to help politicians behind the scenes with advice, speech writing, and other forms of support that appeared to violate the new professional codes. Despite these contradictions, most large newspapers in the United States felt the need to articulate the new professional standards of impartiality. According to Robert W. McChesney, by midcentury "even the laggards" had been brought into line.[21]

The evidence from South Carolina suggests the professionalization narrative that has grown so prominent in journalism history warrants closer study. As the late political communications scholar Timothy H. Cook noted, journalists have often discouraged such scrutiny by downplaying their active role in the political process. Yet a close examination of South Carolina's white press and its role in resisting black equality in the mid-twentieth century reveals a deep and ongoing connection between press and partisan politics in the state, one that would have a significant impact on national political development during and after the civil rights movement. It also shows how partisan journalists had begun to hide their activism from the public to maintain their status as independent sources of information and interpretation. This study takes seriously the notion that journalists often serve as political actors. They frequently influence public opinion and thus wield instrumental power in the democratic process.[22]

In South Carolina, Charleston's *News and Courier* occupied a prominent position near the center of the state's white political world in the mid-twentieth century. In the 1940s, editor William Watts Ball participated in partisan politics openly and proudly. A throwback who had come of age in the late nineteenth century, Ball believed newspaper editors had an obligation to engage fully in the politics of their communities. By the 1950s, however, Ball's successor—Thomas R. Waring Jr.—professed his commitment to contemporary standards of political independence and neutrality. Yet during that decade, *News and Courier* journalists played a leading role in crafting the legal strategy of interposition and in organizing the White Citizens' Council movement that would undergird the white South's campaign of massive resistance. At the same time, the editor of the *Greenville News,* Wayne W. Freeman, served on a committee created by the governor to help the state avoid integrating its schools. Later, when massive resistance began to fail, the South Carolina journalists turned their attention to partisan politics. When the conservative wing of the Republican Party embraced states' rights, Waring and his newspaper's chief political correspondent, William D. Workman Jr., joined that cause and helped the GOP emerge as a viable alternative to the Democrats in the South. But they concealed their party-building activities to avoid violating the norms of their profession. Unlike their mentor, they carried out their political activism while continuing to proclaim their commitment to partisan neutrality and independence. The political activism of the *News and Courier* and other South Carolina journalists during the 1950s and 1960s complicates the consensus view that a professionalized, independent, and nonpartisan press had spread even to the more rural South by then.[23]

The Cultural Struggle Over Civil Rights in South Carolina

The civil rights movement that emerged in South Carolina in the late 1930s had deep ties to the long struggle for black equality that stretches back to the antebellum period and the fight against slavery. But its immediate roots can be traced to the turn of the twentieth century and the cultural struggle that accompanied the rise of Jim Crow rule in the South. Led by men such as South Carolina's "Pitchfork" Ben Tillman, the forces of white supremacy imposed a strict racial caste system and denied southern blacks equal participation in democratic life. Southern whites achieved these goals with both tacit and explicit support of white northern public opinion. Three decades after the Civil War, whites in the North had grown weary of what they called "the Negro problem," and the nation's government ceded to white southerners the power to manage race relations in the region. As the progressive journalist Ray Stannard Baker lamented in 1908: The place of blacks has been settled, "and the less they are talked about the better." Added historian Charles A. Beard, "Agitation of the Negro question had become bad form in the North." A *New York Times* editorial declared that the Supreme Court reflected "this change in public opinion" with its 1896 ruling in *Plessy v. Ferguson* and a series of ensuing cases upholding the constitutionality of racial segregation. Writing for the majority in the *Plessy* case, Justice John H. Brown said, "If one race be inferior to the other socially, the United States constitution cannot put them upon the same plane."[24]

Southern white Democrats had encouraged this racial indifference in the North through a sophisticated propaganda campaign that took advantage of the growing power of mass communication. At a time when industrialization and urbanization had increased the reach and influence of media outlets, white southerners employed newspapers, magazines, novels, plays, popular music, and other forms of media entertainment to demonize and ridicule black Americans. Ignoring evidence of black educational and economic progress achieved during Reconstruction, white southern media depicted

African Americans as violent sexual predators and political naïfs who corrupted civic life. Novelist Thomas Dixon's sympathetic portrayal of the Ku Klux Klan as the defender of a virtuous and democratic white civilization established a cultural benchmark for understanding the meaning of Reconstruction. D. W. Griffith would use much of Dixon's account as source material for his groundbreaking movie, *The Birth of a Nation,* and by the 1920s, academics led by Columbia University's William Dunning would embed this interpretation deep in the historiography of the nation. The *Plessy* ruling and Booker T. Washington's acceptance of white political supremacy in the South appeared to relieve white northerners of moral or constitutional obligations to intervene on behalf of African American equality. Free from federal interference, white supremacist Democrats in the South employed all means necessary, including a violent campaign of terrorism, to dislodge black Americans from the tenuous place in southern politics they had gained during Reconstruction.[25]

In response, W.E.B. Du Bois, the NAACP, and the emerging black press in the North struggled to offer a competing interpretation of the nation's past that emphasized the contradictions at the heart of American democracy. Operating "within the veil" of de facto segregation, the NAACP and the black press embraced the nation's democratic ideals of justice and equality and used them to argue for inclusion in civic life. Their efforts started slowly. By the second decade of the century, however, as the Great Migration of blacks moving from southern farms to northern cities increased, the audience for northern black newspapers grew larger. As Todd Vogel has noted, readers of the black press during this period could "see writers forming and re-forming ideologies, creating and re-creating a public sphere, and staging and restaging race itself." This vigorous black press—particularly the *Chicago Defender*—delivered an indictment of racial injustice that gradually seeped into white, mainstream culture and society. Over time, it would help alter public opinion concerning white supremacy in the South.[26]

Using South Carolina as a case study, this book explores the connection between the rise of an aggressive black public sphere in the North in the early twentieth century and the gradual emergence of the civil rights movement in the South. In 1915, Du Bois's writing in the NAACP's monthly magazine, *The Crisis,* attracted a handful of black followers in South Carolina. They organized an NAACP chapter and launched a promising campaign during World War I, but the black public sphere in the North was not strong enough to rally support for this fledgling civil rights effort in the Deep South. White supremacists in South Carolina crushed the movement violently—without fear of federal government interference or concern about northern public opinion.

By the mid-1930s, when John Henry McCray returned to South Carolina from college, the black public sphere in the North had grown stronger and won more allies. Pressured by black civil rights groups and white liberal activists, the Roosevelt administration slowly began to acknowledge the interests of African Americans. These early steps were tiny and timid: Aid programs like the Works Progress Administration (WPA) offered marginally more relief to black communities; the president created an informal "black cabinet" to brief him on African American issues; and the first lady, Eleanor Roosevelt, began appearing in public with black leaders. These included Mary McLeod Bethune, a prominent South Carolina educator and a heroine to the state's emerging black activists. By the late 1930s, the NAACP's legal assault on Jim Crow began to chip away at the white supremacist ideology that undergirded the *Plessy* ruling. In *Gaines v. Canada* in 1938, the U.S. Supreme Court ordered the state of Missouri to either create a "separate but equal" law school for blacks or admit Lloyd Gaines to the University of Missouri law school.[27]

Taken together, these signals from the North would embolden a new generation of civil rights activists in South Carolina. One of those was Modjeska Monteith Simkins, a Columbia activist who had been attending NAACP meetings since the local chapter was formed during World War I. As a teenager, Simkins had seen a protest movement flourish briefly with the help of a black newspaper. But she had also seen it collapse under the pressure of a white crackdown. Buoyed by FDR's New Deal, Simkins launched a campaign to force the president's white Democratic allies in the state to distribute more federal aid to black Carolinians. Her efforts in the late 1930s helped rouse a sleepy black political network.

In Charleston, John McCray wanted to join this new activism, but cultural ghosts from the past haunted his efforts. Two decades after Booker T. Washington's death, McCray would commit an act of accommodation to white supremacy that would undermine his credibility among the small community of black activists in the state. Chapter 1 addresses this struggle over strategy within the black community. It chronicles McCray's early missteps in Charleston and explores the complex history of accommodationism and protest in the African American struggle for freedom in South Carolina and across the South. The chapter concludes with McCray's comeback two years later, when Simkins recruits the young editor and helps convert his newspaper into a "fighting news organ" willing to oppose conservative forces within the black community in South Carolina.

Chapter 2 introduces one of Simkins's early allies, Osceola E. McKaine. A well-educated and cosmopolitan citizen of the world, McKaine saw in Simkins a true kindred spirit, and the two developed a close alliance in the fight against timidity and accommodation in the black community. To win this political war, they believed the movement needed a newspaper that could carry their message of self-assertion and protest to the larger community. Together, they persuaded McCray to move his paper from Charleston to the state's capital city of Columbia and have it serve as the communications arm of the NAACP effort in South Carolina.[28]

The second chapter details the early years of the *Lighthouse and Informer* and its effort to rally support for confrontation with white rule. In its first major political battle—the fight over black teacher pay in South Carolina— the *Lighthouse and Informer* linked political activism to personal growth and self-fulfillment; it claimed citizenship could never be won through cautious negotiation but must be earned through struggle with white supremacy. McCray, McKaine, and Simkins used their paper to ridicule black leaders who persisted in calling for accommodation with the white government, and demanded the black community embrace the protest strategy.[29]

Chapter 3 focuses on the movement's battle against the all-white Democratic Party primary and its power to exclude African Americans from electoral politics in what was functionally a one-party state. McCray and McKaine used the newspaper to launch an insurgent political organization, the Progressive Democratic Party, designed to challenge party rules and give blacks a voice in the political process in South Carolina. In 1944—twenty years before Fannie Lou Hamer and the Mississippi Freedom Democratic Party famously contested that state's all-white delegation at the 1964 Democratic National Convention in Atlantic City—McCray and a PDP delegation traveled to Chicago to demand seats at the party's nominating convention. Buoyed by growing grassroots support across the state, the movement raised its ambitions. In late 1947, the state conference of NAACP branches announced that it would no longer accept the doctrine of "separate but equal" but would instead battle for full integration in all aspects of civic life of South Carolina.

Chapter 4 turns to the white press of the 1940s and examines its treatment of the rising civil rights movement. Led by William Watts Ball, the editor of the Charleston *News and Courier,* the state's major newspapers embraced an aristocratic form of conservatism that had its origins in the state's planter-class elites who had helped overthrow Reconstruction in the 1870s. Like the old elites, Ball was obsessed with the notion of hierarchy in society; he believed all classes had their "place," with aristocratic elites in charge and working-class whites near the bottom, just one step above the former slaves. Ball had opposed the rise of reform movements led first by Ben Tillman and later by Cole Blease because they empowered small farmers and textile workers and undermined planter-class leadership in the state. Ball was a white supremacist, but he disliked politicians who demonized African Americans to unite working-class white voters. Ball believed blacks were clearly inferior and thus posed no real threat to white rule.

The editor's paternalistic views faded, however, when it became clear that the local civil rights movement had support in the North. In 1948, when President Harry Truman became the first president since Reconstruction to propose civil rights legislation, Ball helped persuade the state's young governor, J. Strom Thurmond, to join the Dixiecrat revolt and challenge Truman's bid for reelection. Formally called the States' Rights Party, the Dixiecrats tried to link their campaign to the Tenth Amendment and the constitution's prohibition against an intrusive federal government. By Election Day, however, the party's rhetoric concerning "mongrelization" and "racial purity" had further undermined the image of white southern segregationists in the eyes of northern public opinion.

In chapter 5, an elder statesman emerges to deliver a new narrative, one that downplayed white supremacy and promised both states' rights and good race relations. James F. Byrnes—a former Roosevelt ally and Washington insider who had served as senator, secretary of state, and Supreme Court justice—came out of retirement in 1950 to win the governorship of South Carolina. He unveiled an expensive school equalization plan designed to strengthen the argument in favor of *Plessy*'s "separate but equal" doctrine by improving the quality of black schools in South Carolina. A month before Byrnes's inauguration, the NAACP had gone to court to challenge the constitutionality of segregated schools in rural Clarendon County. The effort to abolish segregated schools divided the African American community in the South at the time, and Byrnes hoped black parents and teachers in South Carolina would force the NAACP to drop its suit in return for his promise to spend tax dollars to upgrade black schools. Yet McCray's *Lighthouse and Informer* derided the governor's equalization plan as an effort "undertaken in desperation" to fool black southerners and white liberals in the North. His newspaper rallied black South Carolinians in favor of the Clarendon County suit, which would eventually reach the Supreme Court as part of *Brown v. Board of Education of Topeka*.

McCray would pay a price for his militant stance. In 1950, he was indicted on charges of criminal libel after publishing a black defendant's claim of innocence in the rape of a white woman. On advice of his NAACP attorneys, Mc-

Cray pled guilty rather than face an all-white jury, and he eventually served two months on a South Carolina chain gang. McCray and his allies believed his unstinting support for the school integration case prompted a frustrated Byrnes administration to pursue the charges against him. An enraged black community rallied around McCray, and his arrest actually fueled support for the integration suit. But McCray's personal finances suffered during his time on the chain gang, and his newspaper would never fully recover.

The final three chapters examine the role of white journalists in shaping the white backlash in the post-*Brown* years in South Carolina. Waring and Workman—the Charleston *News and Courier*'s editor and chief political writer—played leading roles in organizing the white community's "massive resistance" to the *Brown* ruling. To their dismay, the black public sphere that Du Bois, the NAACP, and the black press had launched at the turn of twentieth century had grown dramatically following World War II. The black community's interpretations of public events now received greater attention in the mainstream white press. In response, Waring launched a campaign to break through the so-called "paper curtain" that he claimed northern media used to silence the voices of white southerners who supported segregation.

The white backlash would have a devastating effect on the civil rights movement in South Carolina. In 1954, just weeks after the *Brown* ruling, the *Lighthouse and Informer* went out of business, depriving the black community of a critical tool of interpretation and organization. McCray continued his journalistic work as Carolina editor of the *Baltimore Afro-American,* but that paper's regional edition never connected with South Carolina's black community in the way the *Lighthouse and Informer* had. The white crackdown increased economic and psychological pressure on the black community and intensified personal conflicts within the movement. A simmering feud between Simkins and McCray escalated in 1954, and the two traded a series of withering denunciations in the *Lighthouse and Informer* and the *Afro-American.* Their split would doom all efforts to save the dying newspaper, and it would undermine black activism in the state.

As 1960 approached, Waring and Workman worked to build a new political home for white racial conservatives in a revamped Republican Party. Waring and his conservative ally, William F. Buckley Jr. of the *National Review,* experimented with arguments designed to unite southern segregationists with the magazine's antistatist and anticommunist readership. With Waring, Workman, and their South Carolina allies playing a central role, the conservative movement emerged as a significant political force in 1960, when Arizona Senator Barry Goldwater challenged the Republican Party's presumptive presidential nominee, Vice President Richard Nixon. In 1962, Workman left journalism to run for the U.S. Senate as a Republican. The effort failed narrowly, yet his campaign signaled the arrival of the conservative Republicans as a new force in Deep South politics.

The book concludes by detailing the effort by Waring and Workman to confront the success of the civil rights movement in the 1960s. After his failed Senate bid in 1962, Workman returned to journalism as editorial page editor at *The State* newspaper in Columbia. With control of the two most influential editorial pages in South Carolina, Workman and Waring worked to undermine black efforts to assert their new political clout in the Deep South. In the early 1960s, the two white editors accepted the integration of higher education in South Carolina and the passage of the Civil Rights and Voting Rights acts as inevitable. Yet they escalated their rhetoric linking blacks to violent crime, and contended that "bloc voting" by African Americans undermined the democratic process. They encouraged white southerners to band together within the conservative wing of Republican Party to limit black political influence. In this way, Workman and Waring enlisted their newspapers in the segregationist countermovement that emerged in the 1960s to blunt the political gains of the black civil rights effort. Espousing a new narrative of "color-blind conservatism," members of this countermovement accepted the change in black legal status in the South, but they claimed that past racial injustices should have no bearing on present-day political debates. According to this view, blacks who raised the issue of race—and who voted based on racial concerns—were simply special pleaders seeking unearned benefits from society.[30]

Though geographically small, South Carolina has always played an outsized role in the racial history of the nation. In many ways it has served as ground zero for the most contentious and vexing issue of American democracy. From the debate over slavery at the constitutional convention through John C. Calhoun's theory of nullification, the first shots at Fort Sumter, the rejection of Reconstruction, and, finally, the rise and fall of Jim Crow, the Palmetto State has taken the lead in the battle to stand still. No state has tried harder to rebel against the arrival of the modern world. And in each of these confrontations, South Carolina newspapers played significant roles. From the secessionist fire-eaters at the *Charleston Mercury* to John McCray's fight for black voting rights and Thomas Waring's embrace of Goldwater Republicanism, the history of journalism in South Carolina has been inseparable from the state's politics. The unending struggle for civil rights in South Carolina is a testament to the courage and tenacity of its African American citizens. Their early success, and the white press' radical response, provides a rich landscape for the study of journalism and its role in shaping political change.

1 Early Struggles

In 1935, John Henry McCray was a college graduate with a good job and his life seemingly mapped out in front of him. Thin and boyishly good looking, the twenty-five-year-old African American had married Satis Victoria Ballou, his campus sweetheart from his college days in Alabama, and the two had come to live in his home state of South Carolina. Despite the ongoing Depression, he had landed a white-collar job with a successful firm in Charleston, the black-owned North Carolina Mutual Life Insurance Company. His wife soon gave birth to their first child, Donald, and the young family appeared to settle into a relatively comfortable life as part of South Carolina's tiny black middle class. But McCray had other plans. Ambitious and headstrong—even arrogant at times—he was a restless soul eager to do more with his life than sell insurance.

McCray majored in chemistry in college, but he had gotten a taste of journalism and political activism as well. Newspapering "gets into your blood," he would later say. The aspiring journalist would eventually launch his own newspaper and deploy it as a political weapon on behalf of black Carolinians. McCray's success as a civil rights activist would not come without a price. His newspaper work would eventually cost him his marriage, land him on a chain gang, and eventually force him to leave South Carolina to look for work. But McCray's efforts at the *Lighthouse and Informer* would have a lasting impact on his home state. His newspaper would help revive and sustain black activism in South Carolina during a critical period in the fight for African American equality.[1]

McCray's career change in the late 1930s should not have been a surprise. The editor's life up to that point had been bound up in the history of black resistance to white supremacy. Born in Florida in 1910, McCray and his family moved to the Charleston area when he was six years old to be closer to his mother's relatives. They settled in the tiny village of Lincolnville, a black community founded during Reconstruction by the African Methodist Episcopal Church. Reverend Richard Harvey Cain had been sent to Charleston after the Civil War to revive the AME denomination. Forced underground after Denmark Vesey's failed slave uprising in 1822, the AME emerged under Cain's leadership as a powerful institution in South Carolina. Cain founded the *Missionary Record,* a church newspaper that proclaimed itself "steeped in the spirit of black independence," and he used the paper to build membership and organize new AME congregations across the region. He solicited donations to purchase property on Calhoun Street, in the heart of Charleston, and hired Vesey's son, Robert, to design and help build a prominent new sanctuary for the Emanuel AME Church. Over the years, the church that came to be known simply as "mother Emanuel" served as a symbol of strength, dignity, and defiance for African Americans during their long struggle for equality in the South. The church would also become a convenient target for acts of white retribution. The latest assault came in 2015, when a teenager inspired by white supremacist literature carried a handgun into the church and shot and killed nine people, including one of Cain's successors as pastor at mother Emanuel, Rev. Clementa Pinckney.[2]

By 1867, Cain had grown disillusioned with the pace of change in postwar Charleston. Concerned by a steady increase in threats against black residents, Cain began to search for land outside the city where African Americans could build their own community and run their own affairs. Aboard a train called the South Carolina Special, Cain and six other AME trustees traveled across the rural Lowcountry to inspect land owned by the South Carolina Railway Commission. They eventually settled on 650 acres near the town of Summerville, located about twenty miles northwest of Charleston. Bordered by swampland, the site known as "Pump Pond" had been used as a refueling stop for the railroad. Cain and the trustees purchased the property for one thousand dollars.[3]

The black press flourished briefly during the decade of Reconstruction in South Carolina. With federal troops protecting black voting rights, a biracial Republican Party rose to power, and slowly rising literacy rates helped African American newspapers establish the beginnings of a black public sphere. During this time, Cain took control of a second newspaper, the *South Carolina Leader,* and used the secular weekly to help build a political career. Cain served as a member of the state's Reconstruction Constitutional Convention in 1868 and helped write a new state constitution that expanded voting rights, empowered state government to invest in roads and other infrastructure, and launched public education to South Carolina. As a member of the Land Commission, he pushed for the redistribution of plantation farmland to poor farmers, both black and white. In 1872, Cain was elected to an at-large seat in the U.S. House of Representatives, becoming the first African American to win a statewide election in South Carolina.[4]

By the mid-1870s, however, Cain had lost faith in the Republican Party and in Reconstruction in the South. Searching for a political alternative, he launched a new party called the Independent-Republicans and even sought an alliance with some of the state's former planter-class slave owners. In the critical election of 1876, white Democrats led by Confederate General Wade Hampton launched a campaign of fraud and violence that reclaimed power in South Carolina. The following year, the new Republican president, Rutherford B. Hayes, agreed to withdraw the last federal troops from South Carolina and bring Reconstruction to an end. Cain left for Texas four years later, and the black community he founded near Summerville soon came under siege. A group of white Democrats in the Lowcountry asserted Cain and the AME trustees had never signed a formal sales agreement with the railroad commission and thus had no legal claim to the land. By that time, however, the small community had established roots, and the AME church had access to formidable legal counsel. By 1889, the South Carolina courts had dismissed the challenge, and the black haven that Cain had launched more than two decades earlier was formally incorporated as the town of Lincolnville, South Carolina.[5]

In 1916, when McCray and his family arrived, the village remained overwhelmingly African American. McCray often claimed that his childhood in what he called "black-ruled" Lincolnville instilled in him the sense of racial pride and assertiveness that led to his political activism. Both of McCray's parents served in leadership roles—his father as the town's top law enforcement officer, his mother on the city council—and as a child he said he believed it was normal to see black adults holding positions of authority. Black children in Lincolnville had a wealth of positive role models, he said, and "you got the feeling that you belonged to an ethnic group that was special . . . and you got away from that feeling [you had] in Charleston where you are hopelessly outnumbered and you're sort of terrified."[6]

McCray excelled in Lincolnville's elementary school and at the Avery Normal Institute, Charleston's high school for black achievers. Founded in 1865 by the American Missionary Association, a New York abolitionist group, the Avery Institute was designed to produce an African American professional and leadership class in the years after the Civil War. At Avery, McCray said he especially benefited from the tutelage of a man named J. Andrew "Pearly" Simmons, a charismatic teacher who encouraged McCray's writing and his activism. McCray called Simmons "a dyed-in-the-wool 'race man' " who would "indoctrinate" his students with the notion that they were the equal of any white person.[7]

McCray graduated as valedictorian at Avery and received a scholarship to attend Talladega College in Alabama. There he honed his editorial skills writing for *The Mule's Ear,* a monthly student magazine, and he experienced his first political protest. In a series of remembrances written late in his life, McCray recounted the story of a Talladega College professor who led a small group of frightened black students in a sit-in at a local soda fountain in the early 1930s. The black professor demanded service for the group at tables that had been reserved for whites only. When the waiter refused, the professor pulled a thick stack of bills from his wallet and said, "Serve this, dammit!" Much to their surprise, the white manager complied. The brief sit-in ended without incident, McCray said, and the relieved students hurried back to campus.[8]

In college, McCray displayed the feistiness—and contrariness—that would often shadow his public career. The young journalist complained about his fellow Talladega students, writing angry editorials chastising their lack of commitment to the cause of black equality. He was especially outraged by their seeming indifference to the Scottsboro case, the racially charged conviction of nine African American teenagers accused of raping two white runaways in northern Alabama in 1931. In one editorial, he criticized students for failing to attend a campus forum on the case. "Talladega and all other Alabama Negro schools are far behind schools of other states in manifesting interest in this cause of justice—this world-wide disgrace to white American citizens," McCray wrote. "We may not possess the financial or political influence to save the lives of the boys, but we can offer our resentment to the manner in which many of the local and neighboring whites regard them."[9]

McCray graduated in 1935 and returned to the South Carolina Lowcountry. One year later, while still employed by the insurance company, McCray began working part-time at the *Charleston Messenger,* a small black weekly, and his aggressive reporting caught the eye of a local activist. Eventually, he was recruited to help revive the NAACP's moribund branch in Charleston. One of his first acts as branch president—the creation of a defense fund to support two black men accused of killing a white police detective—drew mixed reaction from a cautious African American community. Some feared he was, in McCray's words, "stirring up race trouble," but the young activist believed the police had framed the suspects and that it was time for blacks in Charleston to confront local white authority.[10]

By 1937, McCray had established himself as a strong new voice in Charleston's black community. But his next act stunned the NAACP leadership. In April, McCray wrote a letter to Charleston's leading white newspaper announcing his position on one of the NAACP's chief priorities: winning congressional approval of a federal antilynching law. Since its founding in 1909, the national organization had been pushing for legislation that would empower the federal government to investigate and prosecute lynching. Board chairman Louis Wright believed such legislation was central to the "fundamental citizenship struggle in the South." By 1937, NAACP leaders believed they finally had the support they needed to overcome the opposition of powerful white southern Democrats in the Senate and get the bill passed.[11]

Yet in his letter, McCray criticized the "caustic methods" of the national NAACP. The young journalist and local NAACP branch leader maintained that lynching would fade away naturally and that black South Carolinians were "content to wait" for that to occur. He said Charleston's African American community wanted to "promote the basic principles of friendship" with whites and "were not involved in the goings-on beyond the Mason-Dixon line." McCray published his editorial as a letter to Charleston's *News and Courier,* a newspaper whose famously conservative editor, William Watts Ball, had emerged as a leading critic of Roosevelt's New Deal policies. Ball frequently accused the NAACP and other "outside agitators" of stirring up racial problems in the state; McCray's letter appeared to support Ball's claim.[12]

The backlash was immediate. NAACP Executive Director Walter White repudiated McCray in his own letter to the *News and Courier,* claiming the branch president had misused his position and had embarrassed intelligent African Americans in the South. Angry members of the local NAACP branch convened a special meeting to vote McCray out as president. Less than two years after his return to South Carolina, McCray's reputation as a civil rights activist was in tatters. Among the state's small, close-knit group of black activists, he was marked as an accommodator, a man who wanted to appease white supremacy, not confront it. Louise Purvis Bell, a member of the Charleston branch's executive committee, delivered the harshest verdict. In her view, McCray was an "Uncle Tom and a traitor."[13]

McCray never fully explained or apologized for his decision to oppose the NAACP's campaign in favor of the antilynching law. In an oral history interview conducted in 1985, he dismissed the controversy without going into details. The editor claimed his critics in the local NAACP "had been sitting on their hip pockets doing nothing" before his return to Charleston. By the time of that interview, McCray wanted to be remembered as a fearless fighter for civil rights who had always challenged white supremacy, but in 1937 the young activist had clearly embraced a classic accommodationist strategy. McCray wanted to focus on black voting rights in Charleston, not federal law in Washington, and he believed the obsequious tone of his letter would put whites at ease and help persuade them to limit restrictions on voter registration. He tried to ameliorate white concerns about black activism, to assure white supremacists that local black leaders wanted to avoid confrontation.[14]

Two years later, McCray would reemerge to help lead the fight against that type of approach in South Carolina. He would launch his own newspaper and eventually join forces with a new, more militant group of NAACP leaders who wanted to confront white supremacy directly in the courts, at the ballot box, and in the public sphere. One of those leaders, Modjeska Monteith Simkins, would play a key role in luring McCray into the fight. A generation older than McCray, Simkins was a veteran of an earlier movement that flourished briefly in South Carolina during World War I. She had seen first-hand the power a newspaper could play in political organizing. She had also seen a brutal white backlash crush that movement, and Simkins detested the political fear that pervaded the black community in its aftermath. To rise, she believed a new movement in South Carolina needed its own "fighting news organ," one that would confront the accommodationist impulse that dominated black leadership in the 1930s. She wanted a newspaper that would go to war against conservative black leaders who opposed confrontation with white supremacy. Simkins believed McCray's paper could play that role.

Looking back, McCray's sharp turn from an alleged "Uncle Tom" to a fire-breathing opponent of accommodation may seem unfathomable, but it was hardly unique in the black community in the Deep South in the first half of the twentieth century. The debate over how to respond to white oppression had vexed and divided African Americans since the end of Reconstruction. Booker T. Washington had been dead for twenty years when McCray graduated from college and returned to South Carolina, but the strategy of accommodationism that Washington articulated in his famous Atlanta speech of 1895 remained influential among black elites across much of the Deep South. Washington proposed an accommodation with white supremacy to try to avoid an open war between the races that he knew his people could not win. He encouraged blacks to give up their rights to full citizenship and focus instead on economic development and racial uplift. To avoid conflict with whites, Washington remained vague about accommodation's ultimate goal. But for African Americans the strategy was clear: give up the immediate struggle for social and political equality, but obtain those rights over time through economic advancement. Over the next three decades, black Americans, North and South, debated the merits of Washington and his proposals for negotiating the Jim Crow South. As McCray's career showed, the contours of that debate were never simple and clear-cut. Accommodationists sometimes called for confrontation, and protesters occasionally practiced accommodation. In the 1930s, however, most black southerners still accepted one basic premise of the accommodationist strategy: The white leadership in the South had the power and the will to use violent force against blacks with little fear of a northern backlash. A direct confrontation with white supremacists would be suicidal.[15]

The aggressive civil rights movement that emerged in South Carolina in the late 1930s did not arise out of thin air. It was shaped by a long and difficult history of struggle, one that included an intense debate over strategy. To understand the actions of John McCray, Modjeska Simkins, and their newspaper, it is essential to place them in this broader context of African American history in the state and nation in the twentieth century.

Washington, Du Bois, and the Rise of Civil Rights Activism in South Carolina

Washington's 1895 "Atlanta compromise" address had come in the midst of a post-Reconstruction campaign launched by radical white supremacists determined to claim undisputed political power in the South. Led by men such as James K. Vardaman in Mississippi, Charles B. Aycock in North Carolina, and "Pitchfork" Ben Tillman in South Carolina, these "reformers" represented small farmers and working-class whites who had suffered the most during a national economic downturn in the 1880s. As a young militia leader, Tillman had helped Wade Hampton, the former planter and Confederate general, take power in South Carolina in the bloody and contested election of 1876. Although a white supremacist, Hampton had taken a more paternalistic approach to the former slaves. After taking office, he allowed African Americans to continue to vote and to hold some government appointments. By 1890, Tillman had turned on Hampton and led the effort to seize power from the state's planter-class elites. In his campaign for governor, Tillman demonized blacks as an inferior and violent race incapable of assimilating into a civilized and democratic society. He blamed blacks for rising crime rates in the cities, for increased fraud at the polls, and for harboring an uncontrollable lust for white women. In the guise of protecting the honor of southern womanhood, Tillman and other radical white supremacists across the South launched a campaign of violence against blacks that turned public lynching into a common spectacle.[16]

With his Atlanta speech in 1895 and his acclaimed autobiography, *Up from Slavery*, published six years later, Washington articulated a strategy that captivated white America and, in the beginning, appeared to many blacks to be the best available course of action, given the dire circumstances. Washington wooed the southern planter-class elites with soothing language promising black acquiescence to the ways of the white South. He encouraged fellow African Americans to accept the "customs" of the South, including its "prejudices." On the question of black resistance, Washington said black southerners should understand "that the agitation of questions of social equality is the extremist folly." In later speeches, Washington went further, urging African Americans to worry less about white oppression and more about their own improvement. "I fear that the Negro race lays too much stress on its grievances and not enough on its opportunities," he said, opening up a line of conservative criticism that echoes to this day. The paternalistic white elites in the South embraced Washington's vision of a compliant black population eager to focus on economic growth rather than politics, but Tillman and the radical Democrats remained unimpressed. They considered African Americans an existential threat to white rule in the South, and they remained committed to the strategy of political and social exclusion.[17]

The man who emerged as Washington's leading critic, W.E.B. Du Bois, had initially supported the 1895 "Atlanta compromise." The young professor sent Washington a note of congratulations shortly after this speech, and he praised Washington's accommodationist strategy in the *New York Age,* a prominent black newspaper. Washington's proposal could provide "the basis of a real settlement between whites and blacks in the South," Du Bois wrote, "if the South opened to the Negroes the doors of economic opportunity and the Negroes co-operated with the white South in political sympathy." As Washington's popularity and power grew, however, Du Bois grew more concerned. By 1901, Washington had become what his biographer, Louis R. Harlan, called "the most powerful black minority-group boss of his time." From his base at his Tuskegee Institute, Washington used his newfound fundraising prowess to develop a political network—the Tuskegee machine—to empower his supporters and to punish those who dissented. He used his wellspring of white financial donations "to buy black newspapers and bend their editorials to his viewpoint, to control college professors and presidents . . . to infiltrate the leading church denominations and fraternal orders."[18]

As Washington tightened his grip on the black community, Du Bois turned against him. A scholar who wrote with "brooding passion and brilliant pen,"

Du Bois used his literary skills and access to print culture to launch a campaign to counter Washington's growing control over black political leadership. In a review of *Up From Slavery,* Washington's popular autobiography, Du Bois noted that Washington's call for political accommodation and industrial education were not original ideas but had been widely debated among southern blacks over the past decade. More importantly, Du Bois pointed out that despite his newfound fame among whites, Washington did not hold a monopoly on leadership in the black community. Following in the footsteps of Frederick Douglass, who died the same year Washington made his Atlanta speech, black editors William Monroe Trotter and Ida B. Wells had been using newspapers and other forms of print culture to deliver clarion calls urging protest against second-class citizenship.[19]

In 1903, Du Bois followed up with his masterpiece, *The Souls of Black Folk,* a series of probing essays that would help define the African American experience in early twentieth century America. Du Bois's biographer, David Levering Lewis, described the book's publication as an "epochal" event in African American history, and NAACP activist James Weldon Johnson claimed the work had a greater impact on African Americans "than any other single book published since *Uncle Tom's Cabin.*" Through his elegant prose, Du Bois explored "the strange meaning of being black" in America, correctly predicting that "the problem of the Twentieth Century is the problem of the color line." In his opening essay, Du Bois lifted "the veil" shrouding the inner recesses of black life so that white Americans might understand "what it feels like to be a problem." Black Americans who live within that veil, Du Bois argued, experienced a cultural and psychological "two-ness." They were "an American, a Negro; two souls, two thoughts, two unreconciled strivings; two warring ideals in one dark body, whose dogged strength alone keeps it from being torn asunder."[20]

It was in his third essay—"Of Mr. Booker T. Washington and Others"—that Du Bois resumed his criticism of Washington and his strategy of accommodationism. The paternalistic white southerners with whom Washington sought to compromise—South Carolina's Wade Hampton and other remnants of the old planter-class aristocracy—had lost political control, Du Bois contended. They were being replaced by a new generation of radical white Democrats, men such as South Carolina's Ben Tillman who believed blacks should live in permanent subjugation. Du Bois watched violence against black southerners increase while Washington's public rhetoric of accommodation and acceptance remained unchanged. By demanding black submission during this time of "intensified prejudice," Du Bois wrote, Washington was encouraging white repression: "In the history of nearly all other races and peoples, the doctrine preached at such crises has been that manly self-respect is worth more than lands and houses, and that a people who voluntarily surrender such respect, or cease striving for it, are not worth civilizing."[21]

Du Bois argued that Washington's political acquiescence would set back African American progress and lock in white rule for decades to come. Washington's doctrine, Du Bois wrote, allowed whites in the North and South to "shift the burden of the Negro problem to the Negro's shoulders and stand aside as critical and rather pessimistic spectators." Two years later, in 1905, he helped found the Niagara movement, a group of black professionals determined to counter Washington's influence. By the end of the decade, members of the Niagara movement had joined forces with white progressives in the North to form the biracial NAACP.[22]

Founded during a series of meetings in 1909 and 1910, the NAACP sought to rally support for the equal treatment of all races under the law. Though white progressives dominated the founding executive committee, it was Du Bois who served as the voice of the new civil rights organization. Through the pages of *The Crisis,* the group's monthly publication, Du Bois established the interpretive lens through which the NAACP would report on public events. *The Crisis* "first and foremost" would be a newspaper, Du Bois wrote in the first edition, but it was a newspaper with a special mission. "The object of this publication," he declared, "is to set forth those facts and arguments which show the danger of race prejudice." In doing so, the NAACP newspaper would protect "the rights of men, irrespective of color or race, for the highest ideals of American democracy." For the following two decades, Du Bois would use his newspaper to highlight the contradictions at the heart of the American democratic experiment, with legalized discrimination existing in a nation that proclaimed its commitment to equality and justice for all people. He defined black efforts to overcome discrimination as a necessary and patriotic act of citizenship that would restore the nation's damaged civic ideal.[23]

Since the first black newspaper, *Freedom's Journal,* was published in 1827, African Americans have used the press as a vehicle to speak for themselves. Yet with more than 90 percent of their intended audience living in the South, northern black newspapers and pamphlets struggled to find readers. It was not until the beginning of the Great Migration that a robust black public sphere could develop in the North. Since the Civil War, the industrial revolution had been luring white workers from the fields to the cities, creating the giant urban centers of the North. Yet blacks had been mostly excluded from these northern factory jobs. In 1914, the start of World War I halted European immigration to the United States, creating a shortage of industrial workers in the North. Suddenly in demand, southern blacks flocked to industrial boomtowns such as Detroit, Chicago, Pittsburgh, and New York. Abandoning the wide expanses of the rural South, they now lived in close quarters in teeming urban neighborhoods.

Their arrival came at a time when newspapers and magazines were flourishing in the United States. The industrial growth that had created the great cities of the North had increased the demand for advertising and generated a booming media industry. By 1920, the United States had surpassed Europe in the number of periodicals published. Under these promising circumstances, the black press emerged more fully in the North, with Robert Abbott's weekly *Chicago Defender* leading the way. Launched as a one-man operation in 1905, Abbott's *Defender* grew and prospered across the following decade. But like the rest of the black press, it existed in the shadow of white society. Mostly ignored by white readers, black newspapers and magazines carried their interpretations of public events to the growing black population in the North. In 1914, when South Carolina's notorious Governor Cole Blease expressed his support for lynching, the *Defender* railed in anger at the "degenerate . . . foul-mouthed" politician. "The Whole World Holds Its Nose When This Decayed Buffoon Breaks Loose," one *Defender* headline read. By repeatedly highlighting discrimination and demanding justice, the black press helped crystalize black public opinion in the North and create a robust and vital public sphere capable of asserting its democratic rights. With his sharp intellect and fluid writing skills, Du Bois turned *The Crisis* into an influential source of analysis within this public sphere. Closely read by black editors as well as black grassroots activists, *The Crisis* served as a leading voice for black inclusion in the political and economic life of the nation.[24]

By 1915, *The Crisis* had made its way into the hands of attorney Butler W. Nance, a leading black activist in Columbia, South Carolina. Nance had helped established the Capital Civic League, an organization devoted to the fight for African American rights in South Carolina. Describing himself as a "long-time subscriber" to *The Crisis,* Nance wrote Du Bois a letter in June 1915 expressing his interests in having the Capital Civic League become a branch of the NAACP. "There are several things that could be done," Nance wrote, "if you would not be afraid to operate in the South."[25]

Nance's letter arrived at NAACP headquarters at a propitious moment. James Weldon Johnson's emergence as the organization's field director in December 1916 signaled a new effort to organize in the Deep South. By the end of 1916, more than a quarter million African Americans had left the South for jobs in the North. Yet as Johnson noted at the time, the great migration created new possibilities for those who stayed behind. For the first time in decades, whites in the South were forced to acknowledge the value of the black work force. And as Johnson argued in a 1917 speech in Savannah, Georgia, the cracks in the status quo created by the wartime disruption offered "the Negro race the chance to register its first protest against its treatment in the South." Across the first six months of 1917, Johnson traveled from Richmond, Virginia, to Tampa, Florida, and organized more than a dozen local branches. The organization's so-called "Southern Empire" gave the civil rights group what Du Bois called "a real first line of defense facing the enemy at proper range."[26]

As a teenager, Modjeska Monteith Simkins would join this "line of defense" in South Carolina. Her mother and her aunt were early stalwarts of the new NAACP branch in Columbia. Both had been members of Du Bois's Niagara movement before joining the NAACP, and they instilled their commitment to political activism in their children. Simkins had a front-row seat as the fledgling movement gained traction during the war years. She saw how Nance and his Columbia activists took the first tentative steps toward the development of a communications strategy. Slowly, they learned how to use a newspaper to help spread their message and try to shape public debate within the black community. She also saw how frequently those activists had to compete with conservative voices in the community who wanted no part of their protest politics.[27]

Like many black newspapers in the South at the turn of twentieth century, Columbia's *Southern Indicator* had benefited from its close association with Washington's Tuskegee machine. The paper received financial help from Washington's organization, and in return, editor J. A. Roach pushed Washington's strategy of political accommodation, economic prosperity, and racial uplift in his editorials. After Washington's death in 1915, however, Roach offered his support to the new NAACP branch. Yet Nance and his fellow activists were not quite sure how to use this new weapon. At first, they were hesitant to publish the press releases sent by the national NAACP office. During one exchange with national officials, a Columbia activist asked timidly if it was "in keeping with the policy of the office to allow a local newspaper to publish some of the releases." The NAACP national officials seemed bemused by this query, because the news releases were produced with the *hope* that they would be picked up by newspapers and read by the public. In a handwritten note on the letter, one national staff member said emphatically, "Yes, Go Ahead!" But the organization's letter in response was more diplomatic. The director of branches said the national office "should be very pleased" to see the releases run in the Columbia newspaper and in the future would send them directly to the editor.[28]

The *Southern Indicator*'s shift from Washington accommodator to NAACP supporter exemplified the fluid nature of black civil rights strategy at the time. During the early years of World War I, Nance and his colleagues in the NAACP had battled that culture of accommodation in the black community, with mixed results. In his letter to Du Bois in 1915, Nance had included a copy of the Capital Civic League's latest "Address to the People of South Carolina," which the group had distributed as a flyer. The statement called for the creation of an "organized movement" to fight for African American equality, and it criticized "the weak-kneed ministers who claim the church is no place to talk civil rights." This was clearly a shot at the best-known black leader in South Carolina, Reverend Richard Carroll of Columbia, a protégé of Washington's who had come to embody the accommodationist strategy in the state. Carroll urged black Carolinians to forego politics and accept their inferior status in society. "The negro will never be a ruling or dominant race," Carroll told the *Charleston News and Courier* in 1905. "The people who think will always rule, [not] the people who sing, as do the negroes." Of Tillman and the white supremacists who had taken control of the state in the 1890s and carried out a violent campaign against black voting rights, Carroll said: "Their patience has been great. Their tolerance has been marvelous. We have made many friends among them, and what we need to do is strive to make their friendship stronger and more abiding." To accomplish this, Carroll said African Americans should "focus on their own short-comings instead of advising whites about theirs."[29]

Using his own newspaper, the *Plowman,* to help spread his message, Carroll preached a message of racial uplift, but one that emphasized white superiority in the strict hierarchy of southern society. "The white man must stay in his place," Carroll said. "When he uplifts himself, he will be followed by the negro at a respectful distance, but when he lowers himself to the plane of the negro, then the negro will get out of his place and trouble will be brewed."[30]

Like Washington, Carroll's message of appeasement attracted strong support from white leaders, particularly from the Gonzalez brothers, founders of *The State* newspaper in Columbia. Created for the specific political purpose of opposing Ben Tillman and his allies in South Carolina, *The State* advocated a type of white supremacy associated with the state's planter-class elites. Like Carroll, the newspaper placed a great emphasis on hierarchy and the "place" of whites and blacks in southern society. The newspaper supported black aspirations for uplift, as long as they did not interfere with white rule or create racial turmoil. Editor William E. Gonzales embraced Carroll and backed him financially and editorially well into the 1920s. Carroll held an annual conference on race relations in South Carolina where Gonzales and other white leaders often spoke, although Tillman never accepted his many invitations to appear at the event. In March 1909, Booker T. Washington toured South Carolina, with Carroll among the black dignitaries at his side. Washington visited twelve cities and made several whistle-stop speeches in between to spread his vision of both racial uplift and peaceful coexistence with white supremacy. *The State* wrote glowingly of Washington's tour and encouraged whites to go hear him speak. For white South Carolinians, Carroll and his followers represented the best of the black community, and as the nation prepared to enter World War I, they accepted the servile tone of Carroll's public pronouncements as widespread black acceptance of the racial status quo in this state.[31]

Yet Carroll, the state's most famous accommodator, would also come to symbolize black ambivalence toward the strategy. Much like McCray in the late 1930s, Carroll would surprise his white supporters and his black critics with a sudden shift in strategy during the war. His earlier obsequiousness had approached the level of parody, but Carroll had been biding his time looking for an opening to push for black rights. He believed the war and the increase in black migration from the state had created that opening. It was time for black Carolinians to "to come into their own," Carroll argued. He used his access to *The State* newspaper to press publicly for better schools, better wages, and better protection under the law. Lawmakers meet "year after year to make laws for the uplift and salvation of white people" while ignoring the needs of blacks, Carroll wrote in the newspaper. He also demanded that whites stop vilifying African Americans and engineering racial conflicts to rally voters each election cycle—a criticism aimed at Cole Blease, the former governor and frequent political candidate who often defended lynching as a means of controlling the black race.[32]

With Carroll's Baptist ministry now on board, the black civil rights struggle gained momentum during the war years. In February 1919, Butler Nance sent a celebratory letter to Mary White Ovington, executive secretary of the NAACP, announcing a big victory for the South Carolina branches. The state legislature had forced the school board in Charleston to hire black teachers to staff Negro public schools. Until then, Charleston had only allowed whites to teach black children in its public schools. Nance was ecstatic. "This is the culmination of a fight that started thirty-two years ago," he wrote. "Let us continue to fight until twelve million American citizens are PHYSICALLY FREE FROM PEONAGE, MENTALLY FREE FROM IGNORANCE, PO-LITICALLY FREE FROM DISFRANCHISEMENT, SOCIALLY FREE FROM INSULT. God bless the NAACP."[33]

Nance could be excused for his uppercase exuberance. The
had helped launch appeared to be on a roll. Four years after he
the editor of *The Crisis* and asked to join the NAACP, the civil ri
tion had active branches operating in every corner of South C
Charleston on the coast to the capital city of Columbia and the ~~~~
farming town of Orangeburg in the Midlands, up through the Piedmont
cities of Greenville and Spartanburg and across the tobacco-growing region
along the Pee Dee River in the northeast. Those branches had launched a
statewide voter registration drive and pushed local courts to call more blacks
for jury duty. In 1920, after passage of the Nineteenth Amendment allowing
women to vote, Modjeska Monteith and her mother joined a group of black
women who tried to register in Richland County, where Columbia is located.
At first, they were left standing in line for hours without explanation. Some
were eventually allowed to register, but others were denied based on the
state's literacy requirement—even though the majority of the women had
college degrees. A furious Nance pulled the national NAACP into the fray.
The South Carolina women had been treated "in every way, save humane,"
Nance complained, adding, "we mean to stay in the fight until every woman
who possess the qualification is registered."[34]

In Columbia, Nance and his colleagues joined the national NAACP in
denouncing D. W. Griffith's notorious film, *The Birth of a Nation*. Based on
Thomas Dixon's novel, *The Clansman*, Griffith's film depicted Reconstruction
as a period of corruption, plunder, and chaos fueled by black lawlessness.
Griffith's spectacular production used the new medium of motion pictures
to further the white supremacist propaganda campaign against black citizenship. As a powerful communicative institution, the growing feature-film
industry would play a significant role in delivering interpretations and influ-
encing public opinion across the twentieth century. Thus the fight over *Birth
of a Nation* was an important confrontation in the long battle for African
American inclusion within the nation's democratic life. The film fed popular
stereotypes of blacks as both childlike buffoons and violent sexual predators.
And by portraying black lawmakers as the pawns of nefarious white carpetbaggers, Griffith's movie furthered the southern white argument that blacks
were intellectually incapable of participating in the democratic process. In
South Carolina, the new NAACP chapter organized protests against a 1918
screening of *The Birth of a Nation* in Columbia, arguing that the movie promoted "racial antagonism" at a time when brave African American soldiers
were "giving their all for worldwide democracy."[35]

The campaign against *The Birth of a Nation* was part of a surge in black
political activism during the war. Another Columbia black civic group, the

Lincoln Memorial Association, urged lawmakers to prosecute lynching and appoint African American superintendents to manage black school districts. And in Charleston, the NAACP protested the navy's effort to fill jobs at an on-base clothing factory with "white women only." As a result, the navy eventually hired 250 black women. Black Charlestonians also launched their successful effort to replace white teachers with black ones at African American public schools. As the war came to an end, and as black soldiers returned to the state, leaders planned to step up the fight for equality. In a ceremony at Benedict College in Columbia, local physician S. F. Haygood said black soldiers had fought bravely and valiantly for democracy abroad, and now, "We want democracy at home."[36]

The White Crackdown

The spreading black activism shocked a white supremacist leadership more used to the timid ways of the accommodationists. A rising young politician named James F. Byrnes had taken note of the NAACP's rise in South Carolina, and he believed he knew whom to blame for the sudden increase in black assertiveness. Like state NAACP leader Butler Nance, Byrnes had also been reading the *Crisis,* and he accused Du Bois and the civil rights organization of instigating racial unrest in the South. Born to a poor Catholic family in Charleston, Byrnes had scrambled to earn a law degree and become a protégé of Tillman's. A U.S. congressman in 1919, Byrnes would go on to serve in the Senate, on the Supreme Court, as a top aide to President Roosevelt during World War II, and as President Truman's secretary of state. He would be seen as a more moderate southern voice during the civil rights struggle to come. On an August day in 1919, however, he stepped into the well of the U.S. House and delivered what his biographer has called "one of the most inflammatory speeches on race ever read into the *Congressional Record.*" It was near the end of a hot summer of racial violence in small towns and large cities across the nation. In Charleston, two African Americans died and seventeen people of both races were injured when white sailors stationed at the nearby Navy Yard brawled with some black youths. Byrnes claimed the black press, led by De Bois's *The Crisis,* had radicalized black veterans returning from the war and helped incite the spreading violence. He demanded that the editor be charged with treason. Byrnes claimed that "if charging the government with lynching, disfranchising its citizens, encouraging ignorance, and stealing from its citizens, does not constitute a violation of the espionage act, it is difficult to conceive language sufficiently abusive to constitute a violation." The congressman concluded with a stark warning for black Americans: if they did not like postwar America, they were welcome to leave. If necessary, Byrnes said, he would support the forced deportation of black leaders.[37]

Byrnes's strong words on the House floor were part of a national effort to taint civil rights work with the red scare of rising communism in 1919. The congressman made the connection explicit, accusing Du Bois and the rest of the black press of instigating violence in an attempt to create a "little Russia" in the South. Two months after Byrnes's speech, the American Legion in Columbia followed his lead and passed a resolution condemning the NAACP as a group that supported communism. The resolution linked the civil rights organization to the International Workers of the World, a militant labor union cofounded by the American Socialist Party.[38]

Black leaders in South Carolina tried to counter these red-scare attacks with compelling stories of the bravery and heroism exhibited by African Americans who fought for freedom and democracy in Europe. To win this battle of narratives, however, African Americans needed the help of allies within the nation's mainstream culture. They needed the support of empathetic opinion leaders who could help spread their message and sway public opinion. Without such access, black voices were overwhelmed by the arguments put forward by their enemies. White supremacists in South Carolina were free to crush the African American movement without fear of northern intervention. They could use the threat of overwhelming violence and economic retribution to deter black political organization and, most importantly, prevent its spread from the small core of NAACP activists in the cities to the larger African American population in the countryside.

In the months following Byrnes's speech, the NAACP branches in South Carolina began to feel the effects of the white backlash. In October 1919, Nance wrote to James Weldon Johnson to inform the NAACP national office of "a little trouble" that had occurred in the Piedmont town of Anderson. The local NAACP president "was run out of that city—NEVER TO RETURN, so the Anderson paper states," Nance wrote. Tensions were also high in Columbia, where "a race riot was narrowly averted only by the better element of both races putting their heads together," he wrote. "We have not had a lynching yet; but we cannot tell how long."[39]

The threat of lynching remained constant for black South Carolinians across the 1920s. The estimates vary, but studies suggest as many as fourteen African Americans were killed by white mobs between 1919 and 1927. Five of those murders are believed to have occurred in 1921, when white Democrats were eager to halt the civil rights activism that had emerged during the war. White politicians such as Cole Blease signaled their support for the use of mob violence to control the black population during the first three decades

of Jim Crow rule. Blease served as governor from 1911 to 1915 and was elected
to the U.S. Senate in 1924. While governor, he urged white men in South
Carolina to guard against "the black ape and baboon" who lurks in the dark
waiting for the chance to rape a white woman. Lynch mobs were necessary,
Blease argued, because they helped maintain law and order in South Carolina. In 1912, he told the national governors' conference that "whenever the
constitution of my state steps between me and the defense of the virtue of a
white woman, then I say to hell with the constitution!" After receiving reports
of a lynching, Blease would often celebrate publicly with what a northern
newspaper described as a "bizarre death dance."[40]

The use of state-sanctioned terror to enforce the new Jim Crow order had
been a part of life in the Carolinas since the 1890s. Like his protégé Cole
Blease, Ben Tillman had encouraged white mobs to use force to suppress
black political aspirations. Tillman had organized "red shirt" militias that
helped prevent blacks from voting in the 1876 election that ended Republican Party rule in South Carolina. As governor and then U.S. senator, he
organized and led the 1895 convention that rewrote the state's constitution
and imposed Jim Crow laws that enforced segregation and prevented blacks
from participating in politics. As a senator during the volatile election year
of 1898, Tillman would play a significant role in launching violent assaults
on black communities on both sides of the Carolina border.

The first occurred on November 8 in rural Greenwood County, South
Carolina. When a prominent white Republican, Robert "Red" Tolbert, attempted to register black voters to support his congressional run, angry
white Democrats responded with a campaign of terror. Dozens of blacks
were slaughtered, and hundreds more fled the county. Historians note that
the so-called Phoenix massacre—named after the small community where
the violence began—had both political and economic motivations. Triggered
by the effort to register black voters, the white anger also had roots in labor
competition between white and black sharecroppers in Greenwood County.
The massacre not only denied blacks the vote but also forced many to flee
their farms, allowing whites to rent farm land at a lower rate in the county.[41]

Two days after the Phoenix massacre, white Democrats in North Carolina
launched an assault on the black community in the port city of Wilmington,
about fifty miles from the South Carolina border. The massacre came after
a vicious political campaign in which newspapers played a central role and
helped trigger the violence. Led by Josephus Daniels, editor of the *Raleigh
News and Observer*, newspapers supporting the Democratic Party portrayed
blacks and their "white nigger" political allies as thieves, murderers, and
rapists who were destroying white civilization in the South. They vilified

black leaders in Wilmington as "black beasts" and "black brutes" who had
an uncontrollable lust for white women. Daniels hired cartoonist Norman
Jennett to ratchet up the propaganda against the biracial Fusion Party that
had defeated the white Democrats in the elections of 1894 and 1896. One Jennett drawing depicted a giant beast labeled "Negro Rule" over a caption that
read: "The Vampire That Haunts North Carolina." Another cartoon showed
a giant foot labeled "The Negro" crushing a "white man"; that caption asked,
"How Long Will This Last?" Meantime, the *Raleigh News and Observer,* the
Charlotte Daily Observer, and the *Wilmington Messenger* produced a steady
stream of stories describing black assaults on white women that were based
on little more than rumor, innuendo, and urban legend. As Daniels conceded
late in his life, the *News and Observer* was "cruel in its flagellations" and
"never very careful" about running down the details. The tension escalated
when Alexander Manley, editor of Wilmington's black newspaper, the *Daily
Record,* responded with a provocative editorial disputing the rape allegations
and claiming that when interracial sex did occur in Wilmington, it was usually initiated by a white woman.[42]

As Election Day approached, Tillman arrived in North Carolina to rally
the "red shirts," a paramilitary group of white Democrats modeled after the
organization he had helped found back in 1876. In a series of speeches, Tillman ridiculed and shamed the white supremacists for failing to follow the
lead of their South Carolina brethren. He boasted of his exploits as a militia
leader who had helped steal the 1876 election in South Carolina, and he
encouraged North Carolina Democrats to use the same "shotgun policy" to
end black voting in their state.[43]

Tillman's rhetoric and Daniels's press propaganda stoked a fire that could
not be contained. On November 10, after Democrats had swept the elections
statewide, a mob of heavily armed whites burned Manley's newspaper and
marched through the streets of Wilmington killing black residents. Dozens
died in the massacre, and hundreds more fled the city. Wilmington's black
office holders, who were not up for reelection that year, were nonetheless
removed from office in what historians have described as an American coup.[44]

The black press in the North demanded federal authorities intervene in
Wilmington and in Greenwood County, South Carolina, but the northern
white press did little more than note the outrageousness of the violence in
the Carolinas. In Washington, the McKinley administration refused to get
involved. Without the prospect of northern support, African Americans who
faced the threat of open violence in the Carolinas had two choices: leave the
state, which many did, or find ways to accommodate white supremacy and
learn to live with the racial status quo.

The massacres at Wilmington and Phoenix established a precedent that would hold firm across the first three decades of Jim Crow rule. Black Carolinians understood that neither state nor national authorities would step in to protect them from extralegal violence or economic retribution. Rural blacks, who comprised the overwhelming majority of the South's African American population, remained dependent on white landowners for their livelihood. Given those circumstances, it was no surprise that many in the black community would adopt the strategy of accommodation.

Already under siege, the civil rights movement in South Carolina received a devastating final blow in February 1923. A homemade postcard sent to the national NAACP offices by a member of the Columbia branch delivered the sad news: "Pres. Butler W. Nance, atty., died suddenly Monday 2/19/23 four hours after stroke." Nance had been the undisputed leader and chief organizer of the local movement; his departure left the Columbia NAACP branch rudderless. The national office worked furiously to revive the branch and sent emotional pleas encouraging remaining members to inject new life into the organization. But the white crackdown had frightened supporters. In 1926, the city's remaining NAACP members conceded defeat. A letter to the national office stated simply that the branch in South Carolina's capital city was now "inactive."[45]

One South Carolinian who tried to keep up the fight during the white crackdown in the 1920s was attorney Nathaniel Frederick. A staunch Republican, Frederick had launched a newspaper, the *Palmetto Leader,* and used it to demand federal antilynching legislation. Described "as the bravest man in South Carolina" by a national NAACP official, Frederick often defended blacks who had been accused of murder and rape in the state. In 1926, Frederick took on the case of Sam Lowman, his wife, and his son after they were accused of murdering the Aiken County sheriff. The case was so thin against the Lowmans that a white jury could not reach a verdict at their first trial. Before a second trial could be held, however, a white mob kidnapped the Lowmans from jail, took them to a nearby wooded area, and shot and burned them to death. Despite threats against his life, Frederick rushed to Aiken County to gather evidence of the crime, and he printed scathing editorials about the events in the *Palmetto Leader.* During this period, national NAACP officials pleaded with Frederick to try to revive the branch in Columbia, and the attorney and publisher tried. He continued to write hard-hitting editorials in the *Leader* demanding black voting rights and protection from mob violence, but he could not increase NAACP membership or organize collective action in the state.[46]

By 1935, when John McCray graduated from college, the surge in black activism that marked the war years had long passed. He returned to his home state to find a desolate political landscape. The NAACP existed as "little more than a paper organization," with branches in Charleston, Columbia, and Greenville, but none in the rural counties where most African Americans lived. After touring the state, one national NAACP official reported that South Carolina's black community was listless and disengaged: "The traditional organizations of the Negro community, their churches, colleges, civic welfare leagues . . . were generally quiescent." The *Palmetto Leader* had begun to soften its political coverage during the Depression in hopes of retaining some white advertising. With Nathaniel Frederick's death in 1938, the paper turned away from politics altogether and began to publish society and religious news almost exclusively.[47]

Beneath that placid political surface, however, there were rumblings of change. The Depression and Roosevelt's New Deal policies had shifted the political landscape ever so slightly, creating an opening for black activists like Modjeska Monteith Simkins to reassert their influence. As a young woman, Simkins had watched the black demand for civil rights gain traction during World War I, only to see the movement crushed during the early 1920s by a coordinated white backlash. Yet even during those dark days, when the fear of white retribution was pervasive and the call for accommodation grew, she retained faith in black South Carolinians. They did not accept white supremacy willingly, she argued, and they would fight back—if they thought they could win. As Du Bois had noted earlier in the century, "Whenever we submit to humiliation and oppression it is because of superior brute force; and even when bending to the inevitable we bend with unabated protest."[48]

By the time McCray began publishing his first newspaper, the *Charleston Lighthouse*, in 1939, South Carolina's black community was at a turning point. The spirit of protest had reemerged, yet it still had to compete with a powerful culture of accommodation that dominated black political thought in the state. For the movement to expand to the countryside and rally support among a majority of African Americans in the state, the NAACP needed to persuade the mass of black South Carolinians of the efficacy of protest. Otherwise, the emerging activism of the late 1930s would fade in the same way as its predecessor had in the years after World War I. To avoid that fate, NAACP leaders in the state realized the need to build a broad-based opposition movement that united the African American community. To achieve that goal, Simkins said she believed the organization needed a strong communications tool. "We were getting ready to open the statewide fight for the ballot and we needed a newspaper," she recalled. *The Palmetto Leader* was more like a "church paper," she said, and it was not about to join the fight. Simkins had taken note of McCray's work in Charleston. He had "a knack for newspaper writing," she said, and he seemed to enjoy confrontation. She thought he might be the right choice for the job ahead.[49]

2 A Newspaper Joins the Movement

Mary Modjeska Monteith was born on the cusp of a new millennium—December 5, 1899. But for an African American child growing up South Carolina, the coming century hardly looked promising. Later in life, Monteith recalled fond memories of her early childhood in a small neighborhood on the outskirts of Columbia. She remembered her father as a kind and "softhearted" man who bought the children candy on Saturdays. Relatively affluent by the standards of his community, Henry Monteith would often give money to friends and neighbors in need. It was Modjeska's mother, Rachael, who administered the discipline in the Monteith home. More than once, she recalled hearing her mother chastise her father and predict that he "would end up dying in the poorhouse." Modjeska was Rachel's first born, and she demanded that her eldest daughter work hard at school and help take care of her seven siblings at home. She was not a mean woman, Modjeska said, but Rachael Monteith was a realist. To survive, she believed her children must see the world clearly, "no matter how cruel or atrocious it might be."[1]

Modjeska Monteith grew up during the rise of Jim Crow rule in the South, when radical Democrats—men like South Carolina's Ben Tillman—carried out a violent campaign to reimpose the tyranny of white supremacy across the region. Even as a young child, Monteith said her mother made sure she understood what was happening beyond their neighborhood. Rachel Monteith was an educated woman who had been a schoolteacher before marriage. She read to her children frequently, her daughter recalled, and she occasionally focused on current events. In the previous decade, black journalist and activist Ida B. Wells had launched a crusade designed to focus national attention on lynching in the South. Her investigative reporting—

published in northern black newspapers and collected in the book *Southern Horrors*—shone a bright light on the violence. Modjeska Monteith says her mother shared with her young children grim details of this fact of life in the Jim Crow South. In reading to her oldest daughter, Rachael Monteith "made a particular effort to acquaint us with things as they were," Modjeska said. "She read about all the lynchings, and how these people were mutilated and treated during lynchings."[2]

At the turn of the twentieth century, Booker T. Washington's power as leader of the African American community was at its peak. His strategy of having blacks accept second-class citizenship while pursuing economic gain through industrial education had widespread support, particularly in Deep South states like South Carolina. In many ways, the Monteith family appeared to embrace Washington's vision of racial uplift. Henry Monteith was a brick mason who had developed a method for constructing and maintaining safe chimneys that allowed him to build a successful business. His educated wife could stop work as a teacher and stay home to raise their children. The Monteiths would help launch Victory Savings Bank, the first black-owned financial institution in South Carolina. Their lives appeared to be the model of black middle-class virtue that Washington envisioned in the new South. Yet Rachel Monteith in particular had grown wary of the promise of accommodation and uplift. In her world, you weren't given respect. You had to earn it. How could blacks ever expect to be treated as equals if they were not willing to fight for their rights?[3]

Modjeska Monteith said her mother instilled this view in her children. She recalled one story from childhood that made the point dramatically. Her father had been working in Huntsville, Alabama, when a white mob lynched a local black man. Later, one member of the mob came to where Henry Monteith was working to show off a souvenir. As Modjeska recalled, "this fellow came in and showed him this finger that was cut off this Negro. I guess they wanted to intimidate [my father] as a Negro, knowing that he was well thought of." Henry Monteith was "a fearless man," Modjeska said, and he picked up his trowel and hammer and ordered the man to either fight him or leave. The man never bothered her father again. Henry Monteith might have been tender-hearted, his daughter said, but he bowed down to no man, even if it meant risking his life. Modjeska said she often wondered why the white man thought he could intimidate her father so easily. She said, "I guess most of the Negroes in that area were kind of groveling creatures" who had put up with that behavior.[4]

Groveling creatures. In Rachel Monteith's world, it was the worst invective you could use to slander a person. Her daughter, Modjeska, would come to agree. As a civil rights leader, she would often use similar language in her battle to unite the black community behind a strategy of protest in South Carolina.

By 1903, W.E.B. Du Bois's book, *The Souls of Black Folk,* had helped stir opposition to Washington's accommodationist strategy, at least among an educated black elite. Two years later, when Du Bois, Wells, William Monroe Trotter, and other Washington opponents formed the Niagara movement, Rachael Monteith joined the cause. By World War I, when attorney Butler Nance organized the first NAACP chapter in Columbia, Rachael and her daughter Modjeska became regulars at branch meetings. After graduating from Benedict College in 1921, Modjeska Monteith taught mathematics in the Columbia public school system—at Booker T. Washington High School. In 1929, she married J. Andrew Simkins, a businessman who had achieved the sort of independence from white economic control that her father had enjoyed. Simkins owned a service station and, after Prohibition ended, he opened a liquor store in Columbia. He also owned rental properties in the black community. Simkins was not directly dependent on white businesses for his livelihood, a fact that would help insulate Modjeska from white economic retribution during her days as a civil rights organizer.[5]

When she married Simkins, Modjeska Monteith was forced to quit her teaching job, because married women were not allowed to serve in public school classrooms at the time. In 1931, she found new work at the South Carolina Tuberculosis Association, a public health organization funded by private charities. As the organization's first director of Negro work, her primary job was to raise money, a daunting task in a rural state that had been devastated by declining cotton prices even before the Depression began. Over the following decade, Modjeska Simkins would crisscross South Carolina to visit black communities that had been ravaged by tuberculosis, pellagra, and other preventable diseases. She would see first-hand the depths of poverty and public health misery in every corner of the state. And she would develop a rich network of contacts that would eventually help build a civil rights movement in South Carolina.[6]

Simkins credits Franklin Roosevelt's election as president with rekindling black political activism in 1930s South Carolina. With his New Deal policies, Roosevelt "took the jug by the handle," Simkins recalled. "He tried to give the people who were down and had nothing something. . . . It was a shot in the arm for Negroes." Since World War I, the Great Migration had increased the number of black voters in the North. Abandoned by the Republican Party during the 1920s, these new black voters embraced Roosevelt during the Depression and slowly joined his New Deal coalition. In the 1934 midterm elections, the Democratic Party openly campaigned for African American voters in key northern states for the first time; in 1936, African Americans helped sweep Roosevelt to reelection. The emergence of the black vote within the Democratic Party coalition put new pressure on white liberals in the North to challenge the party's southern segregationist wing on the issue of civil rights. With his wife, Eleanor, taking the lead, Roosevelt gradually began to reach out as well. He created a so-called "black cabinet" of African American advisers to consult on national issues. FDR appointed Mary McLeod Bethune, a black educator from South Carolina, to a high-level position in the National Youth Administration, a New Deal relief organization. While he stopped short of formally endorsing federal antilynching legislation, Roosevelt used one of his radio addresses to condemn mob rule and "lynch law." The address angered his southern white allies in the Democratic Party, but his comments, mild as they were, sent a signal of support to liberals in the North and, more importantly, to black activists in the South.[7]

In South Carolina, a tiny vanguard of civil rights activists received the message. In the state capital, Simkins joined forces with Dr. Robert W. Mance and Rev. James Hinton to rouse a sleepy political organization. They launched a furious battle to force the Works Progress Administration and other New Deal agencies to employ more black Carolinians. As Simkins put it, "they tore up" one meeting when they realized the white Democrats in charge of the WPA planned to place unemployed black teachers and other professionals in manual labor jobs. They overturned the policy, and their willingness to challenge the status quo helped stir black activism statewide. The moribund NAACP network in the state slowly flickered back to life. Prodded by Levi G. Byrd, a plumber's aide from the small town of Cheraw, the state's NAACP chapters voted to join forces to coordinate activities. In 1939, they formed the South Carolina Conference of NAACP Branches.[8]

The fledgling movement in South Carolina received another boost with the return of a wandering son. Born in 1892, Osceola E. McKaine grew up in Sumter, South Carolina, but he had since traveled widely and developed a distinctly cosmopolitan worldview. He had studied at Boston College before joining the army, and in 1916 he fought with the 24th Infantry in their failed effort to capture the Mexican revolutionary Francisco "Pancho" Villa. Identified as officer material during the Mexican campaign, McKaine was sent to the new—and controversial—black officer training school at Fort Des Moines, Iowa. In preparing to enter World War I, the Wilson administration had planned for white officers to oversee black units in the segregated U.S. military. But after pressure from prominent black leaders, the army agreed to create the Fort Des Moines training camp to produce a black officer corp.

Southern white supremacists opposed the idea of having black officers at all, and some black leaders believed the existence of a separate training camp for blacks tacitly supported Jim Crow segregation in the military. McKaine excelled at Fort Des Moines, but the experience helped radicalize him as well. He resented the camp's white supremacist leadership, particularly a group of white southern officers who demanded that the new black officers swear allegiance to Jim Crow segregation. In 1917, McKaine emerged from Fort Des Moines as a lieutenant in the all-black 367th Regiment—the so-called "Buffalo Regiment," a named derived from the African American "Buffalo Soldiers" who fought Native Americans in the American West after the Civil War. Lieutenant McKaine and the 367th Regiment would soon join the American Expeditionary Force as it prepared to enter the war in Europe.[9]

While serving in France and Belgium, McKaine and his fellow black doughboys experienced a social world in which skin color played a less significant role than it had in the United States. They found they could socialize with white citizens in France and Belgium, and at times even the strict rules enforcing segregation of U.S. troops began to ease. It turned out that soldiers who fought side-by-side at the front were more likely see each other as equals when the fighting stopped. McKaine had always bristled under the racist policies of the United States, but he had accepted them as inevitable. After his experience in Europe, that was no longer the case. Having fought for his country overseas, McKaine was now determined to fight Jim Crow rule at home. While in Europe, he helped found a secret society of black soldiers— the League for Democracy—that vowed to stand up for black equality once the troops returned to the United States.[10]

On March 14, 1919, McKaine and the rest of the "Buffaloes" in the 367th Regiment marched triumphantly up New York City's Fifth Avenue and into Harlem as thousands lined the street to cheer them on. As the *New York Times* noted, the black infantrymen had earned their grand homecoming. They had seen "hard fighting" in Europe and had earned the respect of German soldiers, who often referred to them as the "black devils." By the war's end, Harlem had emerged as the bustling center of black intellectual and political life. The streets were alive with talk of a "new Negro," one that was entering what the philosopher Alain Locke described as a "dynamic new phase" marked by rising self-respect and political assertiveness. Crowds gathered on Harlem street corners to hear "stepladder" speakers and to participate in impromptu political debates. Newspapers and magazines flourished, with Marcus Garvey's *Negro World,* A. Phillip Randolph's *Messenger,* and Du Bois's NAACP paper *The Crisis* competing for readers and stirring debate over politics, art, and world events. By 1922, the poet Claude McKay had published

Harlem Shadows, launching a decade of artistic output that would come to be known as the Harlem Renaissance.[11]

McKaine found the social and political milieu intoxicating. Rather than return to Sumter, he stayed in Harlem and worked to build the League for Democracy into a national civil rights organization. He edited the group's newspaper, *The Commoner,* and helped organize meetings and rallies in Harlem and throughout New York City. On April 4, the *Amsterdam News,* New York's largest black newspaper, reported on an LFD meeting held in the Palace Casino on 135th Street. "An enthusiastic capacity audience jammed the casino," the newspaper reported, and McKaine's keynote address, which called for the abolition of Jim Crow and an expansion of black voting rights, received "thunderous roars of applause."[12]

The cheers did not last. The red-scare tactics that James F. Byrnes had employed in South Carolina had been used to undermine black political action nationwide in the years following World War I, and McKaine's LFD withered under the government scrutiny. The military had planted spies in the organization before the black troops returned from Europe. Once in Harlem, military and FBI informants reported extensively on McKaine and LFD activities. In his research, historian Miles Richards uncovered documents showing that summaries of McKaine's activities reached the desk of J. Edgar Hoover, the head of the Justice Department's new General Intelligence Division, at least twice in 1920. By 1921, the LFD had lost significant membership and had begun to founder.[13]

In 1924, McKaine left Harlem and struck out on a new adventure, one that would take him back to Europe and see him emerge as a successful businessman. McKaine settled in Ghent, Belgium, and spent the next two decades managing Mac's Place, a popular nightclub that featured live music. Far from his childhood home in the Jim Crow South, McKaine enjoyed the relative racial liberalism of the European continent. Belgians treated him as a respected member of the community, and his staff included numerous white employees. By 1940, when German troops invaded Belgium, Mac's Place was a prominent business in Ghent. At first, the Germans allowed McKaine to keep his nightclub open. But he realized the United States would enter the war soon, and as an American he would surely end up in a Nazi prison—or worse. With nowhere else to go, McKaine returned home to Sumter, South Carolina, the small town he thought he had left for good twenty-five years earlier.[14]

Depressed by what he found in his native state, McKaine resumed the civil rights work he had abandoned when he left United States in 1924. He revived the Sumter NAACP branch and worked to organize a statewide campaign around the issue of black teacher pay. Under the "separate but equal" doctrine handed down in the U.S. Supreme Court's *Plessy v. Ferguson* ruling in 1896, black teachers should have been paid the same salary as their white counterparts. The NAACP made the issue a priority in the late 1930s, but it had a mixed record of success, particularly in the Deep South, where black teachers were wary of confronting white school board officials. In 1940, white teachers in South Carolina earned twice as much as their black counterparts. Yet the NAACP had been unable to find a black teacher willing to challenge the pay discrepancy in court. McKaine wanted to change that.[15]

In the fall of 1940, the teacher-pay effort brought him to the capital city of Columbia, where he met Modjeska Simkins. Similar in age and temperament, the two developed a close friendship and an enduring political alliance. Both were well read and quick-witted, and neither suffered fools easily. They were particularly disdainful of black leaders who refused to challenge injustice for fear of white retribution. For Simkins, these were the "groveling creatures" that her mother had often described, and she was determined to put an end to their influence in South Carolina. Simkins later described the moment when McKaine agreed to join her crusade. The two were enjoying a cold drink on the back porch of her Columbia home. After a few moments of discussion, they realized they shared the same point of view. They believed the time was right to abandon cautious accommodation and confront Jim Crow reign, at least in the courts and at the ballot box, if not yet in the streets. Simkins said the two activists raised their glasses and made a pact: They agreed to challenge the forces of white supremacy directly in South Carolina—and to "destroy" those in the black community who stood in their way.[16]

Simkins and McKaine had declared war that day on both white supremacist rule and the black community's overly cautious response to it. To win, the two activists believed the NAACP needed to develop a distinct voice, one that could rally support among the state's African American citizens and lead them into political battle. They wanted a newspaper whose publisher was committed to the cause and who was unafraid of angering leaders in either the white or black community. They were particularly concerned about black leaders who were unwilling to challenge the white power structure—the sort of leader their newspaper would later describe as the "accommodating Negro" who was willing to serve as a "the stooge for the South."[17]

By 1939, John McCray had rebounded from the humiliation he had endured after his decision to oppose a federal antilynching law two years earlier. He had quit his job at the insurance company and followed his heart into the newspaper business. "There is something about working on a newspaper that haunts you forever," the editor would write years later. "It's more than the smell of printer's ink, the sight of it on you forever. It's more than writing a story, an editorial piece and helping them get into print." A man of no small ego, McCray conceded that he loved the influence—even the power—that came with publishing his own newspaper. Rather than leading an organization or running for office, he said he preferred using "the effectiveness of journalism" to wield political clout behind the scenes. He described it as being "sort of like the puppeteer, the operator who pulls the strings and tries to get other people to do things."[18]

Working with a partner who printed his paper in Savannah, Georgia, McCray had launched the *Charleston Lighthouse*, which he immediately thrust into the middle of one of the hottest controversies in the state's black community. It involved Allen University, a small black college in Columbia run by the AME church. The school's board of trustees had split into competing factions, with one supporting the president and the other accusing him of misusing funds and ruining the university. The conflict grew so heated that students marched out of classes and went on strike. McCray's newspaper came down hard against the Allen president and his supporters on the board. In his usual provocative style, McCray proclaimed in one editorial that, "Hell is going to be so full of AME preachers and presiding elders the rest of us need not worry about where we're going when we die."[19]

McCray's newspaper urged the board to fire the Allen University president and find a new leader who could unite the AME community in support of the college. He suggested Samuel J. Higgins, the principal of Charleston's Burke High School. To McCray's surprise, the board eventually followed his advice. As Allen's new president, Higgins would become a powerful ally and supporter of McCray's newspaper and the NAACP over the following decade. McCray said other black papers in the state had avoided the Allen story because they feared offending the powerful AME church. For the *Lighthouse,* the Allen controversy served as a circulation builder that helped establish the newspaper and its feisty editor as a force in the state's black community.[20]

By 1940, McCray's newspaper had begun to annoy the white community in Charleston and the surrounding Lowcountry. Among other issues, the *Lighthouse* had accused the city's police of mistreating black suspects—"they were whipping heads," McCray said—and the newspaper had demanded the removal of "whites only" signs from the benches in a park that surrounded a city lake. That annoyance had turned to anger when McCray investigated a suspicious rape charge against a black doctor in nearby McClellanville. The *Lighthouse* ran what the editor described as a "tabloid" headline on its front page: "Whites Frame Doctor, Force Him From Town." By the following evening, McCray was in jail. The Charleston police held the editor and several staff members for questioning without pressing charges. Not long after their release, the city raised the fee for the newspaper's business license. The weekly had been paying ten dollars annually; city officials now wanted one hundred dollars, the same amount that the daily newspapers paid. McCray said he realized it was time to leave Charleston.[21]

When McKaine and Simkins reached out to McCray, the editor was eager to hear their plan. McKaine traveled to Charleston with Esau Parker, a Sumter attorney and publisher of a small weekly called the *People's Informer*. Parker was an elderly man who wanted out of the newspaper business. McKaine and Simkins wanted a paper based in Columbia that would work closely with the NAACP and the emerging civil rights movement. The black activists proposed to McCray that he merge his Charleston newspaper with the smaller *Sumter Informer* and move the paper to the state's capital city. Simkins said her husband would provide office space in one of his properties. McCray readily agreed, and by late 1941 the *Lighthouse and Informer* was operating in a building on Washington Street, in the heart of Columbia's black community.[22]

A complete set of all editions of the *Lighthouse and Informer* was never archived and is not available for review. When the paper closed in 1954, most back issues were sold as scrap paper to help pay back taxes. However, fifty full editions have been located over the years, as well as numerous individual pages and articles found in the personal papers of McCray, Simkins, Arthur J. Clement Jr., James F. Byrnes, and William D. Workman Jr. Fortunately, the available editions cover key political events across the life of the newspaper, from its launch in Charleston in 1939 through its demise in Columbia in 1954. Though incomplete, they provide a rich and varied sample of the newspaper's output and capture the essence of its voice and worldview. A close reading of these available editions reveals how McCray and his allies turned the *Lighthouse and Informer* into a leading weapon in the NAACP's effort to reshape political life in South Carolina.[23]

The *Lighthouse and Informer* and Rise of Protest Politics

The first edition of the new *Lighthouse and Informer* hit the streets on a day of infamy—December 7, 1941. The Japanese attack on Pearl Harbor had enraged the American public and ended debate over whether the United States should enter World War II. The nation's black press joined in this new patriotic fervor. Yet it faced a dilemma: how to support the U.S. war effort without appearing to accept the fundamental racism and injustice that permeated American society? In January 1942, a young factory worker from Wichita, Kansas, addressed this issue eloquently in a letter to the *Pittsburgh Courier*. "Should I sacrifice my life to live half American?" James G. Thompson asked. "Would it be demanding too much to demand full citizenship rights in exchange for the sacrificing of my life?" Thompson suggested that African Americans fight for "a Double V . . . the first V for victory over our enemies from without, the second V for victory over our enemies from within." By 1941, Robert Vann's *Courier* had supplanted the *Chicago Defender* as the nation's most widely read black newspaper in part through its aggressive marketing skills. In Thompson's Double V proposal, Vann saw both a smart political strategy and a brilliant public relations ploy. For the rest of the year, the *Courier* splashed the Double V logo across its pages every week. By historian Patrick S. Washburn's count, the weekly newspaper ran 970 Double V items during 1942: "469 articles, editorials, and letters; 380 photographs, and 121 editorial drawings."[24]

McCray embraced the concept of the Double V campaign, but operating in the heart of the Deep South, he was more cautious in how he framed the issue. The editor published a special edition devoted to the topic of "South Carolina Negroes at War." The paper avoided using the *Courier*'s Double V logo, but the *Lighthouse and Informer* made it clear that it believed black troops fighting overseas should be treated as full citizens when they returned home. McCray and his staff profiled African American soldiers and wrote feature stories detailing the black community's support for the war on the home front. The special edition highlighted black patriotism, and it forced the state's white leadership to acknowledge, on the record, the African American contribution to the war effort. In a statement provided to the newspaper, Governor Olin Johnston said, "The people of South Carolina are pleased with the way the negroes of our state are doing their part." Johnston noted what he called "the full cooperation between the colored and white people," and he said the citizens of South Carolina are "not unmindful of what your race is doing . . . to bring a glorious victory to the allied nations." The white governor provided the written statement, but he rejected McCray's request for an accompanying photograph, revealing some misgivings about appearing so prominently in the black press.[25]

McCray's effort to highlight black patriotism did not stop his newspaper from challenging white supremacist leadership in the state. In January 1943, when Governor Richard Jefferies failed to name an African American to a citizens' committee on postwar planning in South Carolina, the newspaper accused the state of hypocrisy. The governor had ignored the democratic ideals the nation had supposedly gone to war to protect. "It is the same old story once again of forgetting and omitting the colored people from responsibility although they comprise forty-four percent of the state's population," the *Lighthouse and Informer* declared. "Many have been the times that we have heard 'our democracy is not perfect but we are working to perfect or improve it while fighting a common war.' The colored people have accepted this explanation and are doing our utmost to win for 'our side.' Such omissions as the one in question discourage and puzzle them. They see no virtue in the repetition of customs contrary to those we now proclaim."[26]

The newspaper's assertiveness surprised white readers in Columbia. McCray ran an exposé on the mistreatment of black inmates serving on chain gangs in South Carolina. New arrivals on these road crews received fifteen lashes with a leather belt on their first day "just to see if they could take it," McCray reported. One inmate received twelve lashes for "acting too stubborn"; another received eight lashes for slipping down while shoveling dirt. The *Lighthouse and Informer* story identified at least one prisoner who had been seriously injured during one of these beatings. State officials complained about McCray's story and at one point suggested he may face a grand jury. Around the same time, a city judge claimed the newspaper "had done more than any 1,000 other things I can think of to agitate" race relations in the capital city.[27]

In the end, the newspaper's reporting on chain gangs had a positive impact. The state eventually launched an investigation into the treatment of prisoners used in road crews and other work sites. Letters to the editor at the *Lighthouse and Informer* showed how pleased—and shocked—black readers were to see this kind of coverage. One black soldier who received the newspaper at his training camp told the editor that his buddies in the barracks loved the newspaper, but "what puzzles them is how is it that you're still alive."[28]

McCray's newspaper frequently questioned police treatment of African Americans in South Carolina. As the years passed and black activism spread in the state, McCray's tone grew bolder. One example involved a burglary suspect who claimed Columbia police had held him without charge for two weeks and "beaten a confession out him." McCray bannered the accusations across the front page and demanded city officials launch a full investigation. "Over the years, we have seen time and again some poor Negro accused hauled into court and confronted with some statement he is alleged to have signed 'of his own free will,' but it is actually a statement he's been forced to sign in order to save himself from further punishment," the newspaper declared in an editorial that also ran on page one. A police department that would sanction such behavior was "illegal, inhumane and vicious," the newspaper said. "It is time this kind of behavior is outlawed and wiped out for good."[29]

McCray's editorial page focused heavily on political issues, but the newspaper found other ways to connect with readers and build a loyal audience.

The paper's society columns served as a type of social media for black communities across the state. Each week, correspondents from big cities, small towns, and rural crossroads sent in items about the comings and goings of local folk. In early January 1943, for example, the newspaper's Cheraw correspondent noted "Miss Virginia Tally of New York City was in town visiting her parents, Mr. and Mrs. Martin Tally," while the Aiken stringer reported that "Mrs. Essie Mason is visiting relatives in Bryn Mawr, Pa." and "Mrs. Janie Bussie has returned to Philadelphia after being called to Aiken by the death of her father, Mr. James G. Bussie." In tiny Graniteville, "a play, 'Aunt Sabiny's Christmas,' was successfully presented at the Valley Fair Baptist Church on Christmas Day," and in Charleston, "Mrs. Anne Elisa Hammond announced the marriage of her daughter, Dorothy Benua, to Mr. James Charles Ellis of Greensboro, N.C."[30]

Each week, the names and hometowns of dozens of black South Carolinians peppered the pages of the *Lighthouse and Informer*. These brief society notes provided an informal geography of the Great Migration and documented the ongoing interaction between North and South. Thousands of black South Carolinians had moved north in search of jobs and to escape Jim Crow, yet many retained close ties with their original communities. By chronicling these interactions so closely on its news pages, the *Lighthouse and Informer* created a personal bond with readers and cemented its ties with the churches, schools, and local organizations that formed the core of black civic life in South Carolina in the 1940s. Perhaps more than any particular editorial comment, it was this commitment to smalltime local journalism that paved the way for the *Lighthouse and Informer* to organize and mobilize black Carolinians for the political fight ahead.

Over time, the newspaper's "letters to the editor" section also developed into a popular sounding board for black South Carolinians, one where the personal often meshed with the political. In 1944, for example, one reader wrote in to praise The Southernaires, a popular gospel group that had performed at Columbia's Township Auditorium. Letter writer John H. Washington said the music was "first class" and "made me feel good all over," but the best moment came at the end, when the group concluded the show with a tune called "We Are Americans, Too." In introducing the song, the group's bass singer, William Edmonston, "got everybody told off in a fine way," Washington wrote, adding that he "wished that a thousand white people had been there to hear him." The concert, he concluded, had "made me much prouder of my race."[31]

McCray's newspaper often found subtle and not-so-subtle ways to raise political issues in its coverage of popular culture. In 1942, for example, the newspaper serialized *Native Son*, the provocative novel from black writer

Richard Wright. Each week, the story of Bigger Thomas, a young black man who kills a white woman and flees from police, unfolded on page four of the *Lighthouse and Informer*. Wright depicted the crushing poverty of Bigger Thomas's life on Chicago's South Side in excruciating detail, and though he did not condone the violence, the author strongly suggested that American racism was the real culprit. Wright's work had been widely acclaimed in the North. Its selection by the Book-of-the-Month Club—a first for a novel by a black author—broadened the book's reach beyond literary circles and into the nation's broader white middle class. Yet for McCray to publish the novel in a weekly newspaper in the heart of the Deep South remained a provocative act. Unfortunately, there is no record of any reader response from black or white South Carolinians.[32]

The newspaper's sports pages usually found a way to insert a social or political comment as well. The paper kept a close eye on Jackie Robinson as he broke the major league baseball color line and began his career with the Brooklyn Dodgers in the late 1940s. In one article, the *Lighthouse and Informer* wondered if other players and the umpires "were ganging up on Jackie"? The newspaper quoted a magazine story that claimed Robinson was a "marked man" who was the frequent target of "pitchers throwing fastballs at his head and runners needlessly spiking him." The newspaper said that Robinson was eager to fight back, but he was prevented from doing so by strict rules laid done by Dodgers' general manager Branch Rickey. Robinson had "made the grade" in the big leagues, the newspaper argued, and "he has the right to beef when he thinks things are wrong." The message for black readers in South Carolina was clear: Jackie Robinson wanted to stand up for his rights, and so should they.[33]

When McCray wrote about sports, he also found ways to connect the story to the black struggle. In early 1943, for example, the editor took aim at a local African American preacher who had criticized Joe Louis shortly after the popular boxing champion had entered the army. The preacher said Louis "ain't nothing" because he had not done enough to help his race. An irate McCray dismissed the preacher as "ignorant," but he said the incident revealed a larger disconnect between black leaders and the black community. "Joe Louis had done more good for his people than 10,000 preachers, 1,000 'militant leaders' and the 12,999,999 other would-be 'leaders' combined," McCray wrote. "What bothers us is that here is a man who makes his living out of the pockets of people who are now as humble and poor as Louis was back in the Alabama cotton fields. He styles himself a 'leader' but we think he should be promptly unfrocked and left aside to be forgotten. He is . . . too far removed from our kind of people to be associating with us."[34]

In the paper's early days, McCray referred several times to this perceived split between "leaders and the little fellows" in the black community. Sometimes he used humor to make the point. When the *Pittsburgh Courier* reported that a new survey showed that 80 percent of black southerners did not believe "national leaders" represented their views on the war, McCray said he was not surprised. "The common colored person knows about as much about what the race 'heads' are seeking as the Negro private who, when asked what he was fighting for in this war, replied: "for fifty dollars a month."[35]

McCray's newspaper complained frequently about the social customs of the segregated South and the indignities black South Carolinians were forced to endure. In one editorial, McCray criticized Columbia police officers for using the word "nigger" on its radio calls. Police radio calls were transmitted on a frequency that could be heard on commercial radio dials, and McCray said some officers routinely used the racial epithet. "On one occasion a week or so ago, the announcer ordered a squad car to proceed to Five Points where a 'little nigger child' was reported struck by a car," he wrote. "Not only is use of such terms offensive to some 25,000 or more citizens of Columbia but it goes further to prove what the department would not admit, namely that to the radio section of the city's police force, a colored citizen is a 'nigger.'"[36]

McCray also ridiculed "the arrogance and egoism" of white South Carolinians who refused to address African Americans with even a modicum of respect and simple decency. In his weekly column, "The Need for Changing," the editor described a phone call he received from a white man whose company advertised in the newspaper. "When I came to the phone he began, 'John, this is Mister Blank.' Get that! I am insignificant but at the very start I must think of him as 'Mister,'" McCray wrote. "As hot under the collar as it made me, I managed to say in an even, civil tongue that I would appreciate it if he would address me as 'McCray'—if under the depravity of racism he found it obnoxious to use the courtesy word 'mister.' When I finished, this man who had seen me but one time started with, 'Now Listen, John.' I hung up. If having his business required a cost in pride and ordinary courtesy, I didn't want it."[37]

From the beginning, the *Lighthouse and Informer* made its political intentions clear. The paper announced explicit plans to help mobilize the black community soon after its move to Columbia. In an unsigned editorial—probably written by Simkins, because it lacked McCray's sarcastic and confrontational tone—the newspaper announced plans to organize a statewide assembly that would bring together those "interested in making South Carolina the democratic community of all races working together for our mutual growth and betterment." To prepare for this "new day just ahead of us," the editorial encouraged those in the black community "to subscribe to the *Lighthouse and Informer* so that all of us can read its pages and know what is taking place amongst our group in this state. Don't learn about what has happened after it has happened. Get in on the ground floor . . . the *Lighthouse and Informer* will keep you informed."[38]

The paper encouraged black Carolinians to join their local NAACP branch and to launch new chapters if their community did not have one. When white officials began taking steps to undermine the civil rights organization, the *Lighthouse and Informer* demanded that the black community fight back. In one column, McCray lamented a new rule that prevented students in black public schools from delivering NAACP membership appeals during school assemblies. "The schools have borne the burden in most drives for community uplift—Red Cross, tuberculosis, hospital building and practically every other matter gets its biggest support from the schools, and with official boosting," McCray wrote. "But the same officials consider the NAACP, working to uplift and protect the rights of Negroes, as 'hostile,' 'radical,' and even 'subversive.' " McCray criticized black school officials who enforced the new policy, saying they were "perpetuating a policy, decreed by white men" that was designed to "enslave" the minds of black children. "At an early age they are taught that to fight for their rights is undesirable; that their fighting leaders . . . are rabble-rousers; that Denmark Vesey was a bad Negro while scoundrels like . . . 'Pitchfork' Ben Tillman were white gentlemen." McCray accused whites of using the new regulation to divide the black community. "If there is one thing the Negroes need now it is to rebel against laws white men lay down for Negroes in their schools and organizations. You can lay your bottom dollar on the fact that such rules . . . are adopted to protect white men from solid unity and resistance among Negroes."[39]

Uniting the black community behind the NAACP was the *Lighthouse and Informer*'s primary goal. McCray's newspaper raged against the injustice of Jim Crow rule in South Carolina, but the paper aimed some of its harshest criticism at black South Carolinians who refused to join the civil rights organization and fight back. McCray often delivered these diatribes in his distinctively sarcastic style. In one column, the editor lashed out at a type of African American that he described as the "I Killits." These were members of the black community who McCray believed were working with white supremacists to try to "kill" the civil rights struggle. The I Killits "are low-down skunks," McCray wrote. In his view, these "vultures" undermined black civil rights efforts in return for a few scraps from the white man's table. "They try to line up on the side of the already well-capable whites, and where possible, hand to these whites ammunition with which to blast away at us," he wrote.

An "I Killit" believed "the white man will win, and if he is at his side some
mercy will come to him, and he'll have a little niche a bit higher than the rest
of his people." McCray went on to compare the "I Killits" to another group
within the black community that he called "I Dunnits." These people mean
well, McCray wrote, but they are "just weakling fatalists who tremble at the
mere suggestion of battling for our rights. They tell you about 'trouble' if you
think about fighting for what you believe and if this should fail, they run
into a hole and hide while the battle rages. But as soon as the victory parade
forms, they dash out and fight like the devil to take over the whole business
and acclaim the credit."[40]

The target of McCray's "I Killit" column was another black editor, a lifelong
nemesis named Davis Lee. Lee had edited the *Savannah Journal* in Georgia
in the late 1930s, then moved north to launch the *Newark Telegram*. Once a
proponent of civil rights, Lee turned on the NAACP in the mid-1940s and
carried out a fierce campaign against the organization's efforts in the South
throughout the rest of his career. McCray published his attack on Lee in 1948,
when black South Carolinians were preparing to vote in a Democratic Party
primary—the only election that mattered in the one-party state—for the first
time since the rise of Jim Crow rule in the state. At the same time, the young
governor, J. Strom Thurmond, was running for president as a leader of the
"Dixiecrats," a group of white southern Democrats who bolted from the national party over its support for black civil rights. Lee had claimed the races
got along fine in the South before black agitators began stirring up trouble.
Their efforts were ruining the region's business climate, Lee said. The average
Negro leader "goes around with a chip on his shoulder looking for prejudice,
discrimination and segregation so that he can holler 'wolf' and keep his
people inflamed and aroused," Lee wrote during the 1948 campaign. "These
leaders are not sincere or consistent," he added. "The Negro preacher who
preaches against jim crowism and segregation doesn't realize he is preaching
against himself, because his church is a jim crow institution."[41]

When Thurmond cited Lee on the campaign trail and described him as the
true voice of black southerners, McCray fired back: "If Governor Thurmond
and the Dixiecrats wish to impress southern Negroes with the thinking of
Negroes they would do well to quote some other person, one for whom there
is respect and esteem among Negroes. Lee has neither," McCray wrote in the
Lighthouse and Informer. He described Lee's newspaper work as "the regrettable type of Negro journalism, if the world 'journalism' can be applied," and
he warned white people not to make a "monstrous blunder" by trusting a
man "who knows nothing about Negroes" in the South.[42]

McCray's attack on Davis Lee and his broadside against the "I Killits" and the "I Dunnits" were not anomalies. The *Lighthouse and Informer* conducted an ongoing assault on conservative forces within the black community—not just outliers like Davis Lee, but more respected black leaders as well. Led by McCray, McKaine, and Simkins, the newspaper demanded black assertiveness and ridiculed accommodation, opportunism, and apathy. It highlighted the injustices of a Jim Crow South that privileged whiteness but saved its greatest outrage for black South Carolinians who refused to demand their rights. With their editorial stance, McCray and his colleagues joined the debate that had animated the black community since the rise of white supremacy and Jim Crow. In the ongoing struggle between accommodation and protest, McCray and his NAACP colleagues used their newspaper to rally support for direct confrontation and undermine the argument for cautious negotiation.

Before they could launch such a campaign, NAACP activists had to persuade a wary African American public that the time was right to confront white supremacy directly. McCray referred to this effort as "beating down the fear" in the black community. The newspaper's push for a campaign of protest was not uncontested. Conservative black leaders in the state believed confrontation would trigger a violent backlash, and they had historical evidence to support their view. McCray and his allies had to overcome this culture of accommodation before they could unite the community behind a strategy of confrontation with white supremacy in South Carolina. As the Davis Lee incident showed, white southerners were eager to make use of the divisions within the African American community to bolster their claims that the Jim Crow system benefited both races in the South—that social segregation and the elimination of most blacks from politics was a necessary act that strengthened rather than undermined American democracy. In prose laced with anger, sarcasm, and occasional bitterness, McCray and his colleagues countered that argument. They used the pages of the *Lighthouse and Informer* to help overcome African American acquiescence and accommodation in the Jim Crow South and communicate a message of agency and activism to black Carolinians.[43]

The Showdown Over Teacher Pay

The first big showdown in the newspaper's campaign to demolish the culture of accommodation and unite the black community behind a strategy of protest came in the early 1940s, when the NAACP began demanding equal pay for black teachers. Conservative black leaders framed the issue in accommodationist terms: they warned against the dangers of overreaching. Black teachers should negotiate with the white boards of education and cut the best deals they could, even if it meant accepting something less than equal pay. McCray and his colleagues presented a starkly different message. The *Lighthouse and Informer* framed the fight for the equalization of teacher salaries as a test of black self-respect. It posed a simple question: Were African Americans ready to assume the rights and responsibilities of full citizenship? South Carolina is "breaking the law," the newspaper declared in late 1941, and the teachers should "invite the attention of the legislature and the city and county authorities to these transgressions." The newspaper published a report from the state board of education that highlighted the discrepancy in school spending. In 1940, South Carolina had spent more than $15 million on white schools but only $2.5 million on black ones. White teachers averaged $1,067 in annual salary; their black counterparts made only $535 a year. "There are no valid reasons why Negro teachers in the employ of the state should DONATE their services . . . while the white teachers are getting real taxpayer dollars" for their work, the *Lighthouse and Informer* said. The newspaper concluded with an argument it would repeat frequently over the following decade. If black citizens refused to stand up for their rights and challenge this obvious discrimination, they deserved their second-class status. To drive the point home, the editorial ended with a quote from Shakespeare's *Julius Caesar*: "The fault, dear Brutus, is not in our stars, but in ourselves, that we are underlings."[44]

The fight over strategy in the teacher pay equalization struggle pitted the NAACP and its allies against the leaders of the Palmetto State Teachers' Association, the black teachers' organization. Across the South, black educators had been wary of the NAACP's legal fight for equal pay for the past decade. Their fear was understandable. Most black teachers depended on white education officials for their jobs, and they feared that legal confrontation could cost them dearly. In South Carolina, the PSTA opposed the NAACP's plan to sue state and local boards of education. Headed by John P. Burgess, a high school principal and a well-known leader in the state's black community, the group sought a negotiated settlement instead. At one meeting of the PSTA membership in Columbia's Township Auditorium, Burgess stood before more than a thousand black educators and told them they were "crazy if you think these white people are going to pay you as much money as they make." The PSTA president said the teachers should be smart and negotiate for something less than equality. Otherwise, they risked being fired. Furthermore, Burgess told the group's rank-and-file to ignore "that ol' crazy newspaper"—the *Lighthouse and Informer*.[45]

For many of the black teachers, Burgess's argument rang true. In the early 1940s in South Carolina, the forces calling for patience and negotiation over direct confrontation had a clear advantage. For the black community in the Jim Crow South, the threat of financial and physical retribution was real and omnipresent. Most families had relatives or friends who had felt the wrath of white anger firsthand. Some PSTA members believed mere membership in the NAACP could be a firing offense. On the other side, advocates of confrontation had few success stories to share.[46]

In 1943, the leadership of the PSTA sent a letter to state education officials requesting a pay increase for its members. Much like McCray's accommodationist letter back in 1937, the teachers' association tried to ease the concerns of the state's white supremacists. Writing to the state board of education, the PSTA said: "We have come to you, a powerful, influential and authoritative group, begging you to help another group that is not so powerful." The language was similar to the tone used so often by Booker T. Washington and his South Carolina protégé, Richard Carroll, during the early years of Jim Crow. In 1895, Washington had written a famous letter to Senator Ben Tillman that requested support for black schools. "I am but an humble member of an unfortunate race; you are a member of the greatest legislative body on earth, and a member of the great, intelligent Caucasian race," Washington's letter began. Historian Leon Litwack has described it as "a classic example of accommodationism." Nearly half a century later, the PSTA leadership appeared to mimic Washington's approach.[47]

Simkins responded with a devastating counterpunch, one in which she would revive her attack on those she considered to be "groveling creatures" in the black community. Published as an editorial in the *Lighthouse and Informer* under the headline "Negro Teachers Called To Arms," Simkins described the PSTA's letter as a "stench bomb" that embarrassed "self-respecting Negroes in all walks of life." She called the PSTA's effort to negotiate "nauseating," and she sent a clear message to the rank and file of the black teachers group:

> Vow to strike forever from the . . . ranks of the PSTA any cringing, groveling creature who is so distorted in his thinking, and so moronic in his power of expression that he removes the Negro teachers of this state from the ranks of the freeborn and places them in the category of whimpering slaves. . . . Resolve now that you will acquit yourselves as American citizens and not as sniveling, crawling nonentities. Believe me, that BEGGING will not improve your economic condition, or any other condition for that matter.

The confrontational tone of Simkins's editorial reflected the bitterness of the contest over strategy. "Swear vengeance against your 'misleaders,' " Simkins urged the black teachers. "Single out your delegates from your county and demand proof of how each stood." Simkins framed the debate clearly to pick a fight with the group's leaders, to create a stark contrast between her will to fight and their desire to negotiate. As she noted in a later interview, she understood their fear and caution. The PSTA leaders were well known in the community and were vulnerable to white retribution. "[They] didn't want the whites to know that they would sit in a meeting and allow black teachers to sue the state of South Carolina," Simkins said years later. However, she was not interested in preserving unity or showing the PSTA leadership any compassion; she wanted to persuade black Carolinians to go into battle—and to shame those too afraid to fight. Simkins wanted to convince them of their agency to confront an unjust system.[48]

In the *Lighthouse and Informer*, Simkins framed the goal of the battle over teacher pay carefully to avoid a debate over winning or losing the court case. Instead, she said black South Carolinians had a choice: they could assert their rights like "American citizens," or they could retreat like "whimpering slaves." She implied that the agency of black South Carolinians is not tied to winning the lawsuit, but from simply filing it in the first place. In this sense, she is redefining "citizenship" in a way that is consistent with Richard H. King's concept of "autonomous freedom." In tracing the "repertory of freedom" as articulated throughout the civil rights movement, King identifies "autonomous freedom" as a kind of self-realization—a rejection of the old, oppressed self and a declaration of personal freedom. Those who embrace autonomous freedom are willing to stand up and demand their rights, even if they expect to face retribution for doing so. In this sense, politics is not the art of the possible; instead, it is a path to self-respect through the assertion of your rights. To fight for those rights—whether you win every battle or not—is a way of declaring yourself a citizen.[49]

McCray made the same case in a 1947 column that looked back on the teacher fight. He described a white "Democrat" who counseled him to be "less conspicuous" in making political demands. "The question about being nice and quiet, just because white folks ask," McCray wrote, "is that it never pays dividends"—perhaps a lesson he learned from his brief foray into accommodationism in 1937.[50]

The Simkins editorial reflected the bitterness of the battle between the accommodationists and the protestors. To reframe the issue and force a choice by the community, the *Lighthouse and Informer* had to draw sharp distinctions between negotiation and confrontation. As McCray knew from personal experience, most black Carolinians vacillated in their support for direct confrontation. Was this the right time, or were African Americans risking a major white backlash? The tone of the debate also engendered criticism. The paper came under fire from those who believed African Americans should remain unified and from those who thought it unseemly to air their debate in public for whites to see and hear. Later in 1943, McKaine addressed the question of unity in the newspaper's signature combative tone: "If, to have unity, we must continue to follow and support a leadership which has, without effective protest or action, permitted the Negroes of this state to become the most illiterate group within the nation . . . if to have unity we must continue to support and follow such leadership then the price is too high."[51]

In the summer of 1943, NAACP activists believed they had found the perfect plaintiff when Malissa Smith, a graduate of the state's black public university, agreed to file suit against the Charleston Board of Education. Smith had taught for three years in Charleston, and she was taking a year's leave to attend graduate school at Columbia University in New York. Bright and well-spoken, Smith could document clearly that she was being paid less than white teachers with the same credentials, and she appeared willing to sue the school board despite opposition from some of her fellow teachers. Yet Smith's case never made it to court. The NAACP Legal Defense Fund, led by a young lawyer named Thurgood Marshall, had made a voting-rights case in Texas a priority over the South Carolina teacher-pay action. The eventual ruling in that Texas case—*Smith v. Allwright*—would outlaw whites-only primary elections in the South and would be critical to the civil rights movement in South Carolina. But Marshall's delay nearly derailed the state NAACP's teacher-pay effort. After waiting for months for the suit to be filed, Smith announced that she had accepted a job in Brooklyn, New York, and would no longer be in a position to sue the Charleston school board. Frustrated NAACP activists scrambled to find a new plaintiff, but many in the black teachers' organization believed Smith had withdrawn in response to some mysterious white retribution. Word spread that pursuing the NAACP strategy and taking the school board to court was a dangerous move.[52]

Within a month, a second Charleston teacher, Viola Louise Duvall, stepped forward to sue the school board. Duvall was a Howard University graduate who taught chemistry at Burke High School. Hinton said he believed she would be a better plaintiff than Smith "in every way," and he pleaded with Marshall to move quickly. But the Texas primary case had reached the U.S. Supreme Court, and the NAACP chief national counsel had to put South Carolina on hold again. Duvall, meantime, began to grow restless. Her white bosses in the school system were not pleased with her decision to sue. And after the *Lighthouse and Informer* ran a story about her case, Duvall said her fellow teachers at Burke began to ostracize her. "Why, it almost seemed as if I had developed a contagious disease," she wrote in a letter to McCray. Concerned about Duvall's state of mind, Hinton wrote to Marshall and said the state's teacher-pay case "is dragging along so slowly that we are losing much prestige daily." He pleaded with Marshall to move the suit forward: "This case will mean the *making* of the NAACP in South Carolina," Hinton said.[53]

In February 1944, Marshall argued the teacher-pay case against the Charleston Board of Education in the federal courthouse there. He had always expected to lose in the U.S. district court and perhaps win on appeal. But Marshall grew even more concerned about the Charleston case when he discovered the name of the judge assigned to hear it: J. Waties Waring. Born into one of the Lowcountry's best-known families, Waring was a member in good standing of the Charleston aristocracy and the Democratic Party. Yet his actions in the Duvall case would stun both white and black South Carolinians. Within moments of opening the proceedings, Waring ordered the Charleston school board to abide by the law and equalize teacher pay in the city's schools. Moreover, he asked Marshall and the NAACP to set the timetable for the equalization to occur. Marshall later said it was the only time in a courtroom when his "jaw almost fell on the table." According to McCray's first-hand account, "pandemonium broke loose in the courtroom" when Waring announced his decision. As well-wishers surrounded Viola Duvall, an amused McCray reported hearing one of her fellow teachers say, "Child, I was with you all this time but I just couldn't show my hand."[54]

A Surprising New Ally

Waring's ruling in the teacher-pay case was the first public indication of his stunning personal evolution. Across the 1940s, he moved from loyal supporter of white supremacy to full-throated proponent of legal, political, and social equality for African Americans. Waring had been a close ally of U.S. Senator "Cotton" Ed Smith, a race-baiting demagogue who broke with Roosevelt in part over civil rights issues. In the 1938 campaign, Smith had rallied supporters across rural South Carolina with his "Philydelphy story"— his account of how he walked out of that city's 1936 Democratic National Convention when a black minister began to deliver the invocation. As the story reached its climax, Smith would proclaim, "when the blue-gummed Senagambian started talking, I started walking—and as I did I believe I heard 'ol John Calhoun say from his mansion in the sky, 'You did good, Ed.' " Smith was one of several southern senators the Roosevelt White House targeted for defeat in the 1938 Democratic primaries, but with Waring serving as a top campaign aide, Smith defied the president and won reelection in a landslide. Smith rewarded Waring for his loyalty by clearing the way for his appointment to the federal judgeship in 1941.[55]

After the teacher-pay cases in 1944 and 1945, Waring's social life underwent a radical change that would help sever his ties with white Charleston—and perhaps nudge forward his new commitment to civil rights. For more than thirty-two years, Waring had been married to Annie Gammell, the daughter of a respected Charleston family and a familiar face at the city's annual society balls in the fashionable neighborhood south of Broad Street. By late 1945, however, rumors began to spread about the Warings' marriage. Sometime earlier that year, Waring had met and fallen in love with Elizabeth Hoffmann, the wife of a wealthy Connecticut textile manufacturer who had a winter home south of Broad. Divorce was still illegal in South Carolina at the time, but Waring was determined to end the marriage. The judge sent his wife to stay with his sister in Florida, where she established residency and filed for divorce. To make matters more tantalizing for the Charleston gossip mill, Judge Waring would be his new wife's third husband. Originally from Detroit, Elizabeth Avery had divorced her first husband, attorney Wilson Mills, to marry Hoffmann. Elizabeth Avery Waring **was** an intelligent and charming person, and Waring's male friends in Charleston would later say they understood why he initially fell in love with her. However, as one former law partner put it, "She was also a Yankee, and she had those characteristics. Those women just don't seem to have the same manner as southern women have. They are a little more aggressive."[56]

It was true that Elizabeth Waring read much more widely and deeply than the judge's former wife. And on the issue of race, the new Mrs. Waring and her husband began to explore points of view beyond the narrow confines of the Charleston *News and Courier* and other southern news media. They were particularly moved by the findings published in *An American Dilemma,* Gunnar Myrdal's investigation into "the Negro problem and American democracy." Funded by the Carnegie Foundation and published in 1944, Myrdal's massive two-volume study depicted in painstaking detail the degree of black misery in America. The book sought to answer one perplexing question: How could a country built on such liberal ideals as freedom and equality allow the wholesale oppression of one-tenth of its citizens? Myrdal provided an optimistic answer. He believed northern whites were unaware of the depth of white oppression in the South, and that they would reject racism and white supremacy once they fully understood its vile impact on the nation's democratic life. Myrdal believed northern public opinion would play a crucial role in the coming fight over black civil rights.[57]

Waring also began to read the black press, including *The Crisis* and McCray's *Lighthouse and Informer*. The federal judge would send the editor hand-written notes to complain when weekly issues did not arrive on schedule. As the Warings expanded their reading, they learned more about the reality of life for African Americans in the South—and they grew increasingly disturbed by what they read. "I couldn't take it at first, I used to say it wasn't true, it couldn't be," Judge Waring later told *Collier's* magazine. "I would put the books down, so troubled I couldn't look at them." Waring's shift in allegiance provided dramatic evidence of change within the nation's public sphere; the African American movement was now gaining empathy and winning allies in the North and the South too.[58]

The victory in the teacher-pay case emboldened African Americans in South Carolina. Encouraged by the *Lighthouse and Informer,* black communities had gradually shifted away from the accommodationist stance and embraced the NAACP. By 1948, the number of dues-paying members in the state exceeded fourteen thousand, up from only about eight hundred a decade earlier. McCray acknowledged this shift in attitude in a celebratory editorial in the *Lighthouse and Informer*. "Once upon a time in South Carolina it was next to being atrocious and ungodly to have it known that you—a Negro—favored taking white people to court and having a showdown for the rights of your race. This is no longer the case," McCray wrote. "Now, seeing how grand it has been, how glorious it was to be out there fighting . . . everybody wants to get into the act."[59]

The movement's initial success in South Carolina in the early 1940s would establish a model for emerging civil rights efforts across the South over the following decade. Simkins's leadership position in South Carolina in the 1940s would foreshadow the prominent role women would play in the movement, both as organizers behind the scenes and as powerful voices in their own right. And her strategy of developing a "fighting news organ" and placing it at the heart of the movement would spread as well. As Roberts and Klibanoff note, southern civil rights campaigns emerging in the following decade often featured black journalists who "ran the newspaper by day and the NAACP by night."[60]

The teacher-pay fight had been an important symbolic victory for the state's NAACP activists, but their goal had been relatively modest. Demanding enforcement of the "separate but equal" doctrine still implied that "separate but equal" was acceptable. The next battle would concern equality in South Carolina—political equality—and it would provoke stronger opposition.

McCray had been arguing in favor of black political involvement since the late 1930s. He repeatedly emphasized the potential political clout of a black community that comprised "46 percent of the population, a majority in 22 of the 46 counties" and in four of six congressional districts in South Carolina. If blacks could get to the ballot box, they could exercise enormous political power. Of course, white Carolinians could do the math as well, and most were determined to keep blacks out of the state's politics. Between 1944 and 1948, McCray's newspaper would move even closer to center stage in the African American fight for full citizenship in the South.[61]

3 A Black Political Insurgency in the Deep South

From the "colored seats" in the balcony, John McCray and Osceola McK-aine looked down into the chamber of the South Carolina statehouse and watched Governor Olin Johnston address the state's lawmakers. What they heard would infuriate them. It was April 14, 1944, and Johnston had called the state's lawmakers back to Columbia for an "extraordinary session" to deal with a new threat to white political rule in the state. Eleven days earlier, the U.S. Supreme Court had surprised both white southerners and NAACP lawyers by siding with the civil rights organization and declaring the Democratic Party's whites-only primary elections to be unconstitutional. Across the South, state parties employed a series of restrictive membership rules to prevent blacks from joining, thus ensuring that African Americans could play no role in party primaries. Democratic primaries were the only elections that mattered in one-party southern states where winning the party nomination was tantamount to being elected to office. If blacks could vote in Democratic Party primaries, they could wield enormous political clout, especially in Deep South states such as South Carolina where blacks comprised nearly half of the population. In the statehouse chamber, a red-faced Johnston vowed never to let this happen, even if it meant defying the law of the land: "White supremacy will be maintained in our primaries," the governor said. "Let the chips fall where they may!"[1]

The Supreme Court justices struck down the use of the whites-only primary in *Smith v. Allwright,* a Texas case brought by Thurgood Marshall and the NAACP. Marshall had argued that the state's system of primary elections violated both the Fourteenth Amendment's equal protection clause and the Fifteenth Amendment's guarantee of African American voting rights. Texas officials claimed the Democratic Party was a private organization, not an extension of the state, and was not bound by these constitutional requirements. As a private entity, they contended, the party could establish membership rules and select candidates for office any way it saw fit. Nine years earlier, the justices had accepted this argument unanimously in *Grovey v. Townsend,* another Texas case. That ruling appeared to set a precedent that would ensure the use of whites-only primaries in the South for decades to come. Between 1935 and 1944, however, the court's makeup changed dramatically. Seven justices left the bench during those years, allowing President Franklin D. Roosevelt to replace some of the court's most conservative members. Nonetheless, Marshall and his colleagues were stunned when the justices voted 8–1 to overturn *Grovey* so soon after appearing to settle the issue. In *Smith v. Allwright,* the court said the nation's "organic law" grants all citizens the right to participate in elections, and no state has the power to nullify that right "by casting its electoral process in a form which permits a private organization to practice racial discrimination in the election."[2]

In South Carolina, Governor Johnston maintained that Texas had not gone far enough in severing party primaries from the state's election machinery, and he urged lawmakers not to make the same mistake. Johnston called on the legislature to abolish all state laws related to political parties—more than one hundred statutes in all—and order the parties to establish new rules and regulations for selecting candidates. If that tactic failed, Johnston and the state's Democratic leaders had other tricks they planned to use to try save the white primary. Their strategy became known as the "South Carolina Plan," and over the next four years, the legal showdown over the future of the white primary played out in the Palmetto State. The outcome would have enormous political implications for the South and the nation. It would open the door for millions of black southerners to enter the political process, and over time it would fundamentally alter the makeup of the nation's two major political parties. As the drama unfolded, John McCray and his newspaper emerged to play a leading role.

In 1944, the governor opened the six-day special session with a demagogic tirade that employed some of the same racist stereotypes "Pitchfork" Ben Tillman had used so effectively during the rise of Jim Crow rule nearly five decades earlier. Johnston said the Supreme Court ruling threatened to return South Carolina to the days of Reconstruction, when a Negro majority dominated the legislature and "fraud, corruption, immorality, and graft" were commonplace. Those black lawmakers had "left a stench in the nostrils of the people in South Carolina that will exist for generations to come," the governor claimed. Tillman and his fellow Democrats had rescued the state from political chaos when they approved a new constitution that virtually eliminated black voting rights, the governor said, and current lawmakers must meet the same challenge now. The state must learn from its history and "keep our white Democratic primaries pure and unadulterated," Johnston said, "so that we might protect the welfare and homes of all the people of our state."[3]

In the statehouse balcony, the black activists sat quietly as Johnston's speech reached its crescendo, but McCray later said "the brilliant Ossie McKaine grew visibly agitated," particularly when the governor concluded with what sounded like a threat of violence against black South Carolinians. Even if legal means failed, Johnston said, whites in the state would "use the necessary methods to retain white supremacy in our primaries." To McKaine, the governor's words sounded like "an open invitation to the Klan to get busy."[4]

Johnston never mentioned McCray or McKaine in his speech, but the governor and his aides had the black editors and their newspaper on his mind that day. Johnston decried that "certain agitators from within and without South Carolina" are taking advantage of events "to create strife and dissension" in the state. To emphasize his point—and perhaps to motivate the lawmakers—the governor and his supporters passed around recent articles from the *Lighthouse and Informer* on the statehouse floor. The "agitators" who are pushing for political change, Johnston said, "are not friends of either race" but are merely out "to further their own selfish gain." In his newspaper, McCray mocked the frequent use of the term "agitator"; he claimed the only "agitating" in South Carolina was done by white leaders who "stir the racial pot" for political gain.[5]

McCray's newspaper had been encouraging the effort to crack open the state's all-white Democratic Party since the paper moved to Columbia in late 1941. Like most African Americans, McCray had once seen the Republican Party as the proper outlet for political participation. But since Roosevelt's election in 1932, he had slowly joined the millions of blacks who turned to FDR because of his New Deal policies. In August 1936, a headline in the *New York Times* captured the political sea change: "Negro Vote Jumps in South Carolina—Rush to Register is Ascribed by Official to Desire to Support Roosevelt."[6]

As African Americans in the South embraced Roosevelt, many white Democratic Party leaders in the region gradually moved away from the president. They feared the administration's relatively liberal positions on labor and racial issues could embolden activists in the South and threaten the political and economic status quo. They were particularly concerned about Roosevelt's wife, Eleanor, and her outreach to African Americans. In 1942, word spread among white South Carolinians that black domestic workers were joining

"Eleanor Clubs" and hatching plans to go on strike. The clubs supposedly had a motto: "A white woman in every kitchen by Christmas." The managing editor of the *News and Courier,* a white daily newspaper in Charleston, assigned reporters to track down the organizers of these clubs, and he pleaded with other southern newspapers to take the threat seriously in their states as well. The rumors grew so strong that Governor Richard Jeffries ordered state law enforcement to join the hunt for the Eleanor Clubs in South Carolina. Neither the state investigators nor the reporters uncovered evidence to support the claims. In fact, domestic workers were leaving white kitchens across the South in 1942, but the reason, the *Richmond Times-Dispatch* noted, "was not because of Eleanor Clubs but because they are able to earn higher wages in war industries." The whole affair seemed to amuse McCray. He would cite the Eleanor Clubs investigation frequently over the years as an example of the white ignorance about black life in South Carolina. If the governor was concerned about black discontent, the editor wrote in one editorial, he should consider trying to help the state's black citizens rather than preaching "antagonism."[7]

The effort to challenge South Carolina's all-white primary had begun after Roosevelt's first election. Black voters had been registering to vote in Democratic Party primaries since the 1934 midterms, but in each election cycle their names had been purged from the voter rolls based on the party's rigid membership rules. The courts had upheld the party's right to establish those rules, despite their clear racial intent. For example, one rule said that only blacks who could prove they had voted in Democratic Party primaries continuously since 1876 could join the party. With the Supreme Court's *Grovey* decision in 1935, the situation appeared hopeless.

In South Carolina, the NAACP's new statewide conference of branches did not agree. By 1942, the group had a new leader, James Hinton, a barrel-chested Baptist preacher whose rumbling baritone was a familiar sound to black residents in every corner of the state. McCray called Hinton "a rebel rouser" who knew how to work a crowd. "He'd be introduced in a place like Anderson, and he'd get up and say, 'all Negro teachers in Anderson, all Negro doctors in Anderson, all Negro big-wigs in Anderson—they ain't worth a damn!" McCray recalled. "He did it all over South Carolina and people liked it. He was telling the truth." Soon after they began working together, McCray said he and Hinton made a pledge: "Every day we live we're gonna do at least one thing to make a white guy squirm—even if it's nothing more than writing a letter to a newspaper or a state official," McCray said. "He would call early in the morning and say, 'Chief, I think I've got something.' I mean we did this religiously."[8]

Modjeska Simkins joined forces with Hinton to form the new leadership of the state conference of branches. She left the South Carolina Tuberculosis Association earlier in 1942 and started working full-time as executive secretary of the NAACP's statewide alliance. The two made a formidable team. With Hinton and Simkins atop the organization, and McCray, McKaine, and their newspaper serving as the group's communications arm, the NAACP in South Carolina geared up to challenge white political rule in the state. Hinton told NAACP counsel Thurgood Marshall that, despite the long odds, the state's African American community was committed to the fight against the white primary and planned to enroll "about 500" Negro voters in the Democratic Party before the 1942 election. "Things are really hot in South Carolina," Hinton wrote, "and we can go over in a big way with the NAACP."[9]

To their surprise, the black activists attracted a small but outspoken number of whites to their voting rights campaign. Columbia attorney R. Beverly Hubert led a group of moderate whites that petitioned the Democratic Party to allow black citizens to join. Hubert told the Richland County board of elections that if black citizens could fight for their country abroad, they should be allowed to vote at home. His speech drew applause, and the board agreed to forward the proposal to state party officials for consideration. At the state Democratic Convention in May, twenty-one white citizens signed a resolution urging the party to "arrive at some plan by which qualified Negroes may vote in the Democratic primaries." The group's spokesman, Dr. J. Heywood Gibbes, said he was convinced that Negroes were "now qualified in mind and character to take part in our form of government." He said black voting in the party primary was inevitable, and that South Carolina could "light a spark" that would benefit the South if it moved first on the issue. State party leaders disagreed. They rejected the request and ordered local election boards to purge the newly enrolled black voters.[10]

The South Carolina activists had no intention of giving up. To avoid the NAACP rules against political partisanship, Hinton and Simkins helped form a new organization, the Negro Citizens Council, which raised $3,000 to prepare for legal battle against the Democratic Party. Hinton told Marshall that "the people are aroused" as never before in South Carolina. Simkins called the 1942 voting-rights push "our very best chance ever" to break down the all-white primary. "We mean to get on this matter now and go through to the end," she wrote to the national office.[11]

Using the subscription list of the *Lighthouse and Informer* to supplement state NAACP membership rolls, Hinton organized mass meetings around the state to discuss "doing something about the ballot." The flyers announcing the meetings included the "Double V" language popularized by the *Pittsburgh*

Courier; they called for "Democracy Abroad" and "Democracy at Home." In Columbia, more than two hundred people showed up at a church to hear from Lottie P. Gaffney, "the main prosecutrix in Spartanburg voting trial." Gaffney had enrolled in the Democratic Party in her hometown and she instructed Columbia's black residents how to go about the process. After the meeting, a fired-up Hinton wrote to Marshall and pleaded with him to get moving on the South Carolina ballot issue. Marshall agreed to come speak to one of the mass meetings. But he pointed out that he was hard at work on "a Texas case" involving the all-white primary that must take precedence over any South Carolina action. A disappointed Hinton conceded the issue reluctantly. Of course, the "Texas case" would be *Smith v. Allwright*. When the Supreme Court sided with Marshall and the NAACP in April 1944, the ruling energized both sides in the fight over the all-white primary in South Carolina.[12]

The Rise of the Progressive Democratic Party

The results of Governor Johnston's "extraordinary session" in response to the *Smith v. Allwright* decision created new hurdles for the black activists in South Carolina. To mount a legal challenge to the new primary system in the state, the NAACP needed to find a black voter who had registered in the Democratic Party but had been denied a vote in the party's primary. This had been easy to accomplish in 1942, when white leaders were confident that the *Grovey* ruling would protect the all-white primary. It became much harder to do after *Smith v. Allwright*. White Democrats controlled the enrollment process and they understood the need to prevent a black applicant from joining the party. White officials moved the party's registration books around surreptitiously, never letting black citizens know when and where they would be open for business. It was like a shell game: A registration book would open at a local store, but when a black voter approached, the book would abruptly close, only to reopen the next day at a different location. The stalling technique worked in the spring and summer of 1944 and ensured another election year with an all-white Democratic primary, despite the Supreme Court decision striking it down. Rather than accept that outcome and wait patiently for the legal process to unfold, McCray responded with an audacious move that would rattle the Democratic Party in South Carolina and Washington as well. He and McKaine used the pages of the *Lighthouse and Informer* to launch a black political organization, one designed to empower the African American community and challenge the white Democrats.[13]

By 1944, the national Democratic Party had begun to splinter. The New Deal coalition that had elected Roosevelt three times was increasingly torn between its staunch segregationist wing in the South and the rising strength of liberal, labor, and black supporters in the North. Roosevelt moved to appease his growing white southern opposition by dumping his liberal vice president, Henry Wallace. The president had been expected to replace Wallace with one of his longtime allies, James F. Byrnes, the former senator from South Carolina, but when northern liberals balked at the choice of such a stalwart segregationist, Roosevelt turned to a little-known senator from Missouri, Harry S. Truman. Many white southerners were not satisfied. After the president's renomination at that summer's Democratic National Convention, the *Charleston News and Courier* and its conservative editor, William Watts Ball, urged state Democrats to place a slate of independent, anti-Roosevelt electors on the ballot so that the incumbent would not receive the state's electoral votes.

Ball's campaign to undermine Roosevelt angered McCray and McKaine. They understood that if Ball succeeded, blacks in South Carolina would be denied the opportunity to vote for FDR in the November general election. They responded by using the *Lighthouse and Informer* to launch a pro-Roosevelt movement they called the "Fourth Term for Roosevelt Club." In a March 1944 editorial, the newspaper complained that black South Carolinians could not join the Democratic Party, "despite [their] overwhelming appreciation for President and Mrs. Roosevelt," so they must find a new way to express their political support. The editorial encouraged readers to launch "Fourth Term Clubs" in their hometowns, and the newspaper offered to provide details on how to go about this to anyone who mailed in a stamped, self-addressed envelope.[14]

McCray said he launched the "Fourth Term Clubs" to highlight the strong African American commitment to the president and to contribute to the effort to overturn the all-white primary. But he did not see the clubs as the beginning of a permanent political organization. However, a local white newspaper, the *Columbia Record,* ran a news story that said the *Lighthouse and Informer* had launched a separate Negro political party. When the Associated Press picked up the *Record'*s story and distributed it statewide, the *Lighthouse and Informer* was inundated with requests for details. As the number of "Fourth Term Clubs" grew, McCray said that he realized he and his newspaper had given birth to something special, a political movement that could challenge both white supremacy and black conservatism in the state. Never one to undersell his accomplishments, McCray later described the creation of a black political party in South Carolina as "brazen, daring and smart . . . a single act of terrorism for white supremacists in a state where by sheer numbers blacks" held enormous political potential. The new party,

McCray said, "was controlled by blacks, by selected people who wanted no 'under the table' payoffs nor . . . pats on the shoulder. That kind of operation scares the daylights out of racist supremacists. It also baffles those blacks who thrive on sell outs."[15]

When McCray suggested the new organization be called the "South Carolina Colored Democratic Party," he received pushback from the tiny number of vocal white moderates in the state who supported black voting rights. In an anonymous letter to the *Lighthouse and Informer,* one man accused McCray of practicing the same exclusionary practices as the regular Democrats. He encouraged the editor to run an editorial inviting "all whites to join your cause." McCray also said an elderly white woman came to the offices of the *Lighthouse and Informer* to confront him directly about the name issue. As McCray later told the story, the woman told the editor that "Colored Democratic Party" made the party sound as "reactionary" as the current Democratic Party. She recommended the group use the word "progressive," and she contributed $5 to launch the party's first fundraising campaign.[16]

McCray agreed to name the organization the Progressive Democratic Party and to welcome white members, but he no longer saw the party as temporary. By May 1944, he began to envision the PDP "a permanent political organization" that could motivate black activism and generate a sense of agency in the African American community. The party would stay in operation, he wrote, "so long as it shall be necessary to have group action in the matter of group rights and privileges."[17]

In one of its first public acts, the PDP signaled its intention to challenge the political status quo and tweak white political leaders in the state. McCray wrote to Secretary of State W. A. Blackwell and requested permission to hold the party's first state convention in the chambers of the statehouse—the same spot where Governor Johnston had stood just three weeks earlier when he had announced plans to defy the Supreme Court and preserve the all-white primary elections. "It is our understanding that use of these facilities is free of cost," McCray wrote to Blackwell, "and they are as accessible to one group as another." The secretary of state passed McCray's request to a lower-level state official who apparently never responded.[18]

Meeting in Columbia's Masonic Hall, more than 170 PDP members representing every county in South Carolina convened on May 24 and formally elected McCray as party chairman. The Associated Press led its story on the PDP convention by describing how the "shouting, stamping and applauding" delegates demanded seats at the upcoming Democratic National Convention in Chicago. The AP focused on Hinton's fiery attack on Governor Olin Johnston and state Representative John Long. In his special session, Johnston had vowed to call out the home guard if necessary to protect white supremacy, and Long had authored a House resolution blaming black protest on "damned Northern agitators." Hinton claimed blacks wanted to avoid violence, but "if it takes shedding blood like Long said it would, he's not the only red-blooded American in South Carolina." To big cheers, the NAACP leader said Long and Johnston should stop all talk of bloodshed and "take that type of bravery over against the Japs and Germans."[19]

McKaine opened his keynote address to the PDP convention by saying, "I am a black man in South Carolina and I'm sure that there will be people who will read carefully what I say." He denounced efforts by the governor and white Democrats to "nullify a lawful decision" of the Supreme Court and prevent blacks from participating in party primaries. "When the courts of a country or state are no longer obeyed," he said, "anarchy and violence are bound to follow." McKaine urged white leaders to see the rise of the PDP as evidence of a new sense of unity and determination among black Carolinians. The new political organization should serve notice to the state's "demagogic, mediocre politicians," that scare tactics will no longer deter the push for equal rights in the state. For McKaine, blacks in South Carolina had stopped living like "spineless serfs" and were ready to challenge the white Democratic Party like "like free men."[20]

When the editor of the *Columbia Record,* the relatively moderate George A. Buchanan Jr., charged in an editorial that McKaine had "talked too much and unwisely," the black activist fired back. "Surely it is not 'talking too much and unwisely' to demand participation in the making and administering of the laws of our state and nation," McKaine wrote in a letter published in the white newspaper. Blacks were tired of being told "no" to every request for change, no matter how minor or reasonable, he continued. Most whites knew little about the state's black residents and failed to grasp the depth of their frustration and bitterness. Such indifference could lead to a conflagration, McKaine wrote: "If the white people don't know what the Negroes are thinking about—that's alarming; if they don't know how they feel—that's dangerous; but if they are not concerned about either—that can be calamitous."[21]

On the eve of the PDP convention, McCray had sent a letter to state Democratic Party chairman Winchester Smith outlining the group's demands. Given the size of the black population in the state and that "the vast majority" are Democrats, McCray said the PDP should be allowed to select eight of the eighteen delegates that would represent South Carolina at the Democratic National Convention in Chicago that summer. McCray argued that a political party should accept "every citizen subscribing to its principles," and he claimed the racial policies of the white Democrats were "unreasonable, undemocratic, and un-Christian-like." Referring to the PDP, McCray said the state now had a party "pledged to uphold the principles of Democratic government, and since the National Democratic Party can not recognize but one organization," the PDP and the white Democrats should work together to send a biracial delegation to Chicago. Smith never replied to McCray's letter.[22]

To the dismay of some national Democrats, McCray and PDP carried out their pledge to challenge the state's white slate of delegates at the party's national convention. Energized by McKaine's keynote speech, which concluded with a call for the PDP to take its fight "on to Chicago," the state delegates selected twenty members of the organization to represent South Carolina's black Democrats at the July convention. In the summer of 1944, Roosevelt was caught between growing black support in the North and an increasingly wary white supremacist wing in the South. It was an alliance that could not hold. Yet despite their strong support for Roosevelt, McCray and the PDP had no intention of walking away quietly and avoiding conflict at the president's convention. If South Carolina's black slate of delegates is not seated, McCray said, "there will be devil to pay." He predicted northern blacks would abandon Roosevelt and perhaps swing the election to the Republicans if the Democrats rebuffed the PDP delegates. "The national [Democratic] party is as responsible as the state party for the denial of membership to Negroes in that it tolerates discrimination in the South," he said.[23]

McCray and a small contingent of PDP leaders met with national party leaders in Washington a week before the Chicago convention. Democratic National Committeeman Robert Hannegan, vice chairman Oscar Ewing, and black congressman William Dawson of Chicago appealed to the editor's loyalty to Roosevelt and urged him to abandon his convention challenge. "Gentlemen," McCray said he told the group, "We are going to Chicago. Now if you care to, we can start talking from that point." McCray said the party officials assured the PDP that Roosevelt and his administration would work through the courts to ensure full black voting rights in the South. For their part, McCray and his colleagues assured the officials that the PDP would support Roosevelt in the fall election. But the Washington meeting would later come back to haunt McCray, as rivals in the PDP would claim that he and the other leaders had "sold out" the group, perhaps even for cash. McCray hotly denied the charge and attributed it to professional jealousy. No evidence emerged to support those accusations.[24]

Twenty years before Fannie Lou Hamer and the Mississippi Freedom Democrats famously challenged that state's all-white delegation in Atlantic City in 1964, McCray and his PDP colleagues traveled to Chicago and launched the first effort to contest the racial makeup of a delegation at the Democratic National Convention. McCray would later recall with amusement that South Carolina's senior senator, Burnett Maybank, was aboard the same Columbia-to-Chicago train that carried most of the PDP delegates, but Maybank refused to come out of his first-class car to mingle with his fellow Democrats. Maybank told reporters just how he felt about the PDP challenge. "As a southern Democrat, I do not propose to be run out of my party by either the Negroes, the Communists or Northern agitators . . . it will be my purpose to see that our party stands where it always has—[for] states' rights and white supremacy."[25]

A large picture of the PDP delegates graced the front page of the *Chicago Defender* as they arrived in Chicago. The black press from across the country followed their convention challenge closely as McCray's PDP contingent and Maybank's white Democrats argued their cases before the party's credentials committee. To no one's surprise, the credentials committee sided with the senator and disqualified McCray's PDP slate on a technicality. The ruling claimed the PDP had violated Democratic Party rules by failing to hold county meetings before holding a state convention and selecting national delegates. Although Maybank's white delegation was seated, McCray used the high-profile moment in Chicago to help organize black activism back home. The PDP nominated McKaine to run for the Senate in the fall and turned his campaign into a recruitment drive to motivate blacks across the state to join both the NAACP and the PDP.[26]

With the *Lighthouse and Informer* publicizing campaign events and offering its full-throated editorial support, McKaine held rallies in nearly every county in the state, and he used this platform to challenge black South Carolinians to join the battle for political rights. In doing so, he again framed the issue to emphasize Richard H. King's concept of "autonomous freedom." The battle will be a "painful, bitter struggle," he said at one stop, but if black men and women reject the idea of being a "ruled" group, they "must be willing to make every sacrifice necessary to obtain the right to vote." In McKaine's view, black agency would come not from winning a tangible victory in the election, but simply from joining the fight for equal rights. In this sense, the PDP's senatorial campaign succeeded.

During his campaign, McKaine encouraged poor whites and blacks to work together to break up the "present oligarchy" governing the state. On the evening of October 18, he stressed this point during a fifteen-minute address on popular Columbia radio station WIS. It was one of the few opportunities the candidate had to address a broad audience of black and white Carolinians. McKaine told his listeners that the PDP was not a "Negro party" but rather an organization that had been founded by "liberal whites and colored citizens" as a last resort, after all efforts to open the Democratic primaries to black voters had failed. McKaine concluded by emphasizing his ties to FDR and the New Deal and his commitment to racial unity. South Carolinians should vote for him, McKaine argued, "because I am the symbol of closer cooperation between the races, the vote-less white and colored South Carolinians."[27]

By the end of the fall, the party claimed to have 45,000 members. However, the final election results showed the PDP with only five thousand votes. An outraged McCray charged that white election officials prevented many blacks from voting and failed to count the ballots of those who did. He reached out to Thurgood Marshall and the NAACP for help. McCray knew the PDP had no chance of winning the election, but he feared that giving in to the fraud without a fight would undermine the momentum and sense of agency the PDP and McKaine's campaign had generated in the black community. As McCray explained in a letter to Marshall: "We have had a hell of a job beating down the fear in these people, in getting their trust and hopes and don't intend to see them come down with their ballot . . . to be robbed, intimidated and frustrated."[28]

Marshall filed a complaint with the U.S. Justice Department and McKaine contested the election in the U.S. Senate, but neither body took action. Nonetheless, the PDP had succeeded in carrying out McCray's primary goals: to move the black community to act and to deliver to the state and the nation a consistent and unified interpretation of how mistreatment of southern blacks undermined and contradicted the ideals of the larger American democracy.

"It Is Time For South Carolina to Rejoin the Union"

In the next election year, 1946, McCray and his colleagues tried again to get a black voter enrolled in the Democratic Party and thus launch a new legal challenge against the all-white primary. The activists had failed to overcome the trickery of the white Democrats throughout the spring of 1946 and were growing desperate. Finally, an unlikely hero emerged. As McCray tells the story, he and three other NAACP activists were standing outside a small store in Columbia's ninth ward. They had seen whites enrolling in the store, but every time a black voter entered the woman behind the counter claimed the enrollment book was not there. As McCray and his colleagues were about to leave, a cab driver named George Elmore drove up. McCray described Elmore as a "pest" who "bugged" everybody with his endless chatter and general nosiness. They barely spoke to him, but soon Elmore learned what they were up to. He asked if he could try to enroll. McCray described the group's response as, "Sure, good riddance and relief!" A light-skinned African American, Elmore walked into the store and, to the amazement of McCray and his colleagues, the woman pulled out the registration book and let him sign up. As soon as she saw his address, however, she realized Elmore was a Negro. By then, she had grown weary of the process as well. She told Elmore that those "other niggers might as well come on in and enroll too." With Elmore, the NAACP had its plaintiff in a new legal assault on the party's all-white primary.[29]

In a remarkable week in South Carolina history, Thurgood Marshall returned to the state in June 1947 to argue two important civil rights cases in federal court in Columbia. In addition to *Elmore v. Rice,* the challenge to the state's all-white primary, Marshall and the NAACP had also filed suit on behalf of John H. Wrighten, a black student from Charleston whose application had been denied by the University of South Carolina law school. In *Wrighten v. Board of Trustees of the University of South Carolina,* Marshall argued that the state's black citizens deserved the same opportunities to pursue a law degree as its white students. In rulings handed down on the same July day, the increasingly liberal federal judge J. Waties Waring delivered sharply worded decisions supporting the NAACP in both cases. He ordered the state to end the all-white Democratic Party primary and to provide legal education for its black citizens, either at the existing law school or at a "separate but equal" facility. "It is time," Waring said in the voting case, "for South Carolina to rejoin the Union."[30]

The state's white Democrats refused to concede defeat. They employed one last trick in a desperate effort to continue barring blacks from voting in Democratic primaries. In May 1948, state party officials passed a new regulation requiring members of the Democratic Party to sign an oath swearing their allegiance to racial segregation and their opposition to President Truman's proposed federal employment protection commission. Obviously, black citizens who wanted to join the party were unwilling to sign such an oath. Yet party election officials vowed to purge 1948 election rolls of any member who had refused to sign. Marshall took the South Carolina Democrats to federal court, and once again Waring delivered a stern rebuke. In *Brown v. Baskin,* the judge declared the party oath unconstitutional, and he vowed to clear his calendar on Election Day so he would be available to imprison any party leader who prevented a registered black voter from casting a ballot in the Democratic primary.[31]

On August 10, 1948, news photographers captured the festive atmosphere as black South Carolinians, dressed in their Sunday best, gathered in long lines to vote in a Democratic Party primary. More than 30,000 black South Carolinians went to the polls that day—by far the largest African American turnout since the Reconstruction era. Marshall returned to South Carolina to monitor voting and said he was moved by what he saw. Despite the predictions of "certain die-hard politicians whose political life depended on white supremacy," Marshall said he saw no evidence of "friction." Large numbers of black citizens voted in the "white primary" for the first time in the twentieth century, he said, and "the skies did not fall."[32]

With his ruling in *Brown v. Baskin,* Waring drove a final stake in the all-white primary in the Deep South. Calling the decision a "landmark of jurisprudence," NAACP executive director Walter White emphasized Waring's personal evolution on racial issues, which he described as a potent symbol of the cultural change occurring in the South. The ruling had added significance, White said, because Waring "is the scion of a distinguished southern family" and is an example of the "new, forward-looking and decent South, the growth of which has struck terror in the hearts" of white supremacist politicians.[33]

White's hopeful words echoed a sentiment that had been a recurring theme in southern discourse. Since the writer George Washington Cable published *The Silent South* in 1885, liberals had been waiting for good and decent whites to rise up in disgust at the excesses of the Jim Crow order. This search for the "silent South" had proved futile so far. By 1948, South Carolina and the rest of the Deep South were changing, but perhaps not as quickly or as decisively as White suggested. Waring would face a harsh backlash from white South Carolinians who believed he had betrayed his homeland. On the streets of Charleston he was routinely referred to as "the guy that let the niggers vote." Congressman Mendel Rivers called Waring a "former white supremacist" who was "as cold as a dead Eskimo in an abandoned igloo . . . with lemon juice . . . in his rigid and calculating veins." He urged fellow lawmakers to impeach the judge and warned that blood would flow in the streets if Waring remained on the bench. The threat of violence seemed valid. Waring and his wife returned home one night to find a cross had been burned on their front yard. On another evening, while playing canasta in the living room, a piece of concrete crashed through the window and flew over their heads. Noting the incident on its editorial page, the *Pee Dee Advocate* in rural Marlboro County said: "Unfortunately, the judge was not hit."[34]

Yet there were small but important signs of cultural and political change in both the North and the South in late 1940s. The most consequential concerned northern public opinion and its reaction to the use of state-sanctioned violence against blacks in the South. When black activists mobilized in South

Carolina during World War I, white supremacists could crush the movement with little fear of its impact on northern public opinion. In the years after Reconstruction, whites in the North had grown weary of what they called "the Negro problem," and the federal government ceded to white southerners the power to manage race relations in their region. At that time, the arguments that Du Bois and the emerging black press delivered concerning racial injustice and the nation's Democratic ideals won few converts in the larger white audience.

By 1943, with the nation now embroiled in another world war, and with northern white Democrats working harder to lure black voters, the cultural milieu had changed. The same arguments Du Bois had made so passionately at the turn of the century began to resonate within mainstream public discourse, and this shift in the cultural landscape began to effect political decision making. The black press and its powerful "Double V" campaign made the link between fascism abroad and racial oppression at home more difficult for whites to ignore. Myrdal's *An American Dilemma,* while hardly a bestseller, had nonetheless influenced elite white opinion leaders and helped to undermine the intellectual credibility of racist and white supremacist arguments. In this shifting cultural and political environment, black activists such as A. Phillip Randolph, leader of the March on Washington movement, could point out the hypocrisy at the heart of the American democratic system and force the nation's president to take his complaints seriously. White supremacists continued to claim that southern blacks were happy under Jim Crow, and that outside agitators, many of them with Communist Party ties, were the source of any discontent. With the emergence of the cold war, red-baiting arguments would gain traction in the late 1940s. But the notion that most southern blacks were content and that white violence was necessary to maintain the natural racial order was growing increasingly difficult to sell in the North.[35]

One southern white leader who appeared to grasp this cultural and political shift was a young World War II veteran named J. Strom Thurmond. Thurmond grew up in Edgefield, South Carolina, hometown of Ben Tillman, the state's foremost white supremacist leader. His father had been such a rabid Tillman supporter that he once killed a man who had criticized his hero. (The jury accepted his claim of self-defense.) Yet when young Thurmond ran for governor in 1946, he campaigned as a New Deal liberal and a racial moderate. In neighboring Georgia that year, Eugene Talmadge rallied white voters with a searing defense of white supremacy in his gubernatorial campaign. He promised to preserve a "Democratic white primary" that would be "unfettered and unhampered by radical, communist, and alien influences."

Without the white primary, Talmadge warned, Georgia's white politicians "will have to go to their homes . . . shake hands with all of them, and kiss their babies. . . ." Yet in South Carolina, just across the Savannah River, Thurmond downplayed race in his campaign. He supported segregation, obviously, but in his stump speeches across the state he championed a prosperous and industrialized South that would benefit both races. In his inaugural address, Thurmond proposed increased spending on African American schools to help prepare the race to thrive in the new economy. The state's black leaders took note of Thurmond's moderate tone. Modjeska Simkins wrote glowingly of the candidate, calling Thurmond the first white politician she had ever seen who campaigned like he wanted to be "governor of all the people of South Carolina." But Simkins was hardly naive. Presciently, she also predicted that the "customary political pressure" could force Thurmond to change his liberal views on race. As she put it, "The vultures are beginning to circle."[36]

As historian Joseph Crespino notes, Thurmond's successful race for governor in 1946 was the only campaign in his long career in which he ran as the more liberal candidate. Yet with his rhetoric in that contest, Thurmond signaled a change in Deep South politics. He was an early proponent of a new interpretation of Jim Crow, one that softened the harsher edges of white supremacy and tried to make it more palatable for white northerners. At the time, Thurmond was concerned more about luring investment to the South rather than ensuring fair play for black citizens, and he would quickly abandon this moderate stance when it served his political interests to do so. But Thurmond's shift to the racial right would come after he had taken a dramatic stand opposing state-sanctioned violence against African Americans in the South.

As black veterans returned from the war, they encountered a new wave of racial violence across the Deep South. Two incidents in South Carolina drew national attention and forced the new governor to respond. In 1946, a veteran named Isaac Woodard was blinded by a Batesburg police officer who beat him after Woodard had a minor dispute with a white bus driver. And in 1947, a group of white taxi drivers from Greenville broke into the nearby Pickens County jail and lynched Willie Earle, a black man accused of murdering a white cab driver. The Woodard case sparked national outrage, but it ended the way most violence against southern blacks had always ended—without any action from local authorities. The Willie Earle case was different, however, and it signaled a slowly shifting political culture in both the North and the South.

Thurmond had been in office less than a year when the Earle lynching occurred. The new governor had an opportunity to employ the tactics of his predecessors, Tillman and Blease. They had criticized mob violence as unfortunate but often complained that the black men had triggered the violence by violating southern mores and customs. Their statements had clearly signaled the government's approval of white violence to contain black aspirations, even though the lawmakers claimed to oppose those who took the law in their own hands. In 1947, Thurmond did just the opposite. He not only criticized the lynching as unacceptable, but the governor encouraged the federal government—the FBI—to investigate the case and bring charges against the white criminals.

The governor's firm support for federal prosecution suggested that some measure of change was underway in the Deep South. Modjeska Simkins and Osceola McKaine praised Thurmond's efforts. In a letter to Thurmond, McKaine said, "it has been a long time since a Governor of South Carolina has shown by his actions that he would really fight for even-handed justice for all citizens regardless of race." Coming generations "will bless you," he added. McKaine noted the worldwide press attention on the Earle case and said Thurmond's "vigorous" response will prompt many to "revise their opinion" of America and the South.[37]

Unlike earlier lynchings in the state, the Earle case attracted press from around the world. Writing in *The New Yorker*, the famed British journalist Rebecca West described the trial as the "Opera in Greenville." Initially, she reported, journalists from the northern black press were allowed to sit with their white counterparts at the crowded press table near the front of the courtroom. Neither the white reporters nor the judge objected to this. In fact, the attorneys representing the white defendants were thrilled. As West noted, one of them said that having "a nigger sitting at the press table along with white men and women" would encourage the all-white jury to acquit. John McCray sat in the "colored seats" in the balcony as he covered the trial for the *Lighthouse and Informer*. And after hearing the defense attorney's remark about blacks sitting at the white press table, the African American reporters from the northern papers decided to head upstairs as well.[38]

In the end, the seating arrangements made no difference. The all-white jury acquitted all thirty-one defendants after a brief deliberation. Infuriated by the decision, McCray called the defendants "vicious and debased murderers," and he declared the verdict to be as "suggestive of savagery as the lynching itself." The editor dismissed the earlier notion that the trial was "the sign of 'progress' that some people are pointing to." Thurmond had done the right thing, he wrote, but the trial's verdict showed that the "Negro-hating element of white people" still controlled judicial outcomes in South Carolina. The answer, he said, was to ensure black people were represented on juries. "White juries reflect the 'mind' of whites when a Negro is involved, but they seldom reflect the 'mind' of Negroes," he concluded. In a separate column, McCray turned his wrath on the "history of hate" in South Carolina and the refusal of educated white society to repudiate lynching long ago. The Ku Klux Klan "probably taught these illiterate and poorly educated [defendants] to hate and lynch, under a tradition of immunity from punishment," he said.[39]

Despite his actions in the Willie Earle case, Thurmond was indeed no liberal on race. He would prove this the following year when he scrambled to lead the "Dixiecrat" revolt against President Truman's civil rights measures. But Thurmond's rhetoric in the 1946 campaign and his decision to call in the FBI in the Earle lynching reflected new concern in the South about the region's image in the North. Thurmond understood that the nation had changed in the past decade. The use of overwhelming, state-sanctioned violence would no longer be accepted by national public opinion. This shift by no means halted all violence in South Carolina, but it did send a small but significant signal of hope to the black community at an important moment in the civil rights struggle. Judge Waring's rulings on teacher pay and the white primary had provided the sort of tangible victories McCray and his NAACP allies needed to convince wary blacks that change was possible in South Carolina, that the 1940s movement would not suffer the same fate as the one that was so brutally crushed in the 1920s. In rural parts of the state, however, African Americans believed white supremacists retained their most powerful weapon—the ability to use violence without fear of retribution. Thurmond's rhetoric on the Earle lynching suggested that could be changing, if slowly. It revealed the growing power of northern public opinion to restrain southern extremism, and it offered hope that black protest in the Deep South might not necessarily end the way it always had in the past. This small opening helped NAACP activists in the region to rally support for their campaign of protest against white supremacy and Jim Crow.[40]

In the *Lighthouse and Informer,* McCray celebrated the death of the all-white primary in April 1948, when the U.S. Supreme Court refused to hear the state party's appeal of Waring's original decision in *Elmore v. Rice.* In an editorial headlined "The White Primary Goes Out," the editor also put South Carolina's black citizens on notice: "The next step is to make certain that the victory is not half a loaf, an empty one. . . . The clarion call against the primary . . . was 'all or none.' And this, henceforth, is the watchword. No membership in the party is complete without all the rights attending that membership. Only through such a stand can the court's ruling be made practical. Only in this fashion can it be said that 'government of all the people by the few of one people' has perished from the earth."[41]

McCray's editorial signaled a change in strategy for the civil rights movement in South Carolina. Earlier in the decade, the NAACP activists had
been willing to ask for "half a loaf." They had demanded the state pay black
teachers the same as their white counterparts, and they had forced the state
to provide a law school for black Carolinians. But they had not challenged
directly the doctrine of "separate but equal" that had been the law of the
land since the *Plessy* ruling in 1896. This would change. Henceforth, the civil
rights activists would demand full integration into the civic and political life
of South Carolina.[42]

During the early 1940s, as the black movement grew in South Carolina,
the state's white press mostly ignored it. They doubted local African Americans had the intelligence or the courage to confront white rule in a serious
way. For McCray and his allies, however, the era of protest politics was just
beginning. By 1948, white editors were forced to confront this new fact of
life, and they began to engage in a serious debate over how to respond.

4 The White Press and the Dixiecrat Revolt

Across the 1940s, South Carolina's white newspapers competed for circulation and influence—the *State* and the *Columbia Record* in the capital; the *News and Courier* and the *Charleston Evening Post* in the historic port city; the *Greenville News,* the *Greenville Piedmont,* and the Spartanburg papers, the *Herald* and the *Journal,* in the foothills of the northwest; and the *Florence Morning News* in the tobacco-growing northeast region along the Pee Dee River. They relied heavily on the national wires services—Associated Press and United Press—and on many days their lead news stories were identical. The differences came on the editorial page, specifically in the unsigned editorials, where each paper tried to distinguish itself through its editorial voice. Publishers competed to hire editors who could deliver compelling commentary, who could be "lively" and "argumentative" to brand their publications and build circulation.[1]

In the early years of the decade, the white editorialists took note of the rising civil rights activism in the state, but most treated it as a minor annoyance, not an existential threat to white political power. In the first year of World War II, they raised concerns about a War Department plan to make it easier for soldiers to vote because they feared it would increase black registration in the state. They were mildly surprised in 1943 when the NAACP launched its bid to equalize pay for black teachers in South Carolina, but the editors supported the legal doctrine of "separate but equal." The next year, when the U.S. Supreme Court ruled in *Smith v. Allwright* that state Democratic parties could no longer exclude primary voters based solely on race, some editors expressed serious concern, but most remained confident that whites would retain control of the party. When John McCray used his black newspaper to form the Progressive Democratic Party and challenge the seating of the state's white delegates at the 1944 Democratic National Convention, the *Columbia Record* reflected the dismissive tone of the white press in its editorial comment. The PDP leaders "talked too much," the paper said.[2]

In the 1930s and early '40s, the leading white editors in South Carolina exhibited characteristics of what the historian Joel Williamson has called the "racial dream world" of white southern paternalism. For these southerners, the question of white supremacy had been settled definitively during the rise of Jim Crow. Since then, black southerners had for the most part been allowed to "escape from the white mind." These educated whites believed black Carolinians accepted their place in the southern caste system and were content with the region's special ways and customs. As Williamson observed, these paternalists developed an abiding belief that racial harmony would prevail through the "sheer power of whites . . . to hold blacks in place and to enforce upon them prescribed behavior." In doing so, these paternalistic whites "slipped further from an understanding of black life."[3]

In a 1933 essay in the *Virginia Quarterly Review,* the outgoing editor of the *Columbia Record,* R. Charlton Wright, offered a glimpse inside the paternalistic "dream world" of the white southern editor in South Carolina. "White supremacy is no longer in danger in the South," Wright proclaimed, because southern blacks have no desire to achieve political equality. Black voters had "played a sinister and dangerous role" during Reconstruction when they were protected by "the guns and bayonets of the federal government." But even then, Wright claimed, it was not the Negro who dominated southern politics. It was the "fanatics of the Freedman's Bureau, the horde of carpetbaggers and low-lived alien politicians from the North [that] did the dominating." They had corrupted and "debauched" the Negro and turned him against his white southern friend. The harshness of the white backlash and the "jim-crowing of the Negro" were unfortunate but understandable responses to the terror of Reconstruction, but the time had come to stop the oppression. Except for a few radicals in the North, Negro leaders were now "conservative" and "educated," Wright concluded, and allowing a handful of respectable Negros to participate in the economic and political life of the South would pose no risk to the region's racial hierarchy.

As 1940 arrived, the majority of the white press in South Carolina agreed with Wright's view. They believed the black community remained politically quiescent, and they had fresh evidence to support their position. In the lead-up to the 1940 elections, an editor at *The State* newspaper in Columbia conducted a survey of county registrars to assess black voter registration. The white registrars who responded were reassuring. Of the 17,000 black residents in Lee County, for example, nine had registered to vote, the registrar reported. In the coastal counties of Georgetown and Horry, which also had large black populations, the numbers were even lower. York County, located just across the border from Charlotte, North Carolina, reported "negligible" black voter registration. The results were same across the state. Only one registrar expressed concern about black voting. In Chester County, fifteen Negros had applied to vote in his jurisdiction, but the registrar was less sanguine about the future. It would be a "grave mistake" to publish a report on Negro voting in the newspaper, he warned the editor. "Only a few Negroes appeared interested" in voting right now, but publicity in *The State* could encourage Negro activists and "start up registration in full blast."[4]

The Chester County registrar was right to be concerned. Led by McCray's *Lighthouse and Informer* and his NAACP allies, the state's black community had by 1940 begun the process of building a vibrant and growing protest movement. A significant portion of black Carolinians had dispensed with the accommodationist strategy and joined the effort to assert their rights as full citizens of the American democracy. They had undergone a political transformation, but the state's white newspapers had failed to see it coming. White journalists living in the "racial dream world" tended to talk to each other, not to black residents—a failing that one NAACP activist emphasized in his letter to a journalist at the *News and Courier*. "The type of Negro I represent you have never met," he wrote. "You have never talked with—you have only a superficial knowledge of." Based on the way African Americans were portrayed in South Carolina's white press, this appeared to be true.[5]

During the 1940s, black South Carolinians appeared in white newspapers as suspects in crime stories and as the butt of jokes based on disparaging stereotypes. The editorial page of the largest newspaper, *The State*, published a regular cartoon series called Hambone that portrayed an elderly "Sambo" character who dispensed pearls of wisdom in deep dialect. In one example, Hambone is shown whittling on a piece of wood as he says: "Doctuhs en Lawyuhs en Preachuhs, dey de onlies' one's gets paid fuh tryin'—win er lose!" In Charleston, the *News and Courier* frequently ran short editorials making fun of the supposedly loose morals of the black community. When the state's General Assembly considered legalizing divorce, for example, the *News and Courier* suggested the new law would be a boon for black attorneys. "Divorce will rapidly come to be fashionable among the colored people," the newspaper said. "Attorneys of their race will soon appear in all counties."[6]

During the early 1940s the largest white newspapers were content to ignore black activism in the state and depict black Carolinians as docile and relatively harmless—perhaps easily swayed by "outside agitators," but posing no existential threat to the status quo. By 1947, however, it became clear that the black push for political equality had gained new support in the North. When President Truman proposed the first civil rights reform measure since Reconstruction, the leading white newspapers in South Carolina were jolted into action. They joined with white politicians to defend the "southern way of life." But they quickly learned that the old arguments conflating white supremacy and racial separation with the protection of "American democracy" had lost their ability to persuade in the shifting public opinion of the North. By the end the decade, after the failed Dixiecrat presidential campaign of South Carolina Governor Strom Thurmond, they would begin the search for new ways of defending white political rule in the South.

In the 1940s, the white press in South Carolina was dominated by a particular brand of conservatism. Led by the *News and Courier* in Charleston and *The State* in Columbia, the state's major newspaper editorial pages favored the aristocratic notions that had been preached by the state's old planter-class elite. They believed in a hierarchical society in which all classes knew their "place." They believed the so-called "Negro question" had been settled and that southern blacks accepted their particular place on society's bottom rung. Northern agitators occasionally stirred up trouble, they contended, but blacks in South Carolina were mostly an affable lot who were content with the status quo.

By 1948, however, the white editors realized what they now confronted. Black activists like Charleston's A. J. Clement did not sound like someone who accepted second-class citizenship. In his letter to the *News and Courier* journalist, Clement sounded like an American patriot appealing to the most sacred values embedded in the nation's democratic heritage. "The things that the modern Negro wants are things of the heart—they are things eternal," Clement wrote. "Mankind has always sought them and in his seeking he will not be denied. For Right and Justice, Fair play, and Understanding—in the long run—always win out."[7]

The state's white press and white politicians struggled to develop a new narrative that could justify the continuation of the old ways in South Carolina. For the past half-century, the leading white editorialists at the state's major newspapers had bemoaned the rise of the white working class as a political power in the state. Obsessed with tradition and hierarchy, their particular type of conservatism worried as much about class as it did race. Ironically, the planter-class elites who first espoused this ideology had lost their great political struggle against "Pitchfork" Ben Tillman, Cole Blease, and other "reformers" at the turn of the century, yet in the 1940s their worldview was thriving on the editorial pages of the state's largest newspapers.

These so-called Bourbon conservatives—led by former Confederate generals Wade Hampton and Matthew Butler—had ruled the state since taking power in the fraudulent election of 1876. With the help of Tillman and other young militia leaders, the former Confederates ousted a Republican government that had come to power with the support of African American votes. In the parlance of the times, Hampton and his supporters had "redeemed" South Carolina from the horrors of Reconstruction. The Bourbons supported economic growth, particularly the push for more industry in the South, but they were most concerned about social order. In their view, the nightmare of Reconstruction had allowed the lower orders—blacks and working-class whites—to abandon their proper place in society and join elite whites in participating in politics and governance.[8]

After taking power in 1876, Hampton and the white Democrats sought to overturn the changes wrought by Reconstruction and restore a strictly regimented society in which all classes knew their place. It was a system that empowered elite landowners at the top and kept poorer whites near the bottom, just one step ahead of the former slaves. Unlike Tillman, Blease, and the radical reformers who would later impose the violent tyranny of Jim Crow, planter-class aristocrats believed they had nothing to fear from the freed blacks. They simply thought blacks were an inferior race and, like poor whites, needed guidance and protection provided by the better class. Even after federal troops had been withdrawn from South Carolina, Hampton's government solicited African American votes, although Tillman and other militia leaders made sure only a handful of blacks would actually cast their ballots.[9]

By 1890, Tillman and his allies had grown weary of Hampton's paternalistic leadership. Tillman's base of support came from the small farmers who had always resented Hampton and the big landowners. They had formed an uneasy alliance in opposition to the Republicans and Reconstruction, but that partnership was coming to an end. The national economic downturn of the 1880s had been especially severe for small farmers in the South, and agrarian uprisings had destabilized the political status quo across the region. In neighboring Georgia, for example, the Populist Party had brought together white yeoman farmers and African Americans in a brief but powerful biracial coalition. In North Carolina, so-called fusionist candidates ran with the support of white Republicans and African American voters. For Tillman, the growth of biracial coalitions posed an unacceptable threat to white rule. He supported the "Mississippi Plan," a strategy that would disenfranchise African Americans in the South and use all means necessary—including violence—to limit black advancement and ensure they remained on society's lowest rung.[10]

In 1890, Tillman rallied the state's small farmers to challenge the Bourbon conservatives for control of the state's Democratic Party. He would ride his "agrarian reform" and white supremacy movement to the governor's mansion and eventually a seat in the U.S. Senate. Later, Blease would add the state's growing number of textile mill workers—the so-called "lint heads"—to the Tillman coalition and also win races for governor and senator.

During the rise of Tillman and Blease, the state's leading newspaper—Charleston's *News and Courier*—sided with Hampton and the planter-class Bourbons. In the postbellum years, editor Francis "Captain" Dawson had turned the Lowcountry newspaper into a journalistic powerhouse. Although born and raised in England, Dawson had fallen in love with the Confederacy and had moved to South Carolina in 1861 to join the cause. After the war, he had worked at the *Charleston Mercury* under the former fire-breathing secessionist Robert Barnwell Rhett. In 1867, Dawson and a partner purchased the struggling *Charleston News*. They added the faltering *Courier* in 1873 and created the *News and Courier*. Though based in Charleston's historic district, the "old lady of Broad Street" was read statewide under Dawson's able leadership. In 1880, the editor created a bureau in the state capital of Columbia and staffed it with an ambitious young journalist named Narciso Gener Gonzalez. N.G., as he was called, was the son of an aristocratic woman from the Lowcountry who had surprised her family by marrying a dashing Cuban expatriate who had fled his homeland after joining a failed revolt against Spanish control.[11]

In 1888, during this first run for governor, Tillman focused his attacks on Dawson and the *News and Courier*. A small "ring" of rich planters rules the state, Tillman said, "and that ring is on Dawson's little finger." These rich planters pump taxpayer money into their pet projects and ignore the needs of the struggling small farmers, he said. Tillman took particular interest in The Citadel, a military college beloved by Charleston high society. Dismissing the school as a "dude factory," he called on the state to build an agricultural college to benefit the small farmers. The *News and Courier* responded in kind to Tillman's attacks. Dawson's paper called Tillman's supporters "red necks" who "carry pistols in their pockets, expectorate on the floor, have no toothbrushes, and comb their hair with their fingers." Tillman lost the 1888 race, and Dawson died one year later, but their clash during that campaign set the tone for the long conflict to come between the state's aristocratic elites and working-class farmers and mill workers.[12]

In 1890, Tillman defeated Hampton's candidate, Alexander Haskell, and claimed the Democratic Party nomination, ending the Bourbon reign in the statehouse. Infuriated by Tillman's victory, Narciso Gonzales decided the *News and Courier* needed more help in the battle against the reformers. He and one of his brothers, Ambrose, raised $30,000 to launch a new daily in Columbia. On February 18, 1891, *The State* rolled off the press and joined the battle against what the paper described as "Tillmanism." For the next thirteen years, under the byline of "N.G.," Narciso Gonzalez hammered away at Tillman's leadership. During that time, Tillman delivered the ag-ricultural college he promised, launching a school that would eventually become Clemson University. But he did little else to help the small farmers economically. Instead, he focused on the perceived threat of black voting rights. At a state constitutional convention held in 1895, Tillman pushed through a new charter that codified Jim Crow laws enforcing racial segre-gation and limiting the African American vote. Of more concern to *The State,* Tillman seemed to excuse the violence of white mobs that lynched blacks in South Carolina. Affiliated with Bourbon conservatism, *The State* supported white supremacy, but despised "lawlessness" and disliked the nasty race baiting of the Tillman and Blease campaigns. For Bourbon con-servatives, it was clear that blacks were inferior and thus it was unnecessary and uncivilized to treat them as a serious threat to white rule. It was this paternalistic view of African Americans in the South that would eventually come to dominate white newspaper opinion in the state during the first half of the twentieth century.[13]

Narciso Gonzales's long struggle with "Tillmanism" came to a violent end in January 1903. The previous year, N.G. had delivered a daily barrage of at-tacks on Tillman's nephew James, who was running for governor that year. *The State* described Jim Tillman as a liar and a gambler who was "the worst and most indefensible man who ever sought the Democratic nomination." The attacks appeared to work. Jim Tillman finished fourth in the Democratic primary.[14]

Five months later, on January 15, 1903, Gonzales left his office one evening and walked down Main Street, where he crossed paths with Jim Tillman, Cole Blease, and two other men. Tillman pulled out a handgun, fired a shot into Gonzales, and calmly turned himself in to a nearby police officer. The injured editor struggled to return to his office, where he dictated an account of the shooting. Four days later, he died in a Columbia hospital. Six months after that, a jury in nearby Lexington County acquitted Jim Tillman on mur-der charges on grounds of self-defense. Some jury members would call the shooting justifiable revenge, given the nature of the newspaper's accusations against Tillman.[15]

The State would survive and prosper after its editor's death, eventually surpassing the *News and Courier* as South Carolina's largest newspaper.

By the 1940s, the two newspapers—along with the *Greenville News* in the northwestern Upstate region—were the dominant news media voices in the state, and all three espoused the distinctly conservative and paternalistic worldview that could be traced back to the Bourbons. Tillman and Blease had once commanded newspapers that did battle with conservative editors at *The State* and the *News and Courier*. Gonzales had derided these political papers as "organettes" that were not built to last, and he was right. By the beginning of the Depression, economic woes had weeded out many weaker papers across the state. Fewer newspapers meant fewer editorial voices, and by the 1940s, the overwhelming majority of those that remained carried on the conservative tradition established by Dawson, Gonzales, and the Bourbon conservatives late in the nineteenth century.[16]

The strongest of these editorial voices belonged to William Watts Ball, the cranky editor of the Charleston *News and Courier*. By the 1940s, Ball was in his seventies and nearing the end of a brilliant career. He had served as an editor at all three of the state's largest newspapers, and he had helped restore *The State*'s political clout after Gonzalez's assassination. As editor from 1913 to 1923, Ball had taken the lead in the fight against Blease, who had been elected governor in 1910 and 1912 and had his eye on a U.S. Senate seat. Ball detested the way Blease stoked class conflict by pushing white mill workers to challenge mill owners over wages and work conditions. His daily attacks have been credited with helping defeat Blease's Senate bid in 1916.[17]

In 1923, Ball left *The State* to become dean of the new journalism school at the University of South Carolina. But the career change did not stick. After four years in academia, Ball longed to return to daily journalism and get back into the political fray. "I long for a 'scrap,' " he wrote to a friend. "I'm not content without a fight on my hands." He got his chance when an old colleague offered him the editorship of the *News and Courier*. It was a good fit from the start. Ball had worked in Charleston before as editor of the competing *Evening Post,* and he was eager to return. He particularly liked the city's rich aristocratic heritage. It is "one of the few communities retaining civilization," Ball said. His biographer, John D. Stark, described Ball's return to Charleston as an "inevitable natural alliance" that had at last been consummated.[18]

An acerbic editorialist, Ball was perhaps even more of a Bourbon conservative than Dawson or Gonzales ever had been. Born in Laurens, South Carolina, in 1868, Ball grew up watching his father battle the forces of Reconstruction following the Civil War. With the protection of federal troops, black residents used their newly acquired right to vote and turned out the white aristocrats like Ball's father who had run all political affairs in Laurens County. As a young boy, Ball cheered Hampton's so-called "red shirt" campaign of

1876. Those childhood experiences helped forge a lif[...]
white supremacy and states' rights. As a true Bourbon [...]
Ball's political views were shaped by two other deepl[...]
belief in the wisdom of the aristocracy and his deep [...]
He liked to say that he "was a Democrat, but not a de[...]
the party, but opposed efforts to extend the franchis[...]

Ball embraced this brand of conservatism as a y[...]
faithful to it throughout his long career. Like his hero Wade Ham[...]
represented the sort of white paternalism that opposed mob violence and
claimed to support the aspirations of South Carolina blacks. Ball summed
up his view on the race question in a 1930 editorial. The editor contended
that his newspaper:

> wishes to defend the Negro from injustice, and to stop lynching; in doing so it
> is opposing a powerful mob element. The task is a dangerous and difficult one.
> Nevertheless, the *News and Courier* and its followers want, in self defense, to
> make Negroes industrious and productive; they want to protect the Negroes'
> property and their persons; they want to oppose beating, killing and cheating
> colored people; they want to improve their health and give them education.
> . . . But they do not propose to invite Negroes to take part in government, and
> when anyone asks this, the South is going to oppose with a solid and unyielding
> front. The question whether we are right or wrong in this attitude, whether or
> not it is savage or civilized, we decline to discuss.[20]

For Ball, race was less important than class. He railed against the populist
politics of Tillman and Blease, who rallied poor, working-class white voters
to win elections in South Carolina. He deplored their appeal for government
aid, which he equated with moral weakness. Ball championed individualism,
self-reliance, and personal resourcefulness; he believed the worthy would find
their way to the top. His 1932 book, *The State That Forgot: South Carolina's
Surrender to Democracy,* was a paean to the aristocratic rule of the Old South,
when educated landowners ran society and the poor—and black—seemed
to know their "place."[21]

Ball's virulent antigovernment views gained national attention in the 1930s
when he challenged Franklin Roosevelt's New Deal policies. They would
lead to a "collectivist state" and "mob" rule, and the "mob disposition," he
wrote, "is now as always to fill guts with food and drink [and] avoid exertion
and responsibility." A lifelong Democrat who despised the Republican Party
of Lincoln and Reconstruction, Ball nonetheless declared after Roosevelt's
1936 reelection that "I have no party." He dreamed of a southern revolt, but
it would be another dozen years before his rebellion arrived.[22]

arrival at the *News and Courier* came in the nick of time. The na-
prosperity of the Roaring '20s had not reached South Carolina, and
newspaper had suffered a steep economic decline. In 1925, editor Frank
Lathan had won a Pulitzer Prize for his editorial decrying the South's lack
of influence on national politics. But by 1927 the "Old Lady of Broad Street"
had slipped dramatically. Once the state's second-largest paper, the *News
and Courier* now trailed even its upstart local competitor, the *Evening Post,*
in daily circulation. By the 1940s, however, Ball's provocative editorial voice
had helped to revive the paper and support its motto as "South Carolina's
most outspoken newspaper." His unsigned opinion pieces, often biting and
sarcastic, ran daily on the editorial page and occasionally on the front page.
They were influential—"read, marked, learned and inwardly digested," as
one newspaper reported. Politicians scrambled to curry his favor.[23]

Ball's former newspaper, *The State,* had promoted longtime newsroom
employee Samuel L. Latimer to the top editor's job in late 1941 after the sudden death of McDavid Horton. Latimer maintained the paper's conservative
editorial line, but without the passion or the flair that Ball possessed. An
editorial in *The State* during the 1940s often read like a bland summation
of the facts rather than a full-throated expression of a deeply held point of
view. For Ball, boring the readers was a cardinal sin, and he could not help
tweaking his old employer in print at times. Without mentioning *The State*
by name, Ball wrote that if "opinions broke loose" on a certain capital city
editorial page, "they would cause more sensation among readers than would
a story of a man biting a dog."[24]

Perhaps Latimer's prose was designed to remain understated and noncon-
troversial. *The State*'s economic fortunes had benefited from the growth of
the capital city, and The State Company had become highly profitable. After
purchasing its afternoon competitor, the *Columbia Record,* The State Company gained a monopoly in the daily newspaper business in the capital city
and began to look like the prosperous chains that would grow to dominate
the industry in the post–World War II years. Though not as conservative as
The State, and certainly not as Bourbon as Ball's *News and Courier,* the *Record,*
under editor George A. Buchanan Jr., was nonetheless a reliable supporter
of segregation and the status quo in South Carolina.

In 1947, a new and slightly different editorial voice began to challenge
the conservative editorial pages in the state. In Florence, about 130 miles
northwest of Charleston, James A. Rogers took over as editor of the *Morning
News* in the summer of 1947. A tobacco market town in the heart of South
Carolina's rural Pee Dee region, Florence had benefitted from the nation's
postwar prosperity. Its population had reached 16,000—a 40 percent increase

since the start of the decade. In his introductory editorial, published June 3, 1947, Rogers noted the growth of the Pee Dee in the postwar years and promised his *Morning News* would be "in the vanguard of this progress." Rogers also used that first editorial to establish his political point of view—and to issue a gentle warning to his readers. He aimed "to publish a liberal, progressive newspaper" that supported "forward strides throughout the Pee Dee," he wrote. In doing so, ". . . we shall not hesitate to voice opinions which may be contrary to those held by some or even many of our readers. That is the traditional spirit of the press, and to that tradition this editorship shall scrupulously cling."[25]

In his opening editorial, Rogers revealed the two forces that would shape his political views during the turbulent years ahead: a deep connection to his community—Florence and the surrounding farmlands—and a commitment to building a progressive and just society. Born in 1905 in the tiny town of Blenheim, South Carolina, the son of a Baptist minister, Rogers fell in love with the rural Pee Dee. Fascinated by farm life, he earned the nickname the "agricultural evangelist" during his years as editor. "Rogers was as much a product of the rural South, particularly the Pee Dee, as cotton," journalist and academic Don Stewart wrote in an obituary of the editor. Like his father, Rogers attended seminary and served as a "country preacher" at churches across the Pee Dee. He wrote a weekly inspirational column, "Hearts Aglow," for the *Morning News* before joining the paper full time. In his first editorial, the new editor summed up his worldview with a quote from John W. Davis, the Democratic Party's failed presidential nominee of 1924: "He deserves to be called progressive who cannot see a wrong persist without an effort to redress it, or a right denied without an effort to protect it."[26]

Where Ball and the conservative editors tended to look back in anger, Rogers looked ahead with cautious optimism. He had grown up in a different South than Ball. Reconstruction had ended more than two decades before his birth. The new century ushered in the Progressive movement in American politics, which reached its peak with the election of Woodrow Wilson in 1912. The movement spawned a growing band of southern liberals—many of them newspaper editors—who emerged as a significant minority voice in the region pressing for economic, educational, and social reforms. They included George Fort Milton of the *Chattanooga News;* Harry Ashmore, a South Carolinian who won a Pulitzer Prize as editor of the *Arkansas Gazette;* Mark Etheridge of the *Macon Telegraph* and later the *Courier-Journal* of Louisville; Virginius Dabney of the *Richmond Times Dispatch;* and, most prominently, Ralph McGill of the *Atlanta Constitution* and Hodding Carter Jr. of Greenville, Mississippi's *Delta Democrat-Times.* These southern liberals embraced industrial development, more spending on education, and improved opportunities for African Americans. They envisioned a prosperous South with good government services and a diversified economy that provided a better life for whites and blacks.[27]

Rogers counted himself proudly in this southern liberal tradition. He emphasized economic progress and improved education, and he frequently quoted McGill to support his editorial point of view. As a southern liberal, however, it should be no surprise that Rogers's introductory editorial failed to mention race. By 1947, race had become what one historian called "the underbelly of Southern liberalism." Like their northern counterparts, southern liberals pressed for reforms on a myriad of issues in the first half of the twentieth Century, but their liberalism stopped short on the question of racial integration. At that time, southern liberals like McGill believed in the necessity of social segregation; they wanted to reform Jim Crow laws, not abandon them. They fought on behalf of blacks in search of better housing, educational facilities, and job prospects. They argued white society should deliver on its promise of "separate but equal." But integration, they said, would lead to "violence and bloodshed"—especially if forced on the South by federal intervention.[28]

In the 1920s and '30s, black leaders embraced southern liberals as their allies. By the '40s, as African Americans grew more assertive politically, the relationship had changed. The new black aggressiveness angered and confused liberals across the South. Mark Etheridge criticized black leaders "who demand 'all or nothing'" and "play into the hands of white demagogues." No power in the world, he warned, "could now force the Southern white people to the abandonment of social segregation." McGill said, "There will be no mixing of the races in schools. There will be no social equality measures. Now or later." And in Richmond, Dabney accused "a small group of Negro agitators and another group of rabble-rousers" of pushing the nation "closer and closer to an interracial explosion." Southern liberals wanted to move slowly on racial issues. But many African Americans no longer supported this strategy.[29]

One bit of evidence that African Americans were beginning to embrace protest politics in South Carolina came in the fall of 1946, when 861 young black and white delegates from around the country gathered in Columbia, South Carolina to plan their ongoing campaign for African American rights. Organized by the Southern Negro Youth Conference, a branch of the National Negro Conference, the delegates met in Township Auditorium, the capital city's largest public meeting hall and performance space. Posters of Robert Smalls and other black, Reconstruction-era leaders lined the auditorium's walls as the delegates heard from such prominent African Americans figures as Paul Robeson and W.E.B. Du Bois. In a powerful keynote speech, Du Bois told his young audience to remain in the South and fight for their democratic rights. "Behold the beautiful land," he said of the South. It would be an act of cowardice to surrender the region to the "thugs and lynchers . . . who choke its soul and steal its resources." To rally support and win allies, Du Bois said, the movement needed "blatant, pitiless publicity" of white acts of injustice and brutality. Since Du Bois launched *The Crisis* in 1910, the black press had been working to draw attention to white atrocities in the Jim Crow South. McCray's newspaper had joined that effort in South Carolina. The *Lighthouse and Informer* used its pages to criticize white oppression to rally local support, but McCray also shared his coverage with the *Chicago Defender*, the *Pittsburgh Courier*, and the *Baltimore Afro-American* in an effort to influence national public opinion.[30]

The city of Columbia had allowed the SNYC to rent Township Auditorium for its convention without complaint, and the white press paid no attention during the first two days of the gathering. The SNYC passed resolutions supporting federal anti–poll tax and anti-lynching laws, called for the creation of a permanent Federal Employment Practices Commission, and praised the AFL and CIO, saying their labor organizing drives had made "distinct contributions to the South." Yet when the group criticized U.S. Secretary of State James F. Byrnes, a South Carolina native, the white newspapers took notice. Byrnes had just returned from peace talks in Paris where he had criticized Soviet efforts to prevent free elections in Bulgaria and other eastern European nations. Du Bois and the SNYC pointed out the hypocrisy of Byrnes claiming to protect democracy abroad while helping to deny it to African Americans at home. Du Bois appeared to take special delight in pillorying the secretary of state. As a young congressman in 1919, Byrnes had called for Du Bois's prosecution under the Espionage Act because of his "treasonous" writings in *The Crisis*. Now it was Du Bois's turn to fire back: "Byrnes is the end of a long series of men whose eternal damnation is the fact that he looked truth in the eye and did not see it," he told the SNYC assembly.[31]

When South Carolina Governor Ransome J. Williams denounced the SNYC attacks on Byrnes, the *Columbia Record* ran his comments on the front page. Williams called it regrettable that "Communistic elements came boldly and brazenly" into South Carolina's capital city to undermine the secretary of state. By linking the event to communism, Williams had resumed the "red scare" tactics that southern whites had used to taint supporters of civil rights since the Bolshevik Revolution of 1917. In an editorial, however, the *Record* downplayed the communist connection. Yet its arguments exemplified the white press' dismissive and paternalistic approach to black activism at the time. The paper agreed that the SNYC's resolutions were "following closely the Communistic line," but it blamed that on a few outside agitators and said most participants were not communists "or fellow travelers." The newspaper suggested the SNYC had underestimated the white community in Columbia and its general support for African Americans. It noted that Du Bois had also criticized Wade Hampton, even though "Hampton believed the Negro in South Carolina should be accorded the ballot." The *Record* said the city granted the SNYC the right to use the auditorium because it believed "in free speech enough to allow the congress to attack South Carolina and South Carolinians without striking back." The *Record* concluded by saying some SNYC leaders were disappointed that white South Carolinians had not given the group a propaganda victory by marching into the arena "hooded and robed" to break up the gathering.[32]

For black leaders in South Carolina, the SNYC meeting was significant, both as a public display of a new and seemingly fearless black assertiveness in the state, but also as a flashpoint in an internal debate over future strategy. McCray was skeptical of the SNYC, which had grown out of the Popular Front movement of the New Deal era and strived to build a biracial coalition of blacks and working-class whites in the South. As such, the SNYC did have ties to both socialist labor organizations and the American Communist Party. To McCray, the SNYC appeared vulnerable to attacks just like the one the governor had made. His chief allies, Modjeska Simkins and Osceola McKaine, embraced coalition building with labor and leftist groups and believed the civil rights movement should stand up to white leaders who employed red-scare arguments. McCray had always said the state movement should remain in local hands, although critics claimed he was merely protecting his own leadership position. The debate over the SNYC and civil rights strategy opened a rift between McCray and his allies that would never entirely heal. As U.S.–Soviet relations worsened and cold war rhetoric grew dominant, white southerners would increase efforts to tie civil rights to a communist plot to destabilize American democracy. By 1949, the SYNC would be out of business, its leaders marginalized and facing legal harassment from the justice department and the House Un-American Activities Committee.[33]

Though angered by criticism of Byrnes, the white press depicted the comments as the work of "troublemakers" and "agitators" like Du Bois. Those could be controlled, they reasoned. Yet when a Democratic president decided to support civil rights legislation, white editorialists were forced on the defensive. They began to take black activism seriously, and their rhetoric grew harsher.

Truman's Civil Rights Push
and the "Dixiecrat" Revolt

Harry Truman assumed the presidency when Roosevelt died in 1945, and he was not expected to win a full term on his own in the election of 1948. A resurgent Republican Party had retaken Congress in a landslide in 1946—in part owing to increased black support in the North—and the GOP appeared ready to move back into the White House after a sixteen-year absence. Truman also faced a rebellion on his left. Henry Wallace, the man he had displaced as FDR's vice presidential running mate in 1944, planned to launch a liberal third-party candidacy for the presidency. Against this backdrop, a young Truman aide named Clark Clifford laid out the president's political strategy in a memo titled "The Politics of 1948." To win, Clifford wrote, Truman must appeal to the emerging urban black vote in four prominent states—California, New York, Illinois, and Ohio. To attract those voters, Clifford advised the president to support a wide-ranging package of civil rights legislation. Clifford knew the plan would enrage southern Democrats, but he thought the "solid South" would stick with the party in the end. "As always, the South can be considered safely Democratic, and in forming national policy can be safely ignored," Clifford wrote.[34]

White southerners were already on edge. They had been rattled by two developments in 1947. In October, the President's Commission on Civil Rights released a report, "To Secure These Rights," that called for an end to discrimination in employment and voting across the South. Truman created the commission partly in response to a string of violent acts against returning black servicemen in the South. One of the worst was the blinding of Isaac Woodard in Batesburg, South Carolina. In the summer of 1946, a white bus driver and two police officers beat Woodard after a dispute on the bus. The driver later claimed that Woodard had been drunk and abusive, but an NAACP investigation found numerous eyewitnesses who disputed that charge. Woodard's story—as well a powerful photograph of the blinded soldier—received widespread attention in the black and white press in the North. The *Chicago Defender* called the beating an "atrocity" carried out by a "hate-crazed Dixie police officer." New York's *Amsterdam News* described how Woodard's eyes "were gouged and torn out by the blunt end of a cracker policeman's billy." Angered by the violence against black veterans, northern white liberals and their African American allies stepped up their pressure on Truman to take action. After the civil rights commission released its report, southern Democrats expressed alarm and warned Truman not to embrace the report's recommendations.[35]

In South Carolina, meantime, white Democrats were more concerned about the imminent demise of the state's all-white primary. In July, U.S. District Judge J. Waties Waring had delivered his ruling in *Elmore v. Rice,* a sharply worded rebuke of the Democratic Party in which Waring suggested "it was time for South Carolina to rejoin the union."[36]

The response from the major white dailies was surprisingly muted. *The State* offered no editorial opinion on Waring's landmark ruling, saying it would rather wait until all appeals were concluded. The *Columbia Record* said Waring's ruling "was not surprising," given the Supreme Court's earlier ruling knocking down the all-white primary in *Smith v. Allwright,* but it encouraged state lawmakers to draft new measures to "control how the ballot is exercised here." In Charleston, Waring's decision angered Ball, and he offered a more forceful response. Ball proposed that white Democrats "abandon completely the name of the Democratic Party" and create "an exclusive white man's political club under a new title." Ball turned the judge's ruling into another exhibit in his case for a white southern revolt.[37]

For the liberal Rogers, just one month on the job, Waring's order offered an early opportunity to deliver on the promise he made in that first editorial: he challenged his community. "The *Florence Morning News* does not share the alarm felt by many South Carolinians at this new development," he wrote on July 13, 1947. "On the contrary, we believe the federal decision was a sober, thoughtful approach to a vexing problem and the opinion handed down was a fair statement of facts, of democracy and of morals." His conclusion was even stronger: " . . . The *Florence Morning News* believes South Carolina has stayed out of the union long enough; that the time has come to make realistic decisions, to cease nurturing political prejudices born out of the distant past, to be able to practice in our own backyard the same principles of justice and democracy we claim are necessities in other parts of the world."[38]

Rogers was not far outside the mainstream of South Carolina's white press. A handful of editors accepted the inevitability of Waring's ruling, but Rogers offered the strongest endorsement, and he knew his editorial ruined a good many breakfasts across the Pee Dee region that Sunday morning. To ease some of those fears, Rogers acknowledged the paper's position was "not a popular one," and he reassured readers that he believed support for black voting rights would not significantly weaken white political rule. "There is no reason to suppose that the average Negro will be more interested in politics than the average white person," he wrote, concluding that blacks would be unlikely to vote in "blocs" to overpower whites politically. With his first major editorial on race, Rogers displayed the pattern he would follow throughout the difficult year head: He sought to lead his community to higher ground, but without marching too far ahead of it.[39]

Truman dropped his civil rights bombshell on February 2, 1948. The president proposed legislation that would abolish the poll tax, end discrimination in interstate transportation, make lynching a federal crime, and create a permanent Federal Employment Practices Commission. The white South reacted virulently. In Jackson, Mississippi, the *Clarion Ledger* set the tone by denouncing the "cold-blooded and treacherous offer by the national leaders to swap destruction of the South for the votes . . . of Negroes who may hold the balance of power in a few states."[40]

Truman's push for civil rights eventually led to a southern revolt at the Democratic Convention in July. One of the key players in the drama turned out to be South Carolina's young governor, J. Strom Thurmond. Just one year into his term, Thurmond was still perceived as the New Deal reformer who had avoided blatant appeals to racism in his campaign. Yet over the next six months, the governor would step into a leadership role in the fight for states' rights and white supremacy in the South. In July 1948, he would bolt from the Democratic Party and run for president on the States' Rights Party ticket. To Ball, Thurmond would become a hero, a defender "of the South against its liberal enemies." To Rogers, the young governor was a great disappointment. His tone grew bitter as he watched Thurmond evolve from New Deal progressive to become one of the "hot heads" and "headline hunters" willing to play on racial fears in search of votes.[41]

The state Democratic Party's response to Judge Waring's ruling angered Rogers as well. With primaries approaching in August, the party faced the prospect of blacks voting in large numbers in Democratic primaries for the first time since Reconstruction. Stunned by the judge's ruling and by Truman's proposals, the state party convened in Columbia in May 1948 and mapped out its response. With Thurmond taking command, the convention confronted Truman first. The party ordered its national convention delegates to support Thurmond as a favorite son candidate and to avoid voting for Truman or any other candidate who supported the civil rights program. To combat Judge Waring's ruling and preserve white primaries, the party had adopted the controversial oath of allegiance. To vote in a primary, Democrats would be required to pledge their support for segregation, their commitment to "the principles of states' rights," and their opposition to the proposed Fair Employment Practices Committee. Rogers mocked the oath as "contrary to every principle of democracy," and he ridiculed the party's decision to debate the oath behind closed doors in executive session. "Does it mean they are

little men without the courage to grapple intelligently with a real problem?"
he asked.[42]

Ball encouraged the party's efforts to fight the judge's ruling. And he suggested a strategy that fit nicely with his belief in aristocratic rule. Abandon
the primaries, he said, and replace them with the nominating convention.
Allow Democratic Party leaders to select the party's candidates. "Why have
primaries?" Ball wrote. "No one, white or colored, appears capable of the
conception that primaries are not sacred and indispensable devices for the
nomination of public offices." Under the convention system, white leaders
would retain control over the party. They could even let in a few blacks, but
only the right kind. "The negroes cooperating with white leaders in conventions would not be tools of the National Society for the Advancement of the
Colored People," he wrote.

Ball clearly meant the NAACP, which he referred to often in his editorials, but rarely by its correct title. He claimed the organization and its leader,
Walter White, would seize political power through "bloc voting." Ball said the
News and Courier is "not condemning them" for voting as a group because,
in his view, "their first, their absorbing aim is not to elect Democrats or Republicans. It is to gain power for negroes." Perhaps Ball was "not condemning
them," but he certainly believed whites should be afraid of potential black
political power. White politicians would be forced to court the black vote,
he argued—was not that what Truman was doing this year?[43]

To accommodate the new medium of television, both national parties
held their conventions in Philadelphia in 1948. The Republicans gathered in
a festive mood in late June and nominated a strong presidential ticket: New
York Gov. Thomas Dewey, seeking to avenge his loss to Roosevelt four years
earlier, and California Gov. Earl Warren. The fractured Democrats arrived in
the city two weeks later with a sense of doom in the air. Wallace had already
launched his third party on the left. Truman's civil rights push had angered
conservative southerners. And northern liberals, led by the young mayor of
Minneapolis, Hubert H. Humphrey, figured to exacerbate the rift by pushing
for an even stronger civil rights plank in the party platform. The question
before white southern Democrats was stark: Should they desert the party of
their fathers and grandfathers—or should they stay and fight from within?[44]

Ball knew what he wanted—and he argued his case forcefully throughout
the month. Southern Democrats had been faithful to the Democratic Party
"because it did not appeal to the negro voters," he wrote on July 2. "The negro question was the basic, overwhelming cause . . . that held the Southern
states in the national Democratic Party. That cause no longer exists. It has

disappeared. . . . What is here said is fact: The sole reason that created and maintained the South solid is gone."[45]

Ball laced his editorials with antigovernment rhetoric, his disdain for what he called "the office holding industry." He claimed the state's incumbent senators, Olin Johnston and Burnett Maybank, secretly supported the national Democratic Party because "the boys can more easily hold their jobs by keeping the machine well greased." He often claimed the Democrats were no different than the Republicans on civil rights, and that neither party "is interested in the Southern white man. He is the forgotten man of 1948."

Rogers also opposed Truman's civil rights package. Like McGill and other southern liberals, Rogers argued against federal coercion, believing it would set back race relations in the region. He also thought the issue would drive white southerners to break with the national Democrats. "While political party lines are deep-seated in the South, it is, nevertheless, true that racial lines are more deeply rooted," the *Morning News* said shortly after Truman's February speech. But Rogers delivered a mixed message on party loyalty. The man who hired him, publisher John G. O'Dowd, was a committed Democratic Party member in 1948. And as the July convention drew closer, Rogers urged state Democrats to stay in the party. But he did so without much conviction. And while he never encouraged readers to vote for Dewey, he joined other southern liberals like McGill in repeatedly bemoaning the lack of a two-party system in the South. "The need for two strong political parties in South Carolina was never so apparent as it is now," he wrote on July 16. The same day he published an editorial from the *Savannah Morning News,* "as Southern a newspaper as the South produces," that actually endorsed the GOP ticket: "The challenge to Southerners this year is crystal clear. It is to put behind them the insufferable fetish that they must vote the Democratic ticket because they have always done so, and because their fathers and grandfathers voted that way."[46]

As the national convention got underway, Thurmond's role in the southern rebellion increased. The South's leading politicians—senators like Richard Russell of Georgia and Harry Byrd of Virginia—had established seniority in Congress that could be jeopardized if they walked away from the party. Some also feared a rabid defense of racial segregation could deter investment and stall economic development in the South. They opposed Truman's civil rights push, but treaded more cautiously. That opened the door for second-tier politicians like Thurmond, and the governor rushed through it. The first night of the convention, he took the lead in urging a caucus of southern delegations to abandon the president. "We have been betrayed," he declared, "and the guilty should not go unpunished." That stirred Rogers to attack: "Frankly, we are becoming tired of little men like Thurmond and [Sen. Olin] Johnston beating their drums to rabble-rouse Southern sentiment. . . . Ostensibly, their fight is against Truman. But in reality, it is all too apparent that their fight is for Thurmond and Johnston." Thurmond was expected to challenge Johnston in the 1950 Senate race, and Rogers believed both men pandered on the race issue to prepare for the political fight ahead. "There is one hope for South Carolina," he wrote. "That hope is this: that the mounting political battle between Johnston and Thurmond will result in each killing the other off politically."[47]

Rogers wrote forcefully about what he opposed that summer. But what did he support, what path forward did he propose? There, he was less specific, more cautious. He condemned the state Democratic Party for ignoring the courts. But he rarely returned to the ethical and moral argument he had used the previous July to support Judge Waring's order striking down whites-only primaries. Now he took a more pragmatic approach. He warned of the dangers of violating federal court orders and looked for ways to reach out to those who feared black political power. "It now appears certain that Negroes will be permitted to vote in the August primary," Rogers wrote July 10. "This newspaper has always feared the problem created by an antagonistic attitude toward the court's decision." But the state party still had time to correct the problem and "eliminate the causes of friction on the racial issue." His solution: create intelligence and educational qualifications for South Carolina voters and apply them equally to both races. "We have frankly admitted, and do so again, that there are Negroes, many of them, who aren't mentally or emotionally prepared to exercise the ballot intelligently. By the same token, we have argued that there are whites who are equally unqualified," he wrote. Again, Rogers leads his community by pressing for black suffrage, but stops short of the more radical idea of universal suffrage. Like other southern liberals at the time, he proposes gradual change with an eye on attracting more whites to his point of view. Critics would mock this approach as "gradualism" and "Jim Crow liberalism." But the editor believed he had pushed hard enough.[48]

Rogers employed the same strategy in the debate over which state party delegation should be seated at the national convention. The state had three slates of delegates going to Philadelphia: the regular white Democrats led by Thurmond; the black Progressive Democrats, led by McCray; and a small group known as the True Democrats, which included several liberal whites angered by the proposed loyalty oath who joined with a handful of blacks to create a third slate. The Progressive Democrats had been battling the white Democratic Party since 1944, when McCray launched the party in the *Lighthouse and Informer* and led its first delegation to the national convention in Chicago to challenge the party's voting rules. McKaine's Senate campaign that fall had mobilized African American political engagement across the state. It was the Progressive Democrats who worked hand-in-hand with Thurgood Marshall and the national NAACP on the legal battle that led to Judge Waring's 1947 ruling overturning the whites-only primary. Clearly, McCray's party represented the overwhelming majority of African Americans in South Carolina; they had worked assiduously within the legal and political systems to earn the right to join the political process. Yet Rogers ignored McCray's party. He argued "logic suggests" the True Democrats should be seated because they are the only ones "representing bi-racial support of Federal Court decisions." It is true that McCray's party started as the South Carolina Colored Democratic Party and initially accepted black members only. But within a month of its founding, the party had changed its name, and by 1948 the Progressive Democrats clearly embraced biracial politics.[49]

With his editorial, Rogers sidestepped the moral and legal issues at the heart of the debate and appeared to search for a "moderate" position that allowed him to chastise the regular Democrats but avoid supporting the activist black organization. Again, he challenged his readers, but stopped short of direct confrontation.

Ball, meanwhile, made it clear where he stood. He called McCray's Progressive Democrats "a creature of the National Society for the Advancement of Colored People, a Northern organization of negroes. It is not a movement of South Carolina negroes." He called for the white Democratic Party to reconvene and open its rolls to "every living organism . . . that could make a letter X," and then "abandon the party to the Office Holding Industry and the Colored People." White South Carolinians should form their own private association and select general election candidates at a nominating convention. White people can "take over the reins of white man's government. They can give the state a fresh new leadership," he wrote, challenging this "new leadership" to confront federal tyranny. "How far will the federal courts go in their decisions? To what extent would white people submit to compulsion upon them exerted by federal authority to wipe out distinctions, to outlaw separation between and of the white and Negro races in South Carolina?"[50]

In Philadelphia, the convention moved toward its dramatic conclusion. On the final day, Humphrey's strengthened civil rights plank passed narrowly 651½ to 582½, sending the hall into pandemonium. With Birmingham's commissioner of public safety, Eugene "Bull" Connor, leading the way, members of the Alabama delegation shouted for recognition to announce their departure in protest. One reporter described Connor's roaring voice as sounding like "the devil's own loudspeaker." But convention chairman Sam Rayburn ignored their pleas and quickly adjourned the session. When the delegates reconvened that evening, Alabama's chairperson, Handy Ellis, told the assembly that his delegation "could not participate" in a convention that could adopt such a strong civil rights plank. "Without hatred and without anger and without fear, but with disillusionment and disappointment . . . we bid you good bye." The sweltering convention hall once again erupted with hoots and jeers as a dozen of Alabama's delegates trudged down the center aisle and out of the building, followed by the entire Mississippi delegation.[51]

Thurmond and the South Carolina delegates stayed in the hall and watched as Truman won the party's presidential nomination on the first ballot. The next day, July 16, Judge Waring issued another blistering order. He rejected the state party's final appeal and demanded the party open its enrollment books to blacks immediately. One day later, a group of rebellious southern Democrats led by Gov. Fielding Wright of Mississippi and former Gov. Frank Dixon of Alabama convened in Birmingham. Initially, Thurmond had said he would not attend, a decision Rogers grudgingly applauded: "Let Governor Thurmond try now as hard to be a good governor as he has tried to plummet himself into the national spotlight."[52]

The editor would quickly be disappointed. Thurmond changed his mind and on the morning of the rebel convention he rearranged his schedule to include a visit to Birmingham. By that evening, he had accepted the presidential nomination of the States' Rights Democratic Party—later nicknamed the Dixiecrats by a *Charlotte News* headline writer. Decades later, Thurmond would claim he cared more about the constitutional question of states' rights than about race. But his acceptance speech suggested otherwise: "I want to tell you that the progress of the Negro race has not been due to these so-called emancipators but to the kindness of the good Southern people. . . . I want to tell you that there's not enough troops in the army to force the Southern people to break down segregation and admit the Negro race into our theaters, into our swimming pools, into our homes and into our churches."[53]

Rogers dismissed the States' Rights convention, calling it "the Birmingham circus" and declaring its leaders "men of small sectional stature whose political ambitions far exceed either their judgment or their ability." The turn of events thrilled Ball, however. They gave him the "rebellion" that he so dearly wanted. He celebrated with a front-page editorial: "Thurmond for President." The Democrats and Republicans "are making a play for negro votes, the former in the belief they have the white Southerners in the bag and the latter in the knowledge that they have no chance to carry the South anyway," Ball said. "The solid South now can demonstrate that it is not in the bag, that it has a mind and a will of its own, and that it offers a tempting bloc of electoral votes for a candidate who will make an honest bid for them." Ball contended the Dixiecrats could carry all eleven states of the old Confederacy and perhaps deny victory to either Truman or Dewey, forcing the election into the House of Representatives. "In the electoral college lies the only chance to save the South for Southerners," he wrote.[54]

Rogers decried the "hot head" and "self-aggrandizing" politician who acted out of anger, and he urged his state to think carefully before embracing the new ticket. "The Birmingham convention was called in the heat of wrath over Philadelphia. It was held amid an atmosphere of hot tempers and high emotionalism," Rogers wrote. "For South Carolina to swallow hook, line and sinker without following first a calm, deliberate, wait-and-see policy would be a harum-scarum invitation to political disaster." In the end, he suspected the Dixiecrats would carry South Carolina, but without "enthusiasm or unanimity." It would be better for the state, however, if the political morass gave birth to a competitive Republican Party. Here he echoed his southern liberal counterparts who believed fervently in the need for a two-party system in the South: "The *Florence Morning News* is unfettered, untied, unpledged to any person or party. Its sole interest is in . . . encouraging good government by whatever party is in power. It has a wholesome faith in the Democratic Party but it would like to see in the South a strong Republican Party as well. It believes this would provide a system of 'checks and balances' which would work to more efficient, more progressive government." Once again, Rogers leavened his argument with caution. He supported a strong GOP in the South, but failed to take the bold step of actually endorsing that year's Republican ticket.[55]

Where Rogers was cautious, Ball was provocative. He chastised the state's "silent" political leaders for failing to support the Dixiecrats more aggressively. "What has happened to the upsurge of enthusiasm that should be greeting the nomination of Thurmond for president?" he asked. "The governor . . . has been a consistent, an able and eloquent supporter of the Southern cause." At the same time, he delivered a warning to white politicians tempted to court black votes in the coming primaries. "Which of the candidates . . . is soliciting the votes of the newly admitted party members of the Negro race? . . . If they welcome the support of the colored Democrats, the white Democrats should know it." Ball hammered away at Truman and the national Democrats as the enemies of white southerners and warned that federal courts would eventually force "amalgamation" of the races in South Carolina. He spoke the language of white supremacy, but claimed his cause was far larger than that.

"Again *The News and Courier* declares that it is not concerned about 'white supremacy.' It is the advocate of supremacy of the worthy." Most of all, Ball advocated rebellion—against the Democratic Party, the federal courts, the New Deal, democracy itself—against all the forces threatening to overwhelm his antiquated vision of South Carolina. "Talk of 'White Supremacy' is filling the minds of some people," he wrote. "It doesn't worry us, but we ARE for Rebel Supremacy, and we've got it! We've got it!"[56]

For McCray and his NAACP allies, Thurmond's sudden turn to the Dixiecrats was a painful disappointment. Just one year earlier, South Carolina's leading black activists had praised Thurmond's response to the lynching of Willie Earle. They had seen the young governor as a new type of southern white Democrat, a gradualist on racial change, perhaps, but one who was ready to abandon the brutality of Ben Tillman and Cole Blease. By joining the Dixiecrats, they feared Thurmond had turned toward the past would unleash dark forces from the state's violent history.

Within a month of the Democratic convention, McCray believed that prophecy had come true. In the *Lighthouse and Informer,* the editor said Thurmond's campaign had empowered the Ku Klux Klan in South Carolina and provoked "several cross burnings" and a "hideous and shameful group attack" on a respected black minister. McCray urged the governor to withdraw from the presidential race to prevent a "calamity" in his home state. "As sincere as he may be," McCray wrote, "Governor Thurmond's pure objectives will be spoiled by associates and supporters he doesn't know and cannot control."[57]

As Election Day approached, McCray's newspaper worked to rally black voters to support Truman. The newspaper launched a fundraising drive urging black southerners to donate one dollar each to the president's reelection campaign to offset the Democrats' loss of white southern support. The weekend before the Tuesday vote, the *Lighthouse and Informer* published an emotional editorial encouraging black voters to "stand with the man who stood by us." President Truman had acted courageously when he defied the white South and proposed civil rights legislation, the paper noted, and it encouraged black voters to treat Election Day as "the second emancipation for our people." The editorial emphasized the high stakes involved. "Millions of people are watching the Tuesday election to decide whether there's any truth in the oft-repeated advice" that it is "political suicide" for a white politician "to fight for the rights of Negroes," the newspaper declared. In a nearby column, McCray warned black voters that the state's Democratic Party leaders were supporting Thurmond and the Dixiecrats and had designed the ballot to make it difficult to vote for "the real Democratic Party." McCray warned his readers not to be "big suckers by staying home and not voting." Blacks who do that will be "giving aid and comfort to Thurmond and the Dixiecrats and the Klan and the Demagogues."[58]

The Dixiecrats won South Carolina and three other Deep South states that November, but they failed to unify the larger South, and finished a distant third in the presidential race. More important, they failed to stop Truman's surprise reelection. The results seemed to support Clark Clifford's analysis: Black voters in the North managed to offset the revolt in the South. In that sense, political analysts considered Thurmond's Dixiecrat campaign an abject failure. Thurmond disagreed, of course. He argued the rebellion had helped the South declare its independence and prove it was "no longer in the bag" for the Democrats.

For William Watts Ball, who had fought so long for his southern revolt, the Dixiecrat campaign was a dream come true. Despite the electoral failure, he depicted it as a grand victory for the region. After the results were in, he summed up his feelings with three short words: "I am free." Yet the Dixiecrat campaign—especially Thurmond's nomination acceptance speech—had damaged the segregationist cause in the national public sphere. Through the use of such loaded language as "mongrelization," Thurmond's campaign appealed to crass white supremacy in a way that would have pleased Cole Blease and Ben Tillman. The Dixiecrat's rhetoric mimicked the shrill tribal cries of the revived Ku Klux Klan in the South, despite Thurmond's attempts to disassociate his campaign from that group. The tone and substance of his campaign had fallen outside the accepted rhetoric of American democracy and had helped encourage civil rights supporters in the North, while further isolating the white South. As the cold war heated up, the United States increasingly found itself on the defensive globally because of racial injustice at home. McCray's *Lighthouse and Informer* would emphasize this point with a political cartoon. It showed an outraged Uncle Sam clasping his hand over the mouth of a southerner who says, "And I still think those Negroes should be barred from the polls." With the letters "UN" hoovering above the two men, the cartoon's caption says: "The Dixiecrats are Embarrassing our Right to Lead."[59]

The Dixiecrat campaign may have rallied white southerners who were eager to embrace the Lost Cause and reunite the Confederacy, but it pained those who believed that a more sober and serious approach could actually preserve the southern way of life. One of those serious men would emerge from South Carolina in the wake of the Dixiecrat debacle and deliver a new message designed to unite the South, but also to try ease concerns and win allies in the North.

5 An Old Warrior Underestimates a New Foe

South Carolina's best-known politician sat out the Dixiecrat campaign of 1948. James F. Byrnes had resigned as U.S. secretary of state in 1947, and since then he had been splitting time between a lucrative Washington law practice and his home in the rolling foothills of South Carolina's Upstate region. Though a generation older than Strom Thurmond, Byrnes was friendly with the young governor from Edgefield, and they appeared to share a similar worldview. In 1946, Thurmond had avoided extreme race baiting in the governor's campaign and had argued that economic progress depended on good race relations in the state. Like Byrnes, Thurmond supported the basic thrust of the early New Deal reforms but chafed at what he considered its more liberal extremes later in FDR's presidency. Neither doubted the correctness or morality of segregation. But both men feared mob violence and an active Ku Klux Klan in South Carolina would scare off business investment and prevent the state from participating in the postwar economic expansion. Yet when Thurmond jumped at the opportunity to lead the Dixiecrat revolt against Truman and the national Democrats, Byrnes refused to endorse his campaign. Ever the canny politician, Byrnes knew better than to oppose the popular Dixiecrat uprising publicly in South Carolina. Instead, he went into hiding. He spent the last six months of 1948 avoiding reporters' calls and, in his words, "sincerely wishing to stay out of politics."[1]

Byrnes's statement was a bit disingenuous. He wanted to stay out of the 1948 presidential campaign, but he had not retired from politics entirely. Like the Dixiecrats, Byrnes despised Truman's push for civil rights reform, but he told friends that he knew a third-party effort would fail. Further, Byrnes suspected the States Rights Party—the Dixiecrats—carried too much racist baggage to be an effective representative of the new South he envisioned. With their harsh rhetoric, the Dixiecrats reeked of the old days, when state leaders praised the Ku Klux Klan and demagogues like Cole Blease rallied white voters by threatening to "lead the lynch mob" to keep blacks in their place. Byrnes had been a national political figure for three decades. As a senator, he had been Roosevelt's chief southern ally pushing New Deal legislation during the 1930s. Rewarded with an appointment to the Supreme Court, Byrnes resigned in 1942 to take a leading role in FDR's White House during the war. Later, he helped negotiate the peace and usher in the cold war as Truman's secretary of state. Byrnes understood how public opinion had shifted in the North since that day in 1919 when he had stood in the well of the House of Representatives and denounced W.E.B. Du Bois and the NAACP as agents of the communist threat. Winning that argument had been relatively easy, given the paucity of national support for civil rights at that time. Now, with black soldiers returning from the war against fascism and the United States presenting itself to the world as a beacon of democracy, the former secretary of state understood the need for white southerners to craft a new message to defend the racial status quo.

Two years after the 1948 Dixiecrat campaign, Byrnes ended his brief retirement and launched a successful campaign for governor of South Carolina. In doing so, the elder statesman unveiled a new narrative in support of white rule in the South, one that replaced the rebel yell of white supremacy with a more modulated and sophisticated argument in favor of states' rights and the "southern custom" of segregation. Under Byrnes's leadership, the state of South Carolina conceded that it had mistreated its African American citizens and failed to abide by the "separate but equal" doctrine that undergirded legal segregation in the South. He claimed that an overwhelming majority of white southerners wanted both races to prosper economically and live in harmony in the South—as long as segregation remained intact. To achieve these goals, Byrnes proposed a new social arrangement in South Carolina. The state would spend the money necessary to create a black school system that was equal to the white one, and it would reform its legal system to abolish lynching and crack down on the Ku Klux Klan and other extremist groups. The state would carry out this generous act to preserve the nation's democratic heritage, protect individual liberties, and enhance race relations, Byrnes argued. Rather than defy the ideals of the founding fathers, such a system would uphold a firmly established American tradition and benefit all citizens, black and white.

Byrnes claimed that Truman and his northern liberal allies, not the white segregationists in the South, presented the greatest threat to the American way of life. In his view, the growing federal government proposed under Truman's Fair Deal policies would eventually overwhelm the states and clear the way for socialist and communist influences to destroy democracy. Such a system would enslave American citizens of both races. Like Thurmond, Byrnes wanted to downplay the issue of race and focus instead on the threat of government repression of individual and states' rights. Unlike the Dixiecrats, however, Byrnes had the national stature required to sell this new argument in the North. At least many in the southern white press thought so. The columnist John Temple Graves, a fixture on editorial pages across the region, said Byrnes gave the states' rights message "the liberal touch it needs, the national prestige, the countrywide scope, the broader gauge, the victory sign."[2]

Byrnes's vision of the South's future included one caveat. African Americans must accept his plan gratefully or risk a violent white backlash. If black activists and their liberal allies pushed too hard—if they challenged southern traditions too aggressively—they would empower the Klan and other white militants, Byrnes said, and they would likely trigger a race war in the South. In stark terms, the elder statesman warned civil rights supporters not to overplay their hand.

Byrnes hoped the carrot and the stick offered in his new approach would appease northern liberal opinion as well as local black leaders. He had some evidence to support his optimism. African American opinion on school integration in the South was far from unanimous at the time. The region's most influential black newspaper, the *Atlanta Daily World*—the only black daily in the nation—did not fully endorse the push for integrated schools. Across the late 1940s, the newspaper strongly supported the legal effort to force southern states to abide by the "separate but equal" doctrine. Editor C. A. Scott called for "complete equalization" of black and white schools and encouraged black citizens to file suit when states failed to meet that standard. But when the NAACP moved to challenge the concept of segregated education directly, Scott's newspaper expressed deep reservations.[3]

If Byrnes had been reading the *Atlanta Daily World* during that time, he may have assumed he could persuade black southerners to accept his vision of race relations in the region. But if he had been reading the leading black newspaper in his home state, John McCray's *Lighthouse and Informer*, Byrnes would have understood how difficult that task would be. In October 1947, state NAACP president Rev. James Hinton had published a letter in the *Lighthouse and Informer* announcing a significant change in the organization's strategy. No longer would the group accept the concept of "separate but equal," Hinton wrote. Legal separation of the races was "unconstitutional, unlawful and immoral," he said, and the state's NAACP would fight to end "all semblances of segregation" in "facilities of tax-supported institutions" in South Carolina.[4]

In December 1950, one month before Byrnes's inauguration as governor, the NAACP formally implemented this new legal strategy. The organization amended an ongoing suit on behalf of Harry Briggs and other parents in rural Clarendon County and asked the courts to outlaw segregation in public schools. The *Briggs v. Elliott* case raised the ante in the civil rights struggle dramatically. Emboldened by its growing support nationally—and nudged along by its new ally, federal judge J. Waties Waring—the movement in South Carolina was challenging the foundation of what Byrnes called the "southern way of life."

The governor understood the stakes in the battle over *Briggs v. Elliott,* and shortly after his inauguration in January 1951, he moved aggressively to smother the suit in its cradle. With the help of white journalists, Byrnes launched a campaign to persuade black citizens in South Carolina to oppose the NAACP action—to step back from a direct assault on segregation and accept his offer to improve black schools in the state. As one journalist noted, Byrnes was working behind the scenes and "marshaling every resource in the state" because the governor realized that "this is it as far as public segregation is concerned."[5]

As a respected elder statesman, Byrnes understood how to craft a new message on segregation that appealed to many white southerners and some of his former colleagues on Capitol Hill. But he misjudged shifting public opinion in the North, and he misread the scope and tenacity of the black political movement in South Carolina. The state had changed since 1919, when Byrnes was a young congressman representing a strip of counties along the Savannah River. It had changed since 1930, when he defeated Cole Blease to claim a seat in the U.S. Senate. Black South Carolinians had been politically invisible and easily intimidated back then. The state now had an engaged and much more united African American community, with NAACP branches operating across the state and coordinating their efforts through the state conference of branches. It had a black political organization, the Progressive Democratic Party, which was registering and mobilizing black voters. And it had a weekly newspaper that was not about to heed the governor's warning and ease the pressure on the white leadership.

McCray's *Lighthouse and Informer* had become the leading public voice of black political activism in South Carolina, and the editor used his newspaper to ridicule Byrnes's new approach to race relations and to rally black support for *Briggs v. Elliott*. McCray called the Clarendon County case "the

most significant event for American Negroes since the abolition of slavery."
And he described the governor's school equalization plan as a frantic effort
"undertaken in desperation" to fool northerners. The state "has never done,
is not now doing, and will never do justice to the Negro until and unless it
is beaten over the head with a federal court blackjack," McCray wrote. The
NAACP and its supporters, he added, were "rapidly putting the blackjack
into the hands of the federal courts."[6]

For Byrnes, McCray and the national black press would emerge as major
obstacles in his bid to establish a new narrative of white southern reasonable-
ness on the question of race. The battle over *Briggs v. Elliott* would dominate
his four years in office, and his bitter reaction to the Supreme Court's eventual
ruling in *Brown v. Board of Education* would tie his legacy to an Old South
narrative he had once promised to transform.

"A coronation instead of a campaign"

Byrnes signaled his return to public life in June 1949 in a commencement address at Virginia's Washington and Lee University. The following day, the *New
York Times* headline declared, "Byrnes Hits Trend to 'Welfare State.'" Without
mentioning Truman by name, and with no references to racial issues, Byrnes
said the nation was "going down the road to statism." He claimed the president's economic policies would eventually transform American citizens into
serfs: "If some of the new programs seriously proposed should be adopted,
there is danger that the individual—whether farmer, worker, manufacturer,
lawyer, or doctor—will soon be an economic slave pulling an oar in the galley
of the state." Of course, Byrnes had been a champion of policies that expanded
federal government power during the New Deal and in the early years of the
war. But FDR had never firmly and unequivocally supported black civil rights
in the South. Truman was different. With his continued push for civil rights
legislation, including passage of anti–poll tax and anti-lynching laws, as well
as the creation of a permanent Federal Employment Protection Commission,
Truman had become the first U.S. president since Reconstruction to place
his administration squarely in support of civil rights reform.[7]

Throughout 1949, Byrnes had been dropping hints to friends and political
allies that he might come out of retirement and run for governor of South
Carolina the next year. By the time he addressed the Southern Governors
Conference in Biloxi, Mississippi, that November, he had made his plans well
known, and the state press paid close attention. In Columbia, the *State* show-
cased the speech with a triple-decker headline across three columns on the
front page: "Byrnes Hits Truman's Spending Policies, Asks Cuts in Taxes and

Debt." In a sidebar story running nearby, the newspaper highlighted a politi-
cal scoop unearthed by Washington syndicated columnist Robert S. Allen:
Bernard Baruch, the financier from South Carolina who had long been close
to Byrnes, was working behind the scenes to put together an Eisenhower-
Byrnes presidential ticket in 1952. Eisenhower would run as a Republican,
Byrnes as a defecting conservative Democrat, and together, Allen reported,
the two would form a winning coalition against Truman and the Democrats.
On Samuel Latimer's editorial page, the *State* cheered the proposed coalition
ticket, saying it would bring "a breath of fresh air to the political situation"
and would have "tremendous appeal to patriotic citizens in every section of
the country."[8] The *News and Courier* also reported Byrnes speech on the front
page and later featured an Associated Press analysis under a three-column
headline: "Byrnes Viewed as New States' Rights Leader." Lower in the news
story, the AP reporter employed a familiar journalistic tactic—quoting the
unnamed but ubiquitous source known as "some observers"—to explain
Byrnes's larger goal. The elder statesman wanted white southern conservatives to break with the "Truman liberals" in the Democratic Party and form
a "solid and lasting coalition" with the Republican Party. In the same way
that McCray and black activists had led blacks out of the Republican Party
in South Carolina a decade earlier, Byrnes now wanted white southerners
to cut their longstanding ties to the Democrats.[9]

Byrnes was following the lead of his South Carolina forebear, John C.
Calhoun, who one hundred years earlier had claimed that southern slave
states had the power to control national politics if they could unite as one
voice and avoid committing to one party. As political free agents, a unified
southern vote could swing elections and win congressional battles by forming ad hoc coalitions with conservative forces elsewhere in the country. In
doing so, the South could dictate policy through its decisive role in creating
what Calhoun called "the concurrent majority." The Dixiecrats may have
been political amateurs, but Byrnes believed they had the correct political
strategy. Whites in the southern states, voting as a bloc, could control the
Electoral College and swing the presidential race toward either major political
party. If the white South could break its historic ties to the Democrats and
"let the leaders of both parties know we are not in the bag of any political
party," Byrnes said, the South could rise again as the most powerful force in
national politics. As governor, he planned to break up the "Solid South" and
lead white southerners away from the Democrats, at least at the presidential
level, but he knew this would not be easy. In early 1950s, many white South
Carolinians still viewed the GOP as "the party of Lincoln," the invading force
that inflicted the horrors of Reconstruction on their beloved Southland.[10]

As he gradually unveiled his plan, Byrnes treaded carefully on the issue of race. He wanted to frame his break with the "Truman liberals" as an honorable difference of opinion about taxes, spending, and the constitutional question of states' rights, not the rejectionist stance of a white supremacist who refused to accept racial progress. Yet Byrnes's decision to reenter politics came at a time when Truman was pressing hard to keep civil rights in the spotlight. In the weeks leading up to Byrnes's Biloxi speech, Truman had been out stumping in support of civil rights reform legislation. "Truman to Stand for No Letup in Battle for Civil Rights Laws," a front-page headline declared in *The State* on November 16. The story detailed Truman's speech honoring civil rights pioneer Mary McLeod Bethune, who was retiring as head of the National Council of Negro Women. A native of South Carolina, Bethune had been a member of FDR's informal "black cabinet" during the 1930s, and her name was anathema to staunch white supremacists in the South. The president praised her work fighting "racial or religious discrimination" and vowed to push forward his civil rights legislation: "We are going to continue to advance in our program of bringing equal rights and equal opportunities to all citizens," Truman said. "In that great cause, there is no retreat and no retirement."[11]

Truman's remarks came five days before Byrnes's speech to the southern governors in Biloxi, yet in their initial coverage, South Carolina's major white newspapers avoided linking Byrnes's attacks on Truman to civil rights and racial issues. They focused instead on his criticism of Truman's Fair Deal spending policies. And that is just how Byrnes wanted it. He hoped to succeed where the Dixiecrats had failed by elevating the discussion to center on economic policy and constitutional issues. The national press was not as cooperative as the state papers, however. An Associated Press Washington reporter highlighted Byrnes's strategy, noting that the former senator wanted to expand the states' rights debate and make it "broader than the racial issues" that prompted the southern split with the national party in 1948.[12]

In his home state, Byrnes did face criticism in the white press, and it mostly came from William Watts Ball, the editor of the *News and Courier*. Deeply conservative, Ball had opposed New Deal spending programs going back to 1933, and he took pleasure in noting Byrnes's sudden reversal on the question of deficit spending. The former senator's attacks on Truman's policies "should be applauded," Ball wrote, but Byrnes's excuse for his support of New Deal spending policies during the Depression "is hollow." Byrnes had claimed in the speech to the governors that the Depression was a crisis that required emergency measures. That crisis was over, Byrnes said, and the need for deficit spending had long passed. Ball had been one of the few southern editors to oppose federal intervention in the economy even during the darkest days of the Depression, and he reveled in the irony of Byrnes now stepping forward to lead the criticism of policies that he had once helped facilitate. The Roosevelt administration "treated the country as a silly mother spoils a whimpering child by giving it candy and making it sick," Ball wrote. He concluded that "morally the country has been sick since 1933" and as FDR's ally in the Senate, Byrnes deserved blame for "the sowing of the germs."[13]

Ball enjoyed tweaking Byrnes about his New Deal connection and his about-face on taxes and spending, but the editor took a more serious tone on the issue of race. Ball had been arguing since 1933 that New Deal reforms would eventually undermine "the southern way of life" and empower both working-class whites and blacks. As Byrnes prepared to reenter politics in South Carolina, Ball returned to the topic in an editorial headlined "Civil Rights and Socialism." The editor claimed that increased federal involvement in state activities would inevitably bring an end to racial segregation in the South. In his typical bombastic style, Ball wrote that when the federal government "shall own and operate the public utilities; when it shall be the insurer of the people against illness, old age and penury; when it shall be the financial patron of schools and colleges; when it shall furnish the free lunches for the children and haul them to the schoolhouses; when it shall assume the medicinal and surgical care of all their health; when it shall be good Old Mother with a whip of nine lashes and millions of spoons in her hand, it will most certainly force the obliteration of distinctions of race." Ball had disliked the spread of democracy when it brought poor, working-class whites into the political system. Now, he feared federal encroachment on state turf would further undermine the foundations of southern society and eventually end white rule in the region. The federal government already had more than two million employees, thanks in part to Byrnes's work during the New Deal, the editor wrote, and under the Truman plan government would expand again and likely bring "many negroes to offices of high power and responsibility" in the South. Ball defined the term "civil rights" as "the wiping out of differences between the races in the United States," and he claimed that Byrnes had contributed to the current crisis through his early support for the New Deal. Byrnes may have wanted to elevate the debate beyond race, but the feisty Charleston editor would not cooperate.[14]

Byrnes announced his candidacy for governor in January 1950, and he coasted to victory in the July Democratic primary. Ralph McGill, the liberal editor of the *Atlanta Constitution*, described the primary race as "more a coronation than a campaign." By the time of Byrnes's inaugural address the following January, United States military forces were fighting on the Korean peninsula, and news about the hot war in Asia and the cold war in Europe dominated the newspapers and benefited Byrnes's effort to downplay the racial issue. On inauguration day, the late edition of the capital city's after-noon newspaper, the *Columbia Record,* bannered an eight-column headline: "100,000 Hear Byrnes Warn Against Russia." Byrnes had made big news in his speech. The former secretary of state said the United States should either bomb communist China or pull its troops out of Korea, and his dramatic statement dominated national and state coverage. Deeper in his inaugural ad-dress, however, Byrnes presented his fullest expression yet of how he intended to frame the white response to the black civil rights reform movement.[15]

Byrnes called for a dramatic increase in spending on black education in South Carolina—$75 million for school-building projects, supported by the sale of state government bonds, plus a new 3 percent sales tax, with revenues to be split equally between black and white school systems. South Carolina had failed to deliver on the promise of "separate but equal" education, Byrnes told the crowd, and if southerners were going to demand states' rights, they must carry out state responsibilities. "We should do it because it is right," Byrnes said. "For me, that is sufficient reason. If any person wants an ad-ditional reason, I say it is wise."[16]

The Battle Over Black Support for *Briggs v. Elliott*

By the late 1940s, black activism had spread well beyond the cities and had even reached one of the most isolated spots in the state: Clarendon County. During the New Deal, the Santee and Cooper rivers had been harnessed in a massive public works project designed to bring electricity to Clarendon and other rural counties in South Carolina's Lowcountry. The resulting lakes became popular recreational areas, but during parts of the year the spider web of feeder streams crisscrossing the tenant farmlands around Santee-Cooper became impass-able. In 1947, a mild-mannered minister and NAACP activist named Joseph A. DeLaine discussed this problem with parents in the Jordon community in the southern tip of the county. One of those parents, a farmer named Harry Briggs, claimed that his son and other black children often had to row across a flooded creek and walk miles to reach their one-room school, while white children rode a school bus. DeLaine helped Briggs and the other black families ask for a school bus of their own. When the local and state boards of education rejected the request, DeLaine persuaded the NAACP to file suit demanding equal facilities for the black schools in Clarendon's school district 22.[17]

On December 22, 1950—one month before Byrnes's inauguration—Thur-good Marshall and the NAACP amended their earlier complaint concerning bus service in Clarendon County. The new case, *Briggs v. Elliott,* demanded an end to segregated schools entirely. It had been three years since the state NAACP had announced its new strategy opposing the "separate but equal" doctrine, but Marshall was unsure if the Clarendon County case provided the right opportunity to risk a frontal assault on segregation. A high-court ruling upholding *Plessy*'s "separate but equal" doctrine could set a precedent that would undermine civil rights efforts for years. Marshall was not sure he had full support from the black community. Just three months earlier, he and his NAACP Legal Defense Fund colleagues had filed a controversial suit in Atlanta that raised the prospect of integrated schools. In *Aaron v. Cook,* the NAACP lawyers demanded city officials either equalize funding for black and white schools *or* end segregation altogether. Even this partial threat to the dual school system drew a swift rebuke from C. A. Scott's *Atlanta Daily World* and his conservative allies in the city's black community. "We seriously doubt the desirability or necessity for our seeking entrance to white (common) schools," Scott wrote.[18]

It took the intervention of the federal judge J. Waties Waring to persuade the NAACP to alter its Clarendon County case. By early 1950, Waring had grown weary of "separate but equal" lawsuits in South Carolina, and he essentially demanded that Marshall turn *Briggs v. Elliott* into a showdown over the constitutionality of segregated schools.[19]

Byrnes and his allies realized the school systems in Clarendon County and the rest of the state were far from equal. As Richard Kluger noted in his definitive study of the *Brown v. Board of Education* case, Clarendon County might have been the one place in America "where life among black folk had changed the least since the end of slavery." Throughout rural South Carolina, many black schools were little more than wooden shacks lacking electricity, running water, and indoor toilets. But the governor wanted to persuade the federal courts to give the state time to fix the problem. He claimed black South Carolinians supported his efforts. "The overwhelming majority of colored people in this state do not want to force their children into white schools," Byrnes argued. "Except for the professional agitators, what the colored people want and what they are entitled to is equal facilities in their schools. We must see that they get them." The governor hoped to undermine northern liberals who supported civil rights by claiming that blacks in South Carolina supported his plan.[20]

Byrnes's promise to raise taxes and borrow money to support black education came with an associated threat: If federal courts refused to grant South Carolina time to reform its school system and insisted on immediate integration, the state would abandon public schools altogether. To back up his

words, Byrnes proposed a referendum to amend the state constitution and
remove the requirement that the state legislature fund public grade-school
education. During Reconstruction, black and white legislators had first included the constitutional requirement that lawmakers fund public education
in the state, and Ben Tillman and other white Democrats who rewrote the
document in 1895 retained the commitment to free grade-school education.
Under Byrnes's plan, a "yes" vote on the referendum would clear the way for
white lawmakers to abolish the public schools in South Carolina if the federal
courts demanded that black and white children attend school together. With
his inaugural address, Byrnes inched closer to the view of southern white
liberals who were eager for at least the appearance of gradual change, but he
refused to rule out militant resistance as well. Byrnes conceded Jim Crow had
failed black families in the state but warned that white southerners would go
only so far in reforming the system. "Whatever is necessary to continue the
separation of the races in the schools of South Carolina is going to be done
by the white people of the state," he said.[21]

Byrnes walked a fine line between promising real reforms in the state and
threatening a white backlash if civil rights supporters and their northern allies
refused to accept his plan. For example, the new governor won praise in the
North and the South for his tough stand against the Klan. Once a powerful
force in state politics, the twentieth-century version of the Ku Klux Klan had
withered since its heyday in the 1920s, when Cole Blease and other South
Carolina politicians routinely signaled their support for the organization.
In the late 1940s, Grand Dragon Thomas Hamilton relocated from Georgia
and tried to build a new hooded empire in South Carolina. His group carried out cross burnings and fiery attacks in several small towns that received
widespread coverage in the press. Despite Thurmond's objections, local Klan
organizations had publicly supported the Dixiecrats in 1948. Determined to
avoid such a connection, Byrnes joined with several other southern governors
in proposing anti-mask and anti–cross burning laws. The measures made it
illegal for an adult to obscure his or her face in public or to burn a cross on
private property without the owner's consent. In proposing the laws, however,
Byrnes again tried to depict the black community as divided, with a majority
in support of "separate but equal" schools and only a tiny minority trying to
stir up trouble. In this case, he linked the Klan and the NAACP and implied
both posed a threat to public safety. It was the governor's job to keep order,
Byrnes said, and "I do not need the assistance of the Ku Klux Klan, nor do
I want interference by the National Association for the Advancement of
Colored People."[22]

The comparison between the NAACP and the Klan infuriated civil rights leaders. In his weekly column in black newspapers, NAACP executive director Walter White accused the governor of suffering from "senility" and the "bile of bitterness." In South Carolina, Hinton responded on behalf of the state NAACP in a statement released to the press shortly after the governor's speech. Unlike the Klan, Hinton said, the NAACP is a law-abiding organization that abhors violence and seeks to "correct existing evils within the framework of the United States." He reminded Byrnes that "you were a most distinguished member of the highest court in our judicial system and we do not believe that you considered it interference on the part of an individual, organization, or racial group if they sought relief through due process of law." When Hinton's statement failed to appear in any of the state's white newspapers, McCray raised concerns of a possible conspiracy. "Is there any truth in the rumor that orders were issued to commentators and news editors to avoid it so as not to 'embarrass' the governor?" McCray asked in the *Lighthouse and Informer*. "Is there any truth in a companion rumor that from here on daily newspapers are going to 'kill' anything released by the NAACP?" The United States is a "free country where there is freedom of speech" and "every side is entitled to be heard," McCray said. The editor wondered if Byrnes and the white press feared "letting white citizens know the truth" in South Carolina.[23]

Most of the state's white press lavished praised on Byrnes's inaugural address and urged South Carolinians to support the new governor. Describing it as a "call for unity," *The State* newspaper in Columbia said the governor's speech should be "read and heeded" because "unity is the great need of the day." The city's afternoon newspaper, the *Columbia Record,* called Byrnes a "true statesman" who had the interest of both races at heart, and it urged South Carolinians to "bend their backs to aid the governor in the task ahead." Among the state's largest white newspapers, only Ball's *News and Courier* expressed a note of dissent. The governor's assault on the Klan "is certain to be applauded," Ball wrote, but he criticized the governor's school-building program and said "South Carolinians who favor low taxes will be disappointed."[24]

For James Rogers, the white liberal editor of the *Florence Morning News,* Byrnes's inaugural speech was nearly perfect. Rogers had detested the "rabble-rousing" of Thurmond and the Dixiecrats. But he also disliked local black activists like McCray and his *Lighthouse and Informer* newspaper as well. Like many of his southern liberal counterparts, Rogers believed in the existence of a "silent" southern majority of both races that supported a safe middle path between white militants who stirred racial passions and black civil rights activists who demanded an immediate end to segregation. With his inaugural message, Byrnes appealed to these "moderate voices," Rogers said. He claimed the governor represented "the assertion of common sense" and "moral conscience," not southern racial prejudice. Rogers predicted "every state in which the races are separate will follow Byrnes and South Carolina in their fight to preserve the segregated system." But to win that battle, he wrote, southerners must keep the argument "on the high plane" and avoid inflaming "the passions of the ignorant and the prejudiced who have brought and can continue to bring immeasurable damage to the cause." Like Byrnes, Rogers placed much of the blame for radical Klan activity on black activists who were asking for too much, too quickly. The editor implied that the state's civil rights movement held the future of public education in its hands: "When the Negro, by his insistence on the end of segregation, destroys tax-supported schools, he has destroyed his own best, if not only, chance of education."[25]

Byrnes focused much of his ire on an old foe—the black press. In 1919, as a young member of Congress, he had accused W.E.B. Du Bois and *The Crisis* of conspiring to bring down U.S. democracy. The magazine's scathing editorials against lynching and white violence in the South were designed to aid the Soviets, Byrnes claimed. He seemed to be arguing that any criticism of the United States, even if well founded, was tantamount to treasonous support for communism. Now, thirty years later, he blamed McCray's *Lighthouse and Informer* and the black press in general for the emergence of racial discord in the state. He claimed the fiery rhetoric of McCray and other black editors had fueled resentment and provoked white militants to embrace mob violence. In a letter to a white minister who complained about the "fascist" Ku Klux Klan, Byrnes pinned the blame on black newspapers: "The attitude of the Negro press has been of wonderful assistance to the Klan. It makes it easy for the Grand Dragon to arouse the prejudices of the people."[26]

In the *Lighthouse and Informer*, McCray dismissed Byrnes's criticism. He was especially irritated by the paternalism inherent in Byrnes's call for blacks to step aside and keep quiet while whites correct the injustices of the state's educational and political systems. "Let the politicians and white supremacists scream all they want," McCray railed in an editorial headlined "Segregation Now in the Negro's Hands." The case against "jimcrowism" was now working its way through the courts, McCray maintained, and the NAACP and its supporters believed both public and legal opinion had shifted in their favor. In his sarcastic style, McCray said white leaders needed to accept that Negros had taken control of their own political fate: "The politician or white supremacist who has backed racial discrimination, especially segregation, suspects it, and the student of civil and legal events knows it: The Negro now can call the tune he wants the white fiddling South to play, and eventually the white South has no alternative but to play, though it may scream, rant and rave." Even if the courts reject the Clarendon County case and refuse to outlaw segregation entirely, McCray argued, they had already ordered states to provide equal facilities, and South Carolina could never afford to fund two truly equal school systems. Such a policy would require massive tax increases and government borrowing and would likely bankrupt the state. If black South Carolinians demanded full equalization, McCray said, eventually "segregation is going to be wiped out." The editor concluded with a zinger that captured in one short paragraph the remarkable change in African American attitudes since Byrnes had last run for office in the state: "So don't go around asking a governor or a major or a police chief what's going to happen and when on this issue. Ask the Negro, the little and big Negro, what he's going to do, how, and when."[27]

In the months after the NAACP filed the suit, McCray's *Lighthouse and Informer* worked to counter the governor's effort to dissuade blacks from supporting the Clarendon County case. *Briggs v. Elliott* is a "new type of lawsuit," the newspaper argued, one designed to end the South's "fallacious theory" of segregated education and "obtain for Negro children equality of opportunity in fact." The paper warned that the case would involve a long and expensive appeals process, but it said readers should "cherish" the opportunity to contribute to the cause. Blacks in South Carolina "were selected as citizens to bring an end to segregation in America, and if this is to come now, in this era, a new kind of history for the state will be written, one which will soften somewhat the bitter memory of the Secession from the Union, the ranting of the Ben Tillmans, the Cole Bleases, the 'Cotton' Ed Smiths, and more recently, the breast beatings of the Dixiecrats and their leader."

McCray's immediate focus in shoring up black support was the Palmetto State Teachers Association, the organization his newspaper had excoriated a decade earlier during the battle over equal pay for teachers. Black educators in South Carolina—and across the South—had always been a relatively cautious group. As public employees who worked in state-funded institutions, they had been particularly vulnerable to white retribution. And as college-educated professionals, they feared losing their tenuous grasp on middle-class status. Understanding this, Byrnes moved to separate the black teachers from the NAACP. The governor targeted the PSTA in his inaugural address, saying, "the negro teachers do not want their pupils to leave them and attend schools for white children." White reporters followed up with stories that emphasized the possibility that black teachers could lose jobs if the schools integrated.

And NAACP leaders in South Carolina began hearing rumors that Byrnes was trying to entice black teachers and parents to testify in court on behalf of the state's segregated educational system.[28]

McCray's newspaper tried to counter Byrnes's effort. Shortly after the governor's inauguration, the *Lighthouse and Informer* addressed an "ugly rumor" that many black teachers opposed the *Briggs v. Elliott* case. "It would be a shame," if the rumor proves to be true, the newspaper said. Citing the legal victory in the teacher-pay case six years earlier, McCray said "no single group in South Carolina has benefited more as the direct result of the NAACP." The editorial later noted that the PSTA leaders had denied any split within the group over *Briggs v. Elliott,* and it encouraged the organization's rank and file to "clear up" the matter at their upcoming annual conference. They should express clear support for the NAACP and its effort to "smash jimcrowism," McCray wrote. Apparently unhappy with the PSTA's response, McCray sharpened his tone in a second editorial. He denounced the "shiftlessness" of teachers who showed "an utter lack of appreciation for the fine civic work of the NAACP." Their actions damaged the reputation of the teaching profession, McCray wrote, adding that such teachers were "as worthless to aiding fights for the race as the most worthless of citizens."[29]

McCray accused Byrnes and his allies of employing what he called "thought-control" and "blackmailing" tactics to bully black South Carolinians and force them to turn on the NAACP. In one editorial, he told the story of young black college graduate who wanted to work as a teacher. During his job interview, the young man said a white school board official asked him two questions: "Do you belong to that subversive organization, the NAACP?" and "Do you read that radical newspaper?" When the man hesitated, the school board official reached in his desk and pulled out a copy of the *Lighthouse and Informer.* "I don't hire any teachers in this county who supports that NAACP or reads this here paper," the official reportedly said. The young man left without getting the teaching job.[30]

McCray said such tactics were part of a "nefarious scheme" that would eventually backfire on the state's "race-indulging" white leadership. The NAACP was not subversive and his newspaper was not radical, the editor wrote. They were simply "free and unbought" and could not be "brow-beaten and induced to support things not in the best interest of the people they serve." Because they could not be "controlled," McCray said, the NAACP and his newspaper were "feared by those who oppose honesty and fair play."[31]

In a clever political ploy, McCray's newspaper joined the *News and Courier* and other conservative white newspapers in denouncing the state's new 3 percent sales tax. He mocked the measure, labeling it the "Byrnes tax" and the "Jim Crow tax." Writing one week after the sales tax went into effect, the *Lighthouse and Informer* attacked its regressive nature. The governor's plan was particularly cruel and senseless, the newspaper said, because it placed the burden of sustaining the "separate but equal" doctrine on those least able to afford it. The sales tax "makes the poorest and hardest-pressed citizens writhe deeper in poverty," he wrote, adding that Byrnes and his allies "would tax to death the poorest wretch in order to give proof to a theory conceived some 53 years ago to hurt Negroes."

Of course, the front line in the battle over *Briggs v. Elliott* was in Clarendon County, where Harry Briggs and his fellow plaintiffs faced enormous pressure to withdraw from the case. Briggs and his wife Eliza would both lose their jobs during their legal battle, and the man who first brought the NAACP to Clarendon County, Rev. Joseph A. DeLaine, would have his Summerton home burned to the ground and eventually be forced to flee the state. Yet they stood firm in their commitment to the case. The *Lighthouse and Informer* chronicled these and other acts of white retribution against the plaintiffs—"Reveal 14 Teachers Fired in Clarendon County 'Revenge,'" blared one double-decker headline on the paper's front page—and the newspaper encouraged readers to attend the many rallies and fundraising drives that were organized by the NAACP and local churches. McCray's editorial page showered the plaintiffs with praise during their ordeal, often focusing on their dignity and grace under fire. "Few Negroes thus far have been able to hold themselves together for an attack on a discriminatory system," McCray declared in one editorial. "One by one they have had to retreat under pressure. But not so in Clarendon County. The more opposition, the more attacks upon them, the firmer and more determined they become." McCray concluded by proclaiming that "under the skins of these plaintiffs beat the kind of heart not easily stopped, one moved only by God's right . . . without malice or bitterness to anyone."[32]

A Case of "Criminal Libel"

McCray would pay a price for his defiance. In January 1950, McCray and an Associated Press reporter, Deling Booth, were indicted on charges of criminal libel. The case centered on their accounts of a rape accusation involving Willie Tolbert, a twenty-five-year-old black man convicted of sexually assaulting a white teenager near Greenwood, South Carolina. The young woman's account of what happened that night was odd, to say the least. She claimed that she and her boyfriend were sitting in a parked car chatting when Tolbert forced his way into the vehicle. Like a scene from *To Kill a Mockingbird*, Harper Lee's famous novel set in 1930s Alabama, the teenager said Tolbert understood the consequences of his actions but was so overcome with sexual desire for her that he proceeded anyway. He said he wanted her to have his child, she claimed. The young woman never explained how an unarmed man who was only five feet nine inches tall and weighed one hundred fifty pounds managed to commit the sexual act while holding the young woman's boyfriend at bay.[33]

Tolbert told a very different story. He claimed the sex had been consensual. He said he helped the teenagers buy liquor and, after a night of drinking, they had invited him to join in the sexual acts. Yet the court never heard Tolbert's story. He was advised not to testify. After a short trial, an all-white jury convicted him and sentenced him to die in the electric chair. Tolbert was electrocuted on October 28, 1949.[34]

Before his execution, Tolbert had granted a death-row interview to the Associated Press reporter, and Tolbert's attorney, Harold Boulware, had conveyed what Tolbert said in that interview to McCray. Both Booth and McCray published Tolbert's claim that the sex was consensual, but neither journalist used the teenage girl's name. Nonetheless, county prosecutor Hugh Beasley—who happened to be the girl's father—charged the two journalists with violating a South Carolina criminal statute prohibiting the media from defaming the victims of sexual assault. Backed by the resources of the AP, Booth had his case dismissed without a trial. When the prosecutor refused to drop the case against McCray, the national black press responded in anger. The *Chicago Defender* called the case "a challenge to freedom of the press, one of the fundamental principles of our democracy."[35]

Thurgood Marshall and the NAACP's legal team helped prepare McCray's case, but they wanted to find a local white lawyer to take the lead role in court. Few would consider it, given the rising racial tension in South Carolina and the political connections of the young woman's family. Jack Greenberg, an NAACP lawyer, said the atmosphere was so hostile in Columbia that a white lawyer who covertly aided McCray asked the editor's legal team "to enter his house through the back door." Greenberg said the lawyer "would have been ruined if his involvement became known." McCray's attorneys won a change-of-venue request and had the trial moved from Greenwood to nearby Newberry County. Despite this small victory, the lawyers persuaded McCray to plead guilty to avoid going in front of an all-white jury. On June 19, 1950, Newberry Circuit Judge Steve C. Griffith fined McCray three thousand dollars and placed the editor on three years' probation. The outcome allowed McCray to continue publishing the *Lighthouse and Informer*, but it prohibited him from traveling outside South Carolina without permission from his probation officer.[36]

One year later, in August 1951, McCray was arrested and charged with violating the rules of his probation. The circumstances around his arrest remain a mystery. The criminal libel charge had received national attention, particularly in the black press, and McCray had accepted several speaking engagements outside South Carolina. In October 1950, he had delivered the keynote address at an event hosted by African American congressman William Dawson of Illinois. He also addressed the New York Press Club, where he accepted an award, and he traveled to Durham, North Carolina to attend the Omega Psi Phi fraternity's Black Achievement Week function. McCray claimed his probation officer, T. R. Patton, had told him that "temporary trips on business" were acceptable under the terms of his plea agreement. Yet nine months after his last out-of-state speech, McCray was arrested without warning and charged with disobeying his probation order. At a hearing before the Newberry circuit judge, Patton denied that he had given McCray permission to travel and said he and the editor had never discussed the issue. Judge Griffith revoked probation and ordered McCray to serve sixty days in jail. When the state Supreme Court rejected McCray's final appeal in late 1952, the editor was taken into custody in Newberry County and forced to spend nearly two months working on a road crew. The symbolism of McCray's sentence was hard to ignore. A decade earlier McCray had published a chilling exposé about South Carolina chain gains and the abusive treatment of black prisoners. The story had helped establish McCray's *Lighthouse and Informer* as the bold and assertive new voice of black activism in the state. Now, in what appeared to be an effort to silence that voice, the editor faced his own stint on a South Carolina chain gang.[37]

McCray always said he believed Byrnes targeted the *Lighthouse and Informer* because of its support for the Clarendon County case. The timing was certainly suspicious. McCray's arrest in the summer of 1951 came in the midst of the governor's campaign to rally black support for his school equalization plan and force the NAACP to drop the Briggs suit. McCray's newspaper was playing a lead role battling the governor's effort. The *Pittsburgh Courier* said McCray's support for *Briggs v. Elliott* and his constant criticism of Byrnes had made him "a marked man" in South Carolina. McCray's NAACP attorneys, Marshall and Greenberg, said they suspected that was the case. Modjeska Simkins was more blunt in her assessment. "The power structure put him in prison," she claimed.[38]

No hard evidence has been found to support accusations of a Byrnes administration conspiracy, and given the heightened tension in South Carolina at the time, it is surprising that the editor traveled outside the state without getting written permission from his probation officer. On the other hand, By-rnes had frequently expressed his anger at the black press, including McCray's newspaper. It is clear that Byrnes kept tabs on the *Lighthouse and Informer* while serving as governor; his gubernatorial and personal papers include several articles and full editions of McCray's newspaper. As the Clarendon County school discrimination case worked its way through the courts, the governor had reason to be concerned about the *Lighthouse and Informer's* impact. Each week, McCray's front-page headlines and aggressive editorials appeared to undermine one of the governor's primary arguments—that most black South Carolinians supported his school equalization plan and opposed the "outside agitators" who were pushing the case against segregation.

If Byrnes and his administration had hoped to silence McCray's newspaper and quell civil rights activism in the South Carolina, the plan backfired, at least initially. Rather than derail the reform movement and end support for the Clarendon County lawsuit, McCray's indictment in January 1950 helped mobilize black South Carolinians. They rallied to McCray's side, eager to resist what they perceived to be an obvious act of intimidation. The National Negro Press Association created the Lighthouse Defense Committee to raise money nationally, but the campaign generated real passion at the grassroots level in South Carolina. Local NAACP branches and Progressive Democratic Party clubs led the effort across the state. They organized John H. McCray Days and held mass meetings and teach-ins to generate support—and to encourage voter registration. They gathered donations from small-business owners, fraternal organizations, and teachers' associations. Students chipped in as well. In Florence, a group of eighth graders raised ten dollars for the cause. The donor lists also show hundreds of individuals digging deep to contribute a dollar or two, at what must have been a great sacrifice to black families in South Carolina in 1950. Along with their hard-earned money, black South Carolinians sent poignant letters tying McCray's fight with their own struggles for dignity and equality in the state. A woman from Charleston told McCray that "the people are depending on you and none others," and a minister from rural Andrews, South Carolina, said the editor "was not alone" but would find many friends fighting alongside him.[39]

Black journalists rallied to McCray's cause as well. Emory O. Jackson, editor of the Scott family's newspaper in Birmingham, Alabama, called Mc-Cray "the chief symbol" of a "free and fearless press," and he admonished black southerners to follow McCray's lead. "Let not a single one of us give in a single inch in the crusade for the kind of justice we believe in," Jackson wrote. The executive editor of the *Pittsburgh Courier* called McCray "one of those brave Negroes, the kind the race must have if it is ever to win full citizenship in this country." P. L. Prattis said McCray and his allies in the Deep South were "slamming their fists in the Lion's mouth" and leading the way in the fight for "full citizenship." Black leaders in the North were "protected by a more supportive public opinion," Prattis argued, but southerners like McCray demonstrated a stronger fighting spirit. "These men abhor gradualism, and rightly so," the editor said. "They know that gradualism is only the resort of cowards, of so-called leaders who want to remain on friendly terms with hostile whites while begging a few indulgences from them."[40]

The Tolbert case and McCray's indictment would become a hot topic in a bitter Senate race in 1950, and it would give African Americans a chance to flex their muscles at the polls and show just how far they had progressed politically in the past decade. The state's junior senator, Olin Johnston, was up for reelection in 1950, and outgoing governor Strom Thurmond, who was prevented by law from seeking a second term, challenged him in the Democratic Party primary. Byrnes's race for governor may have been a "coronation" that year, but the 1950 Senate contest was more like an old-fashioned Carolina "cockfight." The two men disliked each other, and Thurmond, coming off his disappointing Dixiecrat campaign, worried that another poor showing could end his political career. He stayed on the offensive, attacking Johnston daily. Both men supported segregation and white political rule in the state, but Thurmond believed he could use the McCray case to undermine Johnston on the issue.

As the Democratic primary approached, Thurmond's team distributed a flyer and ran a newspaper ad that suggested Johnston had intervened on McCray's behalf and pressured the judge in Greenwood County to grant a change of venue in the case. Thurmond's Dixiecrat campaign had already turned the black community against him, but Johnston was no better on the issue of segregation and civil rights reform. The senator was a staunch supporter of President Truman and his Fair Deal economic policies, however, and for that reason black South Carolinians were already leaning his way. Thurmond's ad vilifying McCray intensified their support. After the ad appeared, the *Lighthouse and Informer* and McCray's PDP clubs came out strongly in favor of Johnston.

In a front-page editorial, McCray launched a voter-registration drive and set an ambitious target: get two hundred thousand black voters registered in time to participate in the Senate primary. Hitting a target that high would require nearly two-thirds of all voting-age African Americans in South Carolina to register in less than two months. In McCray's view, the Senate race was a gift to black voters. It gave them an opportunity to "slap the racial demagogue in the teeth, perhaps knock out a few of them."[41]

During the Senate race, McCray offered his view of how public discourse and political decision making played out in the state's African American community. When black voters gather "in little groups at the barbershop, the beauty parlor, in the college classrooms and after services in the little country church, they exchange views on their common plight," he wrote, "but then they return to their place on the ground, stretch out their necks and allow somebody to place his foot on their throats, and they lay and writhe under the pressure." It was "time for the Negro to get off the ground," he wrote. Black South Carolinians can remove "the foot and the pressure" through "the simple expedient of the ballot."[42]

McCray and the PDP failed to reach their lofty voter-registration target. Based on figures reported in the white press, however, an estimated seventy thousand blacks had qualified to vote in 1950, up from about fifty thousand in 1948. From his perch at the statehouse, Charleston *News and Courier* political reporter William D. Workman Jr. noticed other examples of African Americans exhibiting a new engagement in state politics: more statehouse visits by "negro school groups and individual Negros"; more requests for publications and information and a greater interest in important state agencies; and more Negro letters to the editors of white newspapers. A week before the July 11 primary vote, the *Lighthouse and Informer* sent a strong message to the newly registered black voters: it ran a sample ballot on the front page that encouraged blacks to vote for Johnston over Thurmond in the Senate race. Modjeska Simkins added her voice to the campaign as well, declaring that Thurmond had a "fanatic zeal that makes him a danger to any democracy."[43]

South Carolina's white politicians and press had been eyeing the black vote warily since 1948, when federal judge J. Waties Waring opened the state's Democratic Party primaries. Nonetheless, the results of the 1950 Senate primary were stunning. In what was expected to be a close race, Johnston won by nearly thirty thousand votes. A former textile worker himself, the senator had strong support from labor in the Upstate region he called home. Yet black voters gave him his margin of victory. Returns from predominantly black precincts in Charleston and Columbia revealed that an overwhelming majority had voted for Johnston. Thurmond's advisers later admitted they underestimated the strength of the PDP and its ability to turn out African American voters, particularly in the rural Black Belt region of South Carolina. The results of the Johnston-Thurmond Senate race suggested that African Americans were "much wiser and better informed than yesteryear," McCray argued in the *Lighthouse and Informer*. The black voter of the 1950s could "see through the veil" cast by white politicians and discern "their real intent." Now, McCray said, black South Carolinians know "what is actually possible."[44]

Despite success in the statewide Senate race, McCray was furious at local PDP leaders in Charleston, where businessman and party member Arthur Clement had lost his race against L. Mendel Rivers, a prominent white congressman who had led the effort to impeach Waring after the judge's rulings on the all-white primary. McCray said he had been told that PDP leaders had instructed some party members "not to waste their vote on Arthur" because they disliked Clement and did not think he could win. It was this sort of defeatism and petty infighting that frequently undermined black aspirations in the state, McCray complained. Clement's decision to challenge the powerful white politician—Rivers had been in Congress for ten years and was instrumental in directing military spending toward South Carolina—attracted widespread press attention and probably benefited the black movement, McCray conceded in a letter to Clement. But he said he was no longer interested in symbolic victories. "I am now at the age . . . where I am not so anxious to experiment and gamble just to have it said, 'He made history for his race.' I want to win," McCray wrote.[45]

Byrnes had avoided endorsing a candidate in the heated Senate race between Thurmond and Johnston. The incoming governor presented himself as a wise man who was above politics—a man who had no future ambition other than to help South Carolinians safely navigate dangerous times. He wanted to be seen as a friend and counsel to both races, a calm voice of reason who could stand up to white militant Klansmen and black agitators as well. The white press helped enhance this image. But blacks saw through the veil, McCray said. The Byrnes they saw was not the avuncular elder statesman depicted in the white press. To black South Carolinians, the governor was just another angry white supremacist who wanted to protect the racial status quo. Byrnes wanted blacks to slow down, to temper their request for change. But as McCray had noted back in 1944, black South Carolinians had "beaten down the fear" that white leaders had once used so successfully to divide and crush black political aspirations. By leveraging their growing support from the federal courts, liberal allies in Congress, and northern public opinion, African Americans had gained access to the ballot box in South Carolina and had finally reemerged as a force in the state's electoral politics.[46]

This was a development Byrnes had feared throughout his political career. Although considered a moderate in the early 1950s, Byrnes had launched his political career as a protégé of "Pitchfork" Ben Tillman. As a staunch white supremacist, he regularly expressed his fear that black South Carolinians would one day regain the political power they had lost at the close of Reconstruction. As a young congressman in the summer of 1919, Byrnes had taken to the House floor to accuse the NAACP of communist ties and to encourage

African Americans to leave the country "if they didn't like it here." At the
time, William Watts Ball was editor of *The State* newspaper in Columbia.
To the aristocratic Ball, Byrnes's comments sounded more like the words of
Tillman or Cole Blease, not the more sophisticated and paternalistic conservative that the editor hoped Byrnes would become. In a letter to Byrnes, Ball
accused the congressman of demagoguery. In his reply, Byrnes agreed that
his language had been too harsh. But he also revealed a key motivation that
would drive his political thinking over the years. Byrnes argued that whites
in South Carolina must always remain vigilant against the threat of black
political participation. Given the size of the black population, Byrnes wrote,
"a fair registration" process would grant blacks great political power in the
state. For that reason, he said every issue in South Carolina "must include
this consideration of the race question."[47]

Round One Goes to Byrnes
in the Clarendon County Suit

The NAACP's decision in December 1950 to amend its earlier suit in the
Clarendon County school case had been historic. For the first time in the
twentieth century, a southern court would hear a case challenging the constitutionality of school segregation directly. Columbia's afternoon newspaper,
The Record, placed the story of the suit's filing on the bottom of the front
page, but the much larger morning paper, *The State,* did not. Instead, the
newspaper ran a short Associated Press story on page B8, tucked under an
item about an American Legion toy drive and next to the death and funeral
notices. The paper did give prominent play to another story about black
activism that day. It involved the bombing of the home of a black family that
had challenged racial zoning laws in Birmingham, Alabama. The message
was clear: Black activists who pushed too hard would pay a price. African
Americans in South Carolina understood this all too well.[48]

The State's coverage of *Briggs v. Elliott* underwent a dramatic change in
June 1951 when the three-judge panel hearing the case ruled in favor of the
state. "School segregation sustained," declared an eight-column headline
atop the front page. Byrnes had surprised Marshall and the NAACP by
conceding that South Carolina schools were in fact unequal and asking
the court to focus on the state's effort to remedy the problem. Marshall had
planned to use witness testimony to emphasize the disparity between black
and white schools in South Carolina and to raise doubts about whether
a state that had done so little in the past could be trusted to achieve true

equality in the future. With that option no longer available, Marshall proceeded with witnesses who testified that segregated schools were inherently
unequal, no matter how similar their facilities and resources. As *The State*'s
reporter explained it: "Several high ranking educators, some of them white
men, took the stand today and testified that segregated schools cannot train
young people in a democracy right and are detrimental to the children,
both of the minority, which is isolated, and the majority, which does the
isolating."[49]

The three-judge panel voted 2–1 to reject the NAACP's arguments. They
upheld segregation as constitutionally legal but ordered Byrnes and his government to return in six months with a detailed plan to equalize schools
across South Carolina. In their order, the judges said federal courts "would
be going far outside their constitutional function were they to attempt to
prescribe educational policies" such as integration, "however desirable such
policies might be in the eyes of some sociologists and educators." Chief Judge
John J. Parker of Charlotte and Judge George Bell Timmerman Sr. of Columbia wrote the majority opinion. The lone holdout was Judge Waring of
Charleston, whose fiery dissent would foreshadow the Supreme Court's final
ruling in the case—and would further alienate Waring from white society
in South Carolina. Waring called segregated schools "per se inequality," and
he said testimony in the case had shown "beyond a shadow of a doubt that
the evils of segregation and color prejudices come from early training." The
place to stop it "is in the first grade not in graduate college," Waring wrote.
To their credit, the white daily press gave Waring's dissent prominent play.
The State included a key excerpt on its front page, and the Charleston *News
and Courier* ran a full transcript of Waring's dissent on an inside page.[50]

Byrnes described the court's ruling in one word: "unanswerable." As a former U.S. Supreme Court justice himself, Byrnes believed the legal precedent
was incontrovertible. The court's 1896 ruling in *Plessy v. Ferguson* gave the
states a constitutional right to operate "separate but equal" public facilities—
including educational systems—and the governor saw no legal grounds for
the high court to overrule the three-judge panel's decision in the *Briggs* case.
His allies in the state's white press helped the governor present the court's
ruling as a "Victory of American Rights," as the *News and Courier* called it in
a front-page editorial. The majority opinion had "demolished" the NAACP
claim that segregated schools violated the equal protection clause of the
Fourteenth Amendment, the paper argued. "The court went beyond the
rights of the states, as set out in the Constitution," the editorial continued.
"The court has upheld an older and an even more basic right, the right of

parents to look after the welfare of their children." In doing so, the court had "reaffirmed" the rights of the individual.[51]

After the district court ruling, even some commentators in the national black press began to raise doubts about the wisdom of pursuing the Clarendon case. *Pittsburgh Courier* columnist Marjorie McKenzie said she believed that Byrnes was correct and that the Supreme Court would vote to uphold *Plessy v. Ferguson*. Over the past decade, the court had granted the NAACP victories in a string of graduate-school cases that had chipped away at *Plessy's* "separate but equal" doctrine. But the justices had not overturned it. If the court delivered a similar ruling in the Clarendon case, McKenzie argued, it could establish a precedent that "revives the *Plessy* doctrine [and] gives it modern interpretations and new documentation regarding the state's authority to segregate schools." McKenzie described herself as a liberal who "wants segregation ended now," but the legal analyst said the NAACP lawyers should not force the issue. Faced with the enormous financial burden of supporting truly equal school systems, southern states would eventually abandon segregation on their own, McKenzie argued. The NAACP lawyers should let *Plessy* die a natural death and allow white southerners to integrate schools voluntarily.[52]

The *Courier* column posed a serious problem for McCray and his allies in South Carolina. Worried that McKenzie's concerns could kindle fresh doubts among black South Carolinians, the editor teamed up with Hinton to rebut her arguments in a co-authored response. They maintained that the "separate but equal" doctrine was in fact "ripe" for a direct assault in the courts. But even if the legal case was uncertain, they said, the moral case was undeniable. The real purpose of the Clarendon County case is to "democratize this nation," they said. And in South Carolina, "where every ounce of white supremacy energy is against changing the status quo, and where the Clarendon County plaintiffs have suffered all manner of indignities and atrocities," the black community remains committed to that higher goal. Black Carolinians support the *Briggs v. Elliott* suit "to the last person," they claimed, because they see the case as part of their larger battle for personal dignity and self-respect. McCray and Hinton requested the *Courier* run their column "forthwith, in order that our common battle against segregation shall not suffer further."[53]

Judge Waring's concerns regarding the district court ruling on *Briggs v. Elliott* went deeper than the legal issues raised in his dissent. Waring would later complain that his fellow judges on the panel, Parker and Timmerman, were working closely with Byrnes. He believed they had accepted the governor's arguments before the hearings began and, in their deliberations, "had been throwing aside all the testimony." Waring said Parker and Timmerman urged him to join a unanimous decision to give Byrnes the support he needed to carry out his equalization plan. He claimed the judges backed their argument with a bit of political prophecy. "A Republican victory was assured" in the 1952 presidential election, Waring said he was told, and without the Truman liberals breathing down his neck, Byrnes could then negotiate a deal to bring about gradual change in South Carolina.[54]

Byrnes not only wanted to see "a Republican victory" in the presidential election of 1952, he wanted to be the kingmaker who engineered the GOP win. In November 1951, he returned to the annual Southern Governor's Conference to make his plans clear. On the last day, Byrnes announced he would not support Truman's renomination the next year. He said he had persuaded a majority of southern governors to form a unified bloc and support the best candidate with the best platform, regardless of political party. Byrnes claimed the southerners were prepared to "put loyalty to country above loyalty to party." The Korean War and concerns about the economy had undermined Truman's poll numbers, and the threat of another southern revolt further imperiled his chances in 1952. Three months after Byrnes's comments, Truman announced that he would not seek another term as president. The Democrats would nominate another liberal, Illinois Governor Adlai Stevenson, while the Republicans would defy their party's more conservative wing, led by Senator Robert Taft of Ohio, and turn instead to a war hero, Dwight D. Eisenhower.[55]

Both parties claimed to support civil rights in 1952, but the GOP platform included language bound to please white southerners: "We believe that it is the primary responsibility of each state to order and control its own domestic institutions, and this power, reserved to the states, is essential to the maintenance of our federal government."[56] In the fall, Byrnes announced his support for the Republican candidate, and his political operatives helped create an organization, Independents for Eisenhower, that allowed white southerners to leave the Democratic Party without actually embracing the "party of Lincoln" their grandparents had so despised. Six weeks before the election, Byrnes embraced Eisenhower on the statehouse steps and watched the GOP candidate address a raucous crowd in the capital city. When the band played "Dixie," the general rose and sang along. Afterward, when he said, "I always stand up for that song," the crowd let out a collective rebel yell.[57]

In November, Eisenhower coasted to victory with strong southern support. Although he did not win South Carolina or any Deep South state, the Republican did carry four of the eleven states of the Confederacy. It was the party's best showing in the South since 1928, when southern voters abandoned Democratic nominee and New Yorker Al Smith, a Catholic who opposed Prohibition. *The State* had assured the "dissident Democrats

of South Carolina" that a vote for Eisenhower would not be interpreted as
a vote for a Republican, but "a protest against the policies of the present
Democratic Administration." More than 154,000 of those dissident Democrats joined with about nine thousand Republicans to vote for Eisenhower,
who narrowly lost the state to Stevenson. In its editorials, *The State* never
mentioned race or civil rights as the reason white Democrats were turning
to the Republican candidate. But in Charleston, the *News and Courier* said
race played a significant role in the vote tally. The "Negro bloc vote" had
supported Stevenson and "he carried [South Carolina] with a MINORITY
of traditional Democrats." Take away "Stevenson's Negro vote, and it can be
seen that most of the traditional Democrats voted for Eisenhower." It was
a theme the *News and Courier* would return to frequently over the coming
years: If black voters were joining the Democratic Party, white voters should
look elsewhere for a new political home.[58]

By the end of 1952, Byrnes's plans for reshaping the debate over civil rights
appeared to be working. Truman and his liberal Democratic allies were out
of the White House, and southern white voters had helped show them the
door. The election would be remembered as "independence day," Byrnes
said, because the South was now "out of the bag" and no longer committed
to one party. Truman's civil rights legislation had died in Congress a full
year before Eisenhower's election, and the new administration coming to
power in Washington appeared to support Byrnes's argument in favor of
states' rights. A lower federal court had upheld the doctrine of separate but
equal and refused to outlaw segregated schools in South Carolina. Although
the NAACP had appealed that ruling, Byrnes enjoyed an advantage. He had
served on the nation's highest court with the current chief justice, Fred Vinson, whom he considered an old friend. Byrnes believed the Vinson court
would stand by the precedent set in *Plessy v. Ferguson*. But, as a bit of insurance, the governor had also obtained the services of perhaps the country's
most distinguished jurist to argue the case for the state of South Carolina.
John W. Davis, a former Democratic Party presidential candidate, had participated in at least 250 cases before the U.S. Supreme Court. Even McCray,
ever the optimist, had lost some of the confidence he had expressed in his
rousing response to McKenzie. In the *Lighthouse and Informer,* the editor
conceded that the lower-court ruling "threatens to throw us back." If the
Supreme Court upheld the district court ruling, he said, segregation could
spread beyond the South.[59]

As the case proceeded through the courts, the Byrnes administration
launched a publicity campaign to show off the results of its school equalization program in South Carolina. The department of education produced

glossy brochures featuring new schools and gymnasiums built for black students, and it encouraged national reporters to tour the sites. Positive stories began appearing in national news outlets, raising concerns among state and national NAACP leaders. The black press moved to challenge Byrnes's public relations efforts. The *Pittsburgh Courier* sent two reporters to check out the new facilities in South Carolina. The newspaper conceded that "attractive and modern brick buildings for Negroes are springing up all over the state, replacing old barn-like frame shacks, and brand-new yellow buses are roaming the highways picking up and delivered colored children." But the newspaper dismissed the new spending on black education as "an effort to stave off school desegregation, which can be seen peeping over the horizon." The reporters said "the state of South Carolina is trying to do in three years what it refused to do in the last fifty." And they contended that the new black facilities "were far from being as good and attractive as the new schools being built for white students." The story quoted Modjeska Simkins, who disputed Byrnes's claim that the NAACP had pressured black parents to file the *Briggs* case in Clarendon Country. "You don't have to tell a man when he's hurting," she told the newspaper. This battle to shape the legacy of Byrnes's school equalization plan would play out in the black and white press long after the school segregation case had been settled.[60]

Briggs v. Elliott had been merged with three other cases challenging segregation in southern and border states when it was first scheduled for Supreme Court oral arguments in December 1952. That fall, Byrnes moved to nationalize the case. In an effort to shift the focus from southern segregation to the constitutional issues of states' rights and local self-determination, Byrnes helped persuade the governor of Kansas to file a brief in defense of its segregated school systems, which were also under NAACP attack. The Supreme Court accepted the Kansas case, merged it with other segregation suits, and renamed the case *Brown et al. v. Board of Education of Topeka et al.*[61]

After the December oral arguments, the court announced it would not rule in 1953 but would carry the case over to the next term. Yet Byrnes and Davis remained confident. Byrnes had been talking with his former colleagues on the court, particularly Justice Felix Frankfurter, and the liberal from Boston appeared to agree with Byrnes that "the whole thing was moving too fast" in the South. Harry Ashmore, the liberal newspaper editor from Little Rock, was hearing the same thing from his sources inside the court. Frankfurter was especially supportive of Byrnes's argument concerning the Klan and other extremists. He feared that overturning *Plessy v. Ferguson* and outlawing segregation would mean "the guys who talk nigger would be in charge, there would be riots, and the Army would have to be called out."[62]

By late 1953, however, Byrnes's optimism had been shaken. Three months before the second Supreme Court hearing, Chief Justice Vinson died suddenly. Eisenhower replaced him with former California Governor Earl Warren, a liberal Republican who had no ties to Byrnes and whose sympathies on the question of segregation were unknown. In another setback for the governor, Eisenhower's attorney general, Herbert Brownell, filed an amicus brief in support of Marshall and the NAACP, even though Byrnes thought he had persuaded the president and his administration to remain neutral in the case. The decision undermined Byrnes's credibility. Less than a year earlier, he had urged white southern voters to rally behind the former general because he believed the Republicans supported states' rights. Yet in its first major test, the new administration had acted no differently than the Truman liberals had. The shift in northern opinion on civil rights was more profound than Byrnes had realized, and the governor had overestimated his ability to reverse it. The Republican Party had its conservative wing, but overall the party was not yet as hospitable to the white South as it would become in the next decade.

Byrnes also began to hear favorable chatter about the brief filed by Marshall and the NAACP. The justices had scheduled a second round of oral arguments for December 1953 to explore the NAACP's claim that segregated schools violated the equal protection clause of the Fourteenth Amendment. In response, Marshall had submitted a 235-page brief that made a persuasive case that the amendment should be applied to public education. A lower-court ruling that Byrnes thought was "unanswerable" now seemed in jeopardy.[63]

The latest developments buoyed McCray's spirits, and his writing in the *Lighthouse and Informer* regained its edge. He praised "the magnificence of the people of Clarendon County." And he pointed out an obvious but overlooked fact: Harry Briggs and the African American families in Clarendon County were helping foot the bill for both sides arguing the case—their own NAACP lawyers, and through tax payments, the team defending the state of South Carolina, including the "top-priced lawyer who will work against them." The newspaper's argument apparently had an impact; Byrnes would later announce that Davis had agreed to "donate" his services and defend the state's segregation policies free of charge.[64]

Harry Briggs and his fellow Clarendon County plaintiffs had dug deep in their own pockets to help launch the case and endured economic and physical retribution to carry it through the appeals process. Throughout, they had been bucked up by a local and national black press that rallied public support and fought to stamp out any signs of negativism in the black community. McCray's newspaper and his NAACP allies fought a ferocious battle in the public sphere against a powerful governor, a respected elder statesman who had both national prestige and firm control of the white, mainstream press in South Carolina. McCray would be jailed for two months during the fight with James F. Byrnes, but his efforts would help mobilize the black community and demonstrate its rising political clout in the state.

As 1954 began, South Carolina's governor, its press, and its people waited nervously for the Supreme Court to deliver a final verdict in a battle that had begun deep in the backwoods of Clarendon County.

During World War I, Modjeska Monteith Simkins attended NAACP meetings with her mother and saw a fledgling civil rights movement join forces with a black newspaper. In the late 1930s, Simkins searched for another "fighting news organ" to help reinvigorate black political activism in South Carolina. (Modjeska M. Simkins Papers, South Carolina Political Collections, University of South Carolina)

Charleston editor John Henry McCray agreed to move his newspaper to Columbia, the state capital, and join forces with Simkins and her allies at the NAACP. (John H. McCray Papers, South Caroliniana Library, University of South Carolina)

McCray's paper, the *Lighthouse and Informer*, served as a radical voice for black progress in the state during the 1940s and early 1950s. The paper rallied support for a direct assault on white supremacy and demonized those in the black community who refused to join the fight. (South Caroliniana Library, University of South Carolina)

McCray addresses the Southern Negro Youth Congress in Columbia in 1946. His newspaper rejected cautious accommodation and urged black South Carolinians to "rebel and fight" for their rights. But McCray was skeptical of alliances with outside groups such as the SNYC. (John H. McCray Papers, South Caroliniana Library, University of South Carolina)

On August 10, 1948, black South Carolinians line up to vote in a Democratic Party primary for the first time since the rise of Jim Crow rule in the state. Across the decade, the civil rights movement won legal battles requiring equal pay for black teachers and abolishing the all-white Democratic Party primary. (Associated Press)

In 1951, Governor James F. Byrnes raised taxes and issued bonds to pay for improvements to black schools in part to improve the national image of southern segregation. The governor hoped to appease northern public opinion and persuade black South Carolinians to abandon *Briggs v. Elliott,* the NAACP lawsuit challenging school segregation in Clarendon County. (James F. Byrnes Papers, Special Collections and Archives, Clemson University)

Byrnes' school equalization included such improvements as this brick addition to Scotts Branch School in Clarendon County. McCray's newspaper ridiculed Byrnes's spending plan, calling it an act "taken in desperation" to fool black southerners and white northerners. (Rev. Joseph DeLaine Papers, Courtesy South Caroliniana Library, University of South Carolina)

Clarendon County NAACP leader Rev. Joseph A. DeLaine and his family stood amid the charred remains of their home in Summerton after it was burned to the ground in late 1950. DeLaine and the plaintiffs in the *Briggs v. Elliott* case refused to back down despite physical and economic retribution. (Rev. Joseph A. DeLaine Papers, South Caroliniana Library, University of South Carolina)

McCray's *Lighthouse and Informer* praised the "magnificence of the people of Clarendon County." The newspaper helped publicize mass meetings like this one, which helped to rally black support for the suit. (Rev. Joseph A. DeLaine Papers, South Caroliniana Library, University of South Carolina)

Angered by President Truman's push for civil rights legislation, Byrnes sought to break up the Democratic Party's "solid South" by endorsing Republican Dwight D. Eisenhower in the 1952 presidential race. In October, Byrnes welcomed Eisenhower to Columbia and appeared with the GOP candidate at a statehouse rally where Eisenhower declared his support for states' rights. (James F. Byrnes Papers, Special Collections and Archives, Clemson University)

In Charleston, the newly promoted editor of the *News and Courier*, Thomas R. Waring Jr., urged readers to support Eisenhower in the 1952 race as well. After the Supreme Court's ruling in *Brown v. Board of Education*, Waring and his newspaper played a leading role in the white campaign of "massive resistance." (University Archives and Special Collections, University of the South)

In 1954, Thomas Waring's *News and Courier* supported Strom Thurmond's successful write-in campaign for the U.S. Senate. Three years later, Waring's newspaper denounced southern senators who refused to join Thurmond's one-man filibuster against civil rights legislation. Waring also used his newspaper to help found the White Citizens Council movement in South Carolina and to build the Republican Party in the state. (Strom Thurmond Collection, Special Collections and Archives, Clemson University)

McCray (far right) appeared with state NAACP President Rev. James Hinton, national NAACP executive secretary Roy Wilkins, and Modjeska Simkins at a 1957 event in Orangeburg. At the time, the black movement was splintering in the face of an intense white backlash. A feud between McCray and Simkins hastened the death of the black newspaper, the *Lighthouse and Informer*. (John H. McCray Papers, South Caroliniana Library, University of South Carolina)

In 1960, McCray (left) attorney Harold Boulware (next to McCray) and other members of McCray's political organization, the South Carolina Progressive Democrats, organized a statewide get-out-the-vote effort in the final days of Democrat John F. Kennedy's presidential campaign. (John H. McCray Papers, South Carolinian Library, University of South Carolina)

McCray and the Progressive Democrats held a series of rallies like this one in Columbia. Election analysts believe the effort gave Kennedy and the Democrats their narrow margin of victory in South Carolina. (John H. McCray Papers, South Caroliniana Library, University of South Carolina)

In 1962, political reporter and commentator William D. Workman Jr. left his newspaper job to run for the U.S. Senate as a Republican. With strong support from Thomas Waring's *News and Courier* in Charleston and other newspapers across the state, Workman ran a surprisingly close race against the Democratic incumbent and drew national attention to the rising strength of the GOP in the Deep South. (William D. Workman Jr. Papers, South Carolina Political Collections, University of South Carolina)

In September 1964, Thurmond announced on statewide television that he was switching to the Republican Party and would campaign for GOP presidential candidate Barry Goldwater. Thurmond's announcement came less than two months after President Lyndon Johnson had signed the Civil Rights Act. (Lottie D. "Dolly" Hamby Papers, South Carolina Political Collections, University of South Carolina)

6 Massive Resistance and the Death of a Black Newspaper

On May 22, 1954, the *Lighthouse and Informer* celebrated the U.S. Supreme Court's ruling in *Brown v. Board of Education* with its usual feistiness. The paper's lead editorial cheered the court's rejection of "the lying, moth-eaten 'separate but equal' chicanery," a system of education that had "persisted in the perennial stealing from Negro children." The newspaper ridiculed John W. Davis, the "fabulously-priced" lawyer hired by Governor James F. Byrnes to defend segregation. The "blubbering" Davis may have been famous, but he was no match for the "the legal prowess" of Thurgood Marshall and the NAACP. Most of all, the black newspaper emphasized the connection between the *Brown* ruling and what it saw as the nation's deep-seated desire to fulfill its democratic ideals. By rebuking Byrnes and the white South, the *Lighthouse and Informer* declared, the justices had restored faith in "the sense of American justice and fair play, and the ultimate triumph of right."[1]

The tone of the editorial may have been vintage *Lighthouse and Informer,* but South Carolina's leading black newspaper had undergone a change. The name of its founder and longtime editor, John Henry McCray, no longer graced the masthead. McCray had left earlier in the year to take a job as South Carolina correspondent for the *Baltimore Afro-American.* Always teetering between solvency and financial collapse, the *Lighthouse and Informer* had slipped into bankruptcy in 1954, and the economic struggle had exacerbated a growing rift between McCray and one of the paper's primary benefactors, civil rights activist Modjeska Simkins. Fourteen years earlier, the two had hatched a plan to move the paper to Columbia and create a "fighting news organ" that would mobilize African Americans and jump-start the state's civil rights movement. Now, just weeks after that movement's greatest legal triumph, the paper fell silent for good. In the fall of 1954, the *Lighthouse and Informer* was shuttered and its press sold for $638 to cover back taxes.[2]

The tension between Simkins and McCray had surfaced in the mid-1940s and escalated gradually over the years. In the beginning, Simkins had been one of McCray's biggest fans. Her family had provided office space when McCray moved the *Lighthouse and Informer* to Columbia in 1941, and when fellow activist Osceola McKaine privately criticized the young editor early the next year, Simkins came to his defense. McKaine had complained about spotty delivery of the paper to some residents in his hometown of Sumter, and he claimed that one of McCray's editorials appeared to oppose equal pay for black teachers. "He must surely have been either drunk or in jail when he wrote it," McKaine said. The papers had not arrived because the Sumter residents had not paid their bills, Simkins replied; McCray had no choice but to "cut some of the dead timber" from the subscription list. As for the editorial, she said McKaine had simply misunderstood McCray's point. The young publisher had a tough job, Simkins argued, and she urged McKaine to cut him some slack. As she put it, "the poor boy is working hard and having to pull hills in low gear many times."[3]

The newspaper's precarious finances and the personal debt McCray incurred during his imprisonment in late 1952 ultimately killed the *Lighthouse and Informer*. But the split between Simkins and McCray would doom all efforts to save the newspaper. Their rift was partly a personality clash. Both were strong willed, even arrogant, and both were quick to suspect the worst in others. Yet there were substantive differences as well. They disagreed over strategy concerning electoral politics and coalition building with other progressive organizations. Simkins believed blacks in South Carolina should keep all electoral options open rather than committing to the Democratic Party, and she wanted the movement to work with labor and other outside groups trying or organize in the South. McCray was wary of such alliances. He wanted to maintain tight local control over the civil rights movement and the Progressive Democratic Party, the black political organization he had founded, and he contended that the Democratic Party offered the best political prospects for African Americans in the South. In the spring of 1945, their differences spilled into the open for the first time.

Like most African Americans, McCray had once been a supporter of the Republicans, but by 1940 he had given up on the party of Lincoln and cast his lot with Franklin Roosevelt and the Democrats. Simkins joined McCray and the NAACP in fighting to end the all-white Democratic primary in the South, but she was unwilling to sever ties to the GOP. She supported FDR and the liberal Democrats in the North, but she detested the white supremacist Democrats in the South and believed they would never accept black political equality. Simkins had been active in the state's Republican Party since the 1920s, and despite efforts by national Republicans to turn the party "lily-white" in the South, Simkins held GOP leadership positions into the 1950s. In 1942, her letters urging Thurgood Marshall and the NAACP to help overturn the all-white Democratic Party primary in South Carolina were written on official stationary of the state Republican Party.[4]

In 1945, the tiny GOP in South Carolina had three factions: one led by "Tieless" Joe Tolbert, a longtime white Republican activist from Greenwood County; a conservative "lily white" group headed by J. Carl Hambright of Rock Hill; and a new, more progressive group led by J. Bates Gerald, a white attorney from Summerton, in Clarendon County. Simkins supported the Gerald faction, which actively recruited black members. In 1940, McCray had supported Gerald as well, and even served as the group's Charleston spokesman before breaking ties with the Republicans. African American Republicans were not united behind the Gerald faction, however. A prominent black businessman and NAACP member, Columbia funeral home owner I. S. Leevy, remained loyal to the Tolbert group.[5]

When McCray launched the Progressive Democratic Party in 1944, he told the state Democratic Party chairman that "an overwhelming majority" of South Carolina's African Americans were Democrats. In demanding that blacks be allowed to vote in party primaries and represent the state at the Democratic National Convention, McCray argued that blacks in South Carolina wanted to join the state party—not merely vote for the party's presidential candidate. In McCray's view, being a full-fledged member of the party meant supporting Democrats over Republicans in all elections, not just in the presidential race.[6]

In the summer of 1944, when it became clear that large numbers of black South Carolinians were joining McCray's PDP, the Tolbert faction of the GOP went on the offensive. Leevy ridiculed McCray's organization and moved to compete with it by trying to revive a network of black GOP groups known as "Lincoln Emancipation Clubs" across the state. The Gerald faction was more restrained. In an exchange of letters with McCray, Gerald expressed amazement that the editor would reach out to the white supremacist Democrats in South Carolina. "I have spent thousands of dollars and much time and effort in order that Negroes and Whites might vote in Federal Elections," Gerald wrote. "I have never heard of any others of my race spending a dime in this regard, have you?" After McCray wrote back to defend his strategy, Gerald replied in a more cordial tone. He said he understood what McCray was trying to accomplish with his "new Democratic Party," but he predicted that the editor would eventually rejoin the GOP. "I do believe in all frankness . . . that you are Republican both from choice and for what Republican principles stand for," he wrote. Both Gerald and Simkins argued that McCray and the Progressive Democrats should cast their votes strategically to support the best available candidate, even if that meant supporting Republicans over Democrats in some state and local elections. McCrary remained adamant, however. If integrating the state Democratic Party was the PDP's top priority, he maintained, the group must avoid alliances with the GOP.[7]

McCray's strategy was tested for the first time in March 1945 when Leevy, the black Republican, entered a special election for a seat in the state House of Representatives. As one of six candidates in a low-turnout race, Leevy had a chance to become the first African American elected to the state House since Reconstruction. But to achieve this victory, he needed to unite and mobilize African American voters. Simkins urged McCray to support the black Republican candidate, but the editor refused. Still seething over Leevy's criticism of the PDP the previous summer, McCray said his group would not "support I.S. Leevy in any of his endeavors, he being Tolbert's right-hand man and entirely without repute here."[8]

After some deliberations, the PDP backed a white Democrat named Harold T. Jacobs of Columbia in the House election. Both Jacobs and Leevy lost badly, and a conservative white Democrat won the seat. In his newspaper column, Osceola McKaine sided with Simkins and called the state House election a missed opportunity. Black Carolinians had "a fighting chance to send a member of their race to the state legislature," McKaine wrote, but they failed to unite behind their candidate because of "clashing personalities."[9]

McKaine's column on the 1945 special election had not appeared in McCray's *Lighthouse and Informer;* instead, it ran in the *Norfolk Journal and Guide,* an ambitious black newspaper published in the Virginia coastal city by respected journalist P. B. Young. McKaine and McCray had suffered a falling out after the 1944 Senate campaign, and in early 1945 McKaine had agreed to write a regular column for Young's paper. The following year, Simkins would begin writing for the *Journal and Guide* too.

In addition to their complaints about electoral strategy, Simkins and McKaine had grown increasingly irritated with McCray's desire to avoid alliances between the PDP and other progressive groups. The emergence of a robust black political organization in the heart of the Deep South had drawn national attention in 1944, and left-leaning political and labor organizations that wanted to gain a foothold in the region were eager to link up with McCray and the PDP. McKaine and Simkins supported such biracial coalition building. This was especially true in the fall of 1945, when more than eleven hundred white and black workers went on strike at the American Tobacco Company plant in Charleston. Led by a union associated with the progressive Congress of Industrial Organization (CIO), the striking workers began holding integrated meetings in Charleston, a major breakthrough that suggested working-class blacks and whites could unite to demand reforms in the Deep South. For McKaine, who had often appealed to the white working class in his Senate campaign speeches, the events in Charleston were a sign of genuine progress. "Deep in the grass roots, democracy is beginning to work in the South," he wrote in the *Journal and Guide*. By working closely with labor organizations and other national groups, McKaine argued, McCray and the PDP could help nurture an enduring biracial political coalition in the region.[10]

Simkins and McKaine were particularly interested in building bridges between the South Carolina movement and two outside groups: the Southern Negro Youth Congress (SNYC), founded in 1937 by young African American organizers, and the Southern Conference on Human Welfare (SCHW), launched a year later by former New Deal activists. Both were staffed with experienced and talented political operatives, but both had members with open ties to the American Communist Party, a connection that would grow more problematic as the cold war intensified across the late 1940s. The SCHW was working closely with the CIO, the labor federation, which wielded significant clout within the national Democratic Party. The CIO had planned a major voter-registration drive across the Southeast in advance of the 1946 elections, and it had enlisted the SCHW to carry out the campaign. SCHW leaders wanted McCray's PDP to play a role in this effort.[11]

McCray was wary of all these organizations, but he particularly disliked the Communists. He called communism a "violent theory" and described American Communist Party members as "radical" and "outsiders." Communist Party leaders had "dispatched agents" to South Carolina "for the purpose of taking control" of the movement, McCray said. In the summer of 1944, he claimed, the party placed spies inside the PDP and attempted to "divide and conquer" the black political organization. McCray was less hostile toward the SCHW and the SNYC, but he feared their influence on the PDP. He had acquiesced reluctantly in early 1945 when McKaine said he planned to work for the SCHW. But when SCHW leader James A. Dombrowski offered McCray a $4,000 annual salary if he would quit the *Lighthouse and Informer* and join the group as well, the editor grew suspicious. He rejected the offer and accused the SCHW of trying to take control of the PDP in South Carolina by "buying in" its leadership. "Had I known then what I know now I would have advised against Mr. McKaine's connecting himself with their organization," he wrote to PDP colleague Arthur Clement Jr. When McCray discovered that

McKaine had known beforehand about Dombrowski's plan to lure McCray away from the newspaper, the editor said he realized "something mysterious and queer was going on." McCray called McKaine's actions "treacherous," and he considered launching a campaign to kick the party's former Senate candidate out of the organization. McCray said he rejected the idea because he feared the negative publicity would destroy the PDP. Clement considered McKaine a rival within the party, and he fed McCray's growing paranoia. "McKaine has used you and your paper and you know it!" Clement wrote. Soon after, McKaine's column disappeared from the pages of the *Lighthouse and Informer*.[12]

The SNYC's executive secretary, Esther Cooper Jackson, recalled years later that it was Simkins who had first embraced her group and "welcomed us into South Carolina and into the South." By 1945, both Simkins and McKaine had joined the youth organization's Adult Advisory Board, and the two successfully lobbied the group to hold its annual youth assembly in Columbia. In 1946, as concerns about the group's Communist Party ties spread, Simkins wrote a letter to black activists in South Carolina urging her "fellow-citizens" to ignore the red-scare rhetoric and focus instead on what she identified as the real enemy in their midst. "Some people seem mortally afraid that Communism may sweep our nation," she wrote. "I am unable to evaluate the soundness of their fears. However, thousands of Americans are confident that unvarnished Fascism is far more than a threat in America. Fascism—choking, numbing, murderous, and of a type no less diabolical than Hiterlism—is rampant all about us right here in our Southland." Simkins signed the letter using her title as advisor to the Southern Negro Youth Congress.[13]

In the months leading up to the SNYC Youth Legislature in Columbia, Cooper Jackson recalled a series of difficult discussions in her effort to persuade McCray to support the event. But her charm offensive worked. By August 1946, McCray would describe the SNYC's offer to speak at the conference as a "distinct honor and rare privilege," and he promised Cooper Jackson that he would promote the event by giving it "as much space as possible in our newspaper." Despite his reservations about Communist Party influence, McCray took the stage at Columbia's Township Auditorium that October and urged the SNYC activists to use the PDP as a model for the creation of black political parties throughout the South.[14]

As the cold war escalated, the SNYC and the SCHW were among the first groups to come under siege. By 1949, both organizations had disbanded, and their members suffered increasing government persecution because of their ties to the American Communist Party. As early as 1940, the House Un-American Activities Committee had identified SNYC as a "Soviet front group," which prompted the FBI to investigate its members and supporters. In 1947,

HUAC made public its file on Simkins, which provided pro-segregationist forces in South Carolina with a list of alleged Communist ties to use against her for the rest of her career. As one prominent white columnist would put it, the HUAC report proved that Modjeska Simkins was "bad medicine."[15]

For Osceola McKaine, the SNYC Youth Legislature in October 1946 would turn out to be his last public appearance as a civil rights activist in South Carolina. With the war over, his business partner in Belgium had encouraged him to return to Ghent to revive their nightclub. In December 1946, McKaine boarded a ship for Europe and never returned to his native state. He had not necessarily intended to stay in Belgium, but with his health failing, and his business in far worse shape than he had been led to believe, McKaine never made it back to South Carolina. Despite their disagreements over the previous year, McCray and McKaine mended their relationship. From Belgium, McKaine resumed writing columns for the *Lighthouse and Informer,* and the two "Macs" often traded warm and friendly letters until McKaine's death in 1955.

McCray's relationship with Simkins also seemed to improve in the late 1940s. The civil rights movement they had launched reached its peak during the final years of the decade, with more than fourteen thousand dues-paying NAACP members operating eighty-six branches across the state. The organization recorded a major victory in its battle against the all-white primary, and it displayed rising political clout by mobilizing voters to defeat Strom Thurmond in the 1950 Senate election. With its decision in 1947 to reject the "separate but equal" doctrine and insist on full integration, the movement set in motion a chain of events that would culminate in the U.S. Supreme Court's landmark *Brown* ruling.[16]

The NAACP activists in South Carolina understood the role the *Lighthouse and Informer* had played in the movement's success, and they took steps in the late 1940s to strengthen the paper's finances and formalize its corporate structure. McCray's old friend, Allen University president Samuel R. Higgins, joined with Benedict College professor G. E. Nelson to invest $7,000 in the newspaper. In return, Higgins and Nelson received a majority equity stake and seats on the board of directors of the newly incorporated Lighthouse Publishing Company. Under the arrangement, McCray retained day-to-day control of the business and received the remaining equity shares.[17]

The incorporation of the *Lighthouse and Informer* appeared to ensure its survival as a force in South Carolina's political life for years to come. But McCray's indictment on criminal libel charges in early 1950 undermined the newspaper's finances and led to its eventual collapse. The grassroots campaign that emerged after McCray's arrest may have helped catalyze the black political movement in the state, but it failed to raise enough money to cover all of McCray's bills, and both the editor and his newspaper went into debt. The surprise decision by state and county officials to pursue parole violation charges and to sentence McCray to a chain gang for two months exacerbated McCray's financial problems. If McCray's suspicions were correct and Gov. James F. Byrnes had moved against the editor in an effort to destroy the black press in South Carolina, the governor's plan succeeded spectacularly. The *Lighthouse and Informer* never recovered from McCray's imprisonment.

McCray suffered personally as well. A proud man, McCray and his family received financial aid from Simkins and her husband during his time in jail. It was a benevolent act, but the generosity would nonetheless add another layer of complexity to a relationship that could not bear the strain. Late in her life, Simkins still complained about what she saw as McCray's lack of gratitude. The day McCray began his sentence, she said, "he begged me to see that his family had food and that the paper got off the press, which I did ... without him giving me a quarter." When the editor returned after his two-month sentence, "he walked into the office and walked right by me and didn't even say good morning, or thank you," Simkins said.

McCray told a different story. He contended that Simkins and the *Lighthouse* board never appreciated the sacrifices he and his family had made to keep the paper afloat during tough times. The strain eventually cost McCray his marriage; his wife left South Carolina in the mid-1950s. For all his struggles on behalf of the movement, he believed he deserved more financial support, particularly during his imprisonment.[18]

McCray's final break with Simkins and the newspaper came in 1954. For more than a year, McCray had been complaining to the *Lighthouse* board members. His income was too low, he said in one of letter. And to make matters worse, the newspaper's corporate structure had taken the fun out the job. This last complaint appeared to be aimed at Simkins. She and her husband had always been involved in the effort to keep the newspaper solvent. But in 1953, she took on a more direct role in overseeing day-to-day finances, and she raised questions about some of McCray's spending.

During this time, McCray opened talks with another potential employer, the *Baltimore Afro-American,* a prominent black newspaper owned by the Murphy family. During World War II, black newspapers had grown dramatically, with the *Pittsburgh Courier* leading the pack. The *Courier's* national edition sold more than 350,000 copies each week. White businesses took notice and began to market their products in the black press. In the economic boom of the postwar years, the black newspaper looked like a good business, and the major players in the industry scrambled to compete with the *Courier* and expand their readership. In 1953, McCray approached Carl J. Murphy and his sons at the *Afro-American* and pitched an idea that piqued their interest. He proposed the Baltimore newspaper broaden its reach in the South by launching a Carolina edition and hiring McCray as its editor. With his usual bravado, McCray assured the *Afro-American* executives that he could clear a path for the newspaper in South Carolina. Once he resigned, McCray claimed, the *Lighthouse and Informer* would go out of business because "readers take our paper because of me and would shift with me to any newspaper for which I worked."[19]

In early 1954, when McCray finally left the newspaper and began work for the *Afro-American,* the Lighthouse board members were happy to see the back of him. The newspaper was struggling to pay its bills, and the board members believed McCray had become an obstacle to their financial reform efforts. With the founder now out of the way, Higgins persuaded Simkins to step in and serve as interim manager and editor of the *Lighthouse and Informer* while they worked on a long-term plan to stabilize the newspaper's finances and hire a new editor. It was Simkins who wrote the editorial praising the Supreme Court's ruling in *Brown v. Board of Education.*[20]

In one of her first acts as interim editor, Simkins moved to quash a rumor—apparently spread by McCray—that the *Lighthouse and Informer* had been purchased by the *Afro-American* and would be merged into the new Carolina edition of the Baltimore paper. Simkins sent a letter to "subscribers, agents and friends" that denied the "apparently deliberate report" that the paper had become a "submerged adjunct" to the *Afro-American.* The newspaper is "still alive and slugging," she declared, despite vicious white opposition in this "Dixiecrat stronghold." The newspaper had a "dynamic and indispensable role to play in the historic struggle now being waged in South Carolina," Simkins concluded.[21]

The feud between Simkins and McCray escalated in June 1954 and exploded onto the pages of the *Lighthouse and Informer* and the *Afro-American.* When McCray and his Progressive Democratic Party supported a white candidate rather than Simkins's brother, H. D. Monteith, in a race for a seat in the state House of Representatives, Simkins lambasted the decision. In an editorial headlined "Voice of Jacob," she compared McCray's deceit to the biblical story of the twin brothers Jacob and Esau and their blind father Isaac. "Negroes throughout South Carolina will find it hard to explain such behavior on the part of John H. McCray, whom they have loved as a brother," Simkins' wrote. "But like poor old blind Isaac, if they follow the deal on down they will find that 'The voice is Jacob's voice but the hands are the hands of Esau.'"[22]

McCray responded with reports in the *Afro-American* that suggested Simkins was power hungry and had been conspiring to "take over" McCray's PDP organization. McCray also tried to answer Simkins's criticism in the pages of the *Lighthouse and Informer,* but she refused to run his letter, claiming it was full of "gross misrepresentations" and "nasty lying accusations." Further, Simkins complained that McCray had turned the *Lighthouse and Informer* staffers against her and had made her position at the newspaper untenable. On July 14, she announced her resignation as interim editor and manager, saying "as of this moment I am no longer connected as a volunteer, or in any other capacity, with the *Lighthouse.*"[23]

While Simkins and McCray traded charges, the dunning notes piled up. The Scott family, owners of the *Atlanta Daily World,* hired a collection agency to seek payment for services provided to the *Lighthouse and Informer.* Closer to home, city of Columbia tax authorities demanded Higgins make good on his promise to clear the paper's delinquent tax bill. A prominent white labor lawyer from Greenville, John Bolt Cuthbertson, had approached CIO and NAACP leaders in a last-ditch effort to raise money to save the newspaper. Cuthbertson told McCray that both labor leader Walter Reuther and the NAACP's Thurgood Marshall had supported a financial rescue plan that would keep McCray as editor, but he said "some close friends of yours" had quashed the deal. He refused to identify the friends, saying he was "hesitant to discuss personalities," but by that point McCray's relationship with Simkins and the Lighthouse board was beyond repair. With her close ties to the black-owned Victory Savings Bank, Simkins had always provided the newspaper a financial lifeline during hard times. When she washed her hands of business in the summer of 1954, the *Lighthouse and Informer* had no choice but to shut down. Its assets were auctioned off to cover the tax debt. Many of its archived editions were sold as scrap paper.[24]

McCray had hoped that his journalism in the *Afro-American* and the continuing political work of the PDP could fill the gap left by the death of the *Lighthouse and Informer.* His weekly column, "Need for Changing," continued in the *Afro-American.* He also launched a weekly feature called "Roving About Car'lina," a roundup of news and society items from across the state. But he would soon find that the Murphy family ran a tight ship at the *Afro-American.* The newspaper's managers appeared more interested in building the subscription list and securing new advertisers than in producing local journalism for Carolina readers. McCray's schedule called for only one day a week devoted to newsgathering. He spent most of his time trying to build a reliable distribution network and struggling to collect payments from recalcitrant circulation agents across the state. In the end, the Carolina edition of the *Afro-American* never attracted the local following that had embraced the *Lighthouse and Informer*.[25]

The civil rights struggle in South Carolina suffered a major setback with the collapse of McCray's newspaper. Its demise left only one other locally owned black newspaper, the *Palmetto Leader*, a weekly founded in 1925 by Republican attorney Nathaniel Frederick. Once a strong voice for black rights, the newspaper cut back on political coverage during the Depression, and with Frederick's death in 1938, the *Palmetto Leader* devolved into a religious and society paper that avoided civil rights issues altogether.[26]

The *Lighthouse and Informer* had been instrumental in uniting the black community in South Carolina. Each week for nearly thirteen years, the latest edition of McCray's newspaper had served to rally support for equal rights within a black community still uncertain about its place in civic life. Through the pages of the newspaper, McCray and his allies in the NAACP had challenged white claims about black inferiority and delivered their own interpretation of what white supremacist rule meant for American democracy. The newspaper had defined American citizenship as an act of self-assertion, a right that must be earned by those willing to fight for it. McCray's paper often linked the black community's demand for equal rights to nation's most cherished democratic ideals. In doing so, the *Lighthouse and Informer* helped develop a united black community in South Carolina that was capable of undermining white efforts to depict the "southern custom" of racial segregation as the "natural order" envisioned by the founding fathers. By joining the debate so aggressively, the newspaper helped the black freedom movement in South Carolina break down the barrier that white supremacy had erected to prevent their arguments from being heard in the South and the North. At the same time, McCray and his associates at the *Lighthouse and Informer* had prowled the black public sphere in search of backsliders who instilled fear in the community. They used the paper to ridicule and ostracize fellow African Americans who believed blacks were moving too quickly, or who hoped to win white favor by undermining the movement.

McCray and Simkins could both be stubborn and even petty at times, and their personality clashes certainly contributed to the demise of the newspaper. But it is worth noting the context that helped escalate their feud. By 1953, as the Clarendon County school desegregation case worked its way through the courts, the white response to the black civil rights movement grew harsher. The *Brown* decision in May 1954 served to radicalize white southern politics and heighten efforts to stymie black aspirations. In South Carolina, prominent white newspapers would play a central role in devising the specific tactics and demanding the execution of the massive resistance campaign. For black South Carolinians, the threat of retribution—physical, economic, psychological—grew as white leadership moved to demonize NAACP activity and link it with communist ideology and Soviet tyranny. As the white press in South Carolina helped organize and promote massive resistance in the state, McCray, Simkins, and the rest of the state's black leaders struggled to survive the onslaught.

The *News and Courier* and the Rise of Massive Resistance

In Charleston, the *News and Courier* appeared to represent everything the *Lighthouse and Informer* had been fighting against. The paper believed that the "southern custom" of racial separation was the "natural order," and it described the *Brown* ruling as an attack on the American system of government. In a front-page editorial, the *News and Courier* said the U.S. Supreme Court decision "had cut deep into the sinews of the Republic." By "depriving the states of the right to administer public education," the justices had redefined the Constitution and destroyed the "balance" in race relations that had prevailed in South Carolina since the end of Reconstruction. The *News and Courier* conceded that it was "too late to secede and start another War Between the States," and it urged white southerners to remain calm and not overreact, but the paper said it had no intention of accepting racial integration in the South.[27]

The competing interpretations of the *Brown* decision delivered by the *News and Courier* and the *Lighthouse and Informer* foreshadowed the interpretive battles to come in the state and national public spheres. More than a legal victory, the *Brown* ruling represented a fundamental shift in the culture of the North. The unanimous opinion signaled how far the intellectual credibility of overt racism had fallen over the past decade. In declaring that segregated schools were inherently unequal and illegal, the justices had not only overturned the separate but equal doctrine of *Plessy v. Ferguson,* they established institutional support for the notion that African Americans were full-fledged citizens capable of participating equally in the nation's democratic life. In this sense, *Brown* served as an act of repair intended to heal a wound that had been festering at the heart of American democracy. Yet the issue of black equality was far from settled. Racial conservatives like those at the *News and Courier* would move to resist implementation of the *Brown* ruling. They would take the lead in the effort to delegitimize the ruling in the regional and national public spheres before its egalitarian ethos could harden into an established and accepted cultural reality.

Despite its harsh rhetoric concerning black equality, the *News and Courier* had always maintained a surprisingly hospitable relationship with McCray and his newspaper. McCray had claimed that the *News and Courier*'s legendary editor, William Watts Ball, had inspired him to launch his first paper, the *Charleston Lighthouse*. McCray said he gone to the *News and Courier* offices in the mid-1930s to complain about some long-forgotten editorial policy. Ball had refused to budge on the issue, but he had suggested the black community start its own newspaper. Over the years, Ball and McCray occasionally traded letters and phone calls, usually about some political issue involving African Americans. After the *Lighthouse and Informer* shut down, the *News and Courier*'s Columbia correspondent, William D. Workman Jr., wrote a lengthy obituary. Although mostly objective in tone, the story appeared sympathetic at times. Workman noted McCray's "blunt editorials" had made the *Lighthouse and Informer* a "controversial element in the state's political life," but he accurately reported on the paper's role in fighting for "Negro participation in Democratic primaries, desegregation of public schools, and expansion of the National Association for the Advancement of Colored People." Workman's story described the three goals McCray had set when he launched the newspaper: to provide a medium for Negro expression, to encourage Negro voting, and to enhance Negro education. Workman acknowledged that McCray "takes satisfaction in his conviction" that the newspaper helped South Carolina's black community move closer to achieving those goals. McCray was pleased with the way the *News and Courier* had treated his newspaper, and he wrote to Workman to thank him for his "excellent reporting and analysis." The article may have been "just another routine piece of copy for you," McCray said, but it had been "done up in a most interesting and conclusive way."[28]

Workman's news report on the demise of the *Lighthouse and Informer* reflected the *News and Courier*'s complicated political views. Throughout its existence, the Charleston newspaper had always claimed that it supported African American advancement, as long as that progress did not challenge white rule. The newspaper believed the better class of whites should run the state in a way that retained political control over blacks and working-class whites, but allowed certain gifted members of both of those groups to lift themselves up if possible. In this sense, McCray's goal of creating a newspaper that would "enhance Negro education" fit nicely within the *News and Courier*'s paternalistic worldview. In its reaction to the *Brown* decision, the

News and Courier acknowledged that "Negroes have become more insistent on asserting themselves," and said it "recognizes their rights and ambitions." But like almost all of the southern white press, the Charleston newspaper remained unwilling to accept how widespread the black demand for true equality had become. Instead, it appeared to harken back to the days of Booker T. Washington and industrial education with its call for "advancement for the Negroes both as manpower for the fields and factories as well as customers in the stores." Such economic progress, the paper claimed, would restore racial harmony and "remove many of the social frictions which chafe both races."[29]

In its response to *Brown*, the *News and Courier* hit many of the same paternalistic notes Ball had been delivering since he arrived at the Charleston paper in 1927. But the *News and Courier* was not the same paper. Like the *Lighthouse and Informer*, it too had undergone a major change on its masthead. Ball had retired at the end of 1950 and passed away in 1952. He was replaced by his longtime managing editor, Thomas R. Waring Jr., a familiar name in Charleston society. Waring's father had been editor of the city's afternoon newspaper, the *Charleston Evening Post*. And, in a particularly southern, small-town twist to the story, Waring's uncle was J. Waties Waring, the federal judge whose rulings in favor of the NAACP had made him a despised man in white Charleston. Judge Waring had overturned the all-white Democratic Party primary system in the state of South Carolina in 1947, and he had filed a fiery dissent in the Clarendon County school segregation case that had foreshadowed the eventual U.S. Supreme Court decision in *Brown v. Board of Education*. As a child, the editor had been fond of his uncle. But as an adult, Thomas Waring Jr. had embraced William Watts Ball as his intellectual and professional mentor. Like Ball, the editor believed the South's custom of racial separation had evolved naturally as a means to protect civilization. Despite growing evidence to the contrary, he claimed the majority of both races supported segregation, and thus the federal effort to overturn it was an attack on the nation's democratic values. Judge Waring, in that famous dissent in *Briggs v. Elliott*, had said just the opposite. He argued that racially segregated schools were inherently unequal—he called them "evil"—and thus state-enforced segregation deprived black children of their constitutional right to equal protection under the law. When the Supreme Court sided unanimously with his uncle, Thomas Waring did what *News and Courier* editors had always done—he led his newspaper deep into the political battle.

In its report on the collapse of McCray's *Lighthouse and Informer*, the *News and Courier* had noted that McCray, as editor of the black newspaper and founder of the Progressive Democratic Party, had "become embroiled in politics as well as journalism." The Charleston newspaper could have been describing its own situation at the time. In much the same way that McCray had founded the *Lighthouse and Informer* to further the civil rights movement, Waring and Workman used the *News and Courier* to help push their political aims in the white community. In addition to covering the news, they would work behind the scenes to help shape the white community's "massive resistance" to the *Brown* ruling and to the larger push for black equality. They would help craft the "interposition" strategy to block integration of state schools, help establish the white citizens' council movement in South Carolina, and help launch a campaign to break through the so-called "paper curtain" they believed prevented northerners from hearing the white southern point of view. By the late 1950s, when those efforts appeared to be failing to halt black progress toward full equality, they would play central roles in building a new political home for white southerners in a revamped Republican Party.

Such direct political activism on the part of white southern journalists was hardly unprecedented. In 1954, for example, the liberal editor of the *Arkansas Gazette,* Harry Ashmore, had written a key speech late in the campaign to help gubernatorial candidate Orville Faubus win the Democratic Party primary. It was a bit of political engagement that Ashmore would come to regret. Three years later, Faubus surprised the liberal editor by blocking nine black students from integrating Little Rock's Central High School, a stand that triggered a constitutional crisis and forced President Eisenhower to send federal troops to Arkansas to enforce the *Brown* ruling. At the same time, James J. Kilpatrick, the editor of the *Richmond News Leader,* had joined Virginia's senior U.S. senator, Harry Byrd, in leading the fight against the civil rights movement in that state.[30]

In South Carolina, editors at the *News and Courier* had always engaged openly and directly in political activism. When Waring and Workman joined the paper as young journalists in the 1930s, William Watts Ball supported political candidates in news stories and opinion pieces, and he often consulted with their campaigns on strategy. Ball seemed to be a throwback to the nineteenth century, when powerful editors such as Horace Greely, Thurlow Weed, and the *News and Courier*'s Francis Dawson frequently used their newspapers to promote political ambitions. By the early 1950s, when Waring and Workman emerged as political figures, the *News and Courier*'s top journalists continued to pursue political goals. Yet unlike their predecessors, Waring and Workman began to struggle with the conflict created by their dual roles.[31]

With few large cities to support the professionalized journalism that emerged in twentieth-century America, the South had been especially slow to embrace its norms of impartiality and objectivity. In the years after World War II, as the region grew more prosperous, more urban, and more connected to the rest of the nation, the region's journalists began to accept these new rules of journalism—at least in public. Increasingly across the 1950s, Waring and Workman presented the *News and Courier* as a professional news operation that embodied the ethical standards articulated by organizations such as the American Society of Newspaper Editors and the Associated Press. Despite their deep engagement in political causes, the two Charleston journalists proclaimed their newspaper's commitment to independence, objectivity, and nonpartisanship in news coverage.[32]

Both Workman and Waring had apprenticed under Ball, the paper's editor from 1927 to 1951. After his death in 1952, the *New York Times* called Ball "the last of the great editor personalities." Ball had no doubt about the proper political role of the newspaper editor. He said he believed they had a civic obligation to lead their communities and engage fully in political life. As editor of *The State* from 1913 to 1923, Ball helped organize and lead the opposition to Cole Blease, the populist who served two terms as governor of South Carolina but lost his U.S. Senate bid in 1914. In addition to his editorial support, Ball helped the anti-Blease faction of the Democratic Party select candidates to oppose Blease in the primaries, and he advised those candidates on strategy. Ball was asked to run for office several times and once gave it serious consideration, but he eventually declined. Later, as editor of the *News and Courier,* Ball worked with southern Democrats to try to launch an anti-FDR candidate at the 1944 Democratic National Convention, and he served as an informal adviser to Strom Thurmond's "Dixiecrat" presidential campaign in 1948. Ball frequently wrote about his political involvement openly and proudly in his editorials.[33]

Waring served Ball loyally as city editor and then as managing editor for two decades. Unlike his mentor, however, Waring had spent significant time working outside South Carolina. He graduated from the University of the South in Sewanee, Tennessee, and spent two years at the *New York Herald-Tribune,* where another southerner, respected city editor Stanley Walker of Texas, sharpened his newswriting skills. After taking over as editor of the *News and Courier* on New Year's Day in 1951, Waring emerged as a respected member of the national journalistic community. The Charleston editor served on key editorial committees of both the ASNE and the Associated Press. ASNE colleagues asked him to serve as cochairman of the

Southern Education Reporting Service, an organization created to supply newspapers with impartial and objective news coverage of southern schools in the wake of the *Brown* decision. James Reston of the *New York Times,* perhaps the nation's best-known political reporter of the era, called Waring "the most talented newspaperman in South Carolina."[34]

Waring took steps to modernize the *News and Courier* and separate news reporting from editorial opinion. In one letter to the statehouse staff in 1951, he warned his political reporters to "stick to the facts" and keep their stories impartial. He was especially pointed in his criticism of Workman, his star correspondent. Since 1947, Workman had been given the freedom to write occasional analytical pieces under the byline "editorial correspondent," but Waring thought Workman was abusing this privilege. "Frankly, your copy has slipped," Waring wrote. The new editor chastised his lead reporter for writing too many soft pieces filled with his own opinion instead of "the hard-hitting, original stories from all over the state" that had made his reputation. Unlike Ball, Waring wanted the respect of his peers in the national press, and by the mid-1950s, that demanded at least superficial adherence to the professional norms of independence, impartiality, and objectivity.[35]

The Supreme Court's unanimous decision in the *Brown* case would test Waring's commitment to the new norms of professional journalism. The initial ruling in May 1954 had triggered a torrent of rhetoric from white southerners but a surprisingly timid political response, with little in the way of organized opposition. When the justices returned the following spring with their second *Brown* decision—the so-called Brown II ruling, which addressed the question of an integration timetable—white resistance movements had begun to emerge. The court's decision in Brown II had appeared to be a victory for the white South. The justices set no hard date by which integration had to occur, and the vague wording of their order—"with all deliberate speed"—appeared to give local school districts wide latitude to end school segregation at their own pace. By the summer of 1955, however, white segregationists were in no mood to be appeased.[36]

In South Carolina, a group of white citizens from around the state gathered in Columbia's Roosevelt Hotel on July 20, 1955, to plot their response. Workman and Waring had helped organize the meeting, working closely with two businessmen, Robert Davis of Columbia and Farley Smith of Lynchburg. Smith was the son of former U.S. Senator "Cotton" Ed Smith, the man who had famously walked out of the 1936 Democratic Convention in Philadelphia to protest the presence of a black minister who was invited to deliver the benediction. On the editorial page, the *News and Courier* described the committee as "a cross-section of the better-class moderate white people" who were the state's "leaders in law, clergy, farming, business, education and politics." The group eventually took its name from the number of those who participated. They called themselves the Committee of 52.[37]

During that first meeting, Workman was appointed to a steering committee that was assigned the job of writing a resolution that would be published statewide and delivered to the legislature. Workman wrote several drafts that were distributed to other steering committee members for edits and comments. The final version would come to be known as the "interposition" resolution, and it would serve as a concise summary of the arguments that would dominate southern white rhetoric during the coming years of "massive resistance." The document declared that a "clear and present danger" threatened the nation's constitutional form of government. It claimed the U.S. Supreme Court had trampled on the Tenth Amendment, which reserved to the states all rights not specifically delegated to the federal government. The justices had ignored established legal precedent, the resolution contended, and had based their *Brown* decision on the "dubious conclusions of sociologists and psychologists whose number includes persons tainted by communism." Workman's resolution also noted the shift in northern public opinion, which it blamed on the "pressure and propaganda" applied by the NAACP and other "self-serving organizations." Their efforts had sapped the will of politicians and the general public to "resist encroachments" upon the constitutional rights of the states.[38]

The Committee of 52 called on the South Carolina General Assembly to "maintain the sovereignty guaranteed to it by the constitution." To accomplish that, state lawmakers must "interpose the sovereignty of the State of South Carolina between Federal Courts and local school officials" to halt school integration. Workman would later take pride that he had proposed use of the legal strategy of "interposition" before Kilpatrick, the Richmond editor who made the concept famous during Virginia's battle over school integration. In an exchange of letters, Kilpatrick conceded the point, noting Workman was "in the field three months" before Kilpatrick began using the term publicly.[39]

On August 17, when the Committee of 52 published its resolution as an advertisement in white newspapers across the state, Workman's name appeared as one of the document's signatories. But his editor's name did not. Waring had attended the initial meeting and commented on drafts of the resolution. But he said that, as a professional journalist, he could not sign it. In a letter to one of the committee's organizers, Waring said he preferred to "leave the newspaper free to comment without ties of any kind." Waring said he had told organizers that he would attend the committee's meetings "as a newspaper editor," not as a participant. The *News and Courier* "will continue to hammer in its editorials at the matters treated by the resolution," Waring said, but will retain its independence and reserve the right to "suggest shadings, changes or different strategic approaches" if necessary.[40]

Waring copied Workman on his letter, and not long after, Workman changed his official status on the committee as well. In his letter to a committee organizer, Workman asked to be "relieved of his assignment" and removed from the group's steering committee. He said he based his request on "considerations which arise from my profession." Workman said he was "unwilling to be an active participant in an organization which engages in developments which I, as a newsman, must report." By the time Workman wrote his letter of resignation, the *News and Courier* had already published two news reports on the Committee of 52, one under his byline: W.D. Workman, Jr., Capital Correspondent. Workman's letter concluded by saying, "I do not consider it proper to be at once 'inside' an organization as a member and 'outside' as a reporter."[41]

As the decade wore on, Workman would frequently struggle with the contradiction between his verbal commitments to the standards of professionalized journalism and his deep desire to engage in the white resistance to the civil rights movement. As was the case with the Committee of 52, it appeared to be Waring who demanded *News and Courier* journalists follow the new professional standards, in word and appearance if not in deed.

The Committee of 52 published its resolution in newspapers across the state under the headline "Put Yourself on Record." Within a week, more than seven thousand readers had returned signed copies of the document, a show of support Waring's newspaper hailed as a major victory for the white resistance movement. "If enough of us stand with the 52 no South Carolina politician will ever weaken in the face of pressure from the NAACP," the *News and Courier* proclaimed. "Neither the Supreme Court nor any other body can jail us all, if we insist on retaining our constitutional rights." White newspapers around the state and region agreed. *The State* said "the fight to maintain segregation has stiffened" with the committee's emergence. The *Savannah Morning News* called the South Carolina group "non-political in its motives, non-partisan in make-up, and objective in its approach."[42]

The committee also received a ringing endorsement from the *Greenville News* and its new editor, Wayne W. Freeman. As a reporter for the *News* and its sister paper, the *Greenville Piedmont,* Freeman had competed against Workman at the state capital, and the two were considered the top political writers in the state. In 1955, after moving into the top newsroom job at the *News,* Freeman accepted an invitation from state lawmakers to join a committee that had been engaged in the fight against school integration. Governor

James F. Byrnes had formed the South Carolina School Committee in 1951, shortly after the NAACP filed suit in Clarendon County. Chaired by state Senator L. Marion Gressette, the so-called "Gressette Committee" included fifteen members, split between elected officials and prominent citizens. While remaining editor of the *News,* Gressette served as secretary of the Gressette Committee across the late 1950s and early 1960s. In 1963, Freeman and the committee would play important roles in the peaceful integration of higher education in South Carolina. But when Freeman joined in 1955, the committee's role was clear: map out a legal and political strategy to thwart the *Brown* decision. Rather than see the new Committee of 52 as a rival to his group, Freeman welcomed the new organization. On its editorial page, the *News* said the Committee of 52's resolution on interposition had "put into unmistakable words" the state's commitment to resist the *Brown* decision. The newspaper praised the quality of the men involved, pointing out that they had no ties to the Ku Klux Klan, and "they aren't even in the same category as the so-called citizens' councils, which are an unknown quantity."[43]

Yet the Committee of 52 would soon give way to the white citizens' councils as the primary organizer of white resistance in South Carolina, and Waring and his newspaper would expedite this transition. For the past year, Waring had been in close communication with Robert D. Patterson, a plantation manager near the Mississippi delta town of Indianola who had helped found the citizens' council movement. Patterson had been worried about the future of segregation well before the *Brown* ruling. A World War II veteran and former Mississippi State football star, Patterson said he was driven to act after reading a pamphlet written by fellow Mississippian Tom P. Brady, a Yale-educated lawyer from the small town of Brookhaven. Like Workman's Committee of 52 resolution, Brady's pamphlet ran the gamut of white southern legal arguments against the *Brown* ruling. But it also reached back to the 1948 Dixiecrat campaign to revive harsher rhetoric concerning "amalgamation," "mongrelization," and white subjugation to a "mulatto" race in the South.[44]

Brady expanded the pamphlet into a book, *Black Monday,* in late 1954, and its final chapter detailed several proposed white responses to *Brown.* Some were outlandish, such as the creation of a forty-ninth state as a homeland for all African Americans. But one of Brady's suggestions would gain traction across the South: the creation of "law-abiding" white resistance organizations in every southern state. These groups would be coordinated by a "National Federation of Sovereign States," which would orchestrate southern defiance of federal integration efforts. Brady believed the federation could take the lead in disseminating "correct information" about the "imminent danger" posed by the *Brown* ruling and the civil rights movement. The local organizations would be open and transparent, Brady said. They would be composed of the best people and would eschew violence and intimidation. These organizations would be nothing like "those nefarious Ku Klux Klans."[45]

Following Brady's advice, Patterson convened a group of leading white citizens in his small town and formed the Indianola Citizens' Council in July 1954. By the following summer, Patterson claimed more than sixty thousand Mississippians had joined 215 white citizens' councils across the state. As historian Neil McMillen has shown, the movement received a major boost from the Jackson newspapers, the *Clarion-Ledger* and *Jackson Daily News,* which served as propaganda arms for the citizens' councils. Brady's book and the newspapers in Jackson were part of a communications network that circulated ideas and tactics that could be used in resisting *Brown.* Considered part of the nation's mainstream culture just a few years earlier, these segregationists were now an out group battling the growing consensus in support of the *Brown* decision in national public opinion.[46]

In South Carolina, Waring's editorial page had been urging southern politicians to take the lead in organizing a response since the first *Brown* ruling. By the summer of 1955, the editor had grown frustrated with their inaction. He feared the Ku Klux Klan, with its "terrible" reputation, would step into the vacuum and do the "white South immeasurable" harm in terms of public perception. "The Klan can hurt the aims of those of us who intend to stand up for states' rights—to stand up for them in the daylight and without benefit of bed sheets or masks," the *News and Courier* said. Waring and Workman had both been reading Brady's *Black Monday* and following the rise of the citizens' councils in Mississippi. Brady's call for a resistance movement devoted to the "southern custom" of racial separation but opposed to the Klan appealed to the *News and Courier* journalists.[47]

Waring traveled to Mississippi in 1955 to meet with Patterson and other white citizens' council leaders, and he returned to South Carolina determined to launch the movement in his home state. On September 14, the *News and Courier* published a short editorial posing a question: How should the people of South Carolina respond to the Supreme Court's ruling on segregation? "The people, white and colored, look to their political leaders for guidance," the editorial declared. The next day, on the front page, Waring began answering that question. He launched a three-part series, datelined Jackson, Mississippi, that made the case for the white citizens' council movement as the proper outlet for white resistance to the black push for equality in the South. The councils were mobilizing "to guard both whites and Negroes," Waring argued. Their goal is to preserve segregation "from the assaults" of the NAACP and the federal government. Yet they are also "dedicated to protect the rank and file of Negroes from the wrath of ruffian white people who may resort to violence." By the end of 1955, Waring had become a leading evangelist and recruiter for the white citizens' council movement across the Deep South. Despite his public pronouncements in support of professionalized and independent journalism, he was becoming more engaged as a political organizer and activist.[48]

In South Carolina, a small-town attorney who had helped defend Clarendon County from the NAACP lawsuit on school segregation helped organize South Carolina's first group of citizens' councils. In the weeks after the second *Brown* ruling, the state NAACP had moved beyond the Clarendon case and had begun filing complaints challenging school segregation in other counties in the state. In response, S. Emory Rogers convened a meeting of white citizens in the Orangeburg County town of Elloree. In September, Rogers asked Farley Smith and several other members of the Committee of 52 to meet to discuss strategy. By October, the Committee of 52 had been subsumed into the larger Association of Citizens' Councils of South Carolina. Once again, Workman would cover a political story in which he was deeply engaged personally. In July 1956, the *News and Courier* correspondent reported that between twenty-five and forty thousand South Carolinians had joined local citizens' councils. As in Mississippi and the rest of the Deep South, the council movement was most active in the Black Belt region along the coastal plain in the eastern and southern portions of the state, where African American populations were largest and whites were most concerned about black political power.[49]

Waring used the *News and Courier* to polish the image of the white citizens' councils. Since its inception, the council movement had struggled to present its members as upstanding and peaceful. Yet the specter of the Klan always lingered nearby. In Alabama, for example, *Montgomery Advertiser* editor Grover Hall Jr. described the citizens' councils as nothing more than "manicured Kluxers." Waring tried to overcome these negative images by framing council members as "patriots" who represented the best in the American democratic tradition. They were "private citizens," not politicians, and they had stepped forward only because their political leaders had failed to do so. They were "pillars of the community"—the sort of folks who run "the chamber of commerce and the community chest" and handle all the "civil chores in any town worthy of the name." The council members had a single goal, Waring maintained. They wanted to protect their communities from an unconstitutional intrusion that threatened to destroy their civilized way of life. Waring said the citizens' councils were committed to peaceful resistance and "have no sympathy for the Ku Klux Klan" and "are in no sense architects of an American Fascist movement." The editor assured his readers that the councils were "firm supporters of the Republican and Jeffersonian Democracy."[50]

Yet the actions of the Klan and the citizens' councils often complicated the *News and Courier*'s effort to burnish the image of the state's segregationist movement. Under grand wizard Thomas Hamilton, Klan groups had been active in the state since 1947, and the *Brown* ruling triggered new violence. In Florence, for example, Klan members drew national attention when they attacked the young editor of the daily newspaper. The publisher of the moderately liberal *Morning News*, John G. O'Dowd, had hired his son Jack to replace outgoing editor James Rogers, who had left the paper in 1953 to take a job with an agricultural firm. A graduate of The Citadel who had fought in Korea and worked at newspapers in Texas, Jack O'Dowd was hardly a radical. He believed the U.S. Supreme Court was the law of the land, however, and when the *Brown* ruling came down, he urged the readers of the *Morning News* to accept it. "Segregation is ended in southern schools. This change is law if not fact," the *Morning News* declared the day after the *Brown* decision. "The Supreme Court has ruled that this system of school segregation is a violation of the constitution of these United States, and only a matter of months separates this decision from executed fact." The next day, O'Dowd emphasized that local opposition to *Brown*—no matter how widespread or emotional—would not alter the Court's decision. And the young editor concluded by actually praising the justices: "Since the court decided—without opposition—to end segregation, the court could just as well have included in its decision the date integration is to be completed." Perhaps naively, he believed white southerners should appreciate the court's restraint.[51]

After publishing those two editorials, Jack O'Dowd became a marked man in Florence. Hamilton's Klan group denounced him, and one night a group of men the editor believed were Klansmen chased him as he left the newspaper, forcing him to take refuge in a friend's apartment. Waring would denounce such violent acts, but the attacks on the *Morning News* were not only physical, and they did not come exclusively from the Klan. Local businesses with ties to the white citizens' council withheld advertising in an orchestrated boycott that lasted nearly two years. In a failed effort to appease the public, the *Morning News* announced in the spring of 1956 that it would no longer offer editorial comment on racial matters. When *Time* magazine reported on the paper's struggle and depicted Jack O'Dowd as a courageous voice for reason in his community, Waring's *News and Courier* struck back. An editorial ridiculed the *Morning News*' vow of silence on segregation as "a grandstand play" delivered with "choking voice," and it accused *Time* of trying to make a martyr out of a newspaper "that had allowed public opinion to stop it from saying what it thinks—a newspaper which was fighting for what it said it believed was right, then quit in the face of pressure."[52]

A month later, in June 1956, Jack O'Dowd left his father's newspaper. Facing threats of violence, and with the *Morning News* facing economic collapse, the publisher asked his son to resign. The young journalist left Florence and took a job with the *Chicago Sun-Times*. Before leaving, however, Jack O'Dowd wrote a final editorial headlined "Retreat from Reason." He claimed he had never supported forced integration in South Carolina, but he denounced the tactics of a prosegregationist movement that tried to shut down all debate. In the state's political rhetoric, O'Dowd said, denunciations of the Supreme Court and the NAACP had replaced "home, mother, God, and country."[53]

In Charleston, Waring's *News and Courier* reported the departure of the Florence editor in a short news story that was notable for what was left out. The three-paragraph item made no mention of the *Brown* decision, the Klan attacks, the economic boycott, or O'Dowd's parting-shot editorial. It simply said O'Dowd had "resigned to take a job in Chicago." To replace his son, *Morning News* publisher John G. O'Dowd persuaded James Rogers to return as editor, and Rogers put an end to the boycott by quickly proclaiming the paper's clear opposition to *Brown*. Segregation was not "an evil scheme" to deny the Negro his rights, Rogers wrote. Rather, it was a "high road" that would benefit both races "without tension or ill will."[54]

The campaign against the *Florence Morning News* after its *Brown* editorial illustrated how white resistance operated in 1950s South Carolina and throughout the South. The Klan and other extremist groups intimidated black and white supporters of integration through the use of force, while citizens' councils and so-called "respectable" groups relied on economic retribution. The white press often played a key role in the process. African Americans citizens who signed petitions demanding integrated schools would find their names published in the local newspaper. Thus identified as a "troublemaker," the black citizen would suddenly lose his job, or have his rent raised beyond his ability to pay, or simply be prohibited from purchasing products in local stores. Such tactics did not fit with Waring's framing of the council members as "Jeffersonian Democrats" who cherished American values of freedom and liberty.

In the summer of 1955, in the town of Elloree in the black-belt county of Orangeburg, black parents filed the first petition seeking integrated schools in South Carolina since the *Brown* ruling. A local newspaper published their names, and the economic retribution proved especially brutal. Tenant farmers in the rural area could no longer purchase seed, fertilizer, and other necessities required to grow and sell a crop. Given the thin safety net for the impoverished black communities in rural South Carolina, the boycott inflicted immediate damage. Families were going hungry. As Christmas approached, Modjeska Simkins decided to act. She organized fundraising through the Victory Savings Bank, the black-owned financial institution then run by her brother, Henry. The effort provided money for food and rent to the besieged black community in Orangeburg County.

Simkins also tried to the turn the tables on the local white citizens' council. Working through the state NAACP and local county organizations, she helped organize a black boycott of any business with connections to the citizens' councils in Orangeburg. The tactic helped blunt the councils' impact, she claimed, because "the almighty dollar is the almighty God of the power structure, so that's where you draw blood."[55]

Simkins's handling of the relief effort in Orangeburg put her at odds with the NAACP's national leadership. Angered by the deprivation she saw in the county, Simkins launched a campaign to raise money and supplies for the besieged families in Orangeburg. Prominent black journalist Simeon Booker embraced the campaign and persuaded *Jet* magazine, John H. Johnson's popular African American weekly, to run a small ad requesting help for the South Carolina families. The publicity attracted contributions from across the nation, but Simkins said the ad angered the NAACP's executive director, Roy Wilkins, who admonished her for allegedly violating the organization's guidelines on fundraising. The NAACP was not a relief agency, Simkins was told. When Wilkins demanded the money be returned, a furious Simkins charged the NAACP with hypocrisy. The national NAACP had encouraged black citizens to sign petitions demanding school integration, but "when the power structure stepped down on their necks" the civil rights group refused to help, she claimed. Simkins said she told Wilkins that NAACP leaders in New York "sit up there and drink your Bloody Marys and eat all your sirloin steaks . . . but we are down here under pressure." Although understandable, Simkins's charges were nonetheless overstated. Wilkins and the NAACP did face legal issues concerning fundraising appeals, and Simkins conceded that local officials made changes in their fundraising campaign to accommodate these concerns. However, the situation in Orangeburg County underscored a larger point concerning life in South Carolina in the aftermath of the *Brown* ruling: The white citizens' councils were extracting a high price from black citizens who dared to demand equal rights.[56]

In the *News and Courier,* Waring conceded that segregationists used "economic pressure," but he maintained these efforts were the work of individuals acting alone, not the citizens' council "acting as a group." To protect the image of the segregationist movement, Waring tried to separate the citizens' councils from such anticivil behavior. Workman used his position as a news reporter to support the citizens' council as well. He frequently reported on the growth of the councils and communicated with group leaders to discuss public relations strategy. At one point, he warned the organization to beware of Klansmen who were trying to "infiltrate" the councils to use them for their own "cowardly, secretive ends." One citizens' council leader assured Workman the groups were looking for only the "highest type of conservative leadership" for their local organizations.[57]

Strom Thurmond's Political Rebirth and the "Southern Manifesto"

Waring had embraced the citizens' council movement in part because he believed the state's political leadership had failed to develop an effective strategy for resisting the *Brown* ruling. By early 1956, a politician with close ties to the *News and Courier* would emerge and take a leading role in the fight. Strom Thurmond had returned to public life with a flourish in late 1954. The state's senior senator, Burnett Maybank of Charleston, died suddenly two months before that year's midterm elections. On September 3, just hours after Maybank's funeral, the state party's executive committee convened in Columbia and voted 31–18 to dispense with a primary election. Instead, the party leaders selected the longtime speaker of the state House of Representatives, Edgar Brown, to represent the Democrats on the November ballot. In a Deep South state like South Carolina, where the Republican Party posed no political threat, the November general election was little more than a formality. Securing the Democratic nomination was tantamount to winning the office. Though a powerful figure in the state legislature, Brown had never won a statewide campaign and had little popular support beyond his home district in tiny Barnwell County. His past efforts to win the Democratic Party's nomination for the U.S. Senate had failed badly. With their decision that September evening, the forty-nine members of the party's executive committee had bypassed the voters and essentially named Brown the state's next U.S. senator.

The night before the executive committee meeting, Waring was in his home at 10 Atlantic Street in the heart of Charleston's historic district when he got word of the plan to nominate Brown without a primary. The *News and Courier*'s editorial page had closed hours earlier and gone to the printer, but the editor decided to get the paper on the record opposing the party's action. He called the newsroom and dictated a short, front-page editorial that encouraged the party leaders to schedule a primary and allow voters to determine the nominee. When the executive committee ignored his plea, Waring returned to the front page the next day. The committee had treated South Carolina voters as if they were "unfit to govern themselves," the *News and Courier* declared. To overturn this injustice, the newspaper called for "an upsurge of resentment and an out-pouring of write-in ballots for some popular opponent." Three days later, the *News and Courier* ran another front-page editorial, this one headlined "People Not Yet Licked," that detailed a strategy for a write-in campaign. "To be effective," the editorial said, "[voters] will have to concentrate their votes on one man. We believe South Carolina can produce such a man."[58]

Strom Thurmond had been out of politics since losing the 1950 Senate race to former governor Olin Johnston. Seizing this opportunity for a comeback, Thurmond denounced the Brown candidacy as "backroom politics" and announced a write-in challenge. Waring had his candidate. In yet another front-page editorial, the *News and Courier* endorsed the former Dixiecrat presidential candidate under a headline that proclaimed: "Thurmond is the Man." The Charleston paper was hardly alone in its support, however. Thurmond's successful campaign benefited from the backing of newspapers across South Carolina. During the short campaign, Brown complained about the "Republican-minded press" in the state as he pleaded for Democratic voters to embrace "party loyalty." Yet it did no good. On Election Day, Thurmond crushed Brown, receiving more than 143,000 write-in votes, far surpassing the Democrat's total of 83,000.[59]

Waring called Thurmond's win "the People's Victory"—and he claimed the *News and Courier* deserved the credit. The newspaper's campaign against the Brown nomination had overturned an antidemocratic injustice in South Carolina, the editor declared. Waring was so pleased with the outcome—and so convinced that the newspaper's editorials had swayed public opinion—that he nominated the *News and Courier* for the Pulitzer Prize in the public service category. After consulting past and current Pulitzer judges, Waring concluded that the awarding of journalism's top prize is "governed in some measure by promotion and politics." And he threw himself into the effort. As 1954 wound down, Waring launched an energetic promotional campaign that included soliciting the help of friendly editors across the South. Waring urged his allies to write editorials crediting the *News and Courier* with "protecting the ballot" in South Carolina. Editors in Savannah, Birmingham, Memphis, and Richmond were happy to comply.[60]

Waring's promotional efforts hit a snag, however, when he approached the state's most popular politician for help. Outgoing Governor James F. Byrnes had played a decisive role in Thurmond's victory when he endorsed the write-in effort three weeks before the election. He certainly appreciated Waring's editorial campaign, but other newspaper editors had opposed the Brown nomination with equal fervor, and as a politician Byrnes did not want to take sides in this journalistic squabble. If he wrote a letter crediting the *News and Courier,* Byrnes told Waring, the editor of *The State,* Samuel Latimer, "might not like it."[61]

Waring got even worse news a few days later. He was tipped off that Latimer had submitted *The State*'s coverage for consideration by the Pulitzer judges as well. Waring was furious. *The State* and the *News and Courier* circulated statewide and they competed for readers and influence in South Carolina. Waring accused his competitor of trying to play the spoiler by splitting the southern votes on the Pulitzer Committee and preventing the *News and Courier* from winning the award. In the end, neither paper celebrated a Pulitzer for 1954, but the prize did go to a southern newspaper—the *Columbus Ledger* and *Sunday Ledger-Enquirer* in Georgia, for its investigation of organized crime in neighboring Phenix City, Alabama.[62]

Thurmond's write-in victory would reestablish the former governor as a leading player in South Carolina politics, and his relationship with Waring and Workman, which intensified during the unusual Senate campaign, would place the three at the center of the massive resistance effort in the state. In 1954, Thurmond had based his campaign on his opposition to the party's nomination of Brown without holding a primary election. To emphasize his commitment to the democratic process, Thurmond promised voters that if he won in 1954 he would resign his seat two years later and run again in 1956 rather than serve the full six-year Senate term. With a reelection campaign looming so soon after arriving in Washington, Thurmond was eager to grab national headlines. The massive resistance effort provided the perfect opportunity, just as the Dixiecrat campaign had back in 1948.[63]

In March 1956, Thurmond claimed primary authorship of the so-called Southern Manifesto, a document signed by 101 southern members of Congress. Officially called "The Declaration of Southern Principles," the final version stopped short of using the term "interposition," but it commended "the motives of those states which had declared their intention to resist integration by any lawful means." Like Workman's Committee of 52 resolution, the Southern Manifesto criticized "outside agitators" for destroying the "amicable" relations between the races in the South. In the *News and Courier,* Waring praised the document effusively. He said it was "high time" that southern members of Congress organized "to protect the rights of the states they represent from attack by the federal government." Their decision would benefit all southerners, "both white and colored," the *News and Courier* concluded.[64]

As southern congressmen delivered their manifesto in Washington, state lawmakers met in Columbia, and the two groups seemed to be competing to present the strongest pro-segregation message. As the *News and Courier*'s statehouse reporter, Workman covered the 1956 South Carolina General Assembly. It was the same body that he had petitioned as author of the "interposition" resolution for the Committee of 52, and the state's lawmakers did not disappoint him. In what Workman dubbed "the segregation session," the General Assembly passed a resolution approving of the doctrine of interposition and vowing to fight federal efforts to enforce school integration. The lawmakers passed another resolution commending the work of the white citizens' councils in South Carolina, and they ordered the closing of Edisto State Park, a facility that the NAACP had gone to court to integrate.[65]

More substantively, the South Carolina lawmakers joined other southern states in launching an effort to criminalize the NAACP. The General Assembly passed a bill that would make it illegal for city, county, and state employees in South Carolina to join the civil rights organization. Even some conservative white newspapers believed the measure was unconstitutional. The *Columbia Record* called the new law "ill-advised," but contended the "litigious NAACP" had created the racial animosity in the South. Governor George Bell Timmerman Jr., signed the bill into law March 17.[66]

John McCray denounced these measures in the *Afro-American,* and he tried to rally the Progressive Democratic Party to fight back. McCray disseminated a flyer that included his open letter to Timmerman on behalf of the PDP. He accused the lawmakers of plotting "a course of self-destruction, chaos and rebellion" against the nation's democratic principles, and he compared their actions to the work of "Fascist Italy, storm-trooping Germany" and the "Communists." The anti-NAACP bill, he said, was an act of "punishment and persecution" against those who had been employing legal means to fight for their rights "in keeping with the American way." Appealing to the nation's founding ideals, he depicted the white crackdown on the black civil rights organization as an uncivil and antidemocratic effort to shut down free speech and free association.[67]

The law criminalizing the civil rights organization for public employees had given segregationists a powerful weapon in their effort to curb black political activism. Public school teachers were the backbone of the small but growing black middle class in the Deep South in the mid-1950s. Their organizational skills, as well as their dues, had been instrumental in the growth of the NAACP. Although the law was certain to be overturned in the courts, the appeals would take time. And until then, white leaders could use the measure to harass and intimidate the black community. Across South Carolina, local school boards immediately added a page to their annual review and job application forms asking teachers to list organizational affiliations.[68]

In Charleston, the board of education targeted Septima Clark, one of the black community's foremost political activists. Clark had been active in the NAACP since World War I, when she began teaching on Johns Island in Charleston County. By 1956, she was a veteran organizer who was coordinating efforts with regional and national civil rights organizations. She had led workshops at the Highlander Folk School, an institution founded in east Tennessee to train southern labor activists during the New Deal. It was now helping prepare southern blacks to organize civil rights efforts in their communities. In 1954, Clark had helped lead a workshop at Highlander that included a woman from Alabama named Rosa Parks, who would return to her home in Montgomery and play a leading role in the 1955 bus boycott.[69]

In June 1956, Clark and four other Charleston County teachers received letters from the school board announcing their contracts would not be renewed the following year. The school board gave no explanation for its decision, but Clark said she had been "completely outspoken" on civil rights in the past year, and she believed that had prompted her termination. Clark had hoped to fight the school board's decision, but she found only marginal support from a black community skittish in the face of the white crackdown. She sought to unite black teachers behind their dismissed colleagues, figuring the Charleston County school board could not afford to fire all of them at once. Clark sent more than seven hundred letters to her colleagues asking them to protest the anti-NAACP law and the local firings. Only twenty-six responded. Eleven of those agreed to meet with school officials, but only five actually showed up. Clark would call the effort "one of the failures of my life" because she realized she had "tried to push them into something they were not ready for." The fear of economic retribution from the white community had grown too strong.[70]

As 1956 came to a close, Waring and Workman had reason to be pleased. They had used their dual roles as journalists and political activists to help shape the white response to the *Brown* decisions and the rising push for African American rights in South Carolina. The two had helped craft an "interposition" doctrine that had been embraced as policy by state lawmakers, and they had midwifed the birth of a robust and politically active white citizens' council movement. Through the pages of the *News and Courier*, they had framed the white response as a civil and appropriate rebuke to an unconstitutional federal intrusion into state sovereignty. By trying to force integration in the South, the newspaper repeatedly claimed, the federal government had ignored the will of both races in the region and assumed the role of dictator. Taking advantage of rising fears of Soviet aggression, Waring employed cold war rhetoric to depict opponents of segregation as socialists and communists out to undermine American democracy. The NAACP was "a pawn of the Soviets," Waring claimed. And the effort to end segregation in the South was an attempt "by the Communist Party" to create unrest and generate "anti-U.S. propaganda."[71]

Modjeska Simkins would bear the brunt of this red-scare rhetoric in South Carolina. In 1954, during his successful race for governor, George Timmerman Jr. delivered an entire speech devoted to demonizing the NAACP, the *Lighthouse and Informer,* and "Mrs. Andrew W. Simkins" and her alleged Communist Party ties. Timmerman charged that Simkins's involvement with the Southern Negro Youth Congress and her support for Benjamin J. Davis Jr., a New York City council member who had been jailed because of his Communist Party ties, proved that she was "subversive and communistic."[72]

At the height of the red-baiting campaign against her, Simkins would suffer another acrimonious split with one of her former allies. The state conference of NAACP branches failed to nominate Simkins to a leadership position at the 1957 convention, ending her seventeen-year run as the organization's executive secretary. She accused Rev. James Hinton, the group's president, of working quietly behind the scenes to engineer her ouster, and she would hold a grudge against him for the rest of her life. Simkins accused Hinton of losing his nerve when confronted with the white backlash after the *Brown* ruling. It was true that the state conference of branches failed to hold its annual meeting in 1956, despite the rise of massive resistance in the state. But Hinton's record of civil rights work in South Carolina had otherwise been exemplary. And he had put his life on the line for the cause. In 1949, Hinton had been kidnapped at gunpoint, taken to nearby woods, and threatened with lynching. For some reason, one of the assailants said, "This is the wrong nigger," and Hinton was released unharmed. Seven years later, Hinton's Columbia home had been hit by gunfire. Yet in her attacks, Simkins questioned Hinton's bravery and morality. She accused him of selling out the movement in return for some sort of mysterious and undefined preferential legal treatment for his son. In her words, Hinton had come under pressure "from some element in the power structure that caused him to . . . not push the program he had." In 1958, Hinton formally resigned from his NAACP leadership post.[73]

With McCray, Simkins, and Hinton sidelined, the civil rights movement that had grown so quickly in the 1940s began to falter. The loss of the *Lighthouse and Informer* had denied the movement a powerful communications tool at a decisive moment in the battle with segregationists. The aggressiveness of the white citizens' councils, the continuing presence of the Klan and other extremists, and the signing of the anti-NAACP law combined to intimidate blacks and spread new fear throughout the state. McCray used his limited space in the *Afro-American* as best he could, but with no weekly newspaper dedicated to the task of carrying the movement's interpretation of local events deep into South Carolina's black community, the sense of unity began to fade. The number of active NAACP branches shrank dramatically, falling from eighty-six in the early 1950s to thirty-one by 1957. The overwhelming commitment that had empowered African Americans to defeat the all-white primary and challenge segregation in Clarendon County had begun to dissipate.[74]

Waring and Workman, on the other hand, had used their positions as journalists at a prominent, mainstream newspaper to help shape the politics of South Carolina. While proclaiming their independence and objectivity, they had worked closely with white political leaders to plot and implement the state's response to the *Brown* ruling. Their efforts to emphasize their journalistic independence had been clumsy at times. Anyone watching closely could have seen Workman's name on the Committee of 52 newspaper ads. And it was clear that Waring and Workman had more than a journalistic interest in the growing citizens' council movement in South Carolina. They nonetheless professed their commitment to the new ideals of professional journalism.

If Waring, Workman, and South Carolina's segregationist leaders had reason to cheer in the aftermath of the *Brown* decision, the celebration would be brief. They had helped slow the momentum of the civil rights effort in their home state, but new movements and new battles would emerge elsewhere—in Alabama, Mississippi, Arkansas, and across the South. The national spotlight would grow brighter, and the two South Carolina journalists would find it more difficult to frame the debate over the struggle for African American equality. Eventually, Waring and Workman would turn to partisan politics and begin to build a new political home for southern segregationists. They would continue to espouse the ideals of modern, professionalized journalism, even as they worked tirelessly behind the scenes as political advocates.

7 The Paper Curtain and the New GOP

In the summer of 1958, Charleston *News and Courier* editor Thomas R. Waring Jr. was angry. The white citizens' council movement he had helped launch in South Carolina had lost momentum. Hindered by weak leadership and internal squabbling, the white councils were "taking a siesta" when they should be girding for the battle to come, Waring complained. South Carolina needed a "vigorous" citizens' council movement, he contended, because "it is clear that trouble won't stay away from our door forever." As evidence, he pointed toward the upper South, where states appeared to be backing away from the interposition strategy they had vowed to use to defend segregation of public schools. Even in Virginia, home to interposition's strongest proponents—U.S. Sen. Harry Byrd and Richmond editor James J. Kilpatrick—school officials discussed the merits of accepting "token" integration. For Waring, these were the words of "faint-hearted southerners" who were "suffering from frustration and defeatism." In Columbia, *The State* newspaper agreed. Token integration is still integration, Samuel Latimer's editorial page argued. "When the blows begin to fall" in the southern "core" states of Mississippi, Georgia, Alabama, and South Carolina, leaders must "steadfastly resist the region's ruination by federal force." To accept any breach in racial separation was an act of surrender that would destroy the southern way of life.[1]

Waring's plea for southern unity and stepped-up citizens' council activity came at a precarious time for the segregationists. The nation's political landscape was shifting, and not in the white South's favor. In the fall of 1957, Waring had watched in horror as President Eisenhower sent the 101st Airborne to Arkansas to protect nine African American students who were integrating Little Rock's Central High School. Even before the showdown in Little Rock,

Waring had described the president as "not the man we hoped he would be." In the 1952 presidential election, white conservatives in the South—led by South Carolina Gov. James F. Byrnes—had turned to Eisenhower as a possible political savior. Under his leadership, they hoped the Republican Party would reject its northern liberal wing and embrace states' rights and local control over race relations in the South. That hope faded in 1954 when Eisenhower refused to denounce the *Brown* ruling, and it expired entirely during the president's second term. Not only had Eisenhower deployed federal troops to enforce *Brown,* his administration had proposed ambitious civil rights legislation designed to protect African American voters in the South. In the eyes of Waring and other white southerners, the Republican Party under Eisenhower had turned out to be no different than the national Democrats. Both had abandoned the white South in favor of the growing number of African American voters and their white liberal supporters in the North.[2]

Eisenhower's civil rights bill, drafted in 1956 by Attorney General Herbert Brownell and introduced in Congress the following year, was especially troubling for Waring and his allies in South Carolina. The measure focused on African American voting rights and threatened to further undermine white control of the Democratic Party. Brownell's bill called for the creation of a civil rights division within the Justice Department and an expansion of the agency's power to prosecute voting rights violations. Eisenhower would later say that he focused on voting rights because the ballot was the tool "the American Negro could use to safeguard his other rights." Waring's *News and Courier* saw the administration's civil rights push as another means of "chasing the Negro bloc vote in the North" at the expense of white southerners.[3]

When President Truman had proposed civil rights legislation a decade earlier, the South's powerful Senate delegation had blocked the measure in committee and used the threat of filibuster to kill it. When confronted with Eisenhower's bill, the southern senators pursued a surprising new strategy. Led by Senator Richard Russell of Georgia, the southerners negotiated with the White House and allowed a watered-down version of the voting rights measure to pass. The final bill had been stripped of its most potent enforcement mechanisms, but it still represented a major milestone in the nation's history. Eisenhower's voting rights bill was the first piece of civil rights legislation passed by Congress since Reconstruction. As historian Keith Findley has noted, Russell and his colleagues relented because of growing national support for the civil rights movement. Like Byrnes, who had tried to soften the South's national image with his school equalization plan earlier in the decade, Russell was a cagey politician who had been at the center of the nation's political life since the early 1930s. He feared blatant southern obstructionism would accelerate the shift in northern political opinion and force even greater change in race relations in the South. Additionally, Russell hoped passage of the 1957 civil rights bill—even a weakened version—would help Senate Majority Leader Lyndon Johnson of Texas eventually reach the White House. No southerner could win the Democratic presidential nomination without the support of the party's northern liberals. Russell maintained that Johnson's success in guiding the civil rights bill through the Senate would enhance his image in the North and clear the way for a 1960 presidential bid. Accepting a weak civil rights bill now, Russell argued, would help the South in the long run by placing a southerner in the White House. Russell's strategy took it as a given that Johnson, as a southerner, would slow the push for African American civil rights in the South, not speed it up.[4]

Under Brownell's initial proposal, federal judges would adjudicate charges of voting rights violations in the South. Russell and the southern delegation demanded that suspected violators be allowed to request jury trials, because it was unlikely that the mostly white juries in the South would ever convict in such cases. When the White House agreed, Russell persuaded his southern colleagues not to filibuster the measure and to allow it to pass. Waring loathed this compromise. He considered it a sell-out of the South and a power grab by a federal government eager to encroach on states' rights. Waring compared the measure to the Enforcement Act of 1870, a piece of legislation passed by the Republican Congress during Reconstruction. The so-called "Force Act" gave the president the legal power to enforce the Fifteenth Amendment, which granted African Americans the right to vote. The News and Courier dubbed Brownell's proposed legislation the "Force Bill" and used the term throughout the newspaper, even in the headlines on its news pages. "Passage of Force Bill Urged by Eisenhower" declared the newspaper's front page as the bill moved through Congress. In Waring's view, accepting even a diminished version of the measure would concede to the federal government the power to manage race relations in the South.[5]

The News and Courier was thrilled when the newspaper's friend and ally, Strom Thurmond, defied Russell and broke ranks with his fellow southerners. In a futile effort to derail the bill, Thurmond launched a one-man filibuster that began the evening of August 28. The senator spoke nonstop for twenty-four hours and eighteen minutes, a marathon performance that set a new record for uninterrupted speech on the Senate floor. Thurmond's grand gesture had no impact on the bill's final disposition, but it solidified his reputation as a lone wolf who was more than happy to alienate his Democratic colleagues in the Senate. The day after Thurmond's historic speech, the News and Courier headline read: "South's Senators Desert Thurmond." In a front-page editorial, Waring's newspaper acknowledged that Thurmond had lost the battle but said the southern segregationists would eventually win their war. "Custer's Last Stand is one of the great American stories," the editorial said. "Custer lost the battle with the Indians. He lost his own life. But his name is not forgotten. The Indians finally were defeated."[6]

Eisenhower was a man of conservative temperament who had been born in the South and had always said he wanted to move slowly on civil rights. He had personally expressed his opposition to school integration, and even after the *Brown* ruling the Republican president had told Byrnes that he believed segregation would remain in force for many decades to come in the South. But Eisenhower faced increasing political pressure to act. The black public sphere that W.E.B. Du Bois and the NAACP had helped build at the turn of twentieth century had grown dramatically during World War II. In the postwar years, circulation of the black press boomed; the leading outlets—the *Pittsburgh Courier,* the *Chicago Defender,* the magazines *Ebony* and *Jet*—developed a national audience. Their rising profile prodded white editors to pay more attention to the African American community. It was a *Pittsburgh Courier* sportswriter, for example, who in 1947 helped persuade Branch Rickey and the Brooklyn Dodgers to allow Jackie Robinson to break the color barrier and integrate major league baseball. Robinson's stoic resolve in the face of racial taunts and humiliating treatment by white fans—and some white teammates—served to enhance the growing white liberal support for black civil rights. By the mid-1950s, the northern white media had discovered the civil rights story, and their depictions of southern violence and intransigence helped fuel public outrage. It was a problem Waring had seen coming and had tried hard to prevent.[7]

Piercing the Paper Curtain

Brownell's civil rights proposal had been motivated in part by northern reaction to the 1955 murder of Emmett Louis Till, a Chicago teenager visiting relatives in Mississippi. Till was hardly the first black teen to be lynched in the South. By the summer of 1955, however, the definition of what constituted national news had shifted, and the white media took notice of the events playing out in the Mississippi Delta. For the first time in the twentieth century, the mainstream northern press focused intently on a white act of violence against an African American in the South. Highlighted first by the black press—the *Chicago Defender* covered its front page with stories in the weeks after the murder—Till's abduction and killing eventually drew waves of reporters to the Deep South. As Gene Roberts and Hank Klibanoff have pointed out, public reaction to the coverage was just as Gunnar Myrdal had predicted in *The American Dilemma,* his massive study of the race issue in the United States. Northerners were appalled by the searing images emerging from the drama: the teenager's mutilated body, the arrogant sneers of his killers, the quick and perfunctory verdicts delivered by the all-white jury. In September 1955, the Till case cast into stark relief the gap that existed between the nation's image of itself as a fair and just democracy and the harsh reality of African American life in the South.[8]

In Charleston, the *News and Courier* had run Associated Press stories on the "Mississippi murder" on its front page for seven days running in September 1955. The main headline grew significantly larger and more prominent the morning after the white woman at the heart of the case testified in court. Carolyn Bryant claimed that Till had whistled at her suggestively, grabbed her hand, and "asked her for a date" during an encounter at a small market in Money, Mississippi. In an interview conducted six decades after the incident, Bryant retracted her story, telling historian Timothy B. Tyson that her initial version of what happened in the store was "not true." But the damage had already been done. Three days after Bryant had leveled her accusations against Till, her husband and his half-brother abducted the teenager from his great-uncle's house. The teenager's disfigured and bloated body was later found floating on the surface of the Tallahatchie River.[9]

On the *News and Courier'*s editorial page, Waring called Till's death a "tragedy" and said his killers should be punished, but he quickly moved to his primary argument in the editorial. The murder had provided "race agitators" with "welcome propaganda," but he contended the NAACP was partly responsible for the teenager's death. "Had it not been for the constant dinning in the ears of colored people about denial of their 'rights,'" the editor claimed, "the boy might never have made a remark that caused animosity in the rural community where he was visiting." Waring urged "all decent people" to condemn the violence, but also to "sympathize with the good people of Mississippi" who will be unfairly blamed for it. Waring concluded with a thinly veiled threat for those pushing court-ordered integration in the South: "The death of this boy should remind all who tamper lightly with deep mass emotions that voluntary, friendly approaches are the only way the races can live together in peace."[10]

The jury in tiny Sumner, Mississippi, deliberated sixty-seven minutes before acquitting Carolyn Bryant's husband and his half-brother of Till's murder. The swift verdict helped fuel public anger in the press, both in the North and around the world. Henry Luce's *Life* magazine claimed white southerners who refused to condemn the verdict "were in danger of losing their souls." The Vatican newspaper, *L'Osservatore Romano,* declared that "a crime against an adolescent victim remained unpunished" and thus the jury's decision had left a "stain" on the United States. The *New York Post* said images from the Till case, as well as other "fragments of the southern tragedy," should move the White House to act: "How much more must happen to awaken the humanity and conscience of the president?" Waring dismissed the editorial in the liberal New York tabloid as another example of a "biased" northern press that assumed all white southerners were "bigots."[11]

The *News and Courier* editor had been fighting a public relations battle with the northern media since he took over as the paper's editor in 1951. In the months after the *Brown* ruling, Waring had struggled through three revisions of an essay for *Harper's* magazine before the manuscript was finally published in January 1956. Editor John Fischer had said he wanted to publish a prosegregationist statement that could serve as "a starting point for rational discussion." What he got was a manuscript that "troubled" his conscience. Waring's essay depicted African Americans as immoral, unhealthy, prone to violence, and intellectually inferior. White southerners were decent people who were trying to help African Americans overcome these problems, Waring said. Yet white northerners rarely heard that side of the story because the northern press "has abandoned fair and objective reporting of the race story." In Waring's view, northern editors "almost without exception" have embraced the NAACP interpretation of events in the South and thus have replaced facts with "propaganda."[12]

Waring's experience with *Harper's* appeared to crystalize his thoughts on the media and the role that northern public opinion was playing in the battle over civil rights in the South. At the same time that he was exchanging revisions and caustic letters with the *Harper's* editor, Waring wrote a piece for *The Masthead,* the journal of the National Conference of Editorial Writers. His lead sentence was short and simple: "A paper curtain shuts out the Southern side of the race relations story from the rest of the country." Northern newspapers and magazines have abandoned objective reporting, Waring wrote, and "the deluge of daily and weekly gazettes with anti-Southern slant is molding public opinion." Not since *Uncle Tom's Cabin* has there been "so powerful a blast of propaganda as to becloud the issues with emotion." The states that comprised the old Confederacy must confront this new public relations problem, the editor maintained, because in this battle between North and South "there will be no secession." Instead, public opinion will determine the outcome.[13]

Waring turned his "paper curtain" accusation into a battle cry as he launched a campaign to present the segregationist view in the national media. Biased northern editors claimed to be objective journalists who simply reported the facts, Waring said, but instead they slanted the news to fit their liberal worldview. The liberal slant applied to their editorial pages as well, he claimed. Northern editors frequently published the opinions of liberal southerners and excluded more conservative voices, he said. Waring was particularly angered by the attention paid to Ralph McGill of the *Atlanta Constitution*, Pete McKnight of the *Charlotte Observer*, and Hodding Carter Jr. of Mississippi's *Delta Democrat Times*. Northern editors favored these journalists because they were critics of the South, not defenders, he argued.

In the summer of 1955, Waring reached out to fellow segregationist editors and suggested they send reporters into the North to "expose" the "hypocrisy" of the northern press. Waring claimed northern editors focused on racial problems in the South while ignoring the issue in their own communities. If more African Americans lived in the North, he said, white northerners would understand that "where large numbers of both races are put together, violence is the rule, not the exception." When it came to race, white northerners were no different than white southerners, Waring maintained. Neither group supported forced integration in schools and neighborhoods. It was hypocritical for northern publishers—*Time*'s Henry Luce, for example—to call for school integration and social equality when so few African Americans lived in their neighborhoods. "It is time the North assumed its share of the white man's burden and welcomed Negroes in their communities," he said.[14]

The following year, Waring unveiled a secret weapon in his battle against the "paper curtain." A new byline appeared in the *News and Courier*—Nicholas Stanford—and this columnist pulled no punches. In crisp, well-written prose, Stanford delivered searing jeremiads attacking the "liberal" northern press and its "anti-South bias." Moreover, Stanford's copy revealed a sophisticated knowledge of the media industry and its inner workings.

In his first column, Stanford took on one of Luce's publications, *Life* magazine. In September 1956, *Life* had launched an ambitious five-part series called "The Background of Segregation." The project featured some of the magazine's best-known talent, including photographers Margaret Bourke-White and Gordon Parks. The two spent weeks embedded with families in the Deep South—Bourke-White in South Carolina, Parks in Alabama—and they delivered a series of powerful and award-winning images documenting the everyday life of racial segregation in the region. Stanford was unimpressed. He claimed the first installment in the series made it clear that "mere accuracy will not be allowed to stand in the way of 'colorful reporting,' as they say in the trade." He took particular umbrage at *Life*'s treatment of John Brown, the radical abolitionist who had launched an unsuccessful raid on a federal arsenal in 1859. In Stanford's view, *Life* depicted Brown as a misguided patriot who was dedicated to the eradication of the sin of slavery. In reality, Stanford argued, Brown sought control of the arsenal to "establish a Negro state in the Appalachians" and foment deadly slave rebellions across the South. Among its many other sins, Stanford said *Life's* series was illustrated by a piece of art—"An Old Slave Auction in Charleston"—that left the "bizarre impression" that the South had been settled by "Russians with thick lips, flat noses, and Mongolian fold about the eyes."[15]

Life had not always been so biased, Stanford concluded, but the magazine had begun to slant its coverage in response to pressure from the NAACP and its liberal supporters, an alliance he described as an "unofficial censorship whose power is not even suspected by most Americans." In arguing this point, Stanford laced his prose with references to the black sociologist Franz Boas, the NAACP magazine *The Crisis,* the group's current executive secretary, Roy Wilkins, and a controversy concerning one of *Life's* first stories when the magazine launched in 1936—a negative take on Brazil and its racial "melting pot." Since the critical backlash over the Brazil piece, Stanford maintained, *Life* has "pretty much toed the line on the race question."[16]

Thrilled by the response from readers, Waring encouraged Stanford to send more pieces, and the writer responded with about a dozen columns that ran sporadically in the *News and Courier* between 1956 and 1958. The pieces skewered a wide range of northern media outlets but they usually concluded with the same arguments. Northern editors were hypocrites who criticized the treatment of African Americans in the South but ignored racial conflict in their own communities. They were "muzzled by advertisers" and deathly afraid of offending the "powerful" NAACP and its liberal allies. Fueling this bias were communist sympathizers who had infiltrated northern newsrooms and were shaping the news to benefit the party and its Soviet master.

News and Courier subscribers had been reading similar complaints from Waring for the past year. But Nicholas Stanford claimed a higher level of authority on the issue of northern media bias. Unlike his editor in Charleston, Stanford said he had first-hand knowledge of the anti-South bigotry that pervaded northern newsrooms. That's because he worked in one of them. Nicholas Stanford was actually a pseudonym that he and Waring had concocted to hide the identity of John G. Briggs Jr., the classical music and opera critic for the *New York Times.*

During the 1950s, Briggs's byline appeared regularly in the *Times,* and his literate profiles and witty reviews enlivened the pages of the "old gray lady." A former child prodigy himself, Briggs wrote knowingly about a cultural world that he clearly loved. At the same time, his alter-ego appeared in the Charleston newspaper, delivering a very different style of journalism:

fire-breathing, race-baiting, and occasionally anti-Semitic screeds that were sometimes aimed at his own employer.[17]

The story of John Briggs and his secret work for the Charleston *News and Courier* is more than a historical footnote. It contributes new details to an important inquiry: the effort to trace the origins of the so-called "liberal media" charge that has grown so prominent in political discourse over the past four decades. Historian Nicole Hemmer cites New Deal opponents who took to the media in the 1940s as the originators of the liberal-media claim. Operating in the political wilderness, activists such as Clarence Manion, Henry Regnery, and William Rusher used radio, newsletters, small magazines, and book publishing to deliver their assault on the mainstream media. Historian David Greenberg emphasizes the importance of southern segregationists in helping popularize the "liberal-media" claim in the late 1950s and early '60s during their campaign to undermine northern reporters covering the civil rights movement in the South. Waring's "paper curtain" argument in 1955 bridges those two time periods, and his enlistment of the *New York Times* music critic in the cause reveals an interesting historical twist that is just now coming to light. It turns out that some of the fiercest southern criticism of the "liberal" northern press emanated from the newsroom of the North's most prominent newspaper.[18]

Born and raised in High Point, North Carolina, Briggs graduated from the Curtis Institute of Music in Philadelphia, where he trained as an opera singer. When he moved to New York in 1937, Briggs abandoned plans for a career on the stage and turned instead to journalism and public relations. He started as music editor at NBC, then spent two years as a press agent for the Italian conductor Arturo Toscanini. In 1940, he joined the *New York Post* as music critic. He left the tabloid in 1949 to edit a start-up music magazine, *Etude.* After it folded in 1952, Briggs moved on the *Times,* where he served as opera critic and music writer until 1960. He would also write four books about classical music, including *Requiem for a Yellow Brick Brewery,* a history of the Metropolitan Opera.

Briggs first contacted Waring in the summer of 1955. He told the editor he had picked up a *News and Courier* at a New York newsstand on his way to work one day. After reading the editorial page, he said he realized he had found a kindred spirit. As a supporter of segregation, Briggs detested the Supreme Court's 1954 ruling in *Brown v. Board of Education.* But he also shared Waring's virulent anticommunist views as well. And he agreed with the editor's frequent complaints about liberal, left-wing slant in the northern press. At the time, Briggs was secretly working with a group called AWARE that was urging Congress to investigate communist infiltration in the news and entertainment media. In June 1955, he wrote Waring to complain about news slant in the *Times* and other New York newspapers, and he urged the editor to publish his letter in the *News and Courier*—but without using his name. If he signed the letter, Briggs said, he would be committing "professional suicide." Waring readily agreed.

In his anonymous letter, Briggs declared that "every newspaper and magazine article concerning Southern affairs that emanates from New York is loaded with bias." The journalists' union—the Newspaper Guild—openly supports the NAACP, and northern publishers cower before the civil rights organization because they fear a boycott. This left the South without a voice in the national discussion over race, he wrote. "Talk about Dr. Goebbels and his 'thought control,'" Briggs wrote. "The so-called 'liberals' could give lessons to Dr. Goebbels." Briggs emphasized his status as a working member of the northern press, saying, "one must be on the scene to fully appreciate what is going on." The letter's author was identified simply as "Newspaper Man." Waring weighed in with a nearby editorial that denounced the "national brain-washing" carried out by the media, and he encouraged other journalists "who see through the bias and the slanting of news" to come forward as well.[19]

Briggs's accusations stirred debate among industry insiders. In a letter to Waring, the executive editor of the *Washington Post,* James Russell Wiggins, questioned the basic premise of the "paper curtain" argument. "If there is one thing more than any other that has struck me about this whole crisis, it is the wide variation of opinion, north and south, and the tendency of views to vary in all parts of the country," Wiggins wrote. He also criticized Briggs's call for congressional investigation into media bias. If the "people's right to know is menaced by the bias or inadequacy of a newspaper, under our system the remedy must lie with the people themselves and not with government nor self-constituted professional groups acting instead of or for government." When Waring shared the letter with Briggs, the *Times* journalist dismissed it as "about what one might expect from [owner] Eugene Meyer's leftist, New Dealish *Washington Post.*"[20]

Over the next four years, Waring and Briggs corresponded frequently and often plotted new ways to try to pierce the "paper curtain." In early 1956, for example, Briggs encouraged Waring to complain to the Associated Press about lack of wire service coverage concerning racial conflicts in the North and Midwest. Four years later, Waring would lead a coordinated effort by southern segregationist editors to browbeat AP staff into providing such coverage. Their demands grew so frequent and disruptive that the AP president finally pleaded with Waring to back down. The editor agreed—he always wanted to maintain his good standing in the journalistic community—but he continued his campaign to shred the "paper curtain."[21]

In the war with the northern press, Briggs also served as Waring's chief spy behind enemy lines. By remaining "incognito," Briggs told Waring that he could move around the *Times* newsroom and "observe what's going on" without drawing suspicion. And as their relationship grew, the Charleston editor began to pump Briggs for information about *Times* coverage. When word got out in early 1956 that the New York newspaper was launching a month-long investigation of race relations across the South, Waring urged Briggs to investigate. Briggs replied with a few details: Led by the newspaper's longtime southern correspondent John W. Popham, the project known as "Operation Dixie" would involve in-depth reporting on race relations and the fight over school desegregation in every state in the South. Briggs called it a "typical *Times* push" in which the newspaper would deploy "money or manpower" to try to overwhelm potential critics through the "sheer massiveness" of its coverage. Later, as the project neared publication, Briggs shared some newsroom gossip about fights between reporters and their editors concerning the story of Autherine Lucy, the young African American woman who had been denied admission to the University of Alabama. In Briggs's account, the editors had deleted reporting that had been critical of Lucy's NAACP attorneys. "By the time a piece of copy goes through the process," Briggs wrote to Waring, "it may be taken for granted that there is no deviation from the official line."[22]

Gradually, as their correspondence increased and their conversations grew more casual, Briggs exhibited an even darker side to his politics. He denounced the liberal columnist Murray Kempton as "the great nigger lover." He described the residents of West Harlem as "vermin." And he aimed a steady stream of vitriol at Jews, particular those who worked in the media. "If a clean sweep could be made of Jews in the New York press, radio-TV, magazines and wire services, it would eliminate about 90 percent of the Communist fifth-column threat so far as the dissemination of ideas is concerned," Briggs wrote. The notion is "repugnant and not in accord with our ideas of free speech and freedom of the press," he conceded, but he wondered what alternative loyal Americans had, "aside from that of being elbowed aside in garment-district style."[23]

Briggs's harsh denunciation of the Jews came at a sensitive time for Waring. The editor had developed a warm relationship with Bernard Baruch, the Jewish financier who had been an adviser to Democratic presidents going back to Woodrow Wilson. Born in Camden, South Carolina, Baruch maintained a home along the coast north of Charleston. Waring and Baruch traded letters frequently in the mid-1950s, and the editor and his wife attended social events and private dinners at Baruch's Hobcaw Barony estate. Yet despite his growing friendship with the elder statesman, the editor expressed some sympathy with Briggs's view. Waring said that he was "not as stirred up as you are" about the Jews, perhaps because "there are fewer of them" in Charleston and "you are snowed under by them." He agreed that Jewish influence in the media could be a problem, but he urged Briggs to remain focused on the more "immediate" question of race. "Maybe you think we're too squeamish on the Jewish issue," Waring wrote, "but I believe it is a good strategy to fight a one-front war, at least in this region."[24]

Yet Briggs refused to let up on the Jewish issue. He submitted a Nicholas Stanford column in 1956 that alleged a "Jewish conspiracy" had led to a boycott that kept the conservative journal *American Mercury* off New York newsstands. Waring spiked the column, although he let Briggs down softly by claiming that another correspondent had already mentioned the *American Mercury* boycott in the *News and Courier*. In 1958, Briggs wrote a Nicholas Stanford column on U.S. involvement in the Middle East. It claimed that American problems in the region could be traced to "the existence of the Zionist state of Israel, established in violation of solemn World War I promises of Arab independence . . . and settled by Zionists who on the principle that might makes right drove out the Arabs." Israel had undermined American support in the region, Briggs wrote, and the Russians "were laughing in their sleeves" at the predicament the Jewish state had created for Washington. It was Arthur Wilcox, Waring's associate editor, who spiked this Stanford column. He left a hand-written explanation on Waring's desk. "I didn't like this much," Wilcox wrote. "It seems dated and it sounds like a tirade against the Jews."[25]

Briggs and Waring ended their correspondence sometime in late 1958, and no more Nicholas Stanford columns appeared in the *News and Courier*. In 1960, Briggs left the *New York Times* to take a public relations job in Philadelphia. Ten years later, he wrote to Waring and sent him a copy of his latest book, *Requiem for a Yellow Brick Brewery*. Waring appeared pleased to receive the letter, and also a little wistful about the memories that it stirred. "A lot of newsprint has gone through the webbing since the days of Nicholas Stanford," the editor wrote, "It is hard to say where we are now at, as they say."[26]

Despite his efforts to shred the "paper curtain," it was clear by 1960 that Waring and the southern segregationists were losing the battle over public perception. Their efforts to maintain the racial status quo were increasingly depicted as uncivil and antidemocratic, not in keeping with the nation's ideals. As the civil rights campaign moved from the courtroom to the streets, with freedom riders, student sit-ins, and Martin Luther King Jr.'s Southern Christian Leadership Conference challenging state segregation laws across the South, the northern media flooded the region with reporters and camera crews. As historians have shown, the interpretations of the ongoing confrontations between white police and African American protesters delivered by the national media fueled northern outrage over southern intransigence. Using the relatively new and powerful medium of television, correspondents delivered stark images of courageous African Americans peacefully asserting their democratic rights in the face of a violent and uncivil foe. In the wake of such coverage, Waring and his segregationist allies appeared to be stock villains from an earlier age, their arguments defending racial separation woefully outdated in a nation that now appeared to embrace a racially democratic future. An important pivot had occurred in the nation's public sphere.[27]

Building a New Republican Party

Oddly enough, it was Waring's friendship with a northern journalist that would help revive the fortunes of southern segregationists and point them toward a new and successful political strategy. William F. Buckley Jr. launched the conservative journal *National Review* in 1955, during the height of the massive resistance campaign in the Deep South. Buckley's family owned a home in the horse country near Camden, and Buckley and Waring had gotten to know each other during Buckley's visits to the state. The two traded letters occasionally, and their talk often turned to politics. Like Waring, Buckley despised Eisenhower's "middle-of-the-road" policies, calling them "politically, intellectually, and morally repugnant." Eisenhower Republicans wanted to manage the growth of the welfare state, Buckley charged. He envisioned a more radical conservative movement that would begin to eradicate the vestiges of the New Deal altogether. At the *News and Courier,* Waring and his mentor, William Watts Ball, had been making the same argument for decades. Inevitably, Buckley's conversations with Waring turned to the question of southern conservatives and the issue of race—how did committed economic conservatives like Waring, who was also a segregationist, fit into Buckley's vision of a national conservative movement? Their answer to this question would eventually reshape American politics, and it would transform southern white conservatives. No longer political pariahs, they would reemerge as a dominant force on the national stage.[28]

A small group of intellectual conservatives had been wandering in the political wilderness since Franklin Roosevelt's election in 1932. Like the *News and Courier* editors, they had opposed the New Deal on principle. They believed federal intervention in the economy, even during the darkest days of the Depression, had damaged the nation. It had led to a centralization of federal power at the expense of state and local governments. As Ball had argued so vehemently during the 1930s, the growth of the federal government and its prominent role in the economy amounted to socialism, even communism. The idea ran contrary to the nation's founding principles, Ball had claimed. It would eventually destroy the capitalist spirit and commitment to freedom that had made the country great. Yet those conservative economic arguments had had little political impact, especially in the Deep South. During the 1930s and '40s, those who campaigned against the New Deal occupied the fringes of the two major political parties. The conservative wing of the Republican Party, led by Ohio Sen. Robert Taft, had been active since Roosevelt's first election. Initially, southern conservative Democrats had supported the New Deal, but they had second thoughts when they realized that New Deal policies were helping to empower African Americans to fight for their rights. By 1948, when President Truman's "Fair Deal" proposals included civil rights legislation, even an old FDR ally like James F. Byrnes was ready to desert the Democratic Party. Byrnes had publicly framed his break with Truman as a disagreement over deficit spending and other economic policies. But it was clear from the timing that Truman's civil rights push had been the primary motivator.[29]

When he launched *National Review*, Buckley said the journal had one immediate goal: to "stand athwart history, yelling Stop!" Buckley and his allies at the journal were social as well as economic conservatives. *National Review* opposed government interference in free-market capitalism, but it also supported the concept of social traditionalism. Buckley sought to unite libertarians and traditionalists by arguing that enduring social order grew organically, not through central planning or what he derisively called "social engineering." Communities were bound together by moral and philosophical traditions that had developed naturally over time, and they should not be tampered with lightly. Egalitarianism may sound like an admirable goal to liberals, *National Review* argued, but societal hierarchies had evolved for a reason, and their disruption would cause turmoil and dislocation. Critics contended that Buckley and his allies at the magazine had linked two contradictory ideas. Unfettered capitalism and the constant change that it generated, they claimed, would inevitably clash with the desire to maintain social traditions. Nonetheless, *National Review*'s combination of social and economic conservatism was particularly appealing to Waring. Much like his mentor, William Watts Ball, he was a laissez-faire capitalist who also wanted to maintain the racial status quo in the South.

Buckley had been hearing Waring's side of the segregationist argument at dinners and social gatherings for several years, and he embraced the *News and Courier* editor as a kindred spirit. They shared a common devotion to the preservation of traditions in society, particularly hierarchical order. By 1956, Buckley had decided that southern segregationists were the natural allies of economic conservatives, and he set out to build an intellectual and political relationship. As political scientist Joseph E. Lowndes notes, *National Review* was the first conservative journal to try to link the southern opposition to enforced integration with the antistatist argument that was central to economic conservatism. In doing so, Buckley and his colleagues hoped to persuade southerners to renounce their previous support for New Deal policies that provided the South with federal aid, and convince economic conservatives that southern segregationists were their allies in the broader battle against a centralized and invasive government. Yet *National Review* wanted to do this without appealing to blatant racism. Like Charles Wallace Collins, the Alabama lawyer whose influential book had helped foment the Dixiecrat revolt a decade earlier, *National Review* tried to craft an argument that supported segregationist arguments in principle, but did not appear to violate the foundational and constitutional ideals of the nation. It was a tricky proposition, and Buckley stumbled in his first attempt to make the connection.[30]

In its early efforts, *National Review* supported the interposition argument and the massive resistance campaign, claiming the Tenth Amendment granted states the right to challenge U.S. Supreme Court decisions on constitutional grounds. The magazine had been arguing since its founding in 1955 that the *Brown* ruling and the threat of federal enforcement of school integration was the natural culmination of New Deal policies that increased federal aid to the states. If states took the federal money, they would eventually come under federal control, the editors contended. They urged states' rights supporters to break out of their "opportunistic stupor" and protect their independence by rejecting the government's blandishments.[31]

By 1957—the year of Eisenhower's civil rights bill—Buckley moved beyond school integration and addressed the issue of African American voting rights in the South. Under the headline "Why the South Must Prevail," Buckley delivered the most forthright overture to southern segregationists yet. In its tone and its argument, the editorial sounded strikingly similar to those that had been running for years in Waring's *News and Courier*. For Buckley, the central question was "whether the White community in the South is entitled to take such measures as necessary to prevail, politically and culturally, in areas in which it does not predominate numerically. The sobering answer is

Yes . . . because, for the time being, it is the advanced race." In Buckley's view, "the claims of civilization supersede those of universal suffrage." The *National Review* "believed that the South's premises are correct," he concluded. "If the majority wills what is socially atavistic, then to thwart the majority may be, if undemocratic, enlightened."[32]

Thrilled by Buckley's *National Review* editorial, Waring proclaimed his support in the *News and Courier*. "The right to vote is not more basic than civilization," Waring declared in the newspaper shortly after Buckley's editorial appeared. "Universal suffrage is not the beginning of wisdom or the beginning of freedom." Waring was especially pleased to hear those ideas emanating from outside the South. Yet the *News and Courier* editor realized Buckley's racist argument ran against the grain of the shifting public opinion within the national public sphere. He described Buckley's editorial as "brave words" and made a point of emphasizing that they had been "uttered by a respected northern journal."[33]

Buckley's support for undemocratic measures to thwart African American voting rights in the South had in fact gone too far. Even his colleagues at *National Review* were appalled. Buckley's argument had violated the nation's democratic principles and undermined the constitutional arguments that had been used to link southern segregationists to the new conservative movement. The following week, Buckley's brother-in-law, L. Brent Bozell, took the unusual step of attacking Buckley's editorial in the pages of his own journal. Calling him "dead wrong," Bozell said Buckley's editorial threatened to do "grave hurt to the conservative movement." The Fifteenth Amendment granting African Americans the right to vote was settled law, Bozell said, and thus Buckley's argument was unconstitutional. It was okay to challenge *Brown* through interposition, Bozell said, because the constitution remained vague on whether the U.S. Supreme Court actually had the right to impose federal control over states concerning education. But no such vagueness existed concerning the right to vote. Challenging African American suffrage required the *National Review* to reject the primacy of the constitution in establishing U.S. law. And it asked its readers to accept the harsh and antiquated racial notions of white supremacy and black inferiority. For many, those arguments sounded un-American; they violated the nation's ideals of a pluralistic society based on constitutional government and the rule of law.[34]

Bozell's intervention served as an important course correction for the growing conservative movement as it sought to build a coalition that included southern segregationists. Going forward, conservatives would frame their arguments more carefully to avoid making the claim of white supremacy and thus drawing charges of blatant racism. Instead, they would develop more nuanced interpretations that appealed to white southerners but also aligned more closely with the nation's founding ideals. They would adopt a so-called color-blind ethos that emphasized personal freedom and opportunity, but retained the segregationists' commitment to states' rights. In doing so, the conservative movement would attempt to co-opt the language African Americans had used successfully to demand inclusion as equal citizens in the nation's democratic life.

It was Arizona Senator Barry Goldwater who gave voice to this new conservative interpretation and spread it widely into the mainstream of American party politics. But it was Waring and the emerging South Carolina Republican Party, working closely with the *National Review*, that helped launch Goldwater to national prominence. By 1959, a new breed of white conservative began to take control of the GOP in the state. Roger Milliken of Spartanburg and Greg Shorey of Greenville were industrialists who had moved to South Carolina to make their fortunes in manufacturing. Fiercely antigovernment, they were primarily economic rather than racial conservatives. They opposed new taxes, government regulation, labor unions, and anything that appeared to support the so-called welfare state. They despised the Eisenhower White House and the liberal wing of the GOP, led by New York Governor Nelson Rockefeller. They were Goldwater Republicans.[35]

Shorey and Milliken invited their hero to speak at the South Carolina Republican Convention in Greenville in 1959. The state GOP had few members, and the gathering was small, but Waring and the rest of the conservative press in the state ensured Goldwater's speech would get wide coverage. The Arizona senator delivered the expected indictment of federal spending and intrusive government, but he also linked those concerns to the push for civil rights and school integration in the South. The *Brown* ruling should not be "enforced by arms," Goldwater said, because it was "not based on law."[36]

With the help of the *National Review* editors, Goldwater would refine his message over the next two years as he launched his battle against the Republican Party's liberal wing. In his political autobiography—ghost written by Bozell—Goldwater explained why opponents of civil rights were actually fighting to preserve the American system of government. Goldwater said that civil rights, "defined as rights to desegregated education," do not exist. Despite the *Brown* ruling, he said the constitution prohibits federal involvement in state education. In a nod to the new color-blind ethos of the conservative movement, Goldwater tempered his argument by noting that he did not personally oppose integration. In fact, he said he believed desegregated schools were a good idea. But he emphasized that local officials, not the federal government, should make the choice.[37]

Leaders of the new conservative movement shared many of the same concerns as the southerners, but they expressed their arguments using language that avoided the odor of racism and aligned more closely with acceptable American values. Waring, for example, had long contended that both major political parties had marginalized the white South in their desperate attempt to win the "Negro bloc vote" in the North. It was an argument that resonated with white southerners raised on the overheated mythology of carpetbaggers who manipulated credulous former slaves during Reconstruction. In 1956, Waring had charged that liberal Democrats used "welfare" to bribe "minority blocs" and maintain political control in the United States. He maintained Democratic politicians had been luring black voters with "baskets of food and leniency at the police station" since the New Deal began. "How long other white men will permit this disgrace to continue in the false name of 'civil rights' and 'democracy' may determine the life expectancy of the American Republic," Waring wrote. Four years later, Workman raised the issue of "minority bloc voting," but using language that emphasized the color-blind nature of his appeal. All citizens who meet "the requirements set forth by impersonal, impartial, and color-blind law" should have the right to vote, Workman said, adding that anyone who blocks African Americans from voting illegally is admitting his inability "to out-maneuver them in the give-and-take of political warfare."[38]

Buckley and his colleagues at the *National Review* were teaching southern conservatives how to make their case more palatable in the national public sphere. Goldwater tried to downplay the issue of race and focus on constitutional and economic issues, but some supporters would not go along, even in the North. One of those was William Loeb, the conservative editor of New Hampshire's *Manchester Union-Leader*. In an exchange of letters with Workman and J. Edward Thornton, an attorney in Mobile, Alabama, Loeb praised Goldwater and his southern allies for their efforts to reshape the Republican Party. But Loeb worried that liberal and African American members of the party would never relinquish control to the conservatives. His solution violated the new rule concerning politically correct language: Loeb proposed the Republican Party "become the white man's party." He said he was not "against the Negroes but just FOR the white race." Loeb said his proposal would "leave Democrats with the Negro vote," but give the Republicans the white vote and "white people, thank God, are still in the majority." Sounding much like Waring, the New Hampshire editor believed "Negro outrages" in northern cities would turn voters against the "Northern Democrats' coddling of the Negroes" and ensure Republican gains in the next election.[39]

In Goldwater, Waring and Workman had found a national politician who was actively soliciting their support, and as 1960 approached they were hard at work building a conservative Republican Party in South Carolina. They would once again bring their newspaper into the middle of the state's politics. As they had done earlier in helping launch the citizens' council movement in South Carolina, the journalists publicly defended the new journalistic norms of independence, impartiality, and objectivity. But privately, they operated as political activists and played a central role in GOP party-building efforts. Waring and Workman consulted with party leaders on story ideas, helped to rewrite news releases, withheld significant political news, and developed campaign strategies to help the Republicans compete with the Democrats. In late 1961, Workman would resign from the paper and run for the U.S. Senate as a Republican. Though ultimately unsuccessful, his 1962 campaign against Democratic Sen. Olin Johnston would garner more votes than any Republican since Reconstruction, and his vibrant campaign would lay the groundwork for the growth of the Republicans into the dominant political force in the state.[40]

The *News and Courier* and Partisan Politics

When Workman stepped down as statehouse reporter to run for the Senate, the decision may have raised eyebrows, but it did not violate the professional norms of modern journalism. The revolving door between press and politics has always existed, and the transition from one to the other, if handled transparently and with no overlap, has been an accepted practice. It has been considered unethical, however, when the journalist secretly pursues partisan political goals while claiming to maintain impartiality and independence. As Borden and Pritchard maintain, journalists have a "protected social function" of gathering, interpreting, and disseminating information, and as professionals they are expected to carry out that function without allowing partisan interests to compromise their "independent exercise of judgment." As part of the professionalization of journalism across the twentieth century, news organizations incorporated rules governing partisanship and conflict of interest into both written and unwritten codes of ethics and standards. Workman and his editor violated this code of professional journalism and used their positions at the newspaper to help build a new, conservative version of the Republican Party in the state. Yet Workman felt the need to state when he announced his candidacy that it would be "inappropriate" and "unethical" to combine objective reporting with partisan politics. Workman's decision to hide his political involvement indicates how problematic the issue had become for professional journalists who were tempted to engage in partisan activism.[41]

By the late 1950s, Workman had grown restless with his role as news reporter. He was working on a book called *The Case for the South* that defended segregation, and he yearned to express his opinions in the pages of the *News and Courier*. In June 1958, he told Waring that his reporting job had become a "restricted cul-de-sac," and that he wanted to write a Sunday column on the editorial page. A regular opinion column, Workman argued, would afford him "a sense of editorial release" and allow him to make a "more useful contribution" during this critical moment in South Carolina history. Waring, however, had complained frequently about the growing editorial comment included in the news stories coming out of his Columbia bureau. He told Workman that readers paid more attention to "hot news stories" than political columns. He feared Workman's column would look like just another "$5-a-month syndicated product." But the editor knew Workman had other professional options and did not want to lose his top political reporter. So Waring grudgingly granted Workman a Sunday opinion column in the *News and Courier*, but only if the correspondent agreed to continue his coverage of straight news as well.[42]

Workman's column gave him an outlet to express his support for the conservative Republicans, but the state party appeared to pose little threat to the Democrats. By 1960, white voters in the South had grown comfortable supporting Republicans at the presidential level, but the party had little success in state elections. South Carolina Republican leaders like Milliken and Shorey supported segregation and states' rights in 1960, but, as economic conservatives, they talked more about government intrusion into private business than federal enforcement of civil rights laws. The Republican Party had not been able to compete with South Carolina Democrats on the issue of segregation, but Workman helped to change that. In 1962, his Senate campaign would unite racial and economic conservatives and point the way toward Republican control in the state. For the next two years, however, Workman and his editor continued in their dual roles as activists and journalists as they worked behind the scenes to build the Republican Party in South Carolina.[43]

Workman's evolution from working journalist to political leader took a critical leap forward in January 1960 with the publication of his book. Though deeply racist, it was by the standards of the time an intellectual effort to defend segregation, and its publication transformed Workman into a national spokesman for the white South. Along with James J. Kilpatrick's *The Southern Case for School Segregation*, published in 1962, Workman's book represented a move away from the cruder excesses of earlier southern defenses. Historian George Lewis called it "one of the more erudite" arguments in the defense of segregation. In the book, Workman claimed the *Brown* ruling and federal efforts to force integration had halted progress in race relations in the South. Black civil rights organizations like the NAACP cared more about political power than racial advancement, Workman contended, and their efforts had empowered the Ku Klux Klan and its "unlovely cohorts who substitute muscle and meanness" for intellect in defending the South. The reasonable white southerner is "the man in the middle . . . whose voice needs to be heard," Workman wrote. "He demands for his state the right to administer his own domestic affairs, and he demands for himself the right to rear his children in the school atmosphere most conducive to their learning—all without hurt or harm to his Negro neighbor or to the Negro's children."[44]

Workman rested his case for segregation on one critical argument: Negroes, he said, remain inferior to whites, socially and intellectually, and "race-mixing" would lead to disaster for both races. Workman conceded that some black individuals had overcome remarkable odds to achieve success, "sometimes with direct white opposition." But despite those gains, Workman argued the Negro race remained "a white man's burden"—a "violent" and "indolent" people who needed guidance and leadership from their white superiors. Workman claimed most southern blacks understood this point and had been content with the gradual pace of change in the South before outside forces got involved. He bemoaned what he saw as a rise in hostility between the races brought on by the civil rights movement. For example, he accused southern Negroes of growing "too sensitive" about the word "nigger." Rather than an epithet, Workman considered the word a term of endearment. He called it a harmless mispronunciation by white southerners struggling to say "Negro" in their distinctively slow drawl.[45]

Workman's book drew national attention. In a sympathetic review, the *Wall Street Journal* urged proponents of forced integration to read it. "The case for integrating the schools on moral, legal and political grounds is familiar," the reviewer wrote. "Mr. Workman's list of practical obstacles will be news to many non-Southern readers." Television host Dave Garroway interviewed Workman on the *Today* program, an appearance that received widespread publicity in South Carolina. In introducing him, Garroway said, "Strangely enough, this is a view not frequently heard on television, but whether you agree with the view, open-minded people should allow the opinion to be heard." The morning of the interview, *The State*, South Carolina's largest newspaper, ran a front-page story encouraging its readers to tune in. In Washington, Thurmond sent every member of the U.S. Senate a copy of *The Case for the South*.[46]

In South Carolina, Workman's book was a sensation, and the journalist became a hot commodity on the speaking circuit. Between February and

June 1960, he seemed to be on the agenda at every civic organization across the state: the Women's Club in Columbia; the Kiwanis Club of Greenville; the Rotary Club in Florence; the Historical Society in Sumter; the Citadel Round Table in Charleston; the Sertoma Club in Beaufort; and the Kiwanis Club again, this time back in Columbia. In Lancaster, Workman delivered a speech sponsored by the Chamber of Commerce's Cultural Improvement Committee. In Aiken later that month, the journalist served as keynote speaker for a ceremony marking the Battle of Aiken, billed as the South's last victory in the Civil War. Workman used the occasion to urge the white South to unite politically to restore the region's political clout. In March, the *News and Courier* ran this front-page headline: "Newsman Himself in News." The keynote speaker at the state Democratic Party Convention had urged every delegate to read Workman's book "page for page."[47]

Workman's book tour reached a crescendo in late June, when Gov. Ernest Hollings and four hundred prominent South Carolinians gathered at the Wade Hampton Hotel in Columbia and honored the journalist at a testimonial dinner. *The State* newspaper ran a four-column headline at the top of the front page: "Workman Praised as Major Proponent for South's Cause." At the dinner, Waring playfully described his abstemious friend as "no liquor, no tie, no lie." And another colleague from the Charleston paper announced with great fanfare that a New York newspaper syndication firm would begin syndicating Workman's column, thus holding out the promise that his views would be circulated beyond the South.[48]

For Workman, however, the highlight of the evening must have been the keynote address delivered by Kilpatrick, editor of the *Richmond News Leader* and an intellectual architect of the southern resistance to *Brown* and school integration. In a speech laced with more light humor than serious politics, Kilpatrick said the South believed "the least government is the best government," but he said "society is determined to impose 'a new order,' " on the region. Finally, after all the testimonials, Workman took the stage. In what the newspaper described as a "terse" speech, he made light of the event—"This is the closest a newspaper man ever gets to covering his own funeral"—but ended on a serious note, perhaps foreshadowing the significant role he would play in southern politics: "What else can a man ask for than to be a southerner during times like these?"

Once a mere political journalist in a sleepy state capital, Workman had been transformed into a national spokesman for the white southern cause. He had been expressing some of the same views about segregation in his political reporting since before the *Brown* ruling. But with the book, he had gathered those arguments in one place, and with the support of his New York publisher, had gotten them into the hands of the national media. The television appearances and the reviews in national and regional newspapers spread Workman's arguments far beyond the covers of the actual hard-back book. And they elevated his status, both nationally and at home, as a serious voice in the public sphere. As historian Priscilla Coit Murphy has written, "For a single voice seeking to communicate a message of public interest, publication of a book represented special access" to the media system, and thus wide dissemination of the author's ideas, as well as a "special kind of opportunity for public discussion of an issue." Murphy was writing about a very different book published during the same time period, Rachel Carson's *Silent Spring*. But her point about a book's potential power applies to Workman as well. Publication of *The Case for The South* positioned Workman to play a new and more significant role in the coming transformation of southern politics. His 1962 Senate campaign would unite racial and economic conservatives to create a competitive Republican Party in South Carolina, but only after three years of political activism behind the scenes. While his support for segregation was well known, Workman and his newspaper concealed his political participation while he worked as a political reporter and a columnist.[49]

In late February 1960, state GOP official W. W. "Duck" Wannamaker Jr. saw Workman outside the governor's office in Columbia and gave him a scoop. He told the journalist that Goldwater had just agreed to serve as keynote speaker at the South Carolina Republican Party's state convention in March. Workman was not interested in breaking the news, however. He agreed instead to help the Republicans maximize publicity for the senator's appearance. Workman advised Wannamaker to release the news two weeks before the convention, and to send the release to the state Associated Press bureau on a Saturday so that the story would appear in Sunday newspapers across the state. Wannamaker later showed Workman a draft of the release and asked the journalist if he would "polish it up and put it in good newspaper form." Workman wanted a number of changes. "Start off with Goldwater as the attention-getter," Workman said. He proposed a first sentence: "U.S. Senator Barry Goldwater of Arizona, outspoken leader of conservative elements in the Republican Party, will address the State Republican Convention in Columbia on March 26." Workman recommended including a direct quotation from Greg Shorey "plugging Goldwater and the coincidence of his views with most southerners." He also suggested pointing out that Goldwater "is another in a number of prominent Republicans who have appeared" in South Carolina since Shorey took over as party chairman. Wannamaker wrote back the next day thanking the journalist and telling him that his ideas "are excellent and we shall certainly follow your advice."[50]

Workman was not the only *News and Courier* journalist communicating behind the scenes with state Republicans in early 1960. Roger Milliken, the textile magnate who helped finance the state GOP, gave Waring confidential information about plans for South Carolina Republicans to embarrass the party's presumptive presidential nominee, Vice President Richard Nixon, by nominating Goldwater for president at their state convention in March. Waring passed along the news to Workman, but warned him that even some top GOP figures in the state were unaware of the scheme. The idea, Waring wrote, is to alert "GOP bigwigs and Nixon personally to conservative sentiment in these parts." Once again, Workman had a political scoop, but he and his colleagues at the *News and Courier* made no effort to break the story before the convention. Workman and Waring were more interested in fomenting the Goldwater insurgency than reporting on it.[51]

On the day of Goldwater's appearance at the GOP state convention, the *News and Courier* and the *Greenville News* published Workman's review of Goldwater's book, *The Conscience of a Conservative.* He called the senator "one of the most forthright citizens to appear on the national scene in many a year." Later that day, Goldwater thrilled the state's Republican convention delegates in Columbia with an attack on Democrats who were leading the nation "on the road to socialism." As planned, the GOP delegates nominated their conservative hero for the Republican presidential nomination by acclamation, thus launching Goldwater's long-shot bid to derail the Nixon nomination and put the newly energized conservative wing in charge of the national Republican Party.[52]

Workman served as both political reporter and opinion columnist throughout the 1960 presidential campaign. In July, Workman the reporter covered the debate over a civil rights plank approved at the Democratic national convention in Los Angeles. He described southern Democrats who were "sputtering and gagging over a bitter dose of civil rights medicine" embodied in the party's platform. Disappointed with the nomination of Senator John F. Kennedy of Massachusetts over the southern candidate, Senate majority leader Lyndon Johnson of Texas, Workman predicted the Democrats would struggle to win votes in the South. In one news story, he said "southern independents" were waiting to see whom the GOP nominated before deciding where to place their support.[53]

Workman the columnist wanted those independents to band together behind a reliably conservative candidate. His first choice would be Goldwater, but he knew the senator had no chance of wresting the nomination from Nixon, despite an all-out push by the South Carolina Republicans. On the eve of the Republican convention, when Nixon reached out to appease the liberal

Rockefeller in the so-called "Compact of Fifth Avenue," the South Carolina Republicans girded for war. With national television cameras rolling, state GOP chairman Greg Shorey stepped up to the convention podium and delivered a passionate plea on behalf of Goldwater. Nixon won the nomination, but Goldwater's insurgency at the 1960 convention gave the nation its first up-close look at the new and surprisingly strong conservative wing of the Republican Party, a movement fueled by southern activists like Shorey, Milliken, and Wannamaker of South Carolina.[54]

Faced with a choice between Kennedy and Nixon, a disappointed Workman used his column to bemoan the lack of a stronger conservative candidate. "The sleeping giant of American politics is a bumbling fellow named 'conservative' whose strength is held in check by Lilliputian liberals," Workman wrote. "He is a stout fellow, this 'conservative,' yet placid. He dislikes much of what he sees about him . . . but he cannot guide his mind and his muscles in corrective action." Workman wanted conservatives from both parties to band together to find a new political home. Northern liberals controlled the Democratic Party, he said, and they were actively seeking black support. Despite Goldwater's push, the Republicans remained the moderate and so-called "modern" GOP of Eisenhower's presidency. Until conservative Democrats and conservative Republicans united in one party, Workman said, they would remain politically weak. Greg Shorey read the column with pleasure. "I can't tell you how grateful I am for the splendid article," he wrote to Workman. "This is a significant contribution to not only our efforts but to a better understanding by the electorate of what we are trying to accomplish."[55]

Kennedy won South Carolina with just 51.2 percent of the vote. Black voters supported Kennedy and the Democrats in overwhelming numbers, a fact not lost on the conservative Republicans. Shortly after the election, Milliken sent Waring a letter with details of voting patterns across the state. Waring thanked the GOP activist and assured him he would look into the story. "Loss of the state was surely not due to any failures on your part," the editor wrote to Milliken. "I enjoyed working with you and look forward to many more opportunities to strike a blow for freedom. We have plenty to do."[56]

Waring forwarded Milliken's letter and voting analysis to Workman and asked: "Think this can be interpreted and possibly reproduced?" The same day, Workman wrote a letter to John McCray, the black journalist and a leader of the Progressive Democrats, the mostly African American political organization. Workman asked about the large Democratic vote in three black precincts in Columbia and Darlington. "Do you think this reflects the general pattern of Negro voting throughout the state?" Workman inquired. If McCray replied, no record of it exists. But two weeks later, Workman's analysis appeared as a front-page news story in the *News and Courier* and the *Greenville News*. "The pro-Democratic vote of South Carolina Negroes was a major, perhaps deciding factor," in winning the extremely close race for the Democratic Party, he wrote. By reaching out to allies working with the *News and Courier*, Milliken had helped propel the story of black-voter support for the Democrats to the front pages of the state's newspapers. The message was clear: If new black voters had found a home in the Democratic Party, then it must not be the place for southern white conservatives.[57]

Black voters had indeed provided Kennedy his margin of victory in South Carolina. Kennedy's surprise call to the wife of Dr. Martin Luther King Jr. after the civil rights leader was imprisoned in Georgia certainly boosted his support among African Americans. But in South Carolina McCray's Progressive Democratic Party played a decisive role as well. The PDP worked diligently to turn out votes for Kennedy in the final week of the campaign. McCray and his allies brought in prominent African American speakers to address church and civic groups on Kennedy's behalf. L. Howard Bennett, a South Carolina native who had become the first African American judge in Minnesota, returned to his native state to rally support for Kennedy in Charleston and Columbia. Bennett would go on to serve in the Pentagon during Kennedy's presidency. Arthur Clement Jr., the former Charleston PDP member who had been promoted to a top insurance company job in New Jersey, spoke at churches in Greenville, Spartanburg, and Rock Hill. Long-time NAACP attorney Harold Boulware appeared at rallies in Orangeburg and Columbia, and McCray addressed churches in Florence, Aiken, Darlington, and in the state capital.

McCray also supported Kennedy in his newspaper column, but it is unclear how many readers it had in South Carolina. In the spring of 1960, McCray left the *Baltimore Afro-American* in an acrimonious break-up that included a brief legal battle. He took a job with the *Pittsburgh Courier*, a once mighty newspaper that, like most of the black press, was losing readers and hemorrhaging money by the early 1960s. As the paper's Carolina editor, McCray tried to establish a strong circulation network in the state, but records show he had only marginal success.[58]

The Kennedy campaign's final push in South Carolina in 1960 exemplified the oddly schizophrenic politics of the Democratic Party at that time. McCray and his PDP allies worked to turn out black votes for a presidential campaign that, at the same time, was using racist appeals to attract white segregationist voters. Kennedy's state campaign accused Nixon of supporting integration, socializing with black celebrities, and being a member of the NAACP. Campaign operatives distributed pictures of federal troops enforcing integration in Arkansas in 1957. The caption read: "Remember Little Rock."[59]

McCray had hoped the PDP's success in helping Kennedy win South Carolina would land him a patronage job in the new administration. Clement encouraged Bennett and other contacts in the Kennedy administration "not to overlook" McCray when jobs were handed out. But no offer materialized, and as 1961 arrived, McCray continued to cover South Carolina for the *Pittsburgh Courier*.[60]

Workman's 1962 Senate Race and the Rise of Two-Party Politics in South Carolina

Workman's U.S. Senate campaign of 1962 grew out of a surprise Republican victory in South Carolina a year earlier. A well-known Columbia business-man named Charles Boineau, who had only been a party member for a few months, ran for an open state House seat in a special election in Richland County. The race drew a small turnout, and Boineau won a narrow victory. He became the first Republican elected to the South Carolina House since the 1890s.[61]

Buoyed by Boineau's victory, state Republicans set their sights on the U.S. Senate seat held by Olin D. Johnston, a former textile worker who had held public office since the Depression. The man who ran Boineau's improbable campaign, Republican activist J. Drake Edens, hatched a plan to draft Workman into the 1962 race against Johnston. He organized a committee of Richland County Republicans who called publicly for Workman to run for the GOP nomination. Workman claimed he had no formal ties to the Republican Party and no involvement with the draft effort. However, Workman told Edens that if the Republicans nominated him he would accept the bid and enter the race. For the next three months, Workman continued to serve as a news reporter and opinion columnist while his allies in the GOP ran a de facto campaign for the Senate nomination. The question of the journalistic ethics of such a dual role received no mention in the state's largest newspapers.[62]

Readers of the *News and Courier* could notice Workman's multiple roles. They could pick up the newspaper on November 14, 1961, and see his byline over a column on the editorial page that discussed the new "respectability" of the Republican Party in South Carolina. Deeper in that day's newspaper they would find Workman's byline over a hard news piece on the arguments in a state Supreme Court case involving civil rights demonstrators. The next day, readers would see a brief story from the Associated Press about Edens's effort to draft Workman into the Senate race. Headlined "GOP in Richland County Backs Workman," the story identified the journalist as simply a "political columnist" and did not mention his position at the *News and Courier*. Workman the straight-news reporter appeared again on November 23 with a story on a statehouse hearing about stevedore rates at the Port of Charleston. A week later, Workman the columnist had a piece on the editorial page posing the question: Why is Goldwater so popular? "To this reporter," Workman wrote, "the answer seems to be that Goldwater sticks forthrightly to a relatively simple set of government principles." Finally, on December 2, a front-page story from the Associated Press announced that Workman was officially entering the race for the GOP Senate nomination.[63]

At his campaign's kick-off rally, Workman addressed the ethical questions of what he called "his evolution" from journalist to candidate. Until recently, he said, "my field" had been journalism, and he considered it "highly improper [and] unethical for an individual to seek to combine objective reporting with partisan politics." When Edens proposed the draft movement, Workman said he agreed to push ahead and "see what happens." Workman also said that he wanted to retain his freedom "to go about my business—let me continue in my newspapering." For the past three months, Workman told the crowd, he had been a "passive" candidate and thus could still operate as an impartial and independent journalist. When it became clear that he would have to campaign to win the nomination, Workman said, he decided to end his "passive campaign" and formally enter the race.[64]

At that first rally, Workman could not help bragging to his partisan audience that his "passive" campaign had actually been a lot more active than advertised. He had delivered eighteen speeches to more than 2,500 people in the past two months, he said. "If it gets any more passive I can't stand it," he joked. Workman had been employed in a professional environment at the *News and Courier* where top editors had always been engaged in political activism. By the 1950s, however, the newspaper saw the need to acknowledge expectations of unbiased reporting and journalistic independence. But Workman failed to discuss the contradiction of encouraging the efforts of a campaign draft movement while also covering state politics as a news reporter.[65]

Workman had been a journalist in South Carolina since 1936 and a political correspondent in the capital city for sixteen years. He had close ties with the state's daily newspapers, and none raised ethical concerns about his dual role as journalist and politician. In fact, the press seemed disappointed that he would no longer be reporting from Columbia. The day after Workman launched his campaign, *Greenville News* editor Wayne W. Freeman ran an

editorial under the headline, "An Able Correspondent Resigns." The piece
read more like a salute to a retiring employee than an editorial confronting tricky questions of journalism and politics. "Bill Workman is his own
man," the editorial said. "He is making sure that he will neither embarrass
his former newspaper employers nor be embarrassed by them during the
campaign. In his usual forthright fashion, he resigned rather than ask for
a leave of absence." The newspaper's editors said they would continue running Workman's political columns, which "of course will deal with regional,
national and international matters," not state politics.[66]

The *News and Courier* also announced plans to continue running Workman's column and defended the decision with a pointed example. "Ample
precedent exists for people actively engaged in politics to write newspaper
columns," the paper said. "For example, Senator Barry Goldwater, who actually holds office, syndicates a column to newspapers." Workman's columns
immediately following his campaign announcement did not deal directly
with South Carolina politics. But they did focus on the cold war, a hot-button
issue in a 1962 U.S. senate campaign. Workman's columns were scathing in
their criticism of the Kennedy administration.[67]

With Edens at the helm, Workman ran a vigorous campaign and helped
boost the GOP in South Carolina by establishing volunteer organizations
in every county in the state. In Sumter, Workman played up his journalistic
background, especially his reputation as a dogged news reporter: "Some of
you know me as a columnist you may—or may not—read three times a week.
But many know me without coat and tie—as a shirt-sleeved, shoe-leather
reporter, with pencil in hand and question on tongue, inquiring into the
problems of the people of South Carolina."[68]

By October, the polls showed the Senate race surprisingly tight, and the
national media took interest. James Reston of the *New York Times* came
to South Carolina to investigate the rising Republican phenomenon in the
South. He called Workman a "journalistic Goldwater Republican," and he
described an editorial that Waring had published in the *News and Courier*:
"His theme is a vote for [Democrat Olin] Johnston is a vote of confidence for
the Kennedys . . . while a vote against Johnston is a vote against 'the Kennedy
master-state.' " Reston said he had been hearing the same refrain across the
state from Democrats as well as Republicans.

The political reporter had spotted a trend that was under way across the
Deep South. Workman failed to defeat Johnston, but he won 44 percent of
the vote, a high-water mark for the Republican Party in a statewide race in
South Carolina since the end of Reconstruction. The results signaled the beginning of what political scientists have described as "the great white switch."

Southern conservatives had begun trickling out of the Democratic Party and were laying the foundation for a new political home in the Goldwater wing of the GOP.[69]

Waring and Workman had turned to partisan politics when they realized that the arguments in favor of segregation and white political domination no longer prevailed outside the South. The "paper curtain" that Waring raged about had some basis in reality. Mainstream public opinion had shifted in the rest of the country, and national media outlets had begun to reflect this change. Supporters of black equality had gained the upper hand in the battle over public opinion in the North. Faced with this reality, the two journalists began to work with the emerging conservative movement to develop new means of undermining the civil rights movement, particularly black political advancement. Waring and Workman eagerly joined the effort to take control of Republican Party, but they hid their party-building efforts from their readers to protect their privileged position in the public sphere. As professional journalists who proclaimed their commitment to independence and political neutrality, they held a special status in setting the public agenda and shaping public discourse in their state.

As segregationists, Warning and Workman had publicly opposed school integration in the 1950s and often ignored the professional norms of impartial journalism when reporting on that issue. Because they believed the newspaper's point of view on segregation aligned with the accepted norms of white Charleston at that time, the editor and reporter declared their advocacy openly. Yet, in 1959, when Workman and Waring began their work on behalf of the Republican Party, their advocacy conflicted with the norms of the white community. South Carolina remained a solidly Democratic state at the time. To use Daniel C. Hallin's concept, support for the Republican Party fell outside the white community's "sphere of consensus" and was located instead in the "sphere of legitimate controversy." As a subject of community dispute, partisan politics required impartial treatment under the norms of modern, mainstream American journalism. Waring and Workman felt compelled to abide by the practices of their profession when discussing their journalistic role in public. But that did not stop them from violating those expectations and working behind the scenes on behalf of the Republican Party. During the 1960s, they would continue to use their positions to further the party and the conservative movement. The two journalists would experiment with new arguments in the debate over full citizenship for African Americans.[70]

8   Color-Blind Conservatism
and the Great White Switch

On the evening of September 15, 1964, the *CBS Evening News* broadcast a political scoop: Senator Strom Thurmond of South Carolina planned to leave the Democratic Party and become a Republican. The next day, Thurmond flew home from Washington and confirmed the news in a statewide television address. Angered by President Lyndon Johnson's support for the Civil Rights Act, which had been signed into law two months earlier, Thurmond denounced the national Democrats as the "party of minority groups" and "power-hungry union leaders." Under Johnson's leadership, Thurmond said, the Democrats had embraced liberal policies that "encourage lawlessness, civil unrest, and mob action." Declaring that "the party of our fathers is dead," Thurmond pledged to do "everything in my power" to support the Republican Party and its conservative presidential nominee, Senator Barry Goldwater of Arizona.[1]

The day after his party switch, Thurmond greeted Goldwater on the tarmac at the Greenville-Spartanburg Airport and the two raised clasped hands in triumph before a crowd of twenty thousand southern Republicans. For the next six weeks, Thurmond crisscrossed the South on behalf of the GOP nominee, emphasizing Goldwater's support for states' rights and his vote against Johnson's civil rights legislation. The Republican candidate would halt the spread of communism, defend individual rights, and "protect law-abiding citizens against riots, looting, and assaults in the streets," the South Carolina senator proclaimed. Some Republican political posters made the racial link more explicit. One depicted a white woman in a torn party dress aided by white police officers. The woman had been "seized and beaten by a negro mob" while stopped at a traffic light, the caption read. In bold letters along the bottom, the poster declared: "Barry Goldwater. For States' Rights! For the South!"[2]

Thurmond's support helped Goldwater win South Carolina and four other Deep South states in the 1964 presidential election. But the Republican nominee's appeal to racial conservatives in the South appeared to be out of step with the consensus building in the rest of the nation. Four months after signing the Civil Rights Act, Johnson and his liberal running mate, Senator Hubert Humphrey of Minnesota, won more than 61 percent of the popular vote, the greatest margin of victory in U.S. history. Goldwater captured one state outside the Deep South, his native Arizona, which he won by less than one-half percent of the vote. The morning after the election, a front-page report in the *New York Times* said "the white backlash, on which Mr. Goldwater had counted so strongly, failed to materialize in most parts of the North."[3]

With the passage of the Civil Rights Act, which outlawed segregation in public accommodations, the federal government launched the most comprehensive reforms on behalf of African Americans since Reconstruction. President Kennedy had proposed the measure partly in response to the televised images emanating from Birmingham, Alabama, during the spring of 1963, when the city's police had used fire hoses and attack dogs to suppress peaceful black marchers. After Kennedy's assassination, Johnson and Humphrey led the campaign to overcome a filibuster by southern Senators that had stalled the bill for nearly a year. On August 6, 1964, as the president signed the measure into law, Johnson linked the battle against legalized segregation in the South to the highest ideals of the American nation. "Our Constitution, the foundation of our republic, forbids it. The principles of our freedom forbid it. Morality forbids it. And the law I sign tonight forbids it," the president declared."[4]

A year later, the nation would recoil in horror at more televised images from Alabama, these showing state troopers beating and gassing black marchers as they crossed the Edmund Pettus Bridge outside Selma. The protesters had been marching from Selma to the state capital in Montgomery to demand new laws to protect black voting rights in the South. Although legally obligated by the Fifteenth Amendment to allow blacks to vote, white authorities in the region often prevented African Americans from doing so. After the confrontation near Selma, the national television networks interrupted Sunday night primetime programming to broadcast the violent images into the homes of millions of American families. Infuriated by what he saw that night, the president responded a week later in a televised address to Congress that appealed to what he called "the secret heart of America itself." Echoing

Gunnar Myrdal's idea of a widely held "American Creed" embracing equality and democracy, Johnson said the founding fathers had established the nation with a special purpose in mind. "The great phrases of that purpose still sound in every American heart, North and South: 'All men are created equal'—'government by consent of the governed'—'give me liberty or give me death,'" the president said. To fulfill the nation's historic mission, Johnson said, Americans must embrace black citizenship and welcome African Americans into the nation's democratic family. "Their cause must be our cause, too," he proclaimed. "Because it is not just Negroes, but really it is all of us who must overcome the crippling legacy of bigotry and injustice." Raising his arms in the air, the president stunned even some of his supporters by evoking the spiritual anthem of the civil rights movement. "And we shall overcome," he said, stretching out each word for maximum effect.[5]

Passage of the Civil Rights Act of 1964 and the Voting Rights Act of 1965 signaled a turning point in American democratic life. The federal government's intervention on behalf of African Americans in the South effectively ended the Jim Crow era that South Carolina's "Pitchfork" Ben Tillman had helped usher in more than seventy years earlier. In his various speeches supporting the measures—particularly the 1965 address on voting rights—Johnson had used the communicative power of the presidency to integrate the African American quest for equality seamlessly into the larger American narrative of democracy and freedom. The signing of the Civil Rights Act of 1964 and the Voting Rights Act of 1965 had institutionalized social and political equality for African Americans. The president's powerful declaration of support, delivered by a former segregationist from the South, had resonated emotionally and helped etch the moment deeply in the nation's democratic heritage. Fifty years later, on the anniversary of the violence in Selma, the first African American president would note the power of this shared cultural heritage to influence future political debates. The Selma demonstrations were "not some outlier in the American experience," Barack Obama said. Instead, they were "the manifestation of a creed written into our founding documents: We the People . . . in order to form a more perfect union. We hold these truths to be self-evident, that all men are created equal." These were not mere words, the president said, but "rather a living thing, a call to action."[6]

The African American struggle for freedom across the twentieth century demonstrates the power of this shared culture—this "living thing"—to help generate what the sociologist Jeffrey C. Alexander describes as "social criticism and democratic integration at the same time." Members of a marginalized group that had been denied citizenship rights had launched a protest movement that appealed to the nation's most sacred ideals of justice, liberty, and equality. Using mass media to highlight their commitment to freedom, and to emphasize the antidemocratic acts of their oppressors, the movement gradually built a coalition of empathetic allies within the larger society. The effort had started slowly, and it required the growth of black communicative institutions before the movement could gain traction within white society. Eventually—as the voices of protest spread and their interpretations of public events burrowed deeper into the cultural mainstream—the discrepancy between the ideals of the "American creed" and the reality of the nation's civic life became impossible to ignore. Support for the out-group expanded, and public opinion reached a tipping point. Whether for reasons of morality or ambition, those at the highest levels of the nation's political and economic structure felt compelled to support the cause. In March 1965—one hundred years after the end of Lincoln's war against the slave-holding South—Johnson's speech before both houses of Congress welcomed all African Americans as full-fledged citizens and equal participants in what Alexander describes as the national civil sphere.[7]

While that last sentence is true, it is also far too simple and triumphant to capture the complexity of modern democracy. The civil sphere is a contested space, where outcomes are often contradictory and ambiguous. Just as it offers a means for civic repair, the civil sphere also offers opportunities for civic rupture. In the United States, one group's victory may appear to settle old arguments for good, but inevitably new battle lines emerge, with fresh interpretations used to generate another round of debate over the meaning of citizenship and the boundaries of the civic life. As the sociologist Douglas McAdam and Karina Kloos note in *Deeply Divided,* their study of political polarization in the United States, the white southerners who had opposed black equality in the 1950s did not give up the fight after passage of the civil rights and voting rights acts. In fact, the authors contend, the success of the civil rights movement in the mid-1960s helped mobilize a competing political movement. This "segregationist countermovement," as they call it, was equally intent on demonizing black activism and undermining black political aspirations. In South Carolina, Thomas Waring and William Workman enlisted in this new effort to sway public opinion. Working with conservative politicians, journalists, and other political actors, Waring and Workman joined the white backlash against the civil rights movement and helped develop a new narrative to confront black political clout in the emerging era of African American voting rights.[8]

After his failed Senate race in 1962, Workman returned to journalism, this time as editorial page editor at *The State* in Columbia. He and Waring now controlled the two largest newspapers in South Carolina, and they used their positions to help develop a new rhetorical strategy to maintain white political control through the Republican Party. This new strategy would accept a certain measure of black equality as inevitable. Yet it would develop a political language of "color-blind conservatism" as a means of delegitimizing black political activism. This new rhetoric would define the civil rights movement narrowly as simply an effort to eliminate racial classifications and demand formal equality under U.S. law. For black leaders and their white allies, the goals of the civil rights movement went beyond these limited and legalistic results. They called for a years-long effort to incorporate the historically marginalized black community fully into the political and economic structures of the nation. Color-blind conservatism dismissed such plans as the special pleading of a black community eager to use past racial injustices to demand unearned benefits from present-day society. By stoking white fears of these black demands—and raising doubts about black commitment to the nation's democratic values—the rhetoric of color-blind conservatism helped lure white voters to join the conservative movement within the GOP.[9]

Alexander's theory of the civil sphere helps explain the power of this new Republican rhetoric. He contends that successful political communication eventually links public issues back to the core democratic ideals embedded in the nation's historical memory. These "deep cultural codes" convey the nation's democratic values across society and help citizens distinguish civil from uncivil acts. By the early 1960s, the African American civil rights movement had successfully linked its call for social and political equality with the nation's sense of democratic fairness and civility. Segregationists who used overtly racist arguments found themselves on the wrong side of history. William F. Buckley had discovered this with his 1957 editorial, "Why the South Must Prevail," which opposed black voting rights in the South and drew harsh criticism, even from fellow conservatives. In the mid-1960s, Waring, Workman, and the rising conservative movement in South Carolina moved away from strictly racial arguments and employed more subtle language that intertwined race with issues of law and order, electoral integrity, and economic fairness. The color-blind strategy accepted black success in joining the nation's civil sphere, but suggested that any future consideration of the nation's racial history was an uncivil act that violated the core values of American democracy.[10]

Waring's tone on the editorial page of the Charleston *News and Courier* reflected this shift in strategy. In 1957, in a front-page editorial, he had denounced Eisenhower's civil rights bill as a "force bill" that would require "race-mixing" and initiate an era of bloodshed across the South. But in 1964, when Johnson signed a much stronger bill, the editor avoided predictions of racial violence. He merely urged readers to remain calm, avoid confrontation, and accept the law. But he suggested that the battle over public opinion was not over. Yes, "the Negro leaders and their allies have won enactment of the law they strove so hard to get," Waring said, but no one should celebrate until "the effects of the Civil Rights Act become clear, and until the mood of the entire country—not just the Southern states—begins to jell."[11]

Waring had been arguing for more than a decade that black crime and violence in northern cities would eventually trigger a backlash and turn national public opinion in favor of white southern segregationists. He elaborated on this strategy in a 1963 letter to an old friend from the White Citizens' Council movement. Waring said crime and violence in the North—as he put it, "explosions" now occurring "up in Northern ghettos"—would turn northern whites against African Americans and would "take the liberal's mind off the South." Waring told his friend that he saw indications that the strategy was working during a conference he had attended at the University of Chicago. He was "agreeably impressed" with some of the professors who had expressed concerns about "the social problems" that arise when "mingling different cultures." Waring said. "The troubles in the North," the editor added, appear to be "making an impression on them."[12]

Waring found more evidence of this shift in white public opinion the following year when George Wallace, the segregationist governor of Alabama, entered the Democratic presidential primary in Wisconsin. Initially dismissed as a joke by national media, Wallace won nearly 30 percent the Democratic vote and embarrassed the Johnson White House by nearly defeating a candidate representing the president in the race. The southern firebrand's strong support among working-class whites in the ethnic neighborhoods of Milwaukee stunned the political press. After touring south Milwaukee's 14th Ward—a Polish community with a sprinkling of German, Italian, and Croatian immigrants—political columnists Rowland Evans and Robert Novak described the residents as "neophyte Wallace voters" who had been persuaded by the Alabama governor to "fear the threat of a Negro invasion of their all-white neighborhoods."

Evans and Novak urged Johnson to launch a counterattack against "the lies and innuendo" Wallace had spread about the president's proposed civil rights act, which was working its way through the Senate at the time. In the *News and Courier,* Waring had a different interpretation of the Wisconsin results. He dismissed the racial question and claimed instead that Wallace's success had been fueled by distrust of what he called the "Super State"—the federal government. The debate over the civil rights act "goes past skin color into the bowels of the Constitution and the Republic," Waring wrote. "The man from Alabama has ripped open the bag into which the American people have been stuffed. He has shown them a way to escape. If opponents of the Super State are smart and fast enough to follow up on this break, they just may be able to snatch victory from the jaws of despair and defeat."[13]

By the following summer, the national debate over the meaning of the civil rights movement and African American citizenship had escalated. In June 1965, in a commencement address at Howard University, a flagship institution of African American higher education, Johnson expanded the government's commitment to civil rights beyond the strictly legal issues of segregation and voting rights. Declaring that "freedom is not enough," the president said blacks deserved economic help as well. "You do not wipe away the scars of centuries by saying: Now you are free to go where you want and do as you desire and choose the leaders you please," the president told the Howard graduates. "You do not take a person who, for years, has been hobbled by chains and liberate him, bring him to the starting line of a race, and then say, 'you are free to compete with all the others,' and still justly believe that you have been completely fair." The president said his administration would seek "not just equality as a right and a theory but equality as a fact and equality as a result."[14]

Johnson promised a new government push to aid black economic advance-ment as part of what he called "the next and more profound stage of the battle for civil rights." Yet his Howard speech rallied critics who believed Johnson's commitment to "equality of result," rather than "equality of opportunity," amounted to special treatment for African Americans. For civil rights sup-porters, the effort to overcome the nation's racial past and achieve social, legal, and political equality for blacks resonated with such American ideals as justice, fairness, and simple decency. Waring, Workman, and other conserva-tive critics interpreted Johnson's commitment to "equality of results" to mean just the opposite—an un-American effort to stack the deck in favor of one group of citizens over others. On the editorial page of *The State,* Workman denounced the "preferred status" that he claimed African Americans now had within U.S. society. In his view, African Americans enjoyed "the fawning favoritism of the federal government." The black citizen is "finding economic opportunities flowering before him in a profusion greatly exceeding his own readiness to exploit his good fortune." The success of black political pressure, Workman concluded, had given African Americans everything "except the one thing which cannot be dictated by even so worshipful an administration as that headed by President Lyndon B. Johnson." For Workman, "that elusive but essential element" was white society's acceptance of black equality. That was something the federal government could not grant, he argued; in fact, social programs designed to help African Americans actually undermined this quest for acceptance in the eyes of most white citizens, Workman said. Such early criticism of the Howard speech laid the groundwork for the conservative assault on affirmative action programs the following decade. The issue would play a significant role in attracting new white supporters to the conservative movement across the 1970s and 1980s.[15]

On August 11, 1965, just one week after Johnson signed the historic Voting Rights Act, the Los Angeles community of Watts erupted in flames. During four days of violence, thirty-four people died and property valued in the millions of dollars was destroyed. The tension between the black residents of Watts and the white Los Angeles police officers who patrolled the neighborhood had been building for years. Charges of police brutality were common. Yet for many white television viewers, the violent images were shocking and discordant. Five months earlier, they had seen white state troopers in Alabama beat and gas peaceful black marchers near Selma. Since then, Congress had answered the protesters' pleas with sweeping voting rights reforms in the South, and the nation's president, a white southerner, had aligned himself closely with the black struggle for equality. Yet in Watts, African Americans appeared to be burning down a city neighborhood and threatening to kill those who got in their way. Los Angeles television station KTLA pioneered the use of a helicopter in local news coverage during the early 1960s, and the station delivered live images of the mayhem seen across the nation. As one historian noted: "After Watts, the legions of moderate whites who had been so recently demanding justice for the meek, Christ-like demonstrators at Selma began melting away."[16]

Since the mid-1950s, Waring had been arguing that "race mixing" would inevitably lead to violence, and that the civil rights movement, particularly the acts of civil disobedience led by Rev. Martin Luther King Jr., would encourage black lawlessness in the North. The *News and Courier*'s front page often reflected Waring's obsession with racial conflict in the North. Soon after the *Brown* rulings, the editor began giving even minor racial incidents major news play. In 1956, for example, a five-column, double-decker headline splashed across the front page declared that "Negro mob riots" aboard a ship carrying teenagers to an amusement park north of Buffalo. A melee that left fourteen people injured was certainly newsworthy in upstate New York, but for the South Carolina newspaper, the story's prominent placement had everything to do with Waring's political goals. The editor was so intrigued with the "Negro mob" story that he sent correspondent Anthony Harrigan to Buffalo to investigate. Harrigan returned with a six-part series examining "the problems created by the Negro migration" to the Buffalo area. Later in the series, one of Harrigan's stories explained that "Rochester Also Has Its Negro Problem." Waring was so pleased with the reporter's work in New York that he sent Harrigan to other northern states and out to California that summer to keep Charleston readers abreast of racial conflicts nationwide.[17]

In August 1965, Waring moved quickly to interpret the political meaning of the racial disturbances in Watts. The violence in the impoverished section of Los Angeles, he claimed, indicated that some in the black community were "unworthy of citizenship in a decent community." In the search for causes, he dismissed black anger over the "oft-repeated tale of white oppression" and police brutality in Watts. Instead, he focused on the civil rights movement and the recent legislation "giving unprecedented privileges and support to a minority group." The federal government has been "conferring on Negro Americans extraordinary opportunities to gain public assistance in everything from employment to housing," he wrote. Both the Kennedy and Johnson administrations have "endeavored to meet every demand" made by African Americans, Waring said, "but still there is this terrible outbreak of Negro violence." Waring placed part of the blame on language used by the president, particularly in speeches like the one Johnson delivered at Howard earlier that month. "Only two weeks ago, the president spoke to students as 'fellow revolutionaries,'" Waring said. "Well, Los Angeles is having its street revolution . . . and decent people are dead." In a separate editorial, Waring said the violence in Watts and a recent clash on Chicago's South Side were evidence that some African Americans wanted more from society than equal rights under the law. "Is it voting rights they seek? Nobody is hindering their voting," Waring said. "Do they want to integrate the schools? No segregation laws exist in California or Illinois." The lesson blacks had learned from the civil rights movement, Waring concluded, was "that whites were mistreating them" and that "resisting police authority" was an acceptable response.[18]

In *The State*, Workman depicted Watts as another indication of the black community's disregard for property rights and its unwillingness to accept civic responsibilities. "The only discrimination he can protest is that which he brings upon himself by his own actions and attitudes," Workman wrote. "What white employer wants to hire a Negro by day who may be plundering his store by night? What self-respecting politician will seek the support of a constituency which may turn out to be a riotous mob at the drop of a word? What neighborhood would welcome newcomers who bring them a disregard of property values, a disdain for decent standards, and a manifest distaste of law and order?[19]

The unraveling of the nation's liberal consensus during the traumatic events of the 1960s has been well documented. Johnson's Howard speech would mark the pinnacle of his administration's public commitment to civil rights. During his final three years in office, the escalation of the war in Vietnam would dominate news coverage, spawn an increasingly aggressive antiwar movement, and undermine the president's credibility as a voice for social change. Earlier histories of the time have suggested the fracturing of the civil rights movements and the rise of black power leaders combined with the images of urban rioting to alter white perceptions of the African American political struggle and turn public opinion against the movement. Recently, historians have begun to question the simplicity of this so-called "declension" narrative in civil rights history. Yet most agree that public opinion did undergo a shift in the second half of the 1960s. According to David C. Carter, television furthered the goals of the civil rights movement in the South through the Selma campaign in 1965, but in the three years that followed, the images of blacks rioting in northern cities angered and frightened white viewers. Riding the crest of this backlash, the GOP recovered from the Goldwater rout in 1964 to gain congressional seats in the 1966 midterm elections and to win the White House in 1968. By the late 1970s, the conservative counter-revolution that William F. Buckley Jr. envisioned back in the late 1950s—and that South Carolina's leading white journalists helped him build—would take firm control of the GOP under Ronald Reagan's leadership and would come to dominate American politics over the next three decades.[20]

Race and the "Great White Switch"

Historians have debated the role of race in the rise of the modern conservative movement, particularly its role in the "great white switch"—the decision by white southerners to leave the Democratic Party and join the GOP. In 1995, Dan T. Carter produced an influential interpretation of the backlash thesis in his book *The Politics of Rage,* a biography of Wallace that placed the former Alabama governor at the center of the conservative transformation of U.S. politics. Carter maintained that Wallace's brand of ultra-conservatism had tapped into the fears of whites in the North and the South who saw their world undergoing rapid change. In the mid-1960s, Wallace had catered primarily to their racial fears, Carter maintains, but by the late 1960s he had begun to avoid overt racism and attack a wider range of targets—antiwar protesters, welfare recipients, government bureaucrats. The decision to downplay race was a cosmetic one, Carter contends. Wallace continued to scapegoat African Americans to fuel white resentment, but he delivered his message indirectly, often using a type of code that intertwined race with other issues. Blatantly racist rhetoric was no longer acceptable, but Wallace found that his message of resentment was more popular than ever. As Carter put it, "The politics of rage that George Wallace made his own had moved from the fringes of our society to center stage."[21]

In the past decade, a new group of historians has emerged to question whether race was the dominant issue driving the rise of the conservative Republican Party in the South. Joseph Crespino, author of a book about political change in his native Mississippi, says placing too much emphasis on the backlash thesis attributes to white racism "a mystical, ahistorical quality that explains everything and, thus, explains nothing very well." He maintains that economic and religious issues were at least as important as race in pushing white southerners away from the Democratic Party. In his study of suburban and urban whites in Atlanta, Richmond, and Charlotte, Matthew D. Lassiter argues that members of the "silent majority" in the South opposed "massive resistance" leaders who wanted to close public schools to avoid integration in the late 1950s and early '60s. Yet they also rejected the biracial Democratic coalition that emerged in the early 1970s because they did not trust it to protect their economic prosperity. Two political scientists, Byron E. Shafer and Richard Johnston, take the argument against the backlash thesis further. Their analysis of voting data maintains that race had little to do with partisan realignment in the South in the years after the civil rights movement. White southern voters had embraced the low-tax, small-government economic arguments of Republican conservatives, they argue.[22]

During the 1970s, economic, religious, and cultural issues clearly played significant roles in attracting white southerners to the conservative movement. In 1973, the U.S. Supreme Court's *Roe v. Wade* decision legalizing abortion nationwide politicized white evangelicals in the South, and their growing cultural antipathy to the rising women's movement led them into the conservative wing of the Republican Party. Moreover, the economic trauma created by the oil shortages of the mid-1970s and the escalating interest rates during the Carter administration angered white voters in the prosperous and growing suburbs of the Sunbelt. The Soviet invasion of Afghanistan and the Iranian hostage crisis added to their concerns about the Democratic Party's leadership.

Yet political change is driven as much by rhetoric as by events on the ground. It is the interpretation of those public events that alter perceptions and help citizens make sense of their world. A close look at the role of leading segregationists in South Carolina reveals the centrality of the racial issue and its contribution in transforming the Republican Party into what New Hampshire editor William Loeb called the "white man's party." The conservative voices in the state's major white newspapers had been complaining about the growth of the federal government since the early days of the New Deal. Yet their argument never gained broad public support in the state until the late 1940s, when President Truman proposed civil rights reform in the South. After the *Brown* ruling in 1954, the state's white political leaders, working closely with key journalists, developed a rhetoric of "massive resistance" that linked the call for racial equality to the growth of a tyrannical and oppressive federal government. As one editor had written, "civil rights" would inevitably lead to "socialism." By the early 1960s, when it was clear that massive resistance would fail and that blacks were gaining strength within the Democratic Party, key segregationist leaders embraced a new strategy. The state's best-known journalists—Waring and Workman of the Charleston *News and Courier*—joined forces with a small group of economic conservatives to build a viable Republican Party in the state. It was this union of segregationists and small-government conservatism that laid the foundation for the party's dramatic growth in the South Carolina and the nation over the next two decades. As Dan T. Carter contends, "even though the streams of racial and economic conservatism have sometimes flowed in separate channels, they ultimately joined in the political coalition that reshaped American politics."[23]

By the late 1970s, Reagan had united former segregationists with economic and social conservatives to create a political movement that would come to dominate American politics over the next three decades. The Californian had built this coalition in part through the use of coded rhetoric that referred to race without mentioning the term. During his presidential campaign in 1980, for example, he appeared at the Neshoba County Fair near Philadelphia, Mississippi to court the state's white conservative voters. The symbolism of Reagan's visit was hard to miss. Sixteen years earlier, during the Mississippi Freedom Summer, when black and white civil rights workers poured into the state, three activists had been murdered in Neshoba County and buried in an earthen dam. Because of the murders, Neshoba County held a special place in the history of the African American struggle for equality in the United States. Reagan used his visit to that sacred ground to declare his support for "states' rights"—the same argument the Dixiecrat candidate, Strom Thurmond, had used sixteen years earlier. Yet Reagan's supporters continue to claim that his appeal to Mississippi voters that day was not racial.[24]

It was a political strategist from South Carolina who helped pioneer the use of such coded language to inject race into political debate. Lee Atwater served as White House political director under Reagan and as chief strategist for President George H. W. Bush's 1988 campaign. In a 1981 interview with political scientist Alexander Lamis, Atwater explained the evolution of coded language in Republican political campaigns in the South. "You start out in 1954 by saying, 'nigger, nigger, nigger.' By 1968 you can't say 'nigger'—that hurts you, backfires," Atwater said. "So you say stuff like forced busing, states' rights, and all that stuff, and you're getting so abstract. Now, you're talking about cutting taxes, and all these things you're talking about are totally economic things and a byproduct of them is, blacks get hurt worse than whites. . . ."[25]

One such coded issue that Reagan used effectively to shape white perception of African Americans involved welfare fraud and the so-called "welfare queen." Although he never used that specific term, Reagan delivered frequent rants against "a woman on the south side of Chicago" who received welfare but drove around town in a Cadillac. It was a rhetorical flourish that depicted blacks as lazy, shiftless, and unwilling to carry their proper burden as U.S. citizens. It was a trope that would be repeated frequently by conservatives. A version could be heard in 1994, when Newt Gingrich contrasted "the pristine work ethic" of his overwhelmingly white suburban district with what he called the "welfare values" of the mostly black city of Atlanta. Later that year, Gingrich led a sweeping Republican victory that won control of the House of Representatives for the first time since 1954—and completed the South's transformation into a stronghold of the new GOP.[26]

Republicans dispute the centrality of race in the party's rise to prominence over the past four decades. They are correct to note that economic and social issues have played a significant role. What gets obscured, however, is the way those issues have been racialized in the discourse of American politics. The debate over government spending often focuses on welfare and social programs—which are incorrectly assumed to be primarily black initiatives— and ignore mortgage tax deduction rules and other much more expensive entitlements that benefit middle- and upper-class families. Even marginal efforts to offset a history of inequality through race-based affirmative action programs are depicted as racist and un-American, and those who support such efforts in public discourse are labeled as antidemocratic and uncivil. The white journalists of midcentury South Carolina helped lay the groundwork for this type of "color-blind conservatism." Their shifting narratives and evolving rhetoric during the long struggle over civil rights in South Carolina offers a guide to help us better understand how such cultural interpretations have helped shape our current political discourse.

Epilogue

In 1962, John McCray observed the rise of the new, conservative Republican Party in South Carolina, and he did not like what he saw. In his newspaper column in the *Pittsburgh Courier*, McCray claimed the party was "controlled by the White Citizens' Council, the KKK, and the kindred other white elements." Faced with "race-baiting whites" in the Democratic Party and the conservative GOP, McCray said blacks had nowhere to go in South Carolina politics. In his words, they were "political step-children" yet again.[1]

While certainly true in 1962, the situation would change dramatically over the following decade. Propelled by the Voting Rights Act, which added hundreds of thousands of African Americans to the voting rolls in the South, the biracial Democratic Party that emerged in the 1970s began to elect more progressive candidates across the region. In South Carolina, for example, Richard Riley, a state senator from Greenville, won the governorship in 1978 and followed through on his campaign promise to invest heavily to improve the newly integrated public schools in the state. Candidates promising similar reforms took office in other Deep South and border states during the 1970s and early 1980s—Reubin Askew in Florida, Dale Bumpers in Arkansas, William Winter in Mississippi, and an ambitious Yale Law School graduate named Bill Clinton, also in Arkansas. Even George Wallace campaigned for black votes during his final gubernatorial run in 1982. Downplaying his segregationist rhetoric, Wallace emphasized his support for expanded social and educational programs in Alabama.[2]

The biracial coalition that emerged in the Democratic Party in the 1970s also elected African Americans to state and federal offices in the South, including prominent leaders of the civil rights movement. In 1972, one of

Rev. Martin Luther King Jr.'s former aides, Andrew Young, won a U.S. House race in a white-majority district in Georgia. Young and Barbara Jordan of Texas became the first black members of Congress from the Deep South since Reconstruction. In 1986, Georgian John Lewis, a hero of the Selma voting rights campaign, was elected to Congress as well. That same year, the Democratic Party's biracial coalition in the South delivered a setback to the Reagan presidency and its conservative revolution by defeating four incumbent Republican Senators in the region and returning Senate control to the Democrats.

The political moment would not last, however. In the 1990s—particularly in the years after Clinton's election to the White House in 1992—the great white switch accelerated and reached a tipping point. White Democrats who had voted Republican in presidential elections but remained loyal Democrats at the state and local level finally left the party entirely and joined the GOP. The Democratic Party's biracial coalition no longer could attract enough white members to constitute a majority in most Deep South states. After the 1994 midterm elections, the conservative Republican Party would take firm control of a new "solid South." In South Carolina, after Riley left office in 1987, the Republicans won seven of the next eight gubernatorial elections, the only loss coming after a party split over whether to launch a lottery in the deeply religious state.

John McCray would not be in South Carolina to witness these historic political changes. In 1961, after the Kennedy administration did not offer a job, McCray continued to write for the *Pittsburgh Courier,* but the once powerful black newspaper was struggling financially. At one point, the paper failed to meet its payroll, withholding paychecks for more than two weeks. The paper's chief executive blamed the problem on heavy snows that prevented its distribution in key areas. It was an indication of how far the black newspaper business had fallen in the early 1960s.[3]

Between 1962 and 1964, McCray received offers to leave South Carolina and take top editing positions at the *Chicago Defender* and New York's *Amsterdam News.* But he understood the economic precariousness of the blacks press at the time, and he always said he wanted to stay in the Palmetto State. McCray told a friend that he "grew up in South Carolina, am rooted to it and to leave it, especially under the prevailing circumstances, would be personally grievous and refuting the theory of opportunity and possibility I have been writing about and advocating for many years." McCray wrote a bit for the *Defender* during those years, and in 1964, he did move to Atlanta briefly to work for the Scott family's *Atlanta World.* With the outlook for newspaper work grim, and with no other job prospects in South Carolina, McCray eventually left his home state in late 1964 to take a job at his alma mater, Talladega College, in Alabama. McCray handled public relations and eventually served as a recruitment official and top aid to the school's president.[4]

While at Talladega, McCray reunited with an old classmate from his undergraduate days, Carrie Allen, a prominent social worker who was teaching at the college. They married and lived in Talladega until McCray's death in 1987. Carrie Allen McCray later moved to South Carolina and, at the age of seventy-three, launched a celebrated second career as a poet and memoirist.[5]

McCray managed to build a comfortable new life in Talladega, but he found it hard to leave newspaper work behind. Before departing South Carolina, he took one last shot at reviving the *Lighthouse*. He managed to publish one issue—November 23, 1963, the day after President Kennedy's assassination. The new venture had little capital, however, and McCray gave up after that first issue. While at Talladega, McCray resumed journalistic work in the 1980s, writing a weekly column for the *Charleston Chronicle*, a black newspaper in the South Carolina Lowcountry. His column—"The Way It Was"—ran for more than five years in the *Chronicle,* and it served as an invaluable source of public memory recalling a black social and political movement that had often been marginalized in the Palmetto State's history.

McCray had fallen in love with journalism at an early age, and he never lost his belief in the political power that a newspaper could wield. He frequently wrote about the black press in the *Lighthouse and Informer,* and he clearly saw himself as part of a historically important institution. In one editorial, he honored the nation's first black newspaper, *Freedom's Journal,* calling it the "father and founder" of the black press and urging other newspapers to carry on its legacy. The black newspaper must remain vigilant in battling racism and injustice, McCray said, or the same problems will continue to "divide this country and subject us to the heel of the bigot." Around the same time, McCray's newspaper published a political cartoon showing newspapers labeled "Negro Press" rolling off a printing press and flowing across the sky to form a planet identified as "A New World."[6]

Yet McCray was also a realist. He more than anyone understood the sacrifices required of a black newspaperman operating in the Deep South in the mid-twentieth century. As he put it, only a "plum stomped down fool" would try to publish a black newspaper. "Invariably, you are committed to fighting for an ethnic group that doesn't patronize you enough to pay the rent," he said. "You have to find some way of trading enough with white concerns that will work with you, while you consistently blast away at some other whites. Sort of a crazy business."[7]

McCray never reconciled with Modjeska Simkins, the woman who played such an important role in his newspaper's rise to political prominence in the state. Simkins remained a significant figure in South Carolina until her death in 1992. After stepping down from the state conference of NAACP branches in 1957, she focused her efforts on her home county of Richland. Having pioneered the use of a newspaper to drive activism in the 1940s, Simkins turned to a different medium in the 1960s. She hosted a weekly radio program on WOIC, a popular soul-music station in Columbia. Sponsored by the Richland County Citizens Committee, Simkins's fifteen-minute segment ran most Wednesday evenings from 1966 through the late 1970s. As historian Brian Ward notes, Simkins used her broadcast platform as a way to engage black voters in the community. In her words, she believed radio was the best way for "properly informing our people about candidates and issues, and for getting a full turnout on election day."[8]

As she approached her seventies, Simkins occasionally bristled at the new generation of black activism that emerged. She expressed concerns about the Black Power rhetoric of the era. The "real issue" of Black Power concerns "a united effort in spending our dollars and casting our votes to enrich our future," Simkins said. "This is all that the Black Power idea has ever meant since Frederick Douglass mentioned it generations ago."[9]

McCray also had problems connecting with a new generation of activists. In 1960, the sit-in movement launched by four students challenging segregation laws in Greensboro, North Carolina, had spread quickly to South Carolina. On February 12, more than one hundred students held sit-ins at lunch counters throughout the town of Rock Hill, near the North Carolina border. When young activists launched similar campaigns of civil disobedience in Columbia, McCray criticized them. He had developed a friendly relationship with the white mayor, Lester L. Bates, and he believed Bates was serious about ending segregation voluntarily in the state's capital city. McCray denounced the tactics of civil disobedience and encouraged the demonstrators to "sit and talk" rather than "sit-in." In response, the young protesters accused McCray of selling out. After the city integrated its downtown lunch counters in August 1962, McCray—never one to forgive and forget easily—addressed the young demonstrators again in his *Pittsburgh Courier* column. "It's considered 'bad taste' to say 'I told you so," McCray began, but "I feel justified." McCray's column never addressed the question of whether the sit-in movement had helped motivate the city of Columbia to desegregate so quickly.[10]

By the late 1960s, as the number of African American voters grew and blacks began to exert more political influence, the state of South Carolina began to take a different view of its civil rights pioneers. In 1969, for example, a special committee appointed by the city of Columbia selected former state NAACP president Rev. James M. Hinton as one of five senior citizens to be honored for their services to the community. The timing of Hinton's award was particularly poignant. He received the honor the same year as Samuel L. Latimer, the former editor of *The State* newspaper. A decade earlier, Latimer's editorial page had often denounced Hinton and his organization, calling them subversive and dangerous. When Hinton passed away in 1970, Latimer's former newspaper ran a lengthy and mostly laudatory obituary. In 1992, when Simkins died, the news received front-page play across South Carolina. By that time, Simkins had been awarded the state's highest civilian honor, the Order of the Palmetto.[11]

Across the 1970s, Thomas R. Waring Jr. and William D. Workman Jr. continued their work at two of the state's largest daily newspapers. In 1966, four years after his failed U.S. Senate bid, Workman was elevated to the top job of executive editor at *The State,* overseeing the newsroom and the editorial page. He would remain in that position until 1972, when he gave up his management role to focus on his column writing. He retired from the paper in 1979. In 1982, he came out of retirement to make a second political race, accepting the GOP nomination to challenge Riley, South Carolina's popular Democratic governor. Workman's last hurrah never had a realistic chance of succeeding. He lost badly, garnering a mere 30 percent of the vote. Workman passed away in 1990.

In Charleston, Waring served as editor of the *News and Courier* until 1974, when he moved to its sister paper, the afternoon *Charleston Evening Post,* a newspaper his father had once edited. After three years at the *Post,* Waring retired in 1977. Personal tragedy had sapped some of his vigor, and Waring was less engaged with the state's political life during the final years of his career. In 1965, his wife Celia had died unexpectedly during a vacation trip to see their daughter in Spain. The loss hit Waring hard. As he described it in a letter to his old friend John Briggs, the former *New York Times* music critic, the death of his wife had left him "living alone at 10 Atlantic Street . . . with occasional visits from my children." Waring remained in Charleston until his death in 1993.[12]

Workman, Waring, and McCray had always been linked in the political struggle over the future of South Carolina. In 1935, when McCray returned home from college, he confronted a culture of nearly unquestioned white supremacy in his home state. To fight back, he created a newspaper and used it to deliver his own interpretation of public events. One year later, in 1936, Workman dropped out of George Washington Law School in Washington, D.C., and also returned home. In a long personal memo written at the time, Workman mused about what he really wanted to do with his life. He said he knew he wanted to work in "government and politics" in some way, and he believed "newspaper work is connected" to those endeavors. As the historian

David Paul Nord has noted, newspapers have always been "enmeshed in the political and cultural lives of their communities." Workman understood this. He rejected the legal profession and pursued journalism because he believed newspaper work provided an entrée into the political life of his home state. He landed a night-desk job on the *News and Courier,* where Waring served as city editor and was being groomed for the top job as the paper's editor.[13]

Over the next thirty years, McCray, Workman, and Waring would join the debate over the meaning of citizenship in South Carolina. As much as any politician, the three journalists would engage in the struggle to shape their state's political future.

Notes

Introduction

1. John Henry McCray oral history interview, 1985 (transcript in author's possession).

2. Newby, *Black Carolinians,* 201–67; Edgar, *South Carolina: A History,* 498–511; Hoffman, "The Genesis of the Modern Movement"; Hemmingway, "Beneath the Yoke of Bondage"; Wright, "The Southern White Man and the Negro."; Simon, "Race Relations"; Simon, *A Fabric of Defeat,* 220–25; Hayes, *South Carolina and the New Deal.*

3. Annual report, South Carolina Conference of NAACP Branches, 1948, NAACP papers, B-II 129. For more on the rising civil rights movement in South Carolina in the 1940s, see: Lau, *Democracy Rising;* Sullivan, *Days of Hope;* Roefs, "Leading the Civil Rights Vanguard": Egerton, *Speak Now Against the Day;* Newby, *Black Carolinians;* Hoffman, "Genesis of the Modern Movement": Aba-Mecha, "Black Woman Activist"; Richards, "Osceola E. McKaine"; Charron, *Freedom's Teacher;* Frederickson, *The Dixiecrat Revolt;* Gellman, *Death Blow to Jim Crow.*

4. Sullivan, *Days of Hope,* 142.

5. Klarman, *From Jim Crow to Civil Rights,* 3–7; Sitkoff, *A New Deal for Blacks,* 50–68; Sullivan, *Days of Hope,* 128.

6. Klarman, *From Jim Crow to Civil Rights,* 3–7, 171–235; Sitkoff, *A New Deal for Blacks,* 67; Weiss, *Farewell to the Party of Lincoln;* Gilmore, "False Friends and Avowed Enemies"; Sullivan, *Days of Hope;* Lau, *Democracy Rising;* Hayes, *South Carolina and the New Deal;* Garson, *The Democratic Party and the Politics of Sectionalism;* Morris, *The Origins of the Civil Rights Movement;* Payne, *I've Got the Light of Freedom;* Ditmar, *Local People;* Kruze and Tuck, *Fog of War.*

7. McAdam, *Political Process and the Development of the Black Insurgency,* 2nd ed., viii. See also: Gamson, Fireman, Rytina, *Encounters with Unjust Authority,* 1–22; Snow and Benford, "Ideology, Frame Resonance, and Participant Mobilization," 197–218; Benford and Snow, "Framing Processes and Social Movements," 611–39.

8. Phillips, "The Central Theme of Southern History," 35–42.

9. For more on the shifting historiography of the civil rights movement, see Payne, *I've Got the Light of Freedom,* preface to the 2007 edition, and Hall, "The Long Civil Rights Movement." In addition to Lau, *Democracy Rising* and Charron, *Freedom's Teacher,* other notable works on South Carolina and civil rights include: Sullivan, *Days of Hope*; Richards, "Osceola E. McKaine," Woods, "Modjeska Simkins," Roefs, "Leading the Civil Rights Vanguard," Gellman, *Death Blow to Jim Crow,* Newby, *Black Carolinians,* Hoffman, "The Genesis of the Modern Movement," Hemmingway, "Beneath the Yoke of Bondage," Frederickson, *The Dixiecrat Revolt,* Bass and Thompson, *Strom,* Crespino, *Strom Thurmond's America,* Cahodas, *Strom Thurmond,* Simon, *A Fabric of Defeat,* Hayes, *South Carolina and the New Deal,* Edgar, *South Carolina: A History.*

10. John H. McCray, "The Need for Changing: Our Enslaved Children," *Lighthouse and Informer,* May 11, 1947.

11. Roberts and Klibanoff, *The Race Beat.*

12. Alexander, *The Civil Sphere*; Myrdal, *An American Dilemma.* First published in 1944, Myrdal's massive two-volume study was funded by the Carnegie Foundation and included the work of hundreds of scholars. See also: Jackson, *Gunnar Myrdal and America's Conscience*; Gerstle, *American Crucible: Race and Nation in the Twentieth Century,* 5, 44–80. Gerstle takes the term "civic nationalism" from Michael Ignatieff, *Blood and Belonging: Journeys into to the New Nationalism.*

13. Alexander, *The Civil Sphere*; Alexander, "On the Interpretation of *The Civil Sphere*," 629–39.

14. A. J. Clement Jr. to William D. Workman, WDW Papers, Correspondence, 1948.

15. On black journalism as a "fighting press," see: Myrdal, *An American Dilemma,* vol. 2, 908–27; Roberts and Klibanoff, *The Race Beat,* 12–23; Washburn, *The African American Newspaper,* xvi.

16. For more on the "monitorial" role of journalism, see: Christians et al., *Normative Theories of the Media,* 115–16, 125; or recent examples exploring the question of journalism and partisanship, see: Schudson, "Persistence of Vision—Partisan Journalism in the Mainstream Press," and Kaplan, "From Partisanship to Professionalism: The Transformation of the Daily Press," 116–39.

17. See: Schudson, *Discovering the News,* 14–57; Baldasty, *The Commercialization of News in the Nineteenth Century*; McGerr, *The Decline of Popular Politics,* 107–11; Dicken-Garcia, *Journalistic Standards in Nineteenth-Century America,* 224.

18. Kaplan, *Politics and the American Press,* 16; McGerr, *The Decline of Popular Politics,* 111, 118–20; Kaplan, "From Partisanship to Professionalism: The Transformation of the Daily Press."

19. In addition to McGerr, Kaplan, and Schudson, see also: Campbell, *The Year that Defined Modern Journalism* and Mindich, *Just the Facts*; Pratte, *Gods Within the Machine,* 37; Dickson, *Mass Media Education in Transition,* 8–25; The original canons can be found in the appendix of: Crawford, *The Ethics of Journalism*; the ASNE updated the 1923 canons of journalism in 1975. See http://asne.org/Article_View/ArticleId/325/ASNEs-Statement-of-Principles.aspx (accessed June11, 2015); Christians et al., *Normative Theories of the Media,* 115–16, 125; Borden and Pritchard, "Conflict of Interest in Journalism," 73–91.

20. See, for example, Lippmann, *Public Opinion*; Schudson, *Discovering the News,*

121–23; Kaplan, *Politics and the American Press,* 111; Schudson, "Persistence of Vision—Partisan Journalism in the Mainstream Press," 141.

21. For an extreme example of partisanship in the mid-twentieth century press, see how the Chandler family's *Los Angeles Times* supported the Republican Party, in Halberstam, *The Powers That Be,* 112–22; Also, see the way publisher Eugene Pulliam's *Arizona Republic* used its news pages on behalf of Senator Barry Goldwater, in Perlstein, *Before the Storm,* 40; Also, see the dispute over whether Walter Cronkite, an icon of impartial journalism, secretly encouraged Robert Kennedy to run for the presidency as an anti–Vietnam War candidate, then later interviewed Kennedy about his political plans, in Brinkley, *Cronkite,* 389–92 and Menand, "Seeing It Now: Walter Cronkite and the Legend of CBS News." *The New Yorker,* July 9, 2012, 88–94; Kaplan, "From Partisanship to Professionalism," 116–39 and Schudson, "Persistence of Vision," 140–50; Kaplan, "From Partisanship to Professionalism," 139; McChesney, *The Problem of the Media,* 61–77; Dicken-Garcia, *Journalistic Standards in Nineteenth-Century America,* 32; Schudson, "Persistence of Vision," 146–50; For examples of codes of conduct governing editorial writers and columnists, see Fink, *Writing Opinion for Impact,* 7–10: The National Conference of Editorial Writers Basic Statement of Principles stated: "The writer should be constantly alert to conflicts of interest, real or apparent, including those that may arise from financial holdings, secondary employment, holding public office, or involvement in political, civic, or other organizations." Despite such codes, evidence that rules remained murky for opinion journalists can be found in the dispute over George Will's involvement in debate preparation for presidential candidate Ronald Reagan in 1980. See "Comment: Where There's a Will There's a Way, *Columbia Journalism Review,* September 1, 1983, 25. Adding to the confusion over the role of opinion journalism is the existence of advocacy journalists who wrote for such journals as *The Nation, The National Review,* the alternative and minority press, and other publications of opinion and advocacy; McChesney, *The Political Economy of Media,* 30.

22. See: Christians, et al., *Normative Theories of the Media,* 125; Kaplan, "From Partisanship to Professionalism," 134–35; Cook, *Governing with the News.*

23. Christians, et al., *Normative Theories of the Media,* 125.

24. Baker, *Following the Color Line;* Beard quoted in Sitkoff, *A New Deal for Blacks,* 5; "The 'Jim Crow' Decision," *New York Times,* June 2, 1910, 8; *Plessy v. Ferguson* 163 U.S. 567 (1896); Woodward, *Origins of the New South;* Woodward, *The Strange Career of Jim Crow;* Williamson, *The Crucible of Race;* Brundage, *Lynching in the New South.*

25. Foner, *Reconstruction,* 1–18; Williamson, *The Crucible of Race,* 111–50.

26. Du Bois uses the veil metaphor in *The Souls of Black Folk* (1903) and again in *Darkwater: Voices From Within the Veil* (1920); Vogel, "Introduction," in *The Black Press: New Literary and Historical Essays.*

27. Bartley, *The Rise of Massive Resistance,* 4–5; *Gaines v. Canada* 305 U.S. 337 (1938).

28. John H. McCray, "The Way It Was," *Charleston Chronicle,* February 21, March 6, March 13, 1982.

29. Gamson, Fireman, and Rytina, *Encounters with Unjust Authority,* 1–18; King, *Civil Rights and the Idea of Freedom,* 26–27.

30. For more on the "segregationist countermovement," see McAdam and Kloos, *Deeply Divided,* 23–24.

Chapter 1. Early Struggles

1. John Henry McCray, "The Way It Was," *Charleston Chronicle,* February 2, 1982, JHM papers; McCray oral history interview with Patricia Sullivan, 1985 (transcript in author's possession).

2. McCray oral history, 1985; Hampton and Washington, *The History of Lincolnville, South Carolina;* Robertson, *Denmark Vesey;* Hemingway, "South Carolina," in *The Black Press in the South;* Corasaniti, Perez-Pena, and Alvarez, "Church Massacre Suspect Held as Charleston Grieves," *New York Times,* June 18, 2015.

3. Hampton and Washington, *The History of Lincolnville,* 2–4; for more on Richard Harvey Cain, see Holt, *Black Over White.*

4. La Brie, "Black Newspapers"; Hampton and Washington, "The Story of Lincolnville."

5. Ibid. For more on the end of Reconstruction, see Foner, *Reconstruction.*

6. McCray said two white men lived in Lincolnville when he was a child. McCray oral history, 1985.

7. John H. McCray, "The Way It Was," *Charleston Chronicle,* December 26, 1981, JHM papers, Reel 16, journalism.

8. John H. McCray, "The Way It Was," *Charleston Chronicle,* February. 20, 1982, JHM papers, Reel 16, journalism. McCray oral history interview, 1985; John H. McCray, "The Way It Was," *Charleston Chronicle,* July 25, 1981, JHM papers, Reel 16, journalism.

9. John H. McCray, "The Arraignment of Student Inertia," *The Mule's Ear* 11, no. 3 (February 1935), in JHM papers, Reel 1, journalism; for more on the Scottsboro case, see Carter, *A Tragedy of the American South.*

10. John Henry McCray, "The Way It Was," *Charleston Chronicle,* February 16, 1982, JHM papers, Reel 16, journalism.

11. Sullivan, *Lift Every Voice,* 229.

12. John H. McCray, "States the Position of Southern Negroes," *Charleston News and Courier,* April 13, 1937, clip in NAACP Papers, I-G-196; Walter White to John H. McCray, April 24, 1937, Louise Purvis Bell to the editor, *Charleston News and Courier,* April 16, 1937, NAACP Papers, I-G-196; Stark, *Damned Upcountryman.*

13. "Speaks for Southern Negroes," *Charleston News and Courier,* April 13, 1937; John H. McCray, "The Way It Was," *Charleston Chronicle,* February 16, 1985, JHM papers, Reel 16, journalism; Louise Purvis Bell to Walter White, April 16, 1937, NAACP Papers, I-G-196.

14. McCray oral history, 1985.

15. Harlan, *Booker T. Washington. The Making of a Black Leader,* 218–28; Norrell, *Up from History,* 122–35.

16. Kantrowitz, *Ben Tillman and the Reconstruction of White Supremacy.* See also, Brundage, *Lynching in the New South;* Woodward, *Origins of the New South,* 350–53.

17. Harlan, *Booker T. Washington: The Making of a Black Leader,* 219; from conservative black intellectuals and entertainers, such as Shelby Steele and Bill Cosby, to conservative white politicians such as Ronald Reagan and Newt Gingrich.

18. Harlan, *Booker T. Washington: The Making of a Black Leader,* 225, preface; Harlan, *Booker T. Washington. The Wizard of Tuskegee,* vii.

19. Woodward, *Origins of the New South,* 367.

20. Lewis, *W.E.B. Du Bois,* 277; Johnson, *Along This Way,* 203; Du Bois, "Of Spiritual Strivings," in *The Souls of Black Folk.*

21. Du Bois, "Of Booker T. Washington and Others," in *The Souls of Black Folk.*

22. Ibid.

23. "Editorial: The Crisis," *The Crisis,* November 1910; see also Lewis, *W.E.B. Du Bois,* 410–11; Sullivan, *Lift Every Voice,* 17–19.

24. Baldasty, *The Commercialization of News;* Kaplan, "From Partisanship to Professionalism," 116–39; Washburn, *The African American Newspaper,* 73–112: "Blease, the Degenerate in Another Filthy Tirade . . ." *Chicago Defender,* 1914, 8.

25. Butler W. Nance to W.E.B. Du Bois, June 15, 1915, NAACP papers, I-G-196.

26. Sullivan, *Lift Every Voice,* 61; *Savannah Tribune,* March 10, 1917, NAACP papers, I-G-46; W.E.B. Du Bois, "The Heart of the South," *The Crisis,* May 1917, 18.

27. Modjeska Monteith Simkins oral history interview, 1976, MMS papers, 2–3.

28. Hemingway, "South Carolina," in *The Black Press in the South,* 289–311; R. W. Jackson to Robert Bagnell, June 6, 1923, Robert Bagnell to R. W. Jackson, June 9, 1923, NAACP papers, G-I-196.

29. An Address of the People of South Carolina, Capital Civic League, 1915, NAACP papers, I-G-196; Carroll quoted in Newby, *Black Carolinians,* 16, 174–76.

30. Carroll quoted in Newby, *Black Carolinians,* 16, 174–76.

31. For a full treatment of Washington's 1909 tour of South Carolina, see Jackson, "Booker T. Washington in South Carolina, March 1909."

32. Simon, "The Appeal of Cole Blease."

33. Butler W. Nance to Mary White Ovington, February 5, 1919, NAACP papers, I-G-196.

34. Nance to Walter F. White, September 12, 1920, NAACP Papers, I-G-196.

35. *The State,* March 14, 1918.

36. Hemingway, "Prelude to Change: Black Carolinians in the War Years, 1914–1920"; *The State,* February 21, 1919.

37. Robertson, *Sly and Able,* 85–86; *Congressional Record,* 66th Congress, 1st Session, 4302-B.

38. NAACP secretary (unnamed) to Butler W. Nance, November 2, 1919, NAACP papers, I-G-196.

39. Nance to James Weldon Johnson, October 26, 1919, NAACP papers I-B-196.

40. Lau, *Democracy Rising,* 57–58; Blease quotes come from Coleman Livingston Blease papers, as cited in Simon, "The Appeal of Cole Blease in South Carolina"; see also Newby, *Jim Crow's Defense.*

41. Prather, "The Origins of the Phoenix Racial Massacre."

42. Prather, *We Have A Taken A City;* Cecelski and Tyson, eds., *Democracy Betrayed.*

43. Ibid.

44. Ibid.

45. R. W. Jackson to NAACP, February 21, 1923; R. W. Bagnall to Nathaniel Frederick, September 4, 1926, R. W. Jackson to Robert Bagnell, December 14, 1926, NAACP Papers G-I-196.

46. See Nathaniel J. Frederick Vertical File: Nathaniel Jerome Frederick, Negros and the Law, n.d.; Unfinished (Lowman Case) Statement by N. J. Frederick, n.d.; William Pickens, "Bravest Man in South Carolina," *Palmetto Leader,* n.d.;

47. Hemingway, "Under the Yoke of Bondage," 391; Hoffman, "The Genesis," 354.

48. W.E.B. Du Bois, "The Parting of the Ways," *World Today,* April 1904, 521–23.

49. Modjeska Simkins oral history interview with John Egerton, 1990. Accessed at http://docsouth.unc.edu/sohp/playback.html?base_file=A-0356&duration=01:29:17.

Chapter 2. A Newspaper Joins the Movement

1. Modjeska Monteith Simkins oral history interview with Jacquelyn Dowd Hall, 1976.

2. Ibid., 3; Wells, *Southern Horrors*. For more on Ida B. Wells, see her autobiography: Wells, *Crusade for Justice;* also, Giddins, *Ida: A Sword Among Lions.*

3. Simkins oral history, 4–5.

4. Ibid., 8–10.

5. Ibid., 15.

6. Ibid., 34–35; See also Woods, "Modjeska Simkins and the South Carolina Conference of the NAACP, 1939–1957."

7. Simkins interview with Patricia Sullivan, as quoted in Sullivan, *Days of Hope,* 144; Sitkoff, *A New Deal for Blacks,* 47; Weiss, *Farewell to the Party of Lincoln;* Gilmore, "False Friends and Avowed Enemies," 219–38.

8. Simkins interview with Edwin Hoffman, as quoted in Hoffman, "The Genesis," 355; South Carolina Conference of NAACP Branches, convention program, 1939, MMS papers, NAACP; Lau, *Democracy Rising,* 108–16; Sullivan, *Days of Hope,* 142.

9. Richards, "Osceola E. McKaine and the Struggle for Black Civil Rights." For more on the Fort Des Moines training school, see Nalty, *Strength for the Fight.*

10. Richards, "Osceola E. McKaine," 62–66.

11. "Buffaloes Return Colors From War," *New York Times,* March 15, 1919; Locke, "Introduction," in *The New Negro;* Lewis, *When Harlem was in Vogue.*

12. *New York Amsterdam News,* April 10, 1919.

13. See, for example, "Reds Working Among Negroes," *New York Times,* October 19, 1919; Richards, "Osceola E. McKaine," 60–81.

14. Ibid., 90–94.

15. Newby, *Black Carolinians,* 141; Sullivan, *Days of Hope,* 137; Tushnet, *Making Civil Rights Law,* 20–26; John H. McCray, "The Case That Shocked Thurgood Marshall," n.d., JHM papers, Reel 6; "Your School System, *Lighthouse and Informer,* October 19, 1941, 8.

16. Simkins oral history interview; see also Aba-Mecha, "Black Woman Activist in Twentieth Century South Carolina: Modjeska Monteith Simkins," 44–51.

17. Ibid.; "Not With Us," *Lighthouse and Informer,* October 24, 1948, 8.

18. John H. McCray, "The Way It Was, *Charleston Chronicle,* February 21, 1982, JHM papers, Reel 16, journalism; McCray oral history, 1985.

19. Ibid.

20. Ibid.; McCray oral history interview, 1985.

21. McCray oral history, 1985; John H. McCray, "The Way It Was," *Charleston Chronicle,* February 20, February 27, 1982, JHM papers, Reel 16, journalism.

22. John H. McCray, "The Way It Was," *Charleston Chronicle,* March 6, 1982, JHM papers, Reel 16, journalism; Simkins oral history interview, 1976; Richards, "Osceola E. McKaine," 109; McKaine began as a contributing writer for the paper. When he moved to Columbia from Sumter in 1943, he became associate editor.

23. John H. McCray, "The Way It Was," *Charleston Chronicle,* March 6, 1982, JHM

papers, Reel 16, journalism; Simkins oral history interview, 1976; Richards, "Osceola E. McKaine," 109; McKaine began as a contributing writer for the paper. When he moved to Columbia from Sumter in 1943, he became associate editor.

24. Washburn, *The African American Newspaper,* 143–55.

25. Olin Johnston to John H. McCray, March 20, 1943, JHM papers, Reel 2, journalism.

26. "Comrades Banished," *Lighthouse and Informer,* January 10, 1943, 4.

27. Notes on chain gain story in JHM papers, Reel 2, journalism; McCray Oral History, 1985; John H. McCray, "The Way It Was," *Charleston Chronicle,* March 27, 1982, JHM papers, Reel 16, journalism.

28. Al (no last name provided) to John H. McCray, August 19, 1943, JHM papers, Reel 2, journalism.

29. "Probes City Jail Beating of Accused Man here," *Lighthouse and Informer,* July 12, 1952, 1; "An Editorial: Complaints Against Police Department," *Lighthouse and Informer,* July 12, 1952, 1, 4.

30. "Cheraw Notes," *Lighthouse and Informer,* January 10, 1943, 4; "Here and There," *Lighthouse and Informer,* January 17, 1943, 4; "Aiken Notes," *Lighthouse and Informer,* January 10, 1943, 4.

31. "Americans, Too," Letter to the Editor, *Lighthouse and Informer,* February 6, 1944, 4.

32. Richard Wright, "Native Son," *Lighthouse and Informer,* January 10, 1943, 4.

33. "Are Players, Umps Ganging Up on Jackie?" *Lighthouse and Informer,* August 4, 1947, 7.

34. "Should be Unfrocked," *Lighthouse and Informer,* June 10, 1943, 4.

35. "Leaders—For Whom Do They Speak?" *Lighthouse and Informer,* June 10, 1943, 4.

36. "Police Indiscretion," *Lighthouse and Informer,* February 9, 1947, 4.

37. John H. McCray, "The Need for Changing: Call Me 'Mister'," *Lighthouse and Informer,* February 16, 1947, 4.

38. "Keep Your Lamps Filled with Oil," *Lighthouse and Informer* (n.d., but included with newspaper clips from 1942 to 1943) AJC papers, correspondence, John McCray.

39. John H. McCray, "The Need for Changing: Our Enslaved Children, *Lighthouse and Informer,* May 11, 1947.

40. John H. McCray, "The I Killits," *Lighthouse and Informer,* August 22, 1948, 4.

41. Davis Lee, "What Does the Negro Really Want?" *The Telegram,* September 12, 1948; John H. McCray, "They Might Have First Checked," *Lighthouse and Informer,* August 22, 1948, 4. Davis Lee later returned to South Carolina and edited the *Anderson Herald* in the 1950s and '60s. For more on Lee, see Aiello, "Editing a Paper in Hell," and Hemingway, "South Carolina," in *The Black Press in the South.*

42. "They Might Have First Checked," *Lighthouse and Informer,* August 22, 1948, 4.

43. McCray to Thurgood Marshall, November 9, 1944, NAACP papers, II-B, 209. For extensive examples of white brutality during the Jim Crow era, see Litwack, *Trouble in Mind* and McMillen, *Dark Journey.*

44. "Attention Teachers," *Lighthouse and Informer,* October 19, 1941, 8.

45. For more on the NAACP's teacher-pay fight across the South, see Tushnet, *Making Civil Rights Law,* 20–26; Kluger, *Simple Justice,* 214–15; Brown-Nagin, *Courage to Dissent,* 87–90; McCray oral history, 1985; John McCray, "The Case That Shocked Thurgood Marshall," n.d., JHM papers, Reel 6.

46. Ibid.

47. Litwack, *Trouble in Mind,* 360.

48. Modjeska Monteith Simkins, "Black Teachers Called to Arms," *Lighthouse and Informer,* 1943. Article found in MMS Papers, NAACP; Simkins interview with Barbara Aba-Mecha, as quoted in Aba-Mecha, "Black Woman Activist in Twentieth Century South Carolina," 165.

49. King, *Civil Rights and the Idea of Freedom,* 26–27.

50. John H. McCray, "The Need for Changing," *Lighthouse and Informer,* June 15, 1947, 4.

51. Osceola E. McKaine, "What Price Unity?" *Lighthouse and Informer,* January 10, 1943, 4.

52. James Hinton to Thurgood Marshall, NAACP Papers, Educational Equality, B-II 209; John H. McCray, "The Case That Shocked Thurgood Marshall," n.d., JHM papers, Reel 6.

53. Viola Louise Duvall to John Henry McCray, November 14, 1943, JHM papers, Reel 6; James Hinton to Thurgood Marshall, NAACP Papers, Educational Equality, B-II, 209.

54. John H. McCray, "The Case that Shocked Thurgood Marshall," n.d., JHM papers, Reel 6.

55. Edgar, *South Carolina,* 507; Yarbrough, *A Passion for Justice,* 19–22.

56. D.A. Brockington Jr., interview with Tinsley Yarbrough, as cited in Yarbrough, *A Passion for Justice,* 36.

57. Myrdal, *An American Dilemma;* Jackson, *Gunnar Myrdal and America's Conscience.*

58. J. Waties Waring to John H. McCray, 1952, JHM papers, Reel 6, journalism; Grafton, "Lonesomest Man in Town," 49; see also, Yarbrough, *A Passion for Justice;* Lau, *Democracy Rising,* 129–33; Sullivan, *Days of Hope,* 256; Southern, "Beyond Jim Crow Liberalism."

59. "With Us Now," *Lighthouse and Informer,* June 16, 1950, 8

60. Annual report, South Carolina Conference of NAACP Branches Annual Convention, 1948, NAACP papers, Box B II-129; Roberts and Klibanoff, *The Race Beat,* 150.

61. Some examples: John McCray, "Sticking Together," *Lighthouse and Informer,* January 19, 1947, 4; McCray, "Primary Test Looms," *Lighthouse and Informer,* February 9, 1947, 4; John McCray, "No Apparent Unity," *Lighthouse and Informer,* February 6, 1944, 4.

Chapter 3. A Black Political Insurgency in the Deep South

1. McCray, "The Way It Was," *Charleston Chronicle,* March 13, 1982, Reel 16, journalism; McCray oral history interview, 1985; *Smith v. Allwright* 321 U.S. 649 (1944); Message of Governor Olin D. Johnston Delivered to Joint Assembly and General Assembly of South Carolina, April 14, 1944, John H. McCray Papers, Reel 5, Journalism.

2. *Smith v. Allwright* 321 U.S. 649 (1944). Hine, *Black Victory;* Lawson, *Black Ballots.*

3. Message of Governor Olin Johnston, JHM papers, Reel 7, Politics.

4. John H. McCray, "The Way It Was," *Charleston Chronicle,* March 13, 1982, Reel 16, journalism.

5. Ibid.; *Spartanburg Journal,* April 16, 1944, Olin D. Johnston Gubernatorial Papers, Box 1; "The Apparent Unity," *Lighthouse and Informer,* February 6, 1944, 4.

6. "Negro Vote Jumps . . .," *New York Times,* August 22, 1936.

7. Garson, *The Democratic Party*, 3–53; Frederickson, *The Dixiecrat Revolt*, 34–35; Louis I. Jaffe to Thomas R. Waring, September 5, 1942, TRW papers, Negroes; "The Eleanor Club Myth," *Richmond Times-Dispatch*, August 21, 1942; "The Apparent Unity," *Lighthouse and Informer*, February 6, 1944.

8. McCray oral history, 1985.

9. Rev. James Hinton to Thurgood Marshall, March 18, May 22, 1942, NAACP papers, II-B, 209; Simkins oral history interview, 1976, MMS papers.

10. Rev. James Hinton to Thurgood Marshall, NAACP papers, II-B, 209; "Negro Suffrage in Primaries Urged by 21 White Citizens," *The State*, May 18, 1942; "Negro Voting in Primaries Rejected Here," *Columbia Record*, May 22, 1942, news clips archived in NAACP papers, II-B, 209.

11. Hinton to Marshall, July 21, 1942; Simkins to NAACP, April 20, 1942, NAACP papers, II-B, 209;

12. Marshall to Hinton, April 29, 1942, NAACP papers, II-B, 215.

13. McCray, "The Way It Was," *Charleston Chronicle*, February 21, 1982, JHM papers, Reel 16, journalism.

14. "Fourth Term for Roosevelt," *Lighthouse and Informer*, March 19, 1944.

15. McCray, "The Way It Was," *Charleston Chronicle*, February 27 and March 13, 1982, JHM papers, Reel 16, Journalism.

16. John H. McCray, "The Way It Was," March 13, 1982, JHM papers, Reel 16, journalism; McCray oral history interview, 1985.

17. "South Carolina Colored Democratic Party Organizational Plans," JHM papers, Reel 7, politics; McCray, "The Way It Was," *Charleston Chronicle*, March 13, 1982; McCray oral history interview, 1985; For more on the PDP, see Roefs, "Leading the Civil Rights Vanguard," 474; Lau, *Democracy Rising*, 136–44.

18. McCray to W. A. Blackman, May 18, 1944, JHM papers, reel 7, Politics.

19. "Negro Willing to Shed Blood for Rights," Associated Press, May 24, 1944.

20. McKaine Keynote address to Progressive Democratic Party convention, JHM papers, Reel 7, politics.

21. *Columbia Record*, June 2, 1944, JHM papers, Reel 7, politics.

22. McCray to Winchester Smith, May 10, 1944, JHM papers, Reel 7, politics.

23. McCray oral history interview, 1985; *Norfolk Journal and Guide*, May 20, 1944.

24. McCray oral history interview, 1985.

25. McCray oral history interview; *Columbia Record*, May 27, 1944.

26. *Chicago Defender*, July 20, 1944, JHM papers, Reel 8, politics; McCray oral history interview, 1985; McCray, "The Way It Was," *Charleston Chronicle*, March 13, 4, JHM papers, Reel 16, journalism; Sullivan, *Days of Hope*, 171.

27. Transcript of Osceola E. McKaine's address on WIS radio, October 18, 1944. JHM papers, Reel 8, politics.

28. Osceola E. McKaine campaign speech, 1944, JHM papers, Reel 8, politics; John H. McCray to Thurgood Marshall, November 9, 1944, NAACP papers II-B, 215.

29. McCray, "The Way It Was," *Charleston Chronicle*, December 6, 1980, February 27 and March 13, 1982, JHM papers, reel 16, Politics; McCray oral history interview, 1985.

30. *Elmore v. Rice*, 72 F. Supp. 516, 528; *Wrighten v. Board of Trustees of the University of South Carolina*, 72 F. Supp. 948.

31. *Brown v. Baskin,* 78 F. Supp. 933 (1948).

32. Press Release from Thurgood Marshall, August 18, 1948, NAACP papers, II-B, 209.

33. Walter White Statement to Associated Press, July 18, 1948, NAACP papers, II-B, 209.

34. Cable, *The Silent South;* Kluger, *Simple Justice,* 299–300; Southern, "Beyond Jim Crow Liberalism"; *Pee Dee Advocate,* October 12, 1950.

35. See, for example, Bates, *Pullman Porters;* Bynum, *A. Phillip Randolph.*

36. *Atlanta Constitution,* April 7, April 18, 1946; Simkins, "The Palmetto State," *Norfolk Journal and Guide,* n.d., MMS papers, Political; For details on Thurmond's 1946 campaign and his role in South Carolina and national politics in general, see Crespino, *Strom Thurmond's America;* Bass and Thompson, *Strom;* Cahodas, *Strom Thurmond;* Ward, *Defending White Democracy.*

37. Mrs. Andrew W. Simkins, "The Palmetto State," *Norfolk New Journal and Guide,* March 1, 1947; McKaine to Thurmond, March 12, 1947, JHM papers, Reel 10, Persons.

38. Rebecca West, "Opera in Greenville," *New Yorker,* June 14, 1947, 31–65.

39. "Lynching, An Incorporation," *Lighthouse and Informer,* May 19, 1947, 8; John H. McCray, "The Need for Changing: The Mid-Educated," *Lighthouse and Informer,* May 19, 1947, 8.

40. Bass and Thompson. *Strom,* 42–48; Crespino, *Strom Thurmond's America,* 51–56; West, "Opera in Greenville," *New Yorker,* 31–65.

41. John McCray, "The White Primary Goes Out," *Lighthouse and Informer,* April 25, 1948, 4.

42. Meeting of the Eighth Annual South Carolina Conference of NAACP Branches, 1947, JHP papers, reel 9, Politics.

Chapter 4. The White Press and the Dixiecrat Revolt

1. Stark, *Damned Upcountryman,* 123.

2. Garson, *The Democratic Party and the Politics of Sectionalism,* 1974; *Smith v. Allwright,* 321 U.S. 649 (1944); "Mayberry says Negro Move is Doomed," *Columbia Record,* May 27, 1944, 4A.

3. Williamson, *The Crucible of Race,* 475–82.

4. Survey results found in SJL papers, civil rights, 1930–1966.

5. A. J. Clement to William D. Workman Jr., July 19, 1948. Campaigns, 1948. WDW Papers.

6. J. W Alley, "Hambone," *The State,* November 2, 1949, 4; "Colored Attorneys' Practice," *Charleston News and Courier,* January 6, 1949, 4.

7. A. J. Clement to William D. Workman Jr., July 19, 1948. WDW papers: campaigns, 1948.

8. The name "Bourbon" refers to the reign of Louis XI, which had restored the monarchy in France after the French Revolution and the rise of Napoleon Bonaparte; Kantrowitz, *Ben Tillman,* 64–79; Williamson, *The Crucible of Race,* 79–85.

9. Kantrowitz, *Ben Tillman,* 80–95.

10. Woodward, *Tom Watson;* Woodward, *Origins of the New South;* Kantrowitz, *Ben Tillman.*

11. Jones, *Stormy Petrel,* 66–75.

12. Ibid.

13. Kantrowitz, *Ben Tillman*, 156–66, 198–244.

14. Jones, *Stormy Petrel*, 298–307; Latimer, *The Story of the State*, 53–65.

15. Ibid.

16. Tillman and Blease newspapers included the *Charleston World*, the *Barnwell People*, the *Columbia Register*, and many others that emerged briefly and folded between 1890 and 1930; Jones, *Stormy Petrel*, 288.

17. Stark, *Damned Upcountryman*, 70–73.

18. Ibid.; McNeely, *Fighting Words*; Harrigan, ed., *The Editor and the Republic*; Stark, *Damned Upcountryman*, 121–22.

19. Stark, *Damned Upcountryman*, 14–17; Holden, *In the Great Maelstrom*, 94; Stark, *Damned Upcountryman*, 5.

20. *News and Courier*, May 30, 1930.

21. Ball, *The State That Forgot*.

22. Holden, *In the Great Maelstrom*, 107.

23. Edgar, *South Carolina: A History*; Lathan, "The Plight of the South"; Harrigan, "Introduction," in Ball, *The Editor and the Republic*; Stark, *Damned Upcountryman*; Holden, *In the Great Maelstrom*.

24. "Must Never Break Loose," *Charleston News and Courier*, November 25, 1949, 4A.

25. South Carolina State Legislative Manual, 1948; James A. Rogers. "A Personal Word." *Florence Morning News*, June 3, 1947, 4.

26. Don Stewart. "A Progressive, Courageous Man." *Florence Morning News*, September 30, 1990; A prominent attorney and congressman from West Virginia who also served in the Wilson administration, Davis lost the 1924 election decisively to Republican Calvin Coolidge. Late in his career, Davis would be called up to defend South Carolina in desegregation case that evolved into *Brown v. Board of Education*.

27. Kneebone, *Southern Liberal Journalists*, 4.

28. From the author's review of *Florence Morning News* editorials, 1947–1948; Southern, "Beyond Jim Crow Liberalism"; Teel, *Ralph Emerson McGill*; Carter, *Southern Legacy*; Kneebone, *Southern Liberal Journalists*; Sosna, *In Search of the Silent South*.

29. Sullivan, *Days of Hope*, 145–50; Kneebone, *Southern Liberal Journalists*, 198; McGill, *Atlanta Constitution*, April 9, 1946; Dabney, "Nearer and Nearer the Precipice," *Atlantic Monthly*, January 1943, 94.

30. For more on the SNYC meeting in Columbia, see Lewis, *W.E.B. Du Bois*, 519–24; Gellman, *Death Blow to Jim Crow*, 213.

31. Ibid.

32. "Governor Charges Negro Meeting was Communistic," *Columbia Record*, October 21, 1946, 1A; "Columbia Disappoints," *Columbia Record*, October 22, 1946, 4A.

33. Gellman, *Death Blow to Jim Crow*, 213–53; Lau, *Democracy Rising*, 171–73.

34. Clifford wrote the memo, but he has attributed some of its analysis to longtime Roosevelt aide James Rowe. See, Karabell, *The Last Campaign*, 35–37; Bass and Thompson, *Strom*, 105.

35. Sullivan, *Days of Hope*, 219; Frederickson, *Dixiecrat Revolt*, 54–56; 118–29; Nora Holt, "Blinding of Isaac Woodard American Hero," *New York Amsterdam News*, August 17, 1946, 9.

36. *Elmore v. Rice et al.,* 72 F. Supp. 516, 528.

37. "Judge Waring's Decision, *Columbia Record,* July 13, 1947, 4; "Abandon the Party." *News and Courier,* July 13, 1947, 4.

38. "Judge Waring's Ruling," *Florence Morning News,* July 13, 1947, 4.

39. Southern, "Beyond Jim Crow Liberalism"; Stewart, "A Progressive, Courageous Man": "Judge Waring's Ruling," *Florence Morning News,* July 13 1947, 4.

40. Weill, "Mississippi's Daily Press in Three Crises," 17–54.

41. Bass and Thompson, *Strom;* Cohodas, *Strom Thurmond;* "Thurmond for President," *News and Courier,* July 19, 1948, 1; "Headline Hunters," *Florence Morning News,* July 13, 1948, 4.

42. "No Precedent," *Florence Morning News,* July 15, 1948, 4.

43. "Peril—How to Escape It," *News and Courier,* July 7, 1948, 4. (In 1948, Ball's editorial page at the *News and Courier* never capitalized Negroes; the *Florence Morning News* did)

44. Conway, "Before the Bloggers: The Upstart New Technology of Television at the 1948 Political Conventions"; Warren would play a much larger role in the civil rights struggle six years later. As chief justice of the Supreme Court, he would deliver the opinion overturning school segregation in the case of *Brown v. Board of Education.*

45. W. W. Ball. "Differences Wiped Out," *News and Courier,* July 2, 1948, 4.

46. "Never so Apparent." *Florence Morning News,* July 16, 4; "Voice from Georgia," *Florence Morning News,* July 16, 4.

47. Cohodas, *Strom Thurmond,* 157; "Headline Hunters," *Florence Morning News,* July 12, 1948, 4; "Lone Hope," *Florence Morning News,* July 14, 1948, 4.

48. "Still Not Too Late," *Florence Morning News,* July 10, 1948, 4; Clowse, *Ralph McGill,* 138.

49. "More Confusion," *Florence Morning News,* July 1, 1948, 4; Lau, *Democracy Rising,* 136–40.

50. "Escape from a Corrupt Orgy," *News and Courier,* July 11, 1948, 4; "Time to Abandon Party," *News and Courier,* July 9, 1948, 4; "Wipe Out Distinctions," *News and Courier,* July 2, 1948, 4.

51. Future Alabama governor and presidential candidate George C. Wallace, a protégé of populist Gov. Jim Folsom, was one of the delegates who did not walk out of the convention. Frederickson, *The Dixiecrat Revolt,* 130; Cohodas, *Strom Thurmond,* 167; Bass and Thompson, *Strom,* 116.

52. "The Greater Service," *Florence Morning News,* July 17, 1948, 4.

53. Bass and Thompson, *Strom,* 102; Cohodas, *Strom Thurmond,* 177.

54. "The Birmingham Circus," *Florence Morning News,* July 20, 1948, 4; "Thurmond for President." *News and Courier,* July 19, 1948, 1.

55. "There is Danger in Haste," *Florence Morning News,* July 24, 1948, 4; "S.C. and the Dixiecrats," *Florence Morning News,* July 28, 1948, 4; "Unfettered, Untied," *Florence Morning News,* July 24 1948, 4.

56. "The Silent 'Leaders,'" *News and Courier,* July 23, 1948, 4; "Who Solicits Negro Votes?" *News and Courier,* July 23, 1948, 4; "Supremacy of the Worthy," *News and Courier,* July 13, 1948, 4.

57. "Governor Thurmond Should Withdraw," *Lighthouse and Informer,* August 29, 1948, 8.

58. "Let's Stand By Our Friends," *Lighthouse and Informer*, August 22, 1948. "We Stand By Truman," *Lighthouse and Informer*, October 31, 1948, 8; John H. McCray, "The Need for Changing," *Lighthouse and Informer*, October 31, 1948, 8.

59. "The Dixiecrats are Embarrassing Our Right to Lead," *Lighthouse and Informer*, July 12, 1952, 4.

Chapter 5. An Old Warrior Underestimates a New Foe

1. Robertson, *Sly and Able*, 492–500; Frederickson, *The Dixiecrat Revolt*, 118–150; Crespino, *Strom Thurmond's America*, 34–84; Robertson, *Sly and Able*, 496; Fredrickson, *The Dixiecrat Revolt*, 180.

2. John Temple Graves, "The Press Looks at Jimmy Byrnes and Likes What It Sees," *Winnsboro (S.C.) News and Herald*, January 26, 1951, as quoted in Ward, *Defending White Democracy*. Graves's column appeared in several South Carolina newspapers, including the *Charleston News and Courier* and the *Columbia Record*.

3. For the best account of the *Atlanta Daily World* and its viewpoints during this period, see Brown-Nagin, *Courage to Dissent*, 86–88.

4. The edition of the *Lighthouse and Informer* that included Hinton's letter no longer exists. However, the letter is quoted in news reports such as, "Negro Group Will Battle Segregation," *Columbia Record*, October 20, 1947, clip in NAACP papers, II-B, 209.

5. William M. Bates, United Press, May 6, 1951, copy included in MMS papers.

6. "NAACP Asks Help in Clarendon Suit," *Lighthouse and Informer*, March 17, 1951, 4; "Why Not Tell It all," *Lighthouse and Informer*, July 14, 1951.

7. "Byrnes Hits Trend to 'Welfare State,'" *New York Times*, January 19, 1949, 2; See also Robertson, *Sly and Able*, 497; Crespino, *Strom Thurmond's America*, 87–88.

8. "Byrnes Hits Truman's Spending Policies, Asks Cuts in Taxes and Debt," *The State*, November 22, 1949, 1; "Eisenhower-Byrnes Ticket Said Planned for Presidential Race," *The State*, November 22, 1949, 1; "Ike and Jimmy," *The State*, November 23, 1949.

9. John S. Cutter, "Byrnes Viewed as New States Rights Leader," Associated Press, November 27, 1949, as appeared on page 1 of the *Charleston News and Courier*.

10. Calhoun's unveiled his theory of the "concurrent majority" in his treatise, *A Disquisition on Government*, written in 1850. See also Robertson, *Sly and Able*, 501–2.

11. "Truman to Stand for No Letup in Battle for Civil Rights Laws," *The State*, November 16, 1949, 1.

12. Cutter, "Byrnes Viewed as New States Rights Leader," Associated Press.

13. "Well and Belatedly Said," *Charleston News and Courier*, November 23, 1949, 4.

14. "Civil Rights and Socialism, *News and Courier*, January 7, 1949, 4.

15. Ralph McGill, "What is Jimmy Byrnes Up To Now?" *Saturday Evening Post*, October 14, 1950; "100,000 Hear Byrnes Warn Against Russia," *Columbia Record*, January 16, 1951; "Bomb Red China or Pull Out of Korea—Byrnes," Associated Press, January 16, 1951.

16. Inaugural address of James Francis Byrnes, January 15, 1951, Columbia, South Carolina. James F. Byrnes Gubernatorial Papers.

17. Kluger, *Simple Justice*, 4–25.

18. *Atlanta Daily World* editorials, September 20, 21, 28, 1950; see Brown-Nagin, *Courage to Dissent*, 96–99.

19. "Negro Group Will Battle Segregation," *Columbia Record*, October 20, 1947, clip in NAACP papers, II-B, 209; Kluger, *Simple Justice*, 300–20.

20. "Inaugural Address of James Francis Byrnes, JFB papers; Kluger, *Simple Justice*, 35.

21. Kantrowitz, "Ben Tillman," 214; Holt, *Black Over White*, 152–71; Foner, *Reconstruction*, 185–95. For more on Byrnes's reform effort, see Robertson, *Sly and Able*, 492–525; Ward, *Defending White Democracy*, 139–50; Bartley, *The Rise of Massive Resistance*; for a consideration of Byrnes's reform effort from a Congressional perspective, see Finley, *Defying the Dream*.

22. See Simon, "The Appeal of Cole Blease," 57–86; Robertson, *Sly and Able*, 90–92; Chalmers, *Hooded Americanism*, 337–38; Wade, *The Fiery Cross*, 290–91; Ward, *Defending White Democracy*, 129–30; Byrnes's anti-mask law made an exception for one night a year—Halloween. See "James F. Byrnes Inaugural Address, January 15, 1951," JFB Gubernatorial Papers.

23. Walter White, "Says Byrnes of South Carolina is a White-Face Uncle Tom," *Atlanta Daily World*, February 10, 1951, 7; "NAACP Sets Gov. Byrnes Straight," *Atlanta Daily World*, January 30, 1951, 4; "Was Hinton's Letter Killed?" *Lighthouse and Informer*, as appeared in *Atlanta Daily World*, February 28, 1951, 6.

24. "Mr. Byrnes' Speech," *The State*, January 18, 1951, 4A; "Byrnes Takes Office," *Columbia Record*, January 15, 1951, 4; "Governor's Inaugural Speech," *Charleston News and Courier*, January 16, 1951, 4A.

25. "Governor Byrnes has Sound and Sober Word for Southern Negroes and Their School Fight," *Florence Morning News*, March 18, 1951.

26. James F. Byrnes to R. C. Griffith, November 20, 1951, General Subjects File, Box 1, Folder "Ku Klux Klan," James F. Byrnes Gubernatorial Papers.

27. John H. McCray, "Segregation Now in the Negros Hands," *Lighthouse and Informer*, March 15, 1952.

28. Inaugural address of James Francis Byrnes, January 15, 1951, Columbia, South Carolina. JFB Gubernatorial Papers. See, for example, W. D. Workman Jr. "Segregation End May Mean Loss of Jobs for Negro Teachers," *Charleston News and Courier*, March 10, 1951, 12; Kluger, *Simple Justice*, 338–40.

29. "Ain't It A Shame?" *Lighthouse and Informer*, March 17, 1951; Kluger, *Simple Justice*, 339.

30. "Two They Can't Control," *Lighthouse and Informer*, May 5, 1951, 4.

31. Ibid.

32. "A tribute much deserved," *Lighthouse and Informer*, June 21, 1951, 4; "Reveal 14 Teachers Fired in Clarendon 'Revenge,' " *Lighthouse and Informer*, April 5, 1952, 1; Lau, *Democracy Rising*, 203; Kluger, *Simple Justice*, 1–25.

33. Greenwood County Libel Case, JHM papers, Reel 13; Greenberg, *Crusaders in the Courts*, 55; Frederickson, "The Dixiecrat Revolt," 208–16; Roefs, "Leading the Civil Rights Vanguard," 482–83.

34. Ibid.

35. *Chicago Defender*, January 21, 1950.

36. Greenberg, *Crusaders in the Courts*, 54–57.

37. "State Still Wants Editor Chainganged," *Lighthouse and Informer*, July 26, 1952, 1; notes on chain gain story in JHM papers, Reel 2, journalism; McCray Oral History, 1985; John H. McCray, "The Way It Was," *Charleston Chronicle*, March 27, 1982.

38. Greenberg, *Crusaders in the Courts*, 55; Simkins oral history, 1990; *Pittsburgh Courier*, December 13, 1952.

39. Greenwood County Libel Case, JHM papers, Reel 13 (includes clip of Jackson editorial from the *Birmingham World*).

40. Ibid; P. L. Prattis, "South Carolina Leaders Are Men of Inspiring Courage," *Pittsburgh Courier*, June 21, 1952, 9.

41. "Get Up or Shut Up," *Lighthouse and Informer*, May 6, 1950, 1.

42. Ibid.

43. William D. Workman Jr., Untitled Article for *Charleston News and Courier*, WDW papers, Campaigns, 1950; *Lighthouse and Informer*, July 8, 1950; "To All True Believers in the Fight for True Freedom and True Democracy," July 8, 1950, ODJ papers, campaigns, 1950.

44. "Johnston Beats Thurmond in Senate Primary," *The State*, July 12, 1950; "New Ideas, but Old Lines," *Lighthouse and Informer*, July 5, 1952.

45. John H. McCray to Arthur Clement Jr., July 21, 1950, AJC papers, correspondence, John H. McCray.

46. McCray to Thurgood Marshall, November 9, 1944, NAACP Papers II-B, 2009.

47. Moore, "New South Statesman"; Robertson, *Sly and Able*, 86.

48. Associated Press, "Clarendon Negroes Challenge Segregation in Schools," *Columbia Record*, December 22, 1950, 1A; Associated Press, "Segregation Suit Filed in U.S. Court," *The State*, December 23, 1950, 8B; Associated Press, "Negro Home Bombed in Birmingham," *The State*, December 23, 1950, 2A.

49. Tom McMahon, "School Segregation Sustained," *The State*, June 24, 1951, A1; Tom McMahon, "State Admits Inequalities Exist in Clarendon," *The State*, May 29, 1951.

50. Tom McMahon, "School Segregation Sustained," *The State*, June 24, 1951, A1; "Judge Waring's Dissent," *Charleston News and Courier*, June 24, 1951, A8.

51. McMahon, "School Segregation Sustained"; Robertson, *Sly and Able*, 519; "Victory for American Rights," *Charleston News and Courier*, June 24, 1951.

52. Marjorie McKenzie, "McKenzie in Challenge on Legal Tactics," *Pittsburgh Courier*, July 7, 1951, 6.

53. John H. McCray and James M. Hinton, "S.C. NAACP Answers *Courier's* Writer: 'Time Ain't Ripe' for Miss McKenzie,' " *Lighthouse and Informer*, July 14, 1951, 4.

54. Yarbrough, *A Passion for Justice*, 181–89.

55. Robertson, *Sly and Able*, 511;

56. Ibid., 511; See also Frederickson, *The Dixiecrat Revolt*, 226.

57. "Thousands Hear Eisenhower Pitch for SC Votes," *The State*, September 16, 1952, 1.

58. "Democrats for Ike," *The State*, November 2, 1952, 4; "Two-Party State," *Charleston News and Courier*, November 6, 1952.

59. "Byrnes Says SC is 'Out of the Bag,' Does Not Intend to Get Back Into It," *The State*, November 5, 1952, 1; "The Clarendon Decision Threatens to Throw Us Back," *Lighthouse and Informer*, July 7, 1952, 4.

60. Brochures included in JFB personal papers, education; Robert Ratcliffe and A. M. Rivera Jr., "Can South Carolina Correct a Century of Wrong?" *Pittsburgh Courier*, November 13, 1954, 17.

61. Robertson, *Sly and Able*, 515.

62. Kluger, *Simple Justice*, 760; Harry Ashmore, *Hearts and Minds*, 188.

63. Robertson, *Sly and Able,* 510. For more on Marshall's brief and NAACP legal strategy, see Kluger, *Simple Justice.*

64. John H. McCray, "The Magnificence of Clarendon's Folk," *Lighthouse and Informer,* September 20, 1952, 4.

Chapter 6. Massive Resistance and the Death of a Black Newspaper

1. "Legally Enforced School Segregation Dealt Lethal Blow," *Lighthouse and Informer,* May 22, 1954, 4.

2. John H. McCray oral history interview, 1985; William D. Workman Jr., "Tax Sale Will Mark the End of *Lighthouse and Informer,*" *Charleston News and Courier,* February 5, 1955.

3. Osceola McKaine to Modjeska Simkins, March 20, 1942, Modjeska Simkins to Osceola McKaine, March 23, 1942, MMS papers, General, 1940–1949.

4. Modjeska Simkins to NAACP, April 20, 1942, NAACP papers, II-B, 209.

5. Richards, *Osceola McKaine,* 157–59.

6. John H. McCray to Winchester Smith, May 10, 1944, JHM papers, reel 8, politics.

7. John H. McCray, "The Way It Was," *Charleston Chronicle,* July 19, 1986, reel 16, journalism; J. Bates Gerald to John H. McCray, April 25 and April 30, 1944, Reel 8, politics.

8. John H. McCray to Jesse E. Beard, August 11, 1946, JHM papers, Reel 12, politics, Richland County.

9. Osceola E. McKaine, "The Palmetto State," *Norfolk Journal and Guide,* March 24, April 7, 1945.

10. Osceola E. McKaine, "The Palmetto State," November 11, 1945; for more on the American Tobacco Company strike, see Lau, *Democracy Rising,* 146–53.

11. John H. McCray to Arthur J. Clement Jr., May 14, 1945, September 7, 1945, and March 5, 1946, AJC papers, correspondence, John H. McCray. For more on the SCHW, see Sullivan, *Days of Hope;* for more on the SNYC, see Gellman, *Death Blow to Jim Crow.* See also, Richards, "Osceola McKaine," 226–51.

12. "The Wicked Fleeth in Discord," *Lighthouse and Informer,* April 13, 1947, 4; John H. McCray, "Keeping the Record Straight," text of McCray speech to PDP rally in Bennettsville, South Carolina, March 24, 1946, JHM papers, Reel 8, politics; John H. McCray to Arthur J. Clement Jr., September 7, 1945, AJC papers, correspondence, John H. McCray; Arthur J. Clement Jr., to John H. McCray, November 5, 1945, JHM papers, Reel 9, persons, Arthur Clement.

13. Esther Cooper Jackson interview with the author, July 2011, Cambridge, Massachusetts; Mrs. Andrew W. Simkins, "Dear Fellow-Citizen," n.d., MMS papers, civil rights.

14. Cooper Jackson interview; Esther V. Cooper to John H. McCray, August 3, 1946, John H. McCray to Esther V. Cooper, August 9, 1946, JHM papers, Reel 14, General, Southern Negro Youth Conference.

15. House Committee on Un-American Activities Report, MMS papers, General, 1940–1949; William D. Workman to Don Shoemaker, August 12, 1965, WDW papers, 1965.

16. Report and Recommendations on Membership and Staff, 1957, III-A-37, NAACP papers; See also Lau, *Democracy Rising,* 210.

17. See Audit of Lighthouse Publishing Company, Derrick, Stubbs and Stith, Certified Public Accounts, July 30, 1954. JHM papers, Reel 16, journalism.

18. Simkins oral history interview, 1990; McCray oral history interview, 1985; McCray to Arthur Clement Jr. February 12, 1965, AJC papers.

19. John H. McCray to Samuel R. Higgins and Mrs. Guerny E. Nelson, February 9, 1953; John H. McCray to Cliff MacKay, February 13, 1954, JHM papers, Reel 1, journalism, 1932–1986; Washburn, *The African American Newspaper,* 180.

20. Minutes of the Board of Directors, Lighthouse Publishing Company, March 20, 1954. JHM papers, Reel 16, journalism, Lighthouse and Informer; Derrick, Stubbs and Smith, Certified Public Accounts to Board of Directors Lighthouse Publishing Co, July 30, 1954, JHM papers, Reel 16, journalism, *Lighthouse and Informer.*

21. "The Lighthouse Is Still Alive and Slugging," Mrs. Andrew W. Simkins, March 27, 1954. Transcript of letter found in JHM papers, Reel 16, Journalism, *Lighthouse and Informer.*

22. "Voice of Jacob," *Lighthouse and Informer,* June 12, 1954, 4.

23. "McCray Says: Mrs. Simkins Distorts Facts," Transcript of letter prepared by John H. McCray for publication in *Lighthouse and Informer,* n.d., Modjeska Simkins to John H. McCray, July 14, 1954, JHM papers, Reel 16, Journalism, Lighthouse and Informer.

24. C. A. Scott to John H. McCray, May 18, 1954, Samuel R. Higgins to Thomas F. Maxwell, May 6, 1954, Thomas F. Maxwell to Samuel R. Higgins, May 12, 1954, Paul A. Crouch to Samuel R. Higgins, September 9, 1954, JHM papers, Reel 16, journalism; John Bolt Cuthbertson to John H. McCray, December 15, 1953, JHM papers, Reel 16, journalism.

25. See, for example, John H. McCray to James H. Murphy, April 27, 1955, James H. Murphy to John H. McCray, March 4, 1960, JHM papers, Reel 16, journalism, Afro-American.

26. Hemmingway, "The Black Press in South Carolina," 163–81; William D. Workman Jr., "Tax Sale Will Mark the End of *Lighthouse and Informer*," *Charleston News and Courier,* February 5, 1955, 1B.

27. "The Court's Decision," *Charleston News and Courier,* May 18, 1954, 1.

28. Workman, "Tax Sale Will Mark End of Lighthouse and Informer"; John H. McCray, "The Way Things Were," *Charleston Chronicle,* January 19, 1981; "Won't Try That Again," *Lighthouse and Informer,* July 9, 1943, 4.; John H. McCray to William D. Workman, February 7, 1955, Civil Rights, Correspondence, 1951–1956, WDW papers.

29. "The Court's Decision," *Charleston News and Courier,* May 18, 1954, 1.

30. Roberts and Klibanoff, *The Race Beat,* 144–45; Hustwit, *James K. Kilpatrick;* Heinman, *Harry Byrd of Virginia.*

31. Stark, *Damned Upcountryman,* 61–81, 115–97; Dicken-Garcia, *Journalistic Standards in Nineteenth-Century America,* 31.

32. Crawford, *The Ethics of Journalism,* appendix. See also, Pratte, *Gods Within the Machine,* 37.

33. Stark, *Damned Upcountryman,* 61–81, 153–97.

34. Workman kept a picture of "Dr. Ball" on his office wall in Columbia. See William D. Workman to Thomas R. Waring, December, 6, 1961, TRW papers, Correspondence: William D. Workman; Stark, *Damned Upcountryman,* 8; Rowe, "Pages of History: 200 Years at the *Post and Courier*: The Waring Years"; Walker, *City Editor;* Waring started

serving on Associated Press committees when he was managing editor in the late 1940s. See TRW papers: Correspondence: Associated Press. He was on the ASNE membership committee from 1958 through 1965. See TRW papers: Correspondence: American Society of Newspaper Editors. Both the AP and ASNE had codes of ethics proclaiming their commitment to impartial news coverage; Cumming, "Facing Facts, Facing South," 145–55; James Reston, "How They Fight Elections in South Carolina," *New York Times,* October 19 1962.

35. Waring's letter shortly after becoming editor severely chastised his statehouse reporters for injecting opinion into their reporting. Waring to Workman, January 29, 1951, TRW Papers: Correspondence, William D. Workman, SCHS.

36. Bartley, *The Rise of Massive Resistance,* 67–68.

37. Robert S. Davis to Farley Smith, July 9, 1955, WDW papers, civil rights: Committee of 52, 1955; Edgar, *South Carolina: A History,* 507; Sitkoff, *A New Deal for Blacks,* 70; "Manifesto of Southern Rights," *Charleston News and Courier,* August 19, 1955, 16A.

38. A draft and the final version of the Committee of 52 resolution are available in the Workman papers: WDW papers, Civil Rights: Committee of 52, 1955. The resolution also appeared in the *Charleston News and Courier, The State,* and other South Carolina newspapers on August 18, 1955. Early drafts of the document can found in WDW papers, Civil Rights: Committee of 52, 1955. See also Alva Lumpkin to William D. Workman Jr., July 13, 1955, WDW papers, Civil Rights: Committee of 52, 1955.

39. Ibid.; William D. Workman Jr. to James J. Kilpatrick, April 22, 1957; James J. Kilpatrick to William D. Workman, April 24, 1957, William D. Workman Papers, Correspondence, 1957.

40. Associated Press, "Citizens Urge State Action in Race Issue," *The State,* August 18, 1955; T. R. Waring to Col. James F. Risher, July 27, 1955, WDW papers, Civil Rights: Committee of 52.

41. W. D. Workman Jr., "Citizens Urge State Action in Race Issue," *Charleston News and Courier,* August 19, 1955, B1; W. D. Workman Jr., "State's Committee of 52 Votes to Continue Its Existence and Effort to Gain Public Support," *Charleston News and Courier,* September 8, 1955, B1; W. D. Workman Jr. to Ellison D. Smith Jr., November 1, 1955, WDW papers, Civil Rights: Committee of 52, 1955.

42. "Manifesto of Southern Rights," *Charleston News and Courier,* August 19, 1955, 16A; "Press Supports 'Committee of 52's' Stand," *Charleston News and Courier,* August 25, 1955, 2B.

43. Edgar, South Carolina: A History, 523; "Wayne W. Freeman Biographical Information," WWF papers; Cox, "Integration with (Relative) Dignity," 274; "Press Supports 'Committee of 52's' Stand," *Charleston News and Courier,* August 25, 1955, 2B.

44. McMillen, *The Citizens' Council,* 15–31.

45. Brady, *Black Monday;* a limited first edition, printed on the presses of the *Brookhaven Leader,* was published in June 1954; the original pamphlet was a reprint of a Brady address to the Daughters of the American Revolution in Mississippi.

46. McMillen, *The Citizens' Council,* 25.

47. "Don't Want the Klan," *Charleston News and Courier,* August 16, 1955, 8A; Copies of *Black Monday* can be found in the personal papers of Working and Waring.

48. "Unanswered Questions," *Charleston News and Courier,* September 14, 1955, 12A; Thomas R. Waring, "Mississippi Citizens' Councils Are Protecting Both Races," *Charleston*

News and Courier, September 15, 1955, 1A; For example, Waring's three-part series on the citizens' council movement ran in full in *The Citizens' Council,* a newsletter distributed by the Association of Citizens' Councils of Mississippi. By the next year, Waring was contributing pieces for a newspaper launched by the national citizens' council organization.

49. W. D. Workman Jr., *Charleston News and Courier,* July 1, 1956; McMillen, *The Citizens' Council,* 73–80.

50. Hall quoted in Cumming, *The Southern Press,* 160; Thomas R. Waring, "Private Citizens Formed Citizens Councils," *Charleston News and Courier,* September 16, 1955, 1A.

51. Edgar, South Carolina: A History," 721; "Now That the Court's Decided, Where Do We Go From Here?" *Florence Morning News,* May 18, 1954, 4; "One Area for Appreciation," *Florence Morning News,* May 19, 1954, 4.

52. "*Time* and Florence, *Charleston News and Courier,* March 30, 1956, 4.

53. "Retreat from Reason," *Florence Morning News,* June, 1956, 4A; As Quoted in Quint, *Profile in Black and White,* 99.

54. O'Dowd Resigns Editorial Post at Florence," *Charleston News and Courier,* June 16, 1956, B1; James Rogers, "On This Positive Ground South Can Stake Case for Segregation," *Florence Morning News,* August 5, 1956, 4.

55. Modjeska Simkins oral history interview, 1976, 76–78.

56. Ibid.; McMillen, *The Citizens' Council,* 73–85; Lau, *Democracy Rising,* 215–16.

57. Waring, "Mississippi Citizens' Councils Are Protecting Both Races"; W. D. Workman Jr., "Councils Must be Alert to Keep Out Klansmen," *Charleston News and Courier,* December 7, 1958.

58. "Let the Voters Choose Him," *Charleston News and Courier,* September 3, 1954, 1A; "Unfit to Govern Themselves?" *Charleston News and Courier,* September 4, 1954, 1A; "Thurmond is on the Man," *Charleston News and Courier,* September 8, 1954, 1A. See also: Thomas R. Waring Jr., "Background for Mr. Taylor's Information," an undated memo summarizing the 1954 write-in campaign as part of a Pulitzer Prize submission package. TRW papers, editorial correspondence, Thurmond 1954 Senate Campaign.

59. Thomas R. Waring, "Defense of the Ballot in South Carolina," n.d., TRW papers, editorial correspondence, Thurmond 1954 Senate Campaign.

60. Thomas R. Waring to McClellan Van Der Veer, November 22, 1954, McClellan Van Der Veer to Thomas R. Waring, Nov. 30, 1954, Thomas R. Waring to Virginius Dabney, November 22, 1954, Dabney to Waring, Nov. 29, 1954, TRW papers, editorial correspondence, Thurmond 1954 Senate Campaign.

61. Thomas R. Waring to James F. Byrnes, December 1, 1954, James F. Byrnes to Thomas R. Waring, November 29, 1954, TRW papers, editorial correspondence, Thurmond 1954 Senate Campaign.

62. Thomas R. Waring to W. J. Simmons, December 21, 1955.

63. For example, see: "Where Are Leaders?" *Charleston News and Courier,* September 10, 1955, 8A.

64. Thurmond's actual role in writing the Southern Manifesto remains in dispute. Thurmond claimed he wrote an original draft that was accepted with minor edits. Others have suggested Thurmond overstated his role to boost his political profile in advance of the 1956 election. For a comprehensive overview of the dispute, see Finley, *Defying*

the Dream, 142–46, and Day, "The Southern Manifesto: Making Opposition to the Civil Rights Movement"; "For Southern Action," *Charleston News and Courier,* March 12, 1956, 12A; "96 Congressmen in Solid Front," *Charleston News and Courier,* March 15, 1956, 18A.

65. W. D. Workman Jr., "Lawmakers call for 'interposition' between Supreme Court, state schools," *Charleston News and Courier,* March 11, 1956.

66. Associated Press, "Assembly Passes Anti-NAACP Bill," *Charleston News and Courier,* March 13, 1956; "The South's War Against the N.A.A.C.P.," *Columbia Record,* March 29, 1956, 4.

67. "To the Honorable George Bell Timmerman, Jr, Governor, From: The S.C. Progressive Democrats," March 4, 1956. WDW papers, civil rights: 1956.

68. Charron, *Freedom's Teacher,* 243.

69. Ibid., 220–42.

70. Ibid., 244.

71. "Communism and 'Civil Rights,'" *Charleston News and Courier,* July 25, 1956.

72. "Information from the Files of the Committee on Un-American Activities," July 13, 1965, MMS papers, personal; Transcript of campaign speech delivered by George B. Timmerman Jr., 1954, WDW papers, campaigns, 1954; "Communism and 'Civil Rights,'" *Charleston News and Courier,* July 25, 1956.

73. James M. Hinton to Thurgood Marshall, May 26, 1949, NAACP papers, II-C-182; Simkins oral interview, 1976, 81–84.

74. Annual report on membership and staff, III-A-37, NAACP papers.

Chapter 7. The Paper Curtain and the New GOP

1. "Citizens Councils Must Be Strong To Protect S.C. if Crisis Comes," *Charleston News and Courier,* July 14, 1958; "Many Ways Open for South to Keep Separate Schools Within the Law," *Charleston News and Courier,* March 9, 1958; "Fight Not Lost," *The State,* October 16, 1959, 4A.

2. "Of Mr. Eisenhower," *Charleston News and Courier,* March 1, 1956, 12A; Eisenhower's attorney general, Herbert Brownell, proposed the legislation in April 1956 and the president signed the final measure into law in 1957. See Findley, *Delaying the Dream,* 152–90.

3. Brownell quote as cited in Findley, *Delaying the Dream,* 153; Eisenhower, *The White House Years,* 156; "The Bloc Vote," *Charleston News and Courier,* March 23, 1957, 12A.

4. The original measure would have allowed the Justice Department to adjudicate voting rights violations, but southern senators persuaded Eisenhower to accept local jury trials, knowing full well that all-white juries in the South were unlikely to convict a white southerner of violating a voting-rights law. See Findley, *Delaying the Dream,* 172–88, and Caro, *Master of the Senate,* 848–1004.

5. Associated Press, "Passage of Force Bill Urged by Eisenhower," *Charleston News and Courier,* August 1, 1957.

6. "Never Too Late to Protest," *Charleston News and Courier,* August 7, 1957, 1A.

7. Robertson, *Sly and Able,* 510–12; Washburn, *The African American Press,* 3–4; David Shribman, "Hall of Famer Whose Pen Charted Path for Jackie Robinson," *New York Times,* March 8, 2014, SP2; Carroll, *When to Stop the Cheering?*

8. Roberts and Klibanoff, *The Race Beat,* 86.

9. From author's review of September 1955 issues of *Charleston News and Courier;* Associated Press, "Mrs. Bryant Says Negro Sought Date," *Charleston News and Courier,* September 22, 1955, 1A; from Timothy Tyson's interview for his 2017 book, *The Blood of Emmett Till,* reported by Richard Perez-Pena, "Woman Linked to 1955 Emmett Till Murder Tells Historian Her Claims Were False," *New York Times,* January 27, 2017. Accessed at https://www.nytimes.com/2017/01/27/us/emmett-till-lynching-carolyn-bryant-donham.html.

10. "Mississippi Murder," *Charleston News and Courier,* September 2, 1955, 12A.

11. *Life Magazine,* October 9, 1955, as quoted in Orville Hopkins, "Magazine Rack," *Washington Post and Times Herald,* October 9, 1955; *L'Osservatore Romano* editorial quoted in "Till Case Repercussions," *Chicago Defender,* November 5, 1955, 9; *New York Post* editorial quoted in "Border States Yielding to Pressure But Deep South Can Win Race Battle," *Charleston News and Courier,* September 14, 1956, 12A.

12. John Fischer to Thomas Waring, September 30, 1955; Waring to John Fischer, October 4, 1955. TRW papers: correspondence, John Fischer; Thomas R. Waring Jr., "The Southern Case Against Desegregation," *Harper's,* January 1956, 39–45.

13. Thomas R. Waring, "Paper Curtain Hides South's View," *Charleston News and Courier,* October 30, 1955, 1A.

14. Thomas R. Waring to James J. Kilpatrick, July 27, 1955, TRW papers, correspondence, Kilpatrick; "Opening the North to Negroes," *Charleston News and Courier,* March 28, 1958, 12A.

15. Nicholas Stanford, "Life Magazine Bows to the Censors," *Charleston News and Courier,* September 18, 1956; the series "The Background of Segregation" began in *Life* magazine in September, 1956.

16. Ibid.

17. *Times* columnist Meyer Berger is credited with first attaching the moniker "old gray lady" to the *New York Times.* He did so in a 1951 column in *Life* magazine honoring the Times' one-hundredth birthday. Meyer Berger, "The Gray Lady Reaches 100," *Life* magazine, September 17, 1951.

18. Hemming, *Messengers of the Right,* xi–xvi; Greenberg, "The Idea of the 'Liberal Media' and its Roots in the Civil Rights Movement."

19. "The Biased Northern Press," *Charleston News and Courier,* July 5, 8A; "The National Brain-Washing," *Charleston News and Courier,* July 5, 8A.

20. James Russell Wiggins to Thomas R. Waring, n.d., John Briggs to Thomas R. Waring, n.d., TRW papers, John Briggs.

21. John Briggs to Thomas Waring, 1956, TRW papers, John Briggs; Waring's personal papers document the campaign against the AP. See TRW papers, Associated Press. Roberts and Klibanoff provide an especially detailed and colorful account of the editor's efforts in *The Race Beat,* 216–19.

22. Thomas R. Waring to John Briggs, February 14, 1956, John Briggs to Thomas R. Waring, n.d., Briggs to Waring, n.d., TRW papers, John Briggs.

23. John Briggs to Thomas R. Waring, n.d., Briggs to Waring, n.d., Briggs to Waring, n.d., TRW papers, John Briggs.

24. Thomas Waring to John Briggs, July 24, 1956, Waring to Briggs, July 2, 1957, TRW papers, John Briggs; See also TRW papers, Bernard Baruch.

25. Nicholas Stanford, "A Time of Crisis," unpublished manuscript, TRW papers, John Briggs; Wilcox note to Waring, July 29, 1958, TRW papers, John Briggs.

26. John Briggs to Thomas Waring, June 15, 1970, Thomas Waring to John Briggs, June 18, 1970, TRW papers, John Briggs.

27. See, for example, Roberts and Klibanoff, *The Race Beat,* 270–333.

28. Judis, *William F. Buckley Jr.,* 133; Thomas R. Waring to William F. Buckley Jr.; Buckley to Waring; Waring to Buckley, May–June, 1957. TRW papers, correspondence, William F. Buckley Jr.

29. See chapter 5; see also Robertson, *Sly and Able,* 510–25.

30. Lowndes, *From the New Deal to the New Right,* 2008; Collins, *Whither Solid South?* 1947.

31. "Return to States' Rights," *National Review,* April 18, 1956.

32. William F. Buckley Jr., "Why the South Must Prevail," *National Review,* August 24, 1957.

33. "A Courageous Stand," *Charleston News and Courier,* August 28, 1957.

34. L. Brent Bozell, "The Open Question," *National Review,* September 7, 1957.

35. Buckley launched *National Review* in 1955. See Judis, *William F. Buckley Jr.;* For more on the rise of Republican Party in South Carolina, see Kalk, *The Origins of the Southern Strategy;* Gifford, "'Dixie is No Longer in the Bag': South Carolina Republicans and the Election of 1960"; Perlstein, *Before the Storm.*

36. Perlstein, *Before the Storm,* 115.

37. Barry Goldwater, *The Conscience of a Conservative,* 15–25.

38. "Courting of Negro Vote Gives Balance of U.S. To Its Weakest Group," *Charleston News and Courier,* July 31, 1956, 8A; William D. Workman Jr., *The Case for the South,* 268.

39. William Loeb to J. Edward Thornton, June 7, 1961; J. Edward Thornton to William Loeb, June 9, 1961. WDW Papers: Civil Rights, Correspondence, 1961.

40. Based on evidence gathered from review of the Workman and Waring papers that is detailed in this chapter.

41. Recent examples abound: Tim Russert, George Stephanopoulos, and Pete Williams moved from political and governmental positions to work as impartial journalists on network television; Jay Carney of *Time Magazine* and Linda Douglass of ABC News left journalism to take prominent positions in the Obama administration; Borden and Pritchard, "Conflict of Interest in Journalism," in *Conflict of Interest in the Professions,* 74–75; Davenport and Izard, "Restrictive Policies of the Mass Media," 4–9; Workman discussed journalism ethics when announcing his Senate candidacy. Transcript of Workman speech delivered in Georgetown, South Carolina, December 1, 1961, WDW papers: Campaigns, Senate, 1962.

42. Workman to Waring, June 9, 1958, WDW Papers: Journalism, *Charleston News and Courier,* 1958; Waring to Workman, September 13, 1957, TRW Papers: Correspondence, 1957; Waring to Workman, June 16, 1958, TRW Papers: Correspondence, 1958; The *News and Courier* remained Workman's primary employer throughout the 1950s, but he also filed statehouse news reports for the *Greenville News* and appeared regularly as a political reporter on WIS-TV in Columbia. Waring supported Workman's arrangement with those organizations, but he grew concerned when Workman cut a deal with the *Charlotte Observer.* Waring despised the Charlotte paper, which he saw as a competitor; he granted Workman a raise and approved his new opinion column as long as Workman agreed to cut his ties with the *Observer.* See Waring to Workman, June 16 1958. TRW papers: correspondence, 1958.

43. See, for example, W. D. Workman Jr., "Is Two-Party System Growing in South?" *Charleston News and Courier,* November 14, 1961; their hero, Barry Goldwater, opposed segregation, but he supported states' rights and criticized federal intervention to enforce integration. Kalk, *The Origins of the Southern Strategy,* 25–54; Perlstein, *Before the Storm,* 115–18.

44. William D. Workman Jr., *The Case for the South,* viii.

45. Ibid., 158–63, 46–47.

46. William H. Chamberlain, "News for Non-Southerners," *News and Courier,* December 29, February 7, 1960 (The review was reprinted from the *Wall Street Journal,* and is archived in William D. Workman Papers: Bounded Clips, 1959–1960; "On TV Today," *The State,* February 18, 1960, 1; " 'Case for South' Presented by Thurmond to Colleagues," *News and Courier,* March 4, 1960, 7A.

47. Newspaper clips reporting the civic club speeches are found in WDW papers: bound clips, 1959–1960. "Newsman Himself in the News," *News and Courier,* March 17, 1960, 1.

48. "Workman Praised as Major Proponent for South's Cause," *The State,* June 8, 1960, 1.

49. In addition to the *Today* show, Workman appeared on a CBS News national public affairs program in May 1960; his book was also reviewed in several regional newspapers outside the South, including the *San Francisco Chronicle;* Murphy, "Books and the Media: The *Silent Spring* Debate," in *The History of the Book, Volume 5,* 447–58.

50. Wannamaker to Workman, February 20, 1960, Workman to Wannamaker, February 26, 1960, Wannamaker to Workman, March 3, 1960. WDW papers: politics, 1960.

51. Waring to Workman, March 6, 1960, WDW Papers: Politics, 1960; Gifford, "Dixie is No Longer in the Bag," 207–33.

52. William D. Workman, "Senator Goldwater on States' Rights," *Greenville News,* March 27, 1960; "Goldwater addresses GOP Convention," *The State,* March 27, 1960; Gifford, "'No Longer in the Bag,'" 207–33; See also, Perlstein, *Before the Storm,* 371–406.

53. William D. Workman Jr., "Rights Plank Angers Delegates from South," *Charleston News and Courier,* July 12, 1960; William D. Workman Jr., "Independents Are Waiting on GOP," *Charleston News and Courier,* July 21, 1960.

54. William D. Workman Jr., "Conservatives of Both Parties Cannot Agree on Common Action," *Charleston News and Courier,* July 6, 1960; Perlstein, *Before the Storm;* Gifford, "No Longer 'in the Bag.'"

55. Workman, "Conservatives of Both Parties Cannot Agree on Common Action," *Greenville News,* July 21, 1960, 1A; Shorey to Workman, July 21, 1960. William D. Workman Papers: Correspondence, 1960.

56. Olin D. Johnston Papers: 1960 Clippings, Box 153; Roger Milliken to Waring, November 16, 1960; Waring to Milliken, November 20, 1960. WDW papers: correspondence, 1960. (Copies of the exchange between Milliken and Waring are contained in the Workman papers.)

57. Waring to Workman, November 20, 1960. WDW papers: correspondence, 1960; Workman to McCray, November 20, 1960. WDW papers: correspondence, 1960; William D. Workman Jr., "State's Negroes Backed Kennedy," *Greenville News,* December 2, 1960.

58. John H. McCray to Arthur J. Clement, October 20, 1960, John H. McCray to Mark Tolbert, October 28, 1960, JHM papers, Reel 7, politics; Arthur J. Clement to John H. McCray, October 23, 1960, AJC papers, correspondence: John H. McCray; Pittsburgh Courier Weekly Distributor Report Sheet, July, August, 1960, JHM papers, Reel 5.

59. Kennedy Campaign Flyers, WDW papers, campaigns, 1960.

60. Arthur J. Clement Jr., to L. Howard Bennett, February 7, 1961, AJC papers, correspondence: John H. McCray; John H. McCray to James Murphy, November 7, 1961, JHM papers, Reel 7, journalism; On the decline of the black press, see Washburn, the *African American Newspaper*, 199–201.

61. Charles Evans Boineau Jr., Papers: Biographical Note, SCPC; Boineau's election was something of a fluke; he failed to win reelection in the regularly scheduled election a year later, and he never again held elective office.

62. Associated Press, "GOP in Richland County Back Workman," *Charleston News and Courier*, November 15, 1961, B1; See also "To Seek U.S. Senate Nomination: Workman Resigns Newspaper Post," *Greenville News*, December 2, 1961, 1A, Leverne Prosser, "Workman Will Seek GOP Nomination," *Charleston News and Courier*, December 2, 1961, 1A. Workman recounted his earlier conversations with Edens when he announced his resignation from the newspaper; the lack of ethics discussion in newspaper coverage was based on author's review of major newspapers in South Carolina: *The State, Columbia Record, News and Courier*, and *Greenville News*.

63. W. D. Workman Jr., "Is Two-Party System Growing in South?" *Charleston News and Courier*, November 14, 1961; W. D. Workman Jr., "Supreme Court Hears Case About Negro Sit-ins," *Charleston News and Courier*, November 14, 1961; Associated Press, "GOP in Richland County Back Workman," *News and Courier*, November 15, 1961; W. D. Workman Jr., "Shipping Officials Term Stevedoring Charge Fair," *Charleston News and Courier*, November 23, 1961; W. D. Workman Jr., "Profile of Goldwater," *Charleston News and Courier*, November 25, 1961; Associated Press, "Workman to Seek Nomination," *Charleston News and Courier*, December 2, 1961, 1A.

64. Transcript of Workman speech delivered in Georgetown, South Carolina, December 1, 1961. WDW Papers: Campaigns, Senate, 1962.

65. Ibid.

66. "An Able Correspondent Resigns," *Greenville News*, December 2, 1961, 12A.

67. "Workman's Column," *Charleston News and Courier*, December 13, 1961, 8A; for examples, see W. D. Workman Jr., "Citizens Must Inform Themselves," *Charleston News and Courier*, December 9, 1961; W. D. Workman Jr., "Legal Dilemma Faces Commies," *Charleston News and Courier*, December 11, 1961.

68. Memorandum by J. Drake Edens, July 1962, William D. Workman Papers: Campaigns, Senate, 1962; William D. Workman Jr., "Notes for Sumter, SC, speech," William D. Workman Papers: Campaigns, Senate, 1960.

69. James Reston, "How They Fight Elections in South Carolina," *New York Times*, October 19, 1962; Black and Black, *The Rise of Southern Republicans*, 4. The authors identify two "great white switches"—the increase in the white southern vote for Republicans in presidential elections, which occurred in the 1950s and early 1960s, and the change in white southern political party identification, which came in the 1980s; Jim Martin, a Republican candidate for U.S. Senate in Alabama in 1962, also performed surprisingly well in losing to Democratic incumbent J. Lister Hill; see Black and Black, *The Rise of Southern Republicans*, 1–11; Kalk, *The Origin of the Southern Strategy*, 55–78; Bullock and Rozell, eds., *The New Politics of the Old South*, 1–28.

70. Daniel C. Hallin, *The Uncensored War*, 117.

Chapter 8. Color-Blind Conservatism and the Great White Switch

1. Cohodas, *Strom Thurmond and the Politics of Southern Change,* 359; "My Fellow South Carolinians," Strom Thurmond televised speech, delivered on statewide network from Columbia, September 16, 1964.

2. "Elect Barry Goldwater President of the United States," October 24, 1964. JST papers, speeches, box 11, folder 131; "A Choice for the South," JST papers: box 11, folder 131.

3. Anthony Lewis, "White Backlash Doesn't Develop," *New York Times,* November 6, 1964. 1A.

4. Lyndon B. Johnson, Remarks Upon Signing of Civil Rights Bill of 1964, Public Papers of the Presidents, University of California-Santa Barbara. Accessed March 12, 2014. http://www.presidency.ucsb.edu/ws/index.php?pid=26361&st=&st1=.

5. Lyndon B. Johnson, Special Message to the Congress—The American Promise, Public Papers of the Presidents, University of California-Santa Barbara. Accessed March 12, 2014. http://www.presidency.ucsb.edu/ws/index.php?pid=26805&st=&st1=.

6. Transcript of president Obama's speech in Selma. *Time.* March 7, 2015. Accessed March 8, 2015 at http://time.com/3736357/barack-obama-selma-speech-transcript/.

7. Alexander, *The Civil Sphere,* 4.

8. McAdam and Kloos, *Deeply Divided,* 23, 68; Dowd Hall, "The Long Civil Rights Movement and the Political Uses of the Past."

9. For more on color-blind conservatism, see Jacquelyn Dowd Hall, "The Long Civil Rights Movement and the Political Uses of History," 1233–63; Lassiter, *The Silent Majority,* 4–5; Crespino, *In Search of Another Country,* 9–10; McAdam and Kloos, *Deeply Divided,* 274–76.

10. Alexander, *The Civil Sphere,* 53–61; William F. Buckley Jr., "Why the South Must Prevail," *National Review,* August 24, 1957.

11. "A Time of Testing," *Charleston News and Courier,* July 4, 1964.

12. Waring to William J. Simmons, January 23, 1963. TRW papers: correspondence, 1963.

13. "Wallace in Wisconsin," *Charleston News and Courier,* April 9, 1964.

14. Lyndon B. Johnson, "To Fulfill These Rights," Howard University Commencement Address, June 4, 1965, LBJ Presidential Library. Accessed April 12, 2014. http://www.lbjlib.utexas.edu/johnson/archives.hom/speeches.hom/650604.asp.

15. Ibid.; "A Time of Testing," *The State,* August 18, 1965, 12A.

16. Matusow, *The Unraveling of America,* 196.

17. Associated Press, "Negro Mob Riots on Resort Vessel Sailing to Buffalo," *Charleston News and Courier,* May 31, 1956, 1A; Anthony Harrigan, "Buffalo is Becoming a City of Violence," *Charleston News and Courier,* July 3, 1956, 2A; Anthony Harrigan, "Rochester Also Has Its Negro Problem," *Charleston News and Courier,* July 4, 1956, 2A; Anthony Harrigan, "San Francisco's Negro Problem," *Charleston News and Courier,* July 19, 1956, 19A.

18. "The Los Angeles Riots," *Charleston News and Courier,* August 18, 1965, 12A; "Summer Rioting, *Charleston News and Courier,* August 15, 1965, 8A.

19. "A Time of Testing," *The State,* August 19, 1965, 12A.

20. See, for example, Joseph, *Dark Days, Bright Nights,* 1–10, on the debate over the "declension" view of civil rights efforts in the late 1960s and early 1970s; see also Carter, *The Music Has Gone Out of the Movement,* 2009, 26; Perlstein, *Nixonland,* 2008; Matusow, *The Unraveling of America,* 1984; Hodgson, *America in Our Time,* 1976.

21. Carter, *The Politics of Rage,* 468.

22. Crespino, *In Search of Another Country,* 12; Lassiter, *The Silent Majority*; Shafer and Johnston, *The End of Southern Exceptionalism.*

23. For example, see Willliam Watts Ball, "Civil Rights and Socialism," *Charleston News and Courier,* January 7, 1949, 4A; Carter, *From George Wallace to Newt Gingrich,* xiv.

24. See, for example, Dan McLaughlin, "No, Ronald Reagan Didn't Launch his 1980 Campaign in Philadelphia, MS," Redstate.com, June 2, 2016. Accessed at http://www.redstate.com/dan_mclaughlin/2016/06/02/ronald-reagan-didnt-launch-1980-campaign-philadelphia-ms/; David Brooks, "History and Calumny," *New York Times,* November 9, 2007, A27.

25. Atwater spoke with Lamis and a colleague on condition that his name not be used. Lamis used material from the interview without attributing it to Atwater in Alexander P. Lamis, *The Two-Party South.* After Atwater died, Lamis used quotations from the interview with attribution to Atwater in a 1999 book that he edited: Alexander P. Lamis, ed., *Southern Politics in the 1990s,.*

26. Applebome, *Dixie Rising.*

Epilogue

1. John H. McCray, "Need for Changing," *Pittsburgh Courier,* September 22, 1962, 12.

2. Black and Black, *The Rise of Southern Republicans,* 174–204; Bass and DeVries, *The Transformation of Southern Politics.*

3. P. L Prattis to John H. McCray, December 17, 1962, JHM papers, Reel 16, journalism.

4. John H. McCray to W. G. Edwards, May 17, 1963, JHM papers, reel 14.

5. See "Carrie Allen McCray," Workman Publishing. Accessed at https://www.workman.com/authors/carrie-allen-mccray; see also, Carrie Allen McCray, *Freedom's Child: The Life of a Confederate General's Black Daughter.*

6. "125 Years After the Beginning," *Lighthouse and Informer,* March 15, 1952, 4; Political Cartoon, *Lighthouse and Informer,* July 14, 1952, 4.

7. John Henry McCray, "The Way It Was," *Charleston Chronicle,* February 2, 1982, JHM papers, Reel 16, journalism; McCray oral history, 1985.

8. Ward, *Radio and the Struggle for Civil Rights,* 326–28.

9. Ibid., 326–27.

10. John H. McCray, "Need for Changing," *Pittsburgh Courier,* September 1, 1962, 12.

11. "Rev. J.M. Hinton Sr. Rites To Be Held Wednesday," *The State,* April 15, 1970.

12. Thomas R. Waring to John Briggs, June 18, 1970, TRW papers, editorial correspondence, John Briggs.

13. Unpublished essay, 1936. WDW Papers: Personal; Nord, *Communities of Journalism,* 11.

Bibliography

Primary Sources

Library of Congress
   NAACP Papers
South Caroliniana Library, University of South Carolina–Columbia
   John Henry McCray Papers (JHP)
   Samuel Lowry Latimer Papers (SLL)
   Arthur Clement, Jr. Papers (AJC)
   Wayne W. Freeman Papers (WWF)
   Rev. James Hinton Vertical Files
   Nathaniel Frederick Vertical Files
South Carolina Political Collections, University of South Carolina–Columbia
   Modjeska Monteith Simkins Papers (MMS)
   William D. Workman Jr. Papers (WDW)
   Olin D. Johnston Papers (ODJ)
South Carolina Historical Society–Charleston, S.C.
   Thomas R. Waring Papers (TRW)
South Carolina Department of Archives and History, Columbia, S.C.
   Gubernatorial Papers of James F. Byrnes
   Gubernatorial Papers of Olin D. Johnston
   Gubernatorial Papers of George Bell Timmerman Jr.
Strom Thurmond Institute, Clemson University
   James F. Byrnes Papers (JFB)
   J. Strom Thurmond Papers (JST)

Periodicals

Lighthouse and Informer (Columbia, S.C.)
News and Courier (Charleston, S.C.)
The State (Columbia, S.C.)

Columbia Record (Columbia, S.C.)
Greenville News (Greenville, S.C.)
Florence Morning News (Florence, S.C.)
Palmetto Leader (Columbia, S.C.)
Southern Indicator (Columbia, S.C.)
Charleston Chronicle (Charleston, S.C.)
Atlanta Constitution
Atlanta Daily World
New York Times
New York Post
Washington Post
Baltimore Afro-American
New York Amsterdam News
Pittsburgh Courier
Chicago Defender
The Crisis
Ebony
Jet
Harper's
The Atlantic

Published Primary Sources:

Ashmore, Harry S. *An Epitaph for Dixie*. New York: Norton, 1958.
Ball, William Watts. *The State That Forgot: South Carolina's Surrender to Democracy*. Indianapolis, Ind.: Bobbs-Merrill, 1932.
———. *The Editor and the Republic: The Papers and Addresses of William Watts Ball*, ed. Anthony Harrigan. Chapel Hill: University of North Carolina Press, 1954.
Brady, Tom P. *Black Monday*. Winoa, Miss.: Association of White Citizens' Councils, 1955.
Byrnes, James F. *All in One Lifetime*. New York: Harper, 1958.
———. *The Supreme Court Must Be Curbed*. Greenwood, Miss.: Association of Citizens' Councils, 1956.
Collins, Charles Wallace. *Whither Solid South? A Study in Politics and Race Relations*, New Orleans, La.: Pelican Publishing, 1947.
Du Bois, W.E.B. *The Souls of Black Folk*. Chicago: McClurg, 1903; Dover Thrift, 1994.
———. *The Negro Problem: A Series of Articles by Representative American Negroes of To-Day*. New York: Arno Press and New York Times Books, 1969 (1903).
Kilpatrick, James J. *The Sovereign States: Notes of a Citizen of Virginia*. Chicago: Regnery, 1957.
———. *The Southern Case for School Desegregation*. New York: Crowell-Collier Press, 1962.
Rubin, Louis D., and James J. Kilpatrick. *The Lasting South: Fourteen Southerners Look at Their Home*. Chicago: Regnery, 1957.
West, Rebecca. "Opera in Greenville." *New Yorker*, June 14, 1947, 31–65.
Workman, William D. *The Case for the South*. New York: Devin-Adair, 1960.

Legal Cases

Briggs v. Elliott, 98 F. Supp. 529 (1951)
Brown v. Board of Education of Topeka, Kansas, 347 U.S. 483 (1954, 1955)
Elmore v. Rice, 72 F. Supp. 516 (1947)
Gaines v. Canada, 305 U.S. 338 (1938)
McLaurin v. Oklahoma State Regents, 339 U.S. 637 (1950)
Plessy v. Ferguson, 163 U.S. 537 (1896)
Sipuel v. Board of Regents of University of Oklahoma, 332 U.S. 631 (1948)
Smith v. Allwright, 321 U.S. 649 (1944)
Sweatt v. Painter, 339 U.S. 629 (1950)

Secondary Sources

Aba-Mecha, Barbara. "Black Woman Activist in Twentieth Century South Carolina: Modjeska M. Simkins." PhD diss., Emory University, 1978.

Aiello, Thomas, "Editing a Paper in Hell: Davis Lee and the Exigencies of Smalltime Black Journalism." *American Journalism* 33, no. 2 (Spring 2016): 14–16.

Alexander, Jeffrey C. *The Civil Sphere.* New York: Oxford University Press, 2006.

———. "On the Interpretation of the Civil Sphere: Understanding and Contention in Contemporary Social Science." *Sociological Quarterly* 48 (2007): 641–59.

———. *Performance and Power.* Cambridge, Mass.: Polity Press, 2011.

———. *The Performance of Politics.* New York: Oxford Press, 2012.

———. *The Meaning of Social Life: A Cultural Sociology.* New York: Oxford Press, 2005.

Antonio, Robert J. "Locating *The Civil Sphere.*" *Sociological Quarterly* 48 (2007), 601–13.

Applebome, Peter. *Dixie Rising: How the South is Shaping American Values, Politics and Culture.* New York: New York Times Books, 1996.

Ashmore, Harry S. *Hearts and Minds: The Anatomy of Racism from Roosevelt to Reagan.* New York: McGraw Hill, 1982.

Baldasty, Gerald. *The Commercialization of the News in the Nineteenth Century.* Madison: University of Wisconsin Press, 1992.

Bartley, Numan V. *The Rise of Massive Resistance: Race and Politics in the South During the 1950s.* Baton Rouge: Louisiana State University Press, 1969, 1997.

Bass, Jack, and Marilyn Thompson. *The Complicated Personal and Political Life of Strom Thurmond.* New York: Public Affairs, 2005.

Bates, Beth Tompkins. *Pullman Porters and the Rise of Protest Politics in Black America, 1925–1945.* Chapel Hill: University of North Carolina Press, 2001.

Bedingfield, Sid. "The Dixiecrat Summer of 1948: Two South Carolina Editors—a Liberal and a Conservative—Foreshadow Modern Political Debate in the South. *American Journalism* 27, no. 3 (Summer 2010): 91–114.

———. "John H. McCray, Accommodationism, and the Framing of the Civil Rights Struggle in South Carolina, 1940–1948. *Journalism History* 37, no. 2 (Summer 2011): 91–101.

———. "Partisan Journalism and the Rise of the Republican Party in South Carolina, 1959–1962." *Journalism and Mass Communications Quarterly* 90, no. 1 (2013): 5–22.

Beeby, James, and Donald G. Nieman. "The Rise of Jim Crow, 1880–1920." In *A Companion to the American South,* ed. John B. Boles. Malden, Me.: Blackwell Publishing, 2002.

Benford, Robert D., and David A. Snow. "Framing Processes and Social Movements: An Overview and Assessment." *Annual Review of Sociology* 26 (2000): 611–39.

Benson, Rodney. "Shaping the Public Sphere: Habermas and Beyond," *American Sociology* (2009): 40, 175–97.

Berger, Peter L., and Thomas Luckmann. *The Social Construction of Reality: A Treatise in the Sociology of Knowledge*. New York: Doubleday, 1966.

Black, Earl, and Merle Black. *The Rise of Southern Republicans*. Cambridge, Mass.: Belknap Press of Harvard University, 2002.

Borden, Sandra L., and Michael S. Pritchard. "Conflict of Interest in Journalism." In *Conflict of Interest in the Professions*, eds. Michael Davis and Andrew Stark. New York: Oxford University Press, 2001.

Brinkley, Douglas. *Cronkite*. New York: HarperCollins, 2012.

Brown-Nagin, Tomiko. *Courage to Dissent: Atlanta and the Long History of the Civil Rights Movement*. New York: Oxford University Press, 2011.

Brundage, W. Fitzhugh, *Lynching in the New South: Georgia and Virginia, 1880–1930*. Chapel Hill: University of North Carolina Press, 1993.

———, ed. *Under Sentence of Death: Lynching in the South*. Chapel Hill: University of North Carolina Press, 1997.

Bullock, Charles S. III, and Mark J. Rozell, eds. *The New Politics of the Old South*. Lanham, Md.: Rowman and Littlefield, 2007.

Bynum, Cornelius L. *A. Phillip Randolph and the Struggle for Civil Rights*. Champaign-Urbana: University of Illinois Press, 2010.

Campbell, W. Joseph. *The Year that Defined Modern Journalism: 1897 and the Clash of Paradigms*. New York: Routledge, 2006.

Caragee, Kevin, and Wim Roefs. "The Neglect of Power in Recent Framing Research." *Journal of Communication* 54 (February 2004): 214–23.

Caro, Robert A. *The Years of Lyndon Johnson: Master of the Senate*. New York: Knopf, 2002.

Carroll, Brian. *When to Stop the Cheering? The Black Press, the Black Community, and the Integration of Professional Baseball*. New York: Routledge, 2006.

Carter, Dan T. *Scottsboro: A Tragedy of the American South*. Baton Rouge: Louisiana State University Press, 1979.

———. *The Politics of Rage: George Wallace, the Origins of the New Conservatism, and the Transformation of American Politics*. New York: Simon and Schuster, 1995.

———. *From George Wallace to Newt Gingrich: Race in the Conservative Counterrevolution, 1963–1994*. Baton Rouge: Louisiana State University Press, 1996.

Carter, David C. *The Music Has Gone Out of the Movement: Civil Rights and the Johnson Administration, 1965–1968*. Chapel Hill: University of North Carolina Press, 2009.

Cecelski, David, and Timothy B. Tyson, eds. *Democracy Betrayed: The Wilmington Race Riot of 1898 and its Legacy*. Chapel Hill: University of North Carolina Press, 1998.

Chalmers, David M. *Hooded Americanism: The History of the Ku Klux Klan*. Durham, N.C.: Duke University Press, 1981.

Charron, Katherine Mellen. *Freedom's Teacher: The Life of Septima Clark*. Chapel Hill: University of North Carolina Press, 2009.

Christians, Clifford G., Theodore L. Glasser, Denis McQuail, Kaarle Nordenstreng, and Robert A. White. *Normative Theories of the Media: Journalism in Democratic Societies*. Champaign-Urbana: University of Illinois Press, 2009.

Clemens, Elisabeth S. "Of Tactics and Traumas." *Sociological Quarterly* 48 (2007): 589–599.

Clowse, Barbara Barksdale. *Ralph McGill: A Biography*. Macon, Ga.: Mercer University Press, 1998.

Collins, Randall. "Changing Conceptions in the Sociology of the Professions." In *The Formation of Professions: Knowledge, State and Strategy*, eds. Rolf Torstendahl and Michael Burrage. London: Sage, 1990, 11–24.

Cook, Timothy E. *Governing with the News: The News Media as a Political Institution*. Chicago: University of Chicago Press, 1998.

Critchlow, Donald T. *The Conservative Ascendancy: How the GOP Right Made Political History*. Cambridge, Mass.: Harvard University Press, 2007.

Crespino, Joseph. *In Search of Another Country: Mississippi and the Conservative Counter Revolution*. Princeton, N.J.: Princeton University Press, 2008.

———. *Strom Thurmond's America*. New York: Hill and Wang, 2012.

Cumming, Douglas. *The Southern Press: Literary Legacies and the Challenge of Modernity*. Evanston, Ill.: Northwestern University Press, 2009.

Dailey, Jane, Glenda Elizabeth Gilmore, and Bryant Simon, eds. *Jumpin' Jim Crow: Southern Politics from Civil War to Civil Rights*. Princeton, N.J.: Princeton University Press, 2000.

Day, John Kyle. "The Southern Manifesto: Making Opposition to the Civil Rights Movement." PhD diss., University of Missouri, 2006.

Dewey, John. *Democracy and Education*. New York: Free Press, 1916, 1966.

Dicken-Garcia, Hazel. *Journalistic Standards in Nineteenth-Century America*. Madison: University of Wisconsin Press, 1989.

Dickson, Tom. *Mass Media Education in Transition*. Mahwah, N.J.: Lawrence Erlbaum Associations, 2000.

Dittmer, John. *Local People: The Struggle for Civil Rights in Mississippi*. Champaign: University of Illinois Press, 1995.

Dooley, Patricia L. *Taking Their Political Place: Journalists and the Making of an Occupation*. Westport, Conn.: Praeger, 1997, 2000.

Dudziak, Mary L. *Cold War Civil Rights: Race and the Image of American Democracy*. Princeton, N.J.: Princeton University Press, 2011.

Edgar, Walter. *South Carolina: A History*. Columbia: University of South Carolina Press, 1998.

Egerton, John. *Speak Now Against the Day: The Generation Before the Civil Rights Movement in the South*. Chapel Hill: University of North Carolina Press, 1993.

Entman, Robert M. "Framing: Towards Clarification of a Fractured Paradigm." *Journal of Communication* 43, no. 4 (1993): 51–58.

Entman, Robert M., and Lance Bennett, eds. *Mediated Politics: Communication in the Future of Democracy*. Cambridge, U.K.: Cambridge University Press, 2001.

Ferguson, Karen. *Black Politics in New Deal Atlanta*. Chapel Hill: University of North Carolina Press, 2002.

Ferguson, Jeffrey B. "Introduction." In *The Harlem Renaissance: A Brief History with Documents*. Boston: Bedford/St. Martin's, 2008.

Findley, Keith M. *Defying the Dream: Southern Senators and the Fight Against Civil Rights, 1938–1965*. Baton Rouge: Louisiana State University Press, 2008.

Foner, Eric. *Reconstruction: America's Unfinished Revolution, 1863–1877*. New York: Harper and Row, 1988, 2002.

——. *The Fiery Trial: Abraham Lincoln and American Slavery*. New York: Norton, 2011.

——. *Free Soil, Free Labor, Free Men: The Ideology of the Republican Party Before the Civil War*. New York: Oxford University Press, 1970.

Frederickson, Kari. *The Dixiecrat Revolt and the End of the Solid South, 1932–1968*. Chapel Hill: University of North Carolina Press, 2001.

Fullinwider, S. P. *The Mind and Mood of Black America: 20th Century Thought*. Homewood, Ill.: Dorsey Press, 1969.

Gaines, Kevin K. *Uplifting the Race: Black Leadership, Politics and Culture in the Twentieth Century*. Chapel Hill: University of North Carolina Press, 1996.

Gamson, William A. "Political Discourse and Collective Action." *International Journal of Social Movements, Conflicts and Change* 1 (1988): 219–44.

——. "Promoting Political Engagement." In *Mediated Politics. Communication in the Future of Democracy,* eds., Robert M. Entman and W. Lance Bennett. Cambridge, U.K.: Cambridge University Press, 2001.

——. *Talking Politics*. New York: Cambridge University Press, 1992.

Gamson, William A., and Andre Modigliani. "Media discourse and public opinion on nuclear power: A constructionist approach." *American Journal of Sociology* 95 (1989): 1–37.

Gamson, William A., Bruce A. Fireman, and Steven Rytina. *Encounters with Unjust Authority*. Homewood, Ill.: Dorsey Press, 1982.

Garson, Robert A. *The Democratic Party and the Politics of Sectionalism, 1941–1948*. Baton Rouge: Louisiana State University Press, 1974.

Gellman, Erik S. *Death Blow to Jim Crow: The National Negro Congress and the Rise of Militant Civil Rights*. Chapel Hill: University of North Carolina Press, 2012.

Giddins, Paula J. *A Sword among Lions: Ida B. Wells and the Campaign Against Lynching*. New York: HarperCollins, 2008.

Gifford, Laura Jane. " 'Dixie is No Longer in the Bag': South Carolina Republicans and the Election of 1960. *Journal of Policy History* 19, no. 2 (April 2007): 207–33.

Gilmore, Glenda. *Gender and Jim Crow. Women and the Politics of White Supremacy in North Carolina, 1896–1920*. Chapel Hill: University of North Carolina, 1996.

——. *Defying Dixie: The Radical Roots of Civil Rights 1919–1950*. New York: Norton, 2009.

——. "False Friends and Avowed Enemies: Southern African Americans and Party Allegiances in the 1920s." In *Jumpin' Jim Crow: Southern Politics from Civil War to Civil Rights,* eds. Jane Dailey, Glenda Elizabeth Gilmore, and Bryant Simon. Princeton, N.J.: Princeton University Press, 2000.

Gitlin, Todd. *The Whole World Is Watching: Mass Media in the Making and Unmaking of the New Left*. Berkeley: University of California Press, 1980.

Goffman, Ervin. *Frame Analysis: An Essay on the Organization of Experience*. New York: Free Press, 1974.

Goldberg, Chad Alan. "Reflections on Jeffrey C. Alexander's *The Civil Sphere.*" *Sociological Quarterly* 48 (2007): 629–39.

Greenberg, David. "The Idea of 'the Liberal Media' and its Roots in the Civil Rights Movement." *The Sixties: A Journal of History, Politics, and Culture* 1, no. 2 (December 2008): 167–86.

Greenberg, Jack. *Crusaders in the Courts: How a Dedicated Band of Lawyers Fought for the Civil Rights Legislation.* New York: Basic Books, 1994.

Hahn, Steven. "The Race Man." *New Republic,* October 26, 2009.

———. "Marcus Garvey, the UNIA, and the Hidden History of African Americans." In *The Political Worlds of Slavery and Freedom,* ed. Steven Hahn. Cambridge, Mass.: Harvard University Press, 2009, 115–62.

Halberstam David. *The Powers That Be.* New York: Knopf, 1979.

Hale, Grace Elizabeth. *Making Whiteness: The Culture of Segregation in the South, 1890–1940.* New York: Vintage Books, 1999.

Hall, Jacquelyn Dowd, "The Long Civil Rights Movements and the Political Uses of the Past." *Journal of American History* 91, no. 4 (2005): 1233–63.

Hallin, Daniel C., and Paola Mancini. *Comparing Media Systems: Three Models of Media and Politics.* New York: Cambridge University Press, 2004.

Hampton, Christine W., and Rosalee W. Washington. *The History of Lincolnville, South Carolina.* Charleston, S.C.: Booksurge, 2007.

Harding, Vincent. *There Is a River: The Black Struggle for Freedom in America.* New York: Vintage Books, 1983.

Harlan, Louis R. "Booker T. Washington and the Politics of Accommodation." In *Black Leaders of the Twentieth Century,* eds., John Hope Franklin and August Meier. Urbana: University of Illinois Press, 1982, 2–18.

———. *Booker T. Washington: The Making of a Black Leader, 1856–1901.* New York: Oxford University Press, 1972.

———. *Booker T. Washington: Volume 2: The Wizard of Tuskegee, 1901–1915.* New York: Oxford University Press, 1983.

Haws, Robert, ed. *The Age of Segregation. Race Relations in the South, 1890–1945.* Jackson: University Press of Mississippi, 1978.

Hayes, Jack I. *South Carolina and the New Deal.* Columbia: University of South Carolina Press, 2001.

Hayes, Robert, ed. *The Age of Segregation: Race Relations in the South, 1890–1945.* Jackson: University Press of Mississippi, 1978.

Heinman, Ronald L. *Harry Byrd of Virginia.* Charlottesville: University of Virginia Press, 1996.

Hemmer, Nicole. *Messengers of the Right: Conservative Media and the Transformation of American Politics.* Philadelphia: University of Pennsylvania Press, 2016.

Hemmingway, Theodore. "Black Press in South Carolina." In *The Black Press in the South, 1865–1979,* ed., Henry Louis Suggs. Westport, Conn.: Greenwood Press, 1983.

———. "Beneath the Yoke of Bondage. A History of Black Folks in South Carolina, 1900–1940." PhD diss., University of South Carolina, 1976.

———. "Prelude to Change: Black Carolinians in the War Years, 1914–1920." *Journal of Negro History* 65, no. 3 (Summer 1980): 212–27.

Higginbotham, Evelyn Brooks. *Righteous Discontent: The Women's Movement in the Black Baptist Church, 1880–1920.* Cambridge, Mass.: Harvard University Press, 1993.

Hine, Darlene Clark. "Blacks and the Destruction of the White Primary 1935–1944." *Journal of Negro History* 62, no. 1 (1977): 43–59.

Hoffman, Edwin D. "The Genesis of the Modern Movement for Civil Rights in South Carolina." *Journal of Negro History* 44, no. 4 (1959): 346–69.

Holden, Charles J. *In the Great Maelstrom: Conservatives in Post-Civil War South Carolina*. Columbia: University of South Carolina Press, 2002.

Holt, Michael F. *The Political Crisis of the 1850s*. New York: Norton, 1983.

———. *Black Over White: Negro Leadership in South Carolina During Reconstruction*. Champaign: University of Illinois Press, 1979.

Huggins, Nathan Irvin. *Harlem Renaissance*. New York: Oxford University Press, 1971.

Hustwit, William P., *James J. Kilpatrick: Salesman for Segregation*. Chapel Hill: University of North Carolina Press, 2013.

Ignatieff, Michael, *Blood and Belonging: Journeys into the New Nationalism*. New York: Farrar, Straus and Giroux, 1993.

Jacobs, Ronald N. "Culture, the Public Sphere, and Media Sociology: A Search for a Classical Founder in the Work of Robert Park." *American Sociology* 40 (2009): 149–66.

Jones, Lewis Pinckney. *Stormy Petrel: N.G. Gonzalez and His State*. Columbia: University of South Carolina Press, 1973.

Jordan, William G. " 'The Damnable Dilemma': African-American Accommodation and Protest during World War I." *Journal of American History* 81, no. 4 (March 1995): 1562–83.

———. *Black Newspapers and America's War for Democracy, 1914–1920*. Chapel Hill: University of North Carolina Press, 2001.

Johnston, Hank, and John A. Noakes. *Frames of Protest: Social Movements and the Framing Perspective*. Lanham, Md.: Rowman and Littlefield, 2005.

Judis, John B. *William F. Buckley, Jr.: Patron Saint of the Conservatives*. New York: Simon and Schuster, 1988.

Kalk, Bruce H. *The Origins of the Southern Strategy: Two-Party Competition in South Carolina, 1950–1972*. Lanham, Md.: Lexington Books, 2011.

Kantrowitz, Stephen. *Ben Tillman and the Reconstruction of White Supremacy*. Chapel Hill: University of North Carolina Press, 2000.

Kaplan, Richard L. *Politics and the American Press: The Rise of Objectivity, 1865–1920*. New York: Cambridge University Press, 2002.

———. "From Partisanship to Professionalism: The Transformation of the Daily Press," in *A History of the Book in America: Print in Motion: The Expansion of Publishing and Reading in the United States, 1880–1940*, eds. Carl F. Kaestle and Janice A. Radway. Chapel Hill: University of North Carolina Press, 2009.

Karabell, Zachary. *The Last Campaign: How Harry Truman Won the 1948 Election*. New York: Knopf, 2000.

Katznelson, Ira. *When Affirmative Action was White: An Untold History of Racial Inequality in Twentieth-Century America*. New York: W.W. Norton, 2005.

Kelley, Blair L. M. *Right to Ride: Streetcar Boycotts and African American Citizenship in the Era of Plessy v. Ferguson*. Chapel Hill: University of North Carolina Press, 2010.

Kelley, Robin D. G. " 'We Are Not What We Seem': Rethinking Black Working-Class Opposition in the Jim Crow South." *Journal of American History* (June 1993).

———. *Race Rebels: Culture, Politics and the Black Working Class*. New York: Free Press, 1994.

———. *Hammer and Hoe: Alabama Communists During the Great Depression*. Chapel Hill: University of North Carolina Press, 1990.

Kelly, Brian. " 'Beyond the Talented Tenth' ": Black Elites, Black Workers, and the Limits of Accommodation in Industrial Birmingham, 1900–1921." In *Time Longer Than Rope,* eds. Charles M. Payne and Adam Green. New York: New York University Press, 2003.

King, Richard H. *Civil Rights and the Idea of Freedom.* New York: Oxford University Press. 1992.

Klarman, Michael J. *From Jim Crow to Civil Rights: The Supreme Court and the Struggle for Racial Equality.* New York: Oxford University Press, 2004.

Kluger, Richard. *Simple Justice: The History of Brown v. Board of Education and Black America's Struggle for Equality.* New York: Knopf, 1976; Vintage, 2004.

Kneebone, John T. *Southern Liberal Journalists and the Issue of Race, 1920–1944.* Chapel Hill: University of North Carolina Press, 1985.

Korstad, Robert, and Nelson Lichtenstein. "Opportunities Found and Lost: Labor, Radicals and the Early Civil Rights Movement." *Journal of American History* 75, no. 3 (December 1988): 786–811.

Kruse, Kevin M. *White Flight: Atlanta and the Making of Modern Conservatism.* Princeton, N.J.: Princeton University Press, 2005.

Kruse, Kevin, and Stephen Tuck, eds. *Fog of War: The Second World War and the Civil Rights Movement.* New York: Oxford University Press, 2012.

La Brie, Henry G., III. *Perspectives of the Black Press: 1974.* Kennebunkport, Me.: Mercer House Press, 1974.

Lamis, Alexander P. *The Two-Party South.* New York: Oxford University Press, 1984. 1990.

———, ed. *Southern Politics in the 1990s.* Baton Rouge: Louisiana State University Press, 1999.

Lassiter, Matthew D. *The Silent Majority: Suburban Politics in the Sunbelt South.* Princeton, N.J.: Princeton University Press, 2006.

Latimer, Samuel L., Jr. *The Story of The State and the Gonzales Brothers.* Columbia, S.C.: The State-Record Company, 1970.

Lau, Peter F. *Democracy Rising: South Carolina and the Fight for Black Equality Since 1865.* Lexington: University Press of Kentucky, 2006.

Lepore, Jill. *The Story of America: Essays on Origins.* Princeton, N.J.: Princeton University Press, 2012.

Lewis, David Levering. *W.E.B. Du Bois: The Fight for Equality and the American Century, 1919–1962.* New York: Owl Books, 2000.

———. *W.E.B. Du Bois: Biography of a Race, 1868–1919.* New York: Owl Books, 1994.

———. *When Harlem was in Vogue.* New York: Oxford University Press, 1989.

Levine, Lawrence. *Black Culture and Black Consciousness: Afro-American Folk Thought from Slavery to Freedom.* New York: Oxford University Press, 1977.

Lichtman, Allan J. *White Protestant Nation: The Rise of the American Conservative Movement.* New York: Atlantic Monthly Press, 2008.

Link, William S. *The Paradox of Southern Progressivism, 1880–1930.* Chapel Hill: University of North Carolina Press, 1992.

Lippmann, Walter. *Public Opinion.* New York: Harcourt, Brace, 1922.

Litwack, Leon F. *Trouble in Mind: Black Southerners in the Age of Jim Crow.* New York: Vintage Books, 1998.

Logan, Rayford. *The Negro in American Life and Thought: The Nadir, 1877–1901.* New York: Dial Press, 1954.

Lowndes, Joseph E. *From the New Deal to the New Right: Race and the Southern Origins of Modern Conservatism.* New Haven, Conn.: Yale University Press, 2008.

Matasow, Allen J. *The Unraveling of America: A History of Liberalism in the 1960s.* Athens: University of Georgia Press, 2009.

Maxwell, Angie. The Indicted South: Public Criticism, Southern Inferiority, and the Politics of Whiteness. Chapel Hill: University of North Carolina Press, 2014.

McAdam, Doug. *Political Process and the Development of Black Insurgency, 1930–1970.* Chicago: University of Chicago Press, 1982, 1999.

McAdam, Doug, and Karina Kloos. *Deeply Divided: Racial Politics and Social Movements in Postwar America.* New York: Oxford University Press, 2015.

McChesney, Robert W. *The Problem of the Media: U.S. Communication Politics of the 21st Century.* New York: Monthly Review Press, 2004.

McGerr, Michael E. *The Decline of Popular Politics: The American North, 1865–1928.* New York: Oxford University Press, 1986.

McMillen, Neil R. *Dark Journey: Black Mississippians in the Age of Jim Crow.* Champaign: University of Illinois Press, 1989.

———. *The Citizens' Council: Organized Resistance to the Second Reconstruction.* Champaign: University of Illinois Press, 1994.

McNeely, Patricia. *Fighting Words: The History of the Media in South Carolina.* Columbia: South Carolina Press Association, 1998.

Menand, Louis. "Seeing It Now: Walter Cronkite and the Legend of CBS News." *New Yorker,* July 9, 2012, 88–94.

Megginson, W. J. *African American Life in South Carolina's Upper Piedmont.* Columbia: University of South Carolina Press, 2006.

Meier, August. *Negro Thought in America, 1880–1915: Racial Ideologies in the Age of Booker T. Washington.* Ann Arbor: University of Michigan Press, 1963.

Mindich, David T. Z. *Just the Facts: How "Objectivity" Came to Define American Journalism.* New York: New York University Press, 2000.

Morris, Aldon D. *The Origins of the Civil Rights Movement. Black Communities Organizing for Change.* New York: Free Press, 1984.

———. "Naked Power and the Civil Sphere." *Sociological Quarterly* 48 (2007): 615–28.

Moses, Jeremiah Wilson. *Creative Conflict in African American Thought.* Cambridge, U.K.: Cambridge University Press, 2004.

Newby, I. A. *Black Carolinians: A History of Blacks in South Carolina from 1865–1968.* Columbia: University of South Carolina Press, 1973.

———. *Jim Crow's Defense: Anti-Negro Thought in America, 1900–1930.* Baton Rouge: Louisiana State University Press, 1965.

Nord, David Paul. *Communities of Journalism: A History of American Newspapers and Their Readers.* Urbana and Chicago: University of Illinois Press, 2001.

Norrell, Robert J. *Up from History: The Life of Booker T. Washington.* Cambridge, Mass.: Belknap Press of the Harvard University Press, 2009.

O'Brien, Thomas V. "The Perils of Accommodation: The Case of Joseph W. Holley." *American Educational Research Journal* 44, no. 4 (December 2007): 806–52.

Ortiz, Paul. " 'Eat Your Bread without Butter, but Pay Your Poll Tax!': Roots of the African American Voter Registration Movement in Florida, 1919–1920." In *Time Longer than Rope*, eds. Charles M. Payne and Adam Green New York: New York University Press, 2003.

———. *Emancipation Betrayed: The Hidden History of Black Organizing and White Violence in Florida from Reconstruction to the Bloody Election of 1920.* Berkeley: University of California Press, 2005.

Payne, Charles M. *I've Got the Light of Freedom: The Organizing Tradition and the Mississippi Freedom Struggle.* Berkeley: University of California Press, 1995, 2007.

Prather, H. Leon, Jr. "The Origins of the Phoenix Massacre of 1898." In *Developing Dixie: Modernizing in a Traditional Society,* eds. Winfred B. Moore Jr., Joseph F. Tripp, and Lyon G. Tyler Jr. Westport, Conn.: Greenwood Press, 1988.

Perlstein, Rick. *Before the Storm: Barry Goldwater and the Unmaking of the American Consensus.* New York: Hill and Wang, 2001.

———. *Nixonland: The Rise of a President and the Fracturing of America.* New York: Scribners, 2008.

Phillips, Ulrich B. "The Central Theme of Southern History." *American Historical Review* 34 (October 1928): 35–42.

Quint, Howard H. *Profile in Black and White: A Frank Portrait of South Carolina.* Washington, D.C.: Public Affairs Press, 1958.

Ransby, Barbara. *Ella Baker and the Black Freedom Movement: A Radical Democratic Vision.* Chapel Hill: University of North Carolina Press, 2003.

Rhodes, Jane. "The Black Press and Radical Print Culture." In *A History of the Book in America, Vol. Five,* eds. David Paul Nord, Joan Shelley Rubin, and Michael Schudson. Chapel Hill: University of North Carolina Press, 2009.

Richards, Miles S. "Osceola E. McKaine and the Struggle for Black Civil Rights, 1917- 1946." PhD diss., University of South Carolina, 1994.

Roberts, Gene, and Hank Klibanoff. *The Race Beat: The Press, the Civil Rights Struggle and the Awakening of a Nation.* New York: Knopf, 2006.

Robertson, David. *Sly and Able: A Political Biography of James F. Byrnes.* New York: Norton, 1994.

Roefs, Wim. "Leading the Civil Rights Vanguard in South Carolina: John H. McCray and the *Lighthouse and Informer*, 1939–1954." In *Time Longer Than Rope: A Century of African American Activism,* eds., Charles M. Payne and Adam Green. New York: New York University Press, 2003.

Scheufele, Dietram. "Framing as a Theory of Media Effects." *Journal of Communication* (Winter 1999): 103–18.

———. "Agenda Setting, Priming and Framing Revisited: Another Look at Cognitive Effects of Political Communication." *Mass Communications and Society* 3 (Autumn 2000): 297–316.

Schudson, Michael. *Discovering the News: A Social History of American Newspapers.* New York: Basic Books, 1978.

———. "Persistence of Vision—Partisan Journalism in the Mainstream Press." In *A History of the Book in America, Volume 4, Print in Motion, The Expansion of Publishing and Reading in the United States, 1880–1940,* eds., Carl F. Kaestle and Janice Radway. Chapel Hill: University of North Carolina Press, 2009.

Segrue, Thomas J. *Sweet Land of Liberty: The Forgotten Struggle for Civil Rights in the North*. New York: Random House, 2008.

Shickler, Eric. "New Deal Liberalism and Racial Liberalism in the Mass Public, 1937–1968." *Perspectives on Politics* 11, no. 1 (March 2013): 75–98.

Shafer, Byron E., and Richard Johnston. *The End of Southern Exceptionalism: Class, Race, and Partisan Change in the Postwar South*. Cambridge, Mass.: Harvard University Press, 2006.

Simon, Bryant. *A Fabric of Defeat. The Politics of South Carolina Millhands, 1910–1948*. Chapel Hill: University of North Carolina Press, 1998.

———. "Race Relations: African American Organizing, Liberalism, and White Working-Class Politics in Post-War South Carolina." In *Jumpin' Jim Crow: Southern Politics from Civil War to Civil Rights*, eds., Jane Dailey, Glenda Elizabeth Gilmore, and Bryant Simon. Princeton, N.J.: Princeton University Press, 2000.

———. "The Appeal of Cole Blease of South Carolina: Race, Class, and Sex in the New South." *Journal of Southern History* 62, no. 1 (February 1996): 57–86.

Simmons, Charles. *The African American Press: A History of News Coverage During National Crises, with Special Reference to Four Black Newspapers, 1827–1965*. Jefferson, N.C.: McFarland, 1998.

Sitkoff, Harvard. *A New Deal for Blacks: The Emergence of Civil Rights as a National Issue: The Depression Decade*. New York: Oxford University Press, 1978.

Smock, Raymond W. *Booker T. Washington. Black Leadership in the Age of Jim Crow*. Lanham, Md.: Rowman and Littlefield, 2009.

Snow, David A., and Robert D. Benford. "Ideology, Frame Resonance, and Participant Mobilization," *International Social Movement Research* 1 (1988): 197–218.

———. "Master Frames and Cycles of Protest." In *Frontiers of Social Movement Theory*, eds., Aldon Morris and Carol Mueller. New Haven, Conn.: Yale University Press, 1992.

Sokol, Jason. *There Goes My Everything: White Southerners in the Age of Civil Rights, 1945–1975*. New York: Vintage, 2007.

Southern, David W. "Beyond Jim Crow Liberalism: Judge Waring's Fight Against Segregation in South Carolina, 1942–52." *Journal of Negro History* (1981).

Stark, John D. *Damned Upcountryman: William Watts Ball, A Study in American Conservatism*. Durham, N.C.: Duke University Press, 1968.

Suggs, Henry Louis, and Bernadine Moses Duncan. "The Black Press in North Carolina." In *The Black Press in the South, 1865–1979*, ed., Henry Louis Suggs. Westport, Conn.: Greenwood Press, 1983.

Sullivan, Patricia. *Days of Hope: Race and Democracy in the New Deal Era*. Chapel Hill: University of North Carolina Press, 1996.

———. *Lift Every Voice: The NAACP and the Making of the Civil Rights Movement*. New York: The New Press, 2009.

Tindall, George Brown. *South Carolina Negroes, 1877–1900*. Columbia: University of South Carolina Press, 1952, 2003.

———. *The Emergence of the New South, 1913–1945*. Baton Rouge: Louisiana State University Press, 1967.

Teel, Leonard Ray. *Ralph Emerson McGill: Voice of the Southern Conscience*. Knoxville: University of Tennessee Press, 2001.

———. "W.A. Scott and The Atlanta Daily World." *American Journalism* 6, no. 3 (1989).

Thompson, Julius Eric. "The Black Press in Mississippi." In *The Black Press in the South, 1865–1979*, ed. Henry Louis Suggs. Westport, Conn.: Greenwood Press, 1983.

Tuchman, Gaye. *Making News: A Study in the Social Construction of Reality*. New York: Free Press, 1978.

Tushnet, Mark V. *Making Civil Rights Law: Thurgood Marshall and the Supreme Court, 1936–1951*. New York: Oxford University Press, 1996.

Tyler, Pamela. "The Impact of the New Deal and World War II on the South." In *A Companion to the American South*, ed. John B. Boles. New York: Blackwell Publishing, 2002.

Verney, Kevin. *The Art of the Possible: Booker T. Washington and Black Leadership in the United States, 1881–1925*. New York: Routledge, 2001.

Vogel, Todd, "Introduction," *The Black Press. New Literary and Historical Essays*, ed., Todd Vodel. New Brunswick, N.J.: Rutgers University Press, 2001.

Wade, Wyn Craig. *The Fiery Cross: The Ku Klux Klan in America*. New York: Oxford University Press, 1998.

Walton, Hanes, Jr., *Black Political Parties: An Historical and Political Analysis*. New York: Free Press, 1974.

Ward, Brian. *Radio and the Struggle for Civil Rights in the South*. University of Florida Press, 2006.

Ward, Jason Morgan. *Defending White Democracy: The Making of a Segregationist Movement and the Remaking of Racial Politics, 1936–1965*. Chapel Hill: University of North Carolina Press, 2011.

Washburn, Patrick. *The African American Newspaper. Voice of Freedom*. Evanston, Ill.: Northwestern University Press, 2006.

———. *A Question of Sedition: The Federal Government's Investigation of the Black Press during World War II*. New York: Oxford University Press, 1986.

Webb, Samuel L. "Southern Politics in the Age of Populism and Progressivism: A Historiographical Essay." In *A Companion to the American South*, ed. John B. Boles. New York: Blackwell Publishing, 2002.

Weiss, Nancy J. *Farewell to the Party of Lincoln: Black Politics in the Age of FDR*. Princeton, N.J.: Princeton University Press, 1983.

Wells, Ida B. *Crusade for Justice: The Autobiography of Ida B. Wells*, ed., Alfreda M. Duster. Chicago: University of Chicago Press, 1970.

———. *Southern Horrors and Other Writings: The Anti-Lynching Campaign of Ida B. Wells, 1892–1900*, ed., Jacqueline Jones Royster. Boston and New York: Bedford/St. Martin's, 1996.

West, Michael Rudolph. *The Education of Booker T. Washington. American Democracy and the Idea of Race Relations*. New York: Columbia University Press, 2006.

Williamson, Joel. *The Crucible of Race. Black-White Relations in the American South Since Emancipation*. New York: Oxford University Press, 1984.

Woods, Barbara A. "Modjeska Simkins and the South Carolina Conference of the NAACP, 1937–1959." In *Women in the Civil Rights Movement: Trailblazers and Torchbearers, 1941–1965*, eds. Vicki L. Crawford, Jacqueline Anne Rouse, and Barbara Woods. Bloomington: Indiana University Press, 1993.

Woodruff, Nan Elizabeth. *American Congo: The African American Freedom Struggle in the Delta*. Cambridge, Mass.: Harvard University Press, 2003.

Woodward, C. Vann. *Origins of the New South*. Baton Rouge: Louisiana State University Press, 1951.

———. *The Strange Career of Jim Crow*. New York: Oxford University Press, 1955.

———. *Tom Watson: Agrarian Rebel*. New York: McMillian, 1938; Galaxy Books, 1963.

Wray, Ronald K. "The Anti Pro-Segregationist: Jack K. O'Dowd and the Desegregation Controversy." Thesis, University of South Carolina Honors, 1988.

Yarbrough, Tinsley. *A Passion for Justice: J. Waties Waring and Civil Rights*. New York: Oxford University Press, 1987.

Index

Aaron v. Cook, 117
Abbott, Robert, 27
abortion, 210
accommodationism, 22–24; Richard Carroll on, 29–30; W. E. B. Du Bois' criticism of, 25–26
AFL-CIO, 95, 142
African Americans: accommodationism among, 22–24, 25–26, 29–30; *Briggs v. Elliott* and, 111–12, 116–23; elected to political office, 141, 213–14; Great Migration of, 2, 3, 11, 26–28; growth in activism in the 1930s-40s, 1–3, 41–42; Harlem Renaissance and, 44; life in the South in the 1930s, 1; in the military, 42–43, 47–48, 83; patriotism, 48–49; Progressive Democratic Party and, 1, 69–75, 84, 102–3, 127–29, 140; racial liberalism in Europe and, 44; split between leaders and the community, 52; in sports, 51, 173; teachers, equal pay for, 45, 55–60, 81, 121–22; tenant farmers, 161–62; "two-ness" experienced by, 25; violence against (*see* lynching); voter registrations, 84–85, 127–28; voting rights campaigns, 67–69, 184. *See also* black newspapers; civil rights movement; school segregation
African Methodist Episcopal Church, 18, 46
Alexander, Jeffrey C., 5–6, 202, 204
Allen, Carrie, 215
Allen, Robert S., 113
Allen University, 46, 144

"American creed," 5
American Dilemma, An, 61, 78, 174
American Mercury, 181
American Missionary Association, 19
American Society of Newspaper Editors, 8, 153–54
American Tobacco Company, 142
Amsterdam News, 44, 97, 214
antilynching laws, 21–22, 36, 42, 99, 112
Arkansas Gazette, 152
Ashmore, Harry, 93, 135, 152
Askew, Reubin, 213
Associated Press, 83, 114, 123, 153, 174, 179, 196
Association of Citizens' Councils of South Carolina, 159
"Atlanta compromise," 23–24
Atlanta Constitution, 93, 115, 176
Atlanta Daily World, 4, 110, 117, 147, 214
Atwater, Lee, 211–12
Avery Normal Institute, 19–20
Aycock, Charles B., 23

"Background of Segregation, The," 176
Baker, Ray Stannard, 10
Ball, William Watts, 9, 13–14, 21, 70, 90–92, 107, 150, 151, 182, 183; criticism of James Byrnes, 114–15, 119, 130; on the Democratic Party and civil rights, 98–101, 103, 105–6; on the NAACP, 100; promotion and support for political candidates, 152; response to *Smith v. Allwright*, 98, 100

SID BEDINGFIELD is an assistant professor of journalism and mass communication at the University of Minnesota.

The History of Communication

The University of Illinois Press
is a founding member of the
Association of American University Presses.

_____

University of Illinois Press
1325 South Oak Street
Champaign, IL 61820-6903
www.press.uillinois.edu